CHILDREN'S PLAY, PRETENSE, AND STORY

At the heart of this volume is the recognition that children's engagement with play and story are intrinsically and intricately linked. The contributing authors share a passionate interest in the development and well-being of children, in particular through their use of imagination and adaptation of the everyday into play and stories. Following these principles, the volume explores the connections between play, story, and pretense with regard to many cultural and contextual factors that influence the way these elements vary in children's lives. In a departure from earlier collections on play and story, the authors take a particular focus on normative as compared with atypical development.

This collection begins with an approach to understanding the developmental relationship between play and story, which recognizes their similarities while acknowledging their differences. Much of the collection addresses pretend play and story in children with autism spectrum disorder, an understudied but important group for consideration, as these dimensions of their lives and development have often been considered problematic. The volume also includes sections on play and story in classroom settings and play and story across cultures, including non-English-speaking environments such as Israel, Romania, China, and Mexico. It concludes with a discussion of how play differs across sociocultural and economic contexts, making a unifying claim for the importance of play in children's lives but also calling for an understanding of what play means to very different groups of children.

Susan Douglas is a developmental linguist specializing in language acquisition in children with autism spectrum disorder. Her research interests include syntactic and semantic acquisition, narrative development, and the discourse structure of pretend play.

Lesley Stirling is a linguist and cognitive scientist working on descriptive and typological linguistics, semantics, and discourse analysis, especially of narrative. She has been researching communication in autism for over a decade, focusing on the discourse analysis of children's stories and play interactions.

CHILDREN'S PLAY, PRETENSE, AND STORY

Studies in Culture, Context, and Autism Spectrum Disorder

Edited by
Susan Douglas and Lesley Stirling

NEW YORK AND LONDON

First published 2016
by Routledge
711 Third Avenue, New York, NY 10017

and by Routledge
2 Park Square, Milton Park, Abingdon, Oxon, OX14 4RN

Routledge is an imprint of the Taylor & Francis Group, an informa business

© 2016 Taylor & Francis

The right of the editors to be identified as the authors of the editorial material, and of the authors for their individual chapters, has been asserted in accordance with sections 77 and 78 of the Copyright, Designs and Patents Act 1988.

All rights reserved. No part of this book may be reprinted or reproduced or utilised in any form or by any electronic, mechanical, or other means, now known or hereafter invented, including photocopying and recording, or in any information storage or retrieval system, without permission in writing from the publishers.

Trademark notice: Product or corporate names may be trademarks or registered trademarks, and are used only for identification and explanation without intent to infringe.

Library of Congress Cataloging-in-Publication Data
Children's play, pretense, and story : studies in culture, context, and ASD /
   edited by Susan Douglas and Lesley Stirling.
      pages cm
   Includes bibliographical references and index.
   1. Play—Psychological aspects.   2. Storytelling.   3. Play assessment
(Child psychology)   4. Storytelling ability in children.   5. Autism spectrum
disorders in children.   I. Douglas, Susan Louise, editor.   II. Stirling, Lesley,
editor.
   BF717.C4255 2016
   155.4'18—dc23
   2015029451

ISBN: 978-1-84872-543-0 (hbk)
ISBN: 978-1-84872-544-7 (pbk)
ISBN: 978-1-315-81783-5 (ebk)

Typeset in Bembo
by Apex CoVantage, LLC

Printed and bound in the United States of America by Publishers Graphics, LLC on sustainably sourced paper.

CONTENTS

	Introduction *Lesley Stirling and Susan Douglas*	1
1	Young Children's Pretend Play and Storytelling as Modes of Narrative Activity: From Complementarity to Cross-Fertilization? *Ageliki Nicolopoulou*	7

PART I
Pretense and Storytelling in Autism Spectrum Disorder   29

2	Pretend Play in Children With Autism Spectrum Disorders: A Review of the Literature *Mahwish Chaudry and Cheryl Dissanayake*	31
3	Play, Narrative, and Children With Autism *Karen Stagnitti*	51
4	Developing Reciprocity With Technology and Storytelling: The Design of an Authorable Virtual Peer for Children With Autism Spectrum Disorder *Andrea Tartaro and Justine Cassell*	72

vi Contents

5 Social Robots as Storytellers: Can a Social Robot Encourage Children With Autism Spectrum Disorder to Ask Questions During Playtime? 96
Ramona Simut, Cristina Costescu, Johan Vanderfaeillie, Daniel David, and Bram Vanderborght

6 The Intersection of Pretense and Storytelling in Children With Autism Spectrum Disorder 117
Susan Douglas and Lesley Stirling

7 Dad! You Have to Be . . .: Autism, Narrative, and Family 149
Neil Maclean

PART II
Pretense and Storytelling in the Classroom 173

8 The Wrongheaded Exclusion of Imaginative Storytelling From Kindergarten Writing Instruction 175
Patricia M. Cooper

9 The Development of Subteacher Discourse During Pretend Play in the Wake of Reading a Story 198
Esther Vardi-Rath, Teresa Lewin, Zehava Cohen, Hadassah Aillenberg, and Tamar Eylon

10 The Natural World as Content for Interconnection and Divergence of Pretense and Storytelling in Children's Play 227
Kumara Ward

PART III
Pretense and Storytelling in Cross-Cultural Development 251

11 Using Narratives and Drawings to Assess Creativity in Preschool-Age Children 253
Candice M. Mottweiler

Contents **vii**

12 A Cultural–Historical Reading of Imagination and
    Creativity in Young Children's Shared Narrative
    Creations Across Cultural Contexts   271
    Sue March, Liang Li, and Gloria Quiñones

13 Returning to Play: The Critical Location of Play in
    Children's Sociocultural Lives   294
    Artin Göncü and Jennifer A. Vadeboncoeur

Contributors   *315*
Index   *319*

INTRODUCTION

Lesley Stirling and Susan Douglas

> play … [is] story in action, just as storytelling is play put into narrative form
>
> *(Paley, 1990, p. 4)*

> absorption in fiction is not a short-lived phenomenon of childhood but a capacity that endures a lifetime
>
> *(Harris, 2000, p. 6)*

At the heart of this volume is the recognition that children's play and their engagement with story are intrinsically and intricately linked. The contributors share a passionate interest in and concern for the well-being and development of children, particularly the way in which this relates to their use of imagination and recruitment of elements of their worlds in their play and stories. The goal of the volume is to explore the connections between play, story, and pretense as a function of the many cultural and contextual factors that influence the way in which these elements of children's lives and development vary. In a departure from earlier collections on play and story, we focus specifically on normative as compared with atypical development as one such factor.

Ageliki Nicolopoulou has written extensively about the relationship between children's pretend play and storytelling, and we begin this volume with a reprise of this work and the outline of an approach to understanding the developmental relationship between the two, which balances the recognition of their similarities with an acknowledgement of their complementarities. As she writes in Chapter 1 of the current volume: "Children's pretend play and narrative should not be artificially separated and studied in mutual isolation. Instead, they should be viewed as closely related and often intertwined forms of socially situated symbolic action" (Nicolopoulou, p. 9).

Many of the papers in this volume take Nicolopoulou's work as a catalyst for discussion and, in particular, Douglas and Stirling and Stagnitti also address some of the interrelationships between play and story.

After Nicolopoulou's paper, the volume is divided into three parts, each considering both play and story, but from different, though cross-cutting, perspectives. Children with autism spectrum disorder (ASD) offer a unique population within which to consider the characteristics and dimensions of both pretend play and story. Both of these activities have been considered problematic for these children, although as Chaudry and Dissanayake (this volume) and Stirling, Douglas, Leekam, and Carey (2014) point out, in each case the results of the extensive bodies of research published so far are mixed and difficult to interpret. Hence, research on ASD is of particular relevance to the general themes of this volume. Furthermore, there has been little research that has considered the nexus of play and story within this population of children. In Part I of this volume, we begin to redress this lack.

Chaudry and Dissanayake present a comprehensive review of the research on pretend play in children with ASD. They show that while there are robust findings indicating that these children may have difficulties with at least some kinds of pretend play, there is also substantial evidence that at least some children with ASD can comprehend pretend acts and can participate in pretend play actively and with enjoyment. These findings are reinforced by the papers by Douglas and Stirling and Stagnitti.

Douglas and Stirling begin to address the interaction between play and story as co-occurring within the same contexts of activity, exploring naturalistic interactions in the context of play between five children with ASD and their mother or a researcher and profiling the children's pretend play narrative abilities from the perspective of their focus on plot compared with character and their structural, imaginal, and metacommunicative characteristics. Stagnitti, too, considers the relationship between play and narrative in a case study of application of a learning to play intervention, which indicates developmental gains in both pretend play abilities and separate narrative production abilities in one child with ASD.

While Chaudry and Dissanayake and Douglas and Stirling provide descriptive accounts of play and pretend play narrative, the focus of the paper by Stagnitti, and of those by Simut, Costescu, Vanderfaeillie, David, and Vanderborght and Tartaro and Cassell, is on interventions targeting play behaviours in this atypical population of children. In one of the papers in this volume focusing on a non-English-speaking population, Simut et al. consider the combination of a Social Stories intervention with robot-assisted training to develop one aspect of the ability of children with ASD to take part in social play: that of being able to appropriately ask questions of their interlocutor. They demonstrate that the intervention trialled appeared to effectively support the ability of the six children studied to ask questions but note that additional research is needed to explore whether this skill would generalise beyond the therapeutic context. Tartaro and Cassell describe the design of an instructional environment for children with ASD in which a *virtual peer* may engage with the children in collaborative storytelling and which the children may also control in its interactions with others, demonstrating in a study of seven children what we can learn about the social behaviours and development of children with ASD from their use of such a system.

In the final paper in Part I, Maclean provides a case study of narrative play in one child with ASD—his son—giving a detailed ethnographic description of the activity of *Pretend* that Leo has developed and practiced with his family over a period of more than 7 years. Maclean's work illustrates yet another nexus between story and pretense, as the activity he describes does not involve pretend play, but verges on it, with enactment of creatively produced scenarios, including voicing by the adult participating. Pretend is driven and directed by Leo himself, and Maclean explores the developmental transformation of the play and its intersubjective dynamics within the social relationships it engenders.

In Part II of the book, we turn to a consideration of pretense and storytelling in the classroom and their relationship to children's literacy development, with three papers that take a specific focus on this topic—however, a number of the other papers in this volume are also relevant to children's experiences in institutional, classroom-based interaction—e.g., Nicolopoulou. Cooper begins this section of the book with an impassioned plea for the value of including imaginative storytelling and dramatic play in early-years school classrooms. Vardi-Rath, Lewin, Cohen, Aillenberg, and Eylon describe classroom-based pretend play following story reading, an activity type that is also discussed by Nicolopoulou and by Ward, and show through analysis of the children's metacommunicative discourse how the children manage the pretend play and incorporate aspects of *subteacher* discourse into this metacommunication. Ward describes a longitudinal project in which the introduction of aspects of flora and fauna from the local natural environment manifested over time in changes in the children's preschool creative activities. She studied children's developing use of materials and themes from the environment in their games, stories, dance, and other artistic outputs such as clay modelling and drawing.

While most of the papers in the book discuss English-speaking environments, the papers by Vardi-Rath et al. on Israeli children, Simut et al. on Romanian children, and March, Li, and Quiñones on children in rural Mexico and Australian children of Chinese and Anglo-Australian heritage begin to explore the issues around our cultural conceptualisations of play and story. Part III of the book focuses on the cultural context of play and story. Mottweiler and March et al. link the activities of play and story to the difficult-to-define concepts of *creativity* and *imagination* and, like Ward, to other products of creativity such as children's drawings. Where do children find their material in their creative construction of play and story? This question is a fundamental concern within the research reported by March et al., as well as being discussed elsewhere in the book—for example, by Ward and by Nicolopoulou.

The paper by Göncü and Vadeboncoeur, like the contribution from Nicolopoulou with which we begin the book, makes the strong point that even within an apparently monolithic cultural context, there can be major discontinuities in the understanding of and exposure to play and story. We need only compare the classroom contexts described in Cooper's chapter with those described by Ward to see that within apparently similar, Anglo-cultural environments (the United States and Australia), the way in which the institutions of schooling conceive of and assign comparative value to play and story in the school setting can vary rather extensively. We have chosen to end the volume with the contribution by Göncü and Vadeboncoeur for a number of reasons. As Cooper does for imaginative storytelling, these authors make a strong claim for the importance of play in children's lives, but they frame this within the argument that we need to take a broad and socioculturally sophisticated view of what counts as play. They end with a research and policy agenda that attends to the role of narrative in pretend play and the importance of sustained engagement in research on play.

This book began with a conference held at the University of Melbourne in July 2011, organised by the editors and supported by a Faculty of Arts Conference Support Grant. Entitled "Children's Play, Storytelling and Pretence," the conference brought together more than 40 participants with perspectives representing at least the discipline areas of linguistics, anthropology, psychology, education, and computer science. Nine of the contributions to this volume derive from presentations at the conference, including plenary papers by Dissanayake, Göncü, and Nicolopoulou.

The contributions published here bring together many disciplinary, theoretical, and methodological perspectives. Chaudry and Dissanayake summarise a body of research residing largely in developmental psychology that has emphasised matched-group experimental studies of the pretend play abilities of children with ASD. Both Tartaro and Cassell and Simut et al. explore the possible outcomes of play- or story-based interventions for children with ASD, taking a similarly structured and quantitative approach. On the other hand, many of the papers take a qualitative, case study–oriented approach, and so we get to know children such as Maclean's Leo, Stagnitti's Henry, Douglas and Stirling's Liam, and March et al.'s Mayra in all their individualism and creativity. One theme that emerges across the structural boundaries of the three parts of the book is therefore that of individual as well as cultural difference.

Many of the papers show a concern with how children's play and story unfold within an interactive environment as they engage with adults (e.g., Douglas &

Stirling; Maclean; March et al.; Stagnitti), with peers at home or at school (e.g., March et al.; Vardi-Rath et al.; Ward), or with robotic or virtual playmates (e.g., Simut et al.; Tartaro & Cassell). Play and story are seen as inherently connected with intersubjectivity in human interaction. This perspective also brings with it an interest in the ways in which the pretend or story world and the manifest world relate—and the relationship between play and metaplay talk.

So, what do our authors recommend as next steps in research and policy regarding play and story in children's lives? Without wishing to assume that all the contributors to this volume would necessarily agree on a unified position, we suggest that the following directions have emerged as themes from their collective research and writing on this topic:

1. We have good evidence already—and have had it for many years now—that suggests that both pretend play and narrative are central to children's development. But we need to know more about how play and story in development operate in different sociocultural environments.
2. One type of sociocultural environment in which some children grow up is what Maclean calls *autism world* (p. 154). As Chaudry and Dissanayake indicate, we still don't know enough about the developmental course of pretend play within ASD. The cognitive tasks involved in the production and comprehension of both narrative and social pretend play include tasks such as the negotiation of multiagent mental state ascriptions, the understanding of multiple perspectives, and the maintenance of higher level structural coherence, and it is relevant for developmental, sociocultural, and pedagogical perspectives on play and story to examine these phenomena in children who have a disorder affecting the development of reciprocal social engagement, communication, and the flexible use of objects.
3. As Douglas and Stirling note, we need to know more, too, about the dynamic interplay between the nonverbal and the verbal in pretend play narratives and the way in which these unfold within the social interactive context where a child plays with another. Researching story within pretend play seems likely to provide a new and interesting context for the understanding of language and cognitive development in clinical populations such as ASD. More broadly, as Göncü and Vadeboncoeur suggest, we have "undertheorized the different ways in which narrative genres may be used in different forms of play and everyday practices that include pretense and representation" (p. 307).
4. Finally, the research presented here endorses the position that it is enjoyable and beneficial for children to play freely and to be able to articulate the imaginative stories they produce (no matter how far removed from their everyday lives or how closely based on the media stories to which the children are exposed) within the early-years learning contexts in which they participate. However, for both typical and atypical development, further research will

better inform us as to how best to use and support play and story in educational and therapeutic contexts across different populations of children and for different children as individuals.

On behalf of all the contributors to this volume, we thank the anonymous peer reviewers who so generously took the time to provide comments on the initial proposal and on the individual chapters. Individually and collectively, we have done our best to benefit from these insights, and the papers are the better for their work.

We would also like to acknowledge and thank the children, who—warmly, quirkily, forbearingly, generously and, above all, in all their individuality—shared with all of us their games, their stories, their drawings, and their creative and magical perspectives on their worlds and their lives.

References

Harris, P. (2000). *The work of the imagination*. Oxford, UK: Wiley-Blackwell.

Paley, V. (1990). *The boy who would be a helicopter: The uses of storytelling in the classroom*. Cambridge, MA: Harvard University Press.

Stirling, L., Douglas, S., Leekam, S., & Carey, L. (2014). The use of narrative in studying communication in Autism Spectrum Disorders: A review of methodologies and findings. In J. Arciuli & J. Brock (Eds.), *Communication in autism* (pp. 171–216). Amsterdam, Netherlands: Benjamins.

1

YOUNG CHILDREN'S PRETEND PLAY AND STORYTELLING AS MODES OF NARRATIVE ACTIVITY

From Complementarity to Cross-Fertilization?

Ageliki Nicolopoulou

How should we think about and study the relationship between young children's pretend play and narrative? The emergence and transformations of these symbolic activities in early childhood, along with the development of abilities they require and promote, play important roles in children's experience, development, socialization, and education. It is therefore appropriate that substantial and growing bodies of research have addressed both of these subjects during the past several decades (e.g., Bamberg, 1997; Bruner, 1992; Fireman, McVay, & Flanagan, 2003; McCabe & Bliss, 2003; Nicolopoulou, 1993, 1997a; Roskos & Christie, 2000; Saracho, 2012; Saracho & Spodek, 2003; Singer, Golinkoff, & Hirsh-Pasek, 2006; Tabors, Snow, & Dickinson, 2001). However, there have been fewer efforts to analyze them in an integrated way and to explore the relationship between them concretely and systematically. More systematic examination of the dynamic interplay between pretend play and narrative in development can help enrich both areas of research and, in the process, contribute to our larger understanding of the development of cognition, imagination, language, and socioemotional skills. Along with the other pieces assembled in this volume, the present chapter seeks to contribute to such efforts. It will outline an orienting theoretical approach that may help guide research in this area, illustrate and support it with empirical examples, and suggest some implications for both research and practice. (My discussion will draw on arguments and material from some of my previous publications, particularly Nicolopoulou, 2007.)

Narrative in Play and Story

The lack of sufficient integration between developmental research on pretend play and narrative is both unfortunate and surprising, because theoretical

8 Ageliki Nicolopoulou

considerations and existing empirical research point toward important affinities and interdependence between them (for one overview, see Kavanaugh & Engel, 1998). A key point of intersection, on which I will focus in this chapter, is that pretend play itself has a crucial narrative dimension, since it centers on the enactment of narrative scenarios. In fact, for a number of purposes it is useful to see children's pretend play and storytelling as complementary modes of their narrative activity, on a continuum ranging from the discursive exposition of narratives in storytelling to their enactment in pretend play (Nicolopoulou, 1997a, 2002, 2005, 2007). For enactive as well as discursive narrative, children must develop and employ both production and comprehension skills (a point usefully highlighted, in connection with pretend play, by Kavanaugh, 2006b and Kavanaugh & Engel, 1998).[1]

It is worth emphasizing that this is a continuum rather than a sharp dichotomy. Between the two analytical poles of purely discursive storytelling and purely enacted pretend play, there are various intermediate and hybrid forms. For example, children can use character figurines in a range of ways that include minimally symbolic physical manipulation as a starting point for rudimentary proto-narratives, prompting and illustrating largely discursive storytelling, or engaging in complex and coherent figurine-centered play. And, in practice, children's pretend play often tends to combine enacted narrative with elements of discursive narrative; children use the latter to help set up play scenarios, negotiate adjustments and variations, and offer commentary as the action unfolds (for some illustrations of how this happens, see Douglas & Stirling, this volume). As Boyd (2009, p. 177) aptly put it (drawing on Sawyer, 1997), in children's pretend play, "direction, narration, and enactment flow readily and naturally into one another." This is especially true of the coordinated activity of social pretend play.

The narrative links and parallels between play and story have not gone entirely unexplored, though there is considerable room for further research. Recognition of the narrative dimension in pretend play informed studies of children's *play narratives* and their development (e.g., Eckler & Weininger, 1989; Galda, 1984; Glaubman, Kashi, & Koresh, 2001; Pellegrini, 1985; Sachs, Goldman, & Chaille, 1985; Wolf, Rygh, & Altshuler, 1984). Their guiding premise, summed up by Kavanaugh (2006b, p. 275), was that "there is an implicit narrative structure to the pretend play of young children that bears a striking relationship to their storytelling and story comprehension skill." There have also been some efforts to directly compare the *narrative structures* of children's pretend play and storytelling (Benson, 1993; Ilgaz & Aksu-Koç, 2005). Other work, including some that has not explicitly highlighted the narrative connection between these two symbolic activities, has also helped bring out relevant similarities and affinities. Harris (2000) argued that there are "important continuities" between the cognitive capacities that underpin children's participation in pretend play and the processing of narrative discourse by children and adults (pp. 51–54, 192–194). Both activities entail trying

Children's Pretend Play and Storytelling **9**

to accomplish and combine two key functions: creating and transforming an adequately coherent mental model of an imagined world (playworld or storyworld) while also entering into the point of view of the characters being portrayed.

Furthermore, several partly independent, partly intersecting lines of research have helped illuminate another set of similarities between pretend play and storytelling: both represent the union of expressive imagination with rule-governed cultural form in the context of social life, and this helps them serve as key contexts for children's construction of reality and identity (Nicolopoulou, 1993, 1997a). In both pretend play and storytelling, children are required, encouraged, and increasingly enabled to appropriate the rich array of themes, images, roles, genres, models, and other symbolic resources available in their culture and to use these flexibly and creatively—for the intrinsic satisfactions offered by these activities and, simultaneously, to help make sense of the world and of themselves. In the process, children also use play and story as vehicles for expressing and working over emotionally important themes that preoccupy them and symbolically managing or resolving the concerns they represent. Engaging in either or both of these symbolic activities—as actors, listeners, or storytellers; in solitary forms or in practices shared with adults and peers—offers children opportunities and motivations to use and master the narrative genres and other symbolic resources they embody, to explore and extend their inherent possibilities through performance and experimentation, and to push on to greater range and proficiency. (I am synthesizing arguments, analyses, findings, and implications from a range of sources that include Bruner, 1986; Cohen & MacKeith, 1991; Fein, 1987, 1995; Feldman, Bruner, Kalmar, & Renderer, 1993; Miller, Hengst, Alexander, & Sperry, 2000; Miller, Hoogstra, Mintz, Fung, & Williams, 1993; Nicolopoulou, 1997a, 1997b; Nicolopoulou, Scales, & Weintraub, 1994; Richner & Nicolopoulou, 2001; Rowe, 1998, 2000; Wells, 1986; Wolf & Heath, 1992.) So we should not be surprised by indications that, in significant respects, "[t]he complexity and structure of children's stories seem to develop in a manner parallel to the development of their dramatic play" (Galda, 1984, p. 28), nor by accumulated evidence that children's participation in various forms of pretend play can help promote skills necessary for the production and comprehension of stories (Nicolopoulou & Ilgaz, 2013).

The key insights here have perhaps been formulated most vividly by Vivian Paley (1990), who has consistently argued that "play . . . [is] story in action, just as storytelling is play put into narrative form" (p. 4); that children's "fantasy play and storytelling are never far apart" (p. 8); and "that this view of play makes play, along with its alter ego, storytelling and acting, the universal learning medium" (p. 10). Following the lead of Paley and others in this respect, I have argued that we should approach children's pretend play and narrative as closely related and often intertwined forms of socially situated symbolic action—and that one source of valuable theoretical resources for grasping the interplay between the two is

Vygotsky's sociocultural analysis of children's play (Nicolopoulou, 1997a, 2002; Nicolopoulou, Cortina, Ilgaz, Cates, & de Sá, 2015; Nicolopoulou, de Sá, Ilgaz, & Brockmeyer, 2010; Vygotsky, 1933/1967). Both pretend play and storytelling should be viewed as expressions of children's symbolic imagination that draw from and reflect back upon the interrelated domains of emotional, intellectual, and social life.

From Complementarity to Convergence?

Now for the other side of the coin. Understanding and appreciating these similarities and interconnections between children's pretend play and storytelling is an essential starting point. But the two are not identical—which is why they can play complementary and mutually enriching roles in development. Their differences have to do with the intrinsic characteristics of play and story production and comprehension as activities, their roles in children's social relations and group life, and the kinds of skills and capacities they require and promote. We need theoretical and empirical approaches that can do justice to those developmental and experiential differences as well as the overlaps and similarities.

Building on elements from previous research and my own ongoing studies of preschool children in naturalistic contexts, I have argued (e.g., in Nicolopoulou, 2007) that the active interplay and cross-fertilization between children's pretend play and storytelling can significantly advance their development in a range of domains but that this active interplay is neither given nor automatic. Rather, they seem to start out as mostly separate and parallel activities, and the potential for fruitful coordination and cross-fertilization between them is a developmental achievement—which then serves as a catalyst for accelerating further development. I thus propose a model that sees young children's pretend play and storytelling as initially parallel and complementary modes of their narrative activity, with at least partially distinct developmental origins and trajectories, which children are only gradually able to integrate effectively. To put it another way, the relationship between the two moves from complementarity to convergence in the course of development. It is important to add that this convergence is not a once-and-for-all event that can be located at a specific age, but a gradual, complex, and uneven process (with cross-cultural variations, as suggested by Reese, 2013) that we still need to map out and analyze. Broadly speaking, however, the period from roughly 3 to 5 years seems to be especially critical in this respect.

From Initial Disjunction to Growing Cross-Fertilization: Developmental Patterns and Possible Explanations

One type of evidence supporting the model just proposed is a pattern I have consistently observed in preschool classes I have studied over several decades.

Toward the beginning of the school year, especially among younger preschoolers and those with weaker narrative skills, there tends to be a significant disjunction between the themes, scenarios, and other symbolic elements that the children use in their pretend play and in their storytelling. Over time, however, there is an increasing integration and cross-fertilization between the two, with similar themes and scenarios used flexibly and effectively in both activities. I offer two contrasting examples to illustrate this pattern.

Thematic Disjunction Versus Overlap and Interchange: Two Snapshots

One example of sharp thematic disjunction comes from a Head Start classroom in a large metropolitan area, a few weeks after I had begun to introduce a storytelling and story-acting practice that will be described later in this chapter.[2] During one of my visits to this classroom, before taking stories from the children, I was observing a group of them at a waist-high sand table while they played with figurines representing animals, cars, and superheroes. What follows is an excerpt from my field notes (February 28, 2003):

> At one moment I was playing with some kids at the sand table. I noticed that the children were rather imaginative in their play, taking on the role of a character/superhero flying around, hitting others, etc. I pretended I did not know what to do with my character and some of the kids were directing me. A regular volunteer in this classroom, an older woman from the community, urged me to take down a story from one of these children, Dasai,[3] because she mentioned he was very imaginative. I had noticed his imaginative engagement in the sand table play (that is, having his action hero character perform various stereotypic actions). After he lost interest in the sand table and was looking around for another activity, I asked him whether he wanted to tell me (i.e., dictate) a story. He was eager to do that, and I thought that he would tell me a story that followed (or had some elements of) his sand table play. However, his story just recounted some simple ordinary events and resembled a number of stories I was getting from the children in this and other Head Start classrooms.

> **Dasai:** Me and my brother played outside. We went to the store.
> **AN:** *[Because he stopped, I asked]* What kind of store?
> **Dasai:** Gumstore. That's it.

This incident helped bring home to me a phenomenon of which I had gradually become aware—the extent to which some young children, especially during early phases of their preschool years, viewed their pretend play and storytelling as

12 Ageliki Nicolopoulou

separate and disconnected activities. One manifestation of this disconnection was the minimal or, in this case, nonexistent overlap between the thematic content in their pretend play and storytelling.

For contrast, here is an example from a different preschool classroom serving children from predominantly middle-class families, which illustrates the possibility for children to engage in effective and flexible interchange between their pretend play and storytelling. For several weeks, the teacher had been using a variety of activities to highlight the theme of dinosaurs. Her goal was to build on and enrich the children's interest in this theme, which was present in a good deal of their pretend play, especially among the boys. But whereas the boys tended to use dinosaurs exclusively in scenarios featuring aggression and violence, she tried to complement this by suggesting that dinosaurs also had families and children and engaged in some nonviolent activities. Over time, the dinosaur theme became prominent in a number of children's stories as well as their play, and this was especially true for children who had already experienced the storytelling and story-acting practice during the previous year. In the incident I am about to describe, the child storyteller not only used the dinosaur theme in his story but also went a step further and used his story to reflect back on his dinosaur-themed play.

Two children, Mason and Kellen, had been excluding another child, Ben, from their play. The teacher had a discussion with Mason and Kellen in which she expressed her disappointment about this. After their discussion, Mason went to the storytelling corner and composed the following story. It is apparent that he tried to make up with Ben by including him in the activity described in the story and in effect included him in their play as well, since this story was acted out by the children involved:

> Once upon a time there was Kellen. Mason and Ben and then Cooper came. And then Mason and Ben and Cooper and Kellen went home to watch TV. And then a dinosaur came and then Mason hopped on the dinosaur that was named Pterodactyl and the dinosaur named Pterodactyl flopped his wings and went up in the air. And then Mason said, "Down for a landing, Pterodactyl!" And he said, "Wait a minute, I forgot Kellen and Ben and Cooper." And then he flew like this [flops hands] and Cooper, Ben, and Kellen hopped on the pterodactyl and flew off together to Dinosaur Land and then they all went home. The end.
>
> *(Mason, 4;5)*

In preschool classrooms I have studied, children often displayed this kind of thematic continuity between their pretend play and storytelling. But they rarely did so from the beginning of the school year. The ability and inclination to engage in this flexible interchange took time to develop—and it developed to different degrees, and with different rhythms, for different children.

Making Sense of This Pattern

These and other findings support the idea that young children's pretend play and storytelling start out as relatively distinct and parallel symbolic activities, and the ability to engage in flexible coordination and cross-fertilization between them is a developmental achievement that requires some time and effort to accomplish. The explanation I propose for this developmental pattern remains tentative and exploratory, but it is possible to suggest some orienting hypotheses.

The narrative dimension shared by pretend play and the production and comprehension of stories offers a starting point for making sense of their somewhat distinct but ultimately interrelated developmental trajectories. As noted previously, a key point of contact between these two symbolic activities is that both involve constructing and understanding narrative scenarios. However, fully developed narrative combines a number of different elements, and achieving full narrative competence requires being able to integrate them effectively. I would argue that, especially in their early phases, young children's pretend play and storytelling require and promote partly distinctive but complementary clusters of narrative-related skills. They emphasize different elements of narrative, build to some degree on different cognitive and linguistic abilities, pose different challenges, and offer different possibilities. This complementary relationship between the two activities is an important reason why their coordination and cross-fertilization can be beneficial, but it also helps explain why integrating them requires significant effort and development.

What are the elements into which well-formed narrative can be analytically decomposed in order to pursue these hypotheses? Here, we might draw on the influential suggestion by Bruner (1986) that successful narrative must simultaneously construct and effectively integrate two landscapes: a *landscape of action* that links sequences of actions and events in physical settings and a *landscape of consciousness* that portrays "what those involved in the action know, think, and feel" (p. 14). These two landscapes are analytically distinct, but it is their integration that gives successful narrative its full power and coherence. To reframe this distinction somewhat, constructing (and comprehending) fully developed narrative requires both (a) coordinating actions and events into a coherent *plot* and (b) rich and effective representation of *characters*, including the portrayal and coordination of their subjective points of view. How are pretend play and story involved in the processes by which young children develop the abilities necessary for accomplishing these complementary tasks—and the ability to integrate them effectively?

Complementary Narrative Emphases in Early Pretend Play and Storytelling

From the beginning, of course, young children struggle with both plot construction and character representation in both pretend play and storytelling, and these

14 Ageliki Nicolopoulou

two aspects of narrative can never be entirely independent. But there are good reasons to believe that in the earliest phases of development the two activities tend to emphasize and promote different dimensions of narrative and narrative skills. In comparative terms, the narrative dimension in early pretend play involves more emphasis on character representation and perspective taking, whereas early storytelling offers more opportunities and motivations for increasing complexity, coherence, and sophistication in plot construction.

There is considerable evidence (summed up by Kavanaugh & Engel, 1998) that pretend play, especially sociodramatic role-play, highlights and fosters children's abilities to understand and coordinate multiple mental perspectives. Several characteristic features of pretend play, whether solitary or interactive, contribute to these effects. Children's identification with characters whose roles they enact heightens their interest and emotional engagement in the activity. This role playing also has an important cognitive dimension, since it pushes the child to see the world from the point of view of the character being represented—which entails constructing a relatively consistent perspective for this character—and also to coordinate this imagined perspective with those of other protagonists in the play scenario. Thus, it promotes the ability and inclination to understand people's actions in terms of motives, beliefs, desires, and other internal mental states in addition to externally observable phenomena—skills that are critical for constructing a landscape of consciousness in narrative. This is true not only for children's participation in play enactment itself, which involves portraying and identifying with characters, but also for the "metaplay" communication and interaction used in setting up, negotiating, and managing play (e.g., Farver, 1992; Goldman, 1998; Göncü, 1993a, 1993b; Sachs et al., 1984; Sawyer, 1997; Trawick-Smith, 1998). Wolf et al. (1984) found that, in pretend play with figurines, even 3-year-olds began to explicitly attribute to characters emotions, cognitions, obligations, and moral judgments; this is several years younger than the earliest age at which such mentalistic descriptions have been found in children's stories in the great bulk of research on narrative (e.g., Berman & Slobin, 1994; for an overview, see Nicolopoulou & Richner, 2007). There is also ample research suggesting that children who participate more frequently in role-play and other forms of joint pretend play demonstrate greater understanding of internal mental processes, including the role of false beliefs (e.g., Astington & Jenkins, 1995; Kavanaugh, 2006a; Schwebel, Rosen, & Singer, 1999; Taylor & Carlson, 1997; Youngblade & Dunn, 1995).

At the same time, the strongly improvisational style of children's pretend play (Sawyer, 1997) makes it more difficult to develop complex, sophisticated, or even coherent plots, and these difficulties are increased by the negotiated multiparty improvisations of cooperative pretend play. As Sawyer and others have recognized, analyses of intersubjectivity in pretend play (and metaplay) interaction still need to be coordinated more fully with developmental analyses that explore the structure and symbolic content of the enacted play narratives themselves. But existing play research already offers evidence—in effect, if not explicitly—for the developmental priority of character representation over plot in young children's pretend play narratives (e.g., Howes, Unger, & Matheson, 1992; Sachs et al., 1984). Even as the characters in their play scenarios are increasingly fleshed out, individuated, and portrayed with psychological depth, the plots tend to remain rudimentary, with minimal complexity or coherence. It is not until later that children begin to construct and enact well-articulated plots in their pretend play, thus moving toward the effective integration of plot and character representation in their play narratives.

In their storytelling, by comparison, young children initially show greater preoccupation with and success in constructing, elaborating, and extending coherent plots. Some children may start out with proto-stories in which they simply list characters, but as soon as they grasp that the characters' actions have to be described explicitly, they begin to construct sequences of actions and events that become increasingly extended, complex, and imaginative. My own observations accord with Benson's (1993) finding that the plots of preschoolers' stories are usually more complex and sophisticated than those of their pretend play narratives. For some time, however, this increasing strength in plot construction is not usually matched in the development of character representation. Young children are certainly capable of including a range of characters in their stories, and some of them (particularly girls) begin quite early to link characters in family or quasifamily relationships. However, at first, these characters tend to remain generic types, described with little detail or psychological depth. They are portrayed largely in terms of their actions, especially by boys, or in terms of their social ties, especially by girls (Richner & Nicolopoulou, 2001). Only later do the children's stories begin to portray individuated characters with more detailed characteristics, perspectives on the world, and internal mental states (Nicolopoulou & Richner, 2007; Richner & Nicolopoulou, 2001).

Before proceeding, I want to reiterate that these comparisons between pretend play and story should not be taken as suggesting a rigid or complete separation between the two activities and their developmental dynamics. For example, I have emphasized the ways that pretend play can encourage and facilitate children's identification with characters being enacted. But it seems clear that, under some circumstances, even very young children can sometimes experience vivid identification and deep imaginative involvement with characters in stories they hear and tell (e.g., the 2-year-old described in Miller et al., 1993). The actual developmental pathways followed by individual children are always complex and diverse, in narrative as in other domains, and they are influenced in various ways by specific social contexts and practices. In general terms, however, the available evidence supports the broad tendencies and contrasts outlined here.

Integrating the Elements of a Complete Narrative Scenario

In both their pretend play and their storytelling, young children gradually master the ability to construct a full narrative scenario. That is, they achieve the capacity to routinely produce and understand narrative scenarios that effectively combine coherent and complex plots with rich and substantial character representations, including the portrayal of a landscape of consciousness. This is a developmental goal toward which they are working in both contexts, though from different and complementary directions. I would provisionally suggest that achieving this level of development in at least one of their two central narrative activities—pretend play or storytelling—is a key factor that accelerates active and fruitful narrative cross-fertilization between them. One reason is that the ability to produce and understand a full narrative scenario, if only in minimal form, integrates the two crucial elements of narrative emphasized by early pretend play and storytelling, respectively, and helps enable children to build cognitive bridges between the two activities. We still need to determine the degree to which achieving this capacity to integrate the enactive narrative of pretend play and the discursive narrative of story production and comprehension takes the form of a gradual and self-reinforcing process or a more sharply defined developmental breakthrough. But, in either case, it constitutes an important developmental threshold that serves, in turn, as a basis and impetus for further development.

Promoting Convergence, Cross-Fertilization, and Development: Reports from a Preschool Storytelling and Story-Acting Practice

The argument I have been making has practical as well as analytical implications. To contribute to promoting children's learning and development, it is important for us to understand, encourage, support, and design activities that can help young children achieve effective narrative integration and cross-fertilization between pretend play and storytelling. And it so happens that much of my work for several decades has involved studying the operation and effects of a preschool practice with precisely these characteristics. This is an activity combining storytelling and story-acting—also described as story dictation and dramatization—pioneered by the teacher and author Vivian Paley (1990) and used in many preschool and kindergarten classes in the United States and abroad (Cooper, 2005, 2009; McNamee, 1987; Nicolopoulou, 1997a, 2002). I have been able to demonstrate that participation in this practice helps promote young children's narrative abilities as well as other skills in the interconnected domains of oral language, emergent literacy, and social competence (Nicolopoulou, 1996, 2002; Nicolopoulou et al., 2010, 2015; see also McNamee, McLane, Cooper, & Kerwin, 1985). And one key to its effectiveness is the way it integrates elements of storytelling (discursive narrative) and pretend play (narrative enactment). In addition to helping demonstrate the practical value of such narrative- and play-based practices in early childhood education, the findings from my research also provide further evidence to support the developmental model proposed in this chapter.

This practice is conducted with variations in different contexts, but its main outlines tend to be fairly consistent. At a certain period during each day (usually during some version of "choice time"), any child who wishes can dictate a story to a designated teacher or teacher's aide, who writes down the story as the child tells it. This storytelling is voluntary, and each story dictation is typically child-initiated. Although children are not required to compose any specific type of story or guided toward suggested topics, these are usually fictional or fantasy stories, rather than "factual" accounts of personal experience characteristic of "show and tell" or "sharing time." Later that day, each of these stories is read aloud by the teacher to the entire class, assembled for "group time," while the child/author and other children, whom he or she chooses, act out the story.

This is an apparently simple activity with complex and powerful effects. Several features are especially worth noting. Although this is a structured and teacher-facilitated activity, the children's storytelling is voluntary, self-initiated, and relatively spontaneous. Their stories are neither solicited directly by adults nor channeled by props, story stems, or suggested topics. Because this practice runs through the entire school year and the children control their own storytelling, it provides them with the opportunity to work over, refine, and elaborate their narratives and to use them for their own diverse purposes—cognitive, symbolic, expressive, and social-relational (Nicolopoulou, 1996, 1997b; Nicolopoulou et al., 1994, 2014; Richner & Nicolopoulou, 2001). At the same time, having their stories written down by an adult and then later read to the class can help familiarize children with writing and its uses in a concrete and engaging manner (Nicolopoulou, McDowell, & Brockmeyer, 2006).

Furthermore, the way that this practice combines story*telling* with story-*acting* has several important implications. Children typically enjoy storytelling for its own sake, but the prospect of having their story acted out, together with other children whom they choose, offers them a powerful additional motivation to compose and dictate stories. And one result of having the stories read to and dramatized for the entire class at group time is that the children tell their stories not only to adults but also primarily to *each other*; they do so not in one-to-one interaction but in a shared public setting. Children are thus given opportunities to borrow elements from each other's stories and rework them, facilitating narrative cross-fertilization. When this practice is established as a regular part of classroom activities, all children typically participate over time in three interrelated roles: (a) composing and dictating stories, (b) taking part in the group enactment of stories (their own and those of other children), and (c) listening to and watching the performance of the stories of other children. Thus, the children's storytelling and story-acting are embedded in the ongoing context of the classroom miniculture and the children's everyday group life, with their strong relational and emotional significance (see Nicolopoulou, 2002, and Nicolopoulou et al., 2014, for some elaboration). To borrow a telling formulation from Paley (1986), this public arena offers children an "experimental theater" (p. xv) in which they can reciprocally try out, elaborate, and refine their own narrative efforts while getting the responses of an engaged and emotionally significant peer group audience. And, of course, this practice systematically integrates elements from two symbolic activities of special interest to children: the discursive exposition of narratives in storytelling and the enactment of narratives in pretend play. Some reasons why that combination might be valuable have already been discussed.

I have studied the use of this storytelling and story-acting practice as a regular part of the curriculum in 20 preschool classes (not counting control classes) of 3- to 5-year-old children that differed by geography and social class composition. Eleven were in preschools in California and Massachusetts serving children from middle-class backgrounds; the other nine were in programs serving children from poor and otherwise disadvantaged backgrounds, including two Head Start classes, one in Massachusetts and one in Pennsylvania, and seven classes in a preschool and childcare program in Pennsylvania studied from 2005 to 2007. In most cases, collection and analysis of the children's stories were complemented by regular ethnographic observations of the classroom activities, friendship patterns, and group life of the children involved, including their unstructured free play.

In certain respects, the patterns have been strikingly consistent across all the classrooms studied, though every classroom also has its own unique features. In all cases, children became enthusiastically involved in this storytelling and story-acting practice and brought considerable energy and creativity to it. As the school year progressed, children's stories became more complex and sophisticated, manifesting significant advances in narrative competence and cognitive abilities. But along with these broad similarities, it is also worth noting some systematic differences between the predominantly middle-class preschools and those serving low-income and otherwise disadvantaged children—whose backgrounds also included higher degrees of family disorganization and instability. In the latter, children tended to begin the year with weaker oral language skills, including narrative skills (as one would expect from, e.g., Hart and Risley, 1995; Hoff, 2006; Peterson, 1994), and less familiarity with the basic conventions for constructing freestanding, self-contextualizing fictional narratives (for some elaboration, see Nicolopoulou, 2002, pp. 128–129, 139–141). Thus, by comparison with the middle-class preschoolers, they were much more in the position of building up the basic foundations for their participation in this narrative activity from scratch rather than simply applying and expanding narrative skills they had already mastered.

In constructing their stories, the children drew themes, characters, images, plots, and other elements from a wide range of sources, including fairy tales; children's books; various media of popular culture, including TV and video games;

and their own experiences; they also drew elements from each other's stories. However, they did not simply imitate other children's stories, nor did they just passively absorb messages from adults and the larger culture. It is clear that, even at this early age, they were able to appropriate these elements *selectively* and to *use* and rework them for their own purposes (Nicolopoulou, 1996, 1997b; Nicolopoulou et al., 1994, 2014; Richner & Nicolopoulou, 2001). These processes of active and selective appropriation and narrative cross-fertilization became increasingly conspicuous as the children achieved greater mastery of narrative skills. So they took off more rapidly in the middle-class preschool classes, but in the long run they flourished in the low-income preschool classes as well.

Given this lively profusion of narrative appropriation and cross-fertilization, which includes an ongoing interchange and reworking of themes between different children's stories, one might also expect to find extensive thematic interchange between the children's storytelling and their unstructured pretend play. In fact, preschoolers often do use common themes in their stories and play scenarios. However, as I have already indicated, I have consistently found that among the younger preschoolers and those with weaker narrative and play skills, the overlap of themes and other symbolic elements between their discursive narratives and the narrative scenarios they enact in pretend play is at first minimal or absent. At that stage, as I have suggested, the children's pretend play and storytelling appear to operate as parallel activities with surprisingly little thematic interchange or mutual influence. Integration between them, as expressed by the use of common themes in both activities, takes some time to become established. Some research findings from middle-class preschools and from Head Start classes can help flesh out and illuminate different aspects of this overall pattern.

Middle-Class Preschools

In Paley's rich ethnographic accounts of her preschool classes (e.g., 1986, 1988, 1990), one encounters numerous examples of children using (and reworking) similar themes in their pretend play and storytelling. In my own studies of middle- and upper-middle-class preschoolers, I have also observed frequent continuity of themes between children's play and their stories. However, there is at first a sharp disjunction between the themes that children use in these two activities, and thematic continuity between them has to be developed over time.

To provide one illustration of this pervasive pattern, I will use a middle-class preschool classroom studied during the 1999–2000 school year. This class included 17 children (nine girls and eight boys). My examples come from two time periods (in December and May) in which the children's classroom play was observed and audiotaped for 2 consecutive days. In both observational periods, the children who told stories also engaged in pretend play episodes. However, in December, as in previous months, the extent to which they used common themes in their pretend play and storytelling was minimal, whereas by May it had increased substantially.

During the first day of the December observation period, we did not see much sustained pretend play, but the next day, five children, later joined by two more, participated in a joint play episode lasting over an hour that centered on fire truck and firefighter themes. This play episode seems to have been at least partly inspired by props that the teacher brought into the classroom (i.e., she placed tires next to a large block structure on which children could sit), and during the play she actively but gently scaffolded it (e.g., adding hoses once the firefighter theme was established). Different children took on the firefighter paradigm and actively elaborated on it in their own way, responding only intermittently to the teacher's suggestions. The children engaged in the play episode developed and recycled a cluster of loosely connected themes: putting out a fire, helping a dead person, washing the fire truck, driving the fire truck around, and putting gas in the fire truck.

Later in the day, two of the dominant children in this play episode dictated stories to the teacher, but their stories showed barely a trace of the central play themes. There was no mention of fires, fire trucks, or firefighters. One story did mention a hose—"Ben blowed on the hole of the hose" (Jason, 5;0)—which may have been a reference to the hoses used to put gas in the make-believe fire truck. In the other story, told by Rhys (5;1), there was mention of a dead person—a role that this child had played briefly during the play episode. In both stories, these were no more than brief (and ambiguous) references to isolated elements from the play episode, with no effort to incorporate and elaborate on the central themes of the pretend play narrative. This lack of sustained thematic interchange was a pattern we observed consistently in this class throughout the fall semester.

By May, in contrast, themes from the children's pretend play appeared frequently in their stories and vice versa, and there was often a fluid continuity between the narrative scenarios in the two activities. For example, two boys, Tillian and Jason, played together with the themes of Power Rangers and fighting. Later that day, they coauthored a story using the same themes:

> A story about fighting.
> One day there was two men. Then there was a Power Ranger. Then one man punched the other man. And then that man fell down a mountain. And then he climbed back again. And punched the guy back. Then the Power Ranger chased those fighting guys out of the world forever. And then came the end.
>
> *(Tillian, 5;2 & Jason, 5;6, May 25, 2000)*

That same day, Holly, one of the youngest children in the class, was playing with figurines of various farm animals, arranging and rearranging them in different configurations. At one point she announced to a teacher and a nearby child that she had created a "horse school." This other child joined her briefly in playing with the figurines. Later that day, Holly told the following story:

> A toy story.
> Once upon a time there was a big horse. And then there was a little sheep. And there was a goose and a chicken. They both had babies, two babies and three babies. And then there was a little horse and a little goat. And there was a black cat. They played Candy Land. The end.
>
> *(Holly, 3;9, May 25, 2000)*

These examples capture the larger pattern indicated by the analyses of pretend play and storytelling of children in the middle-class preschools studied. At first, the use of common themes in these two modes of narrative activity was minimal and tended to include only isolated elements. (The main exceptions were children in their second year of preschool who began the school year already having participated in this storytelling and story-acting practice the previous year.) By the spring, however, thematic continuity and cross-fertilization between their pretend play and storytelling were considerably more frequent and comprehensive.

Low-Income Preschools: Two Head Start Classrooms

This initial disjunction between the thematic content of children's stories and their pretend play scenarios has been even more striking in preschools serving poor and otherwise disadvantaged children that I have studied. Earlier I offered one example from a Head Start classroom in a large city, a few weeks after I had introduced the storytelling and story-acting practice in that class. The typical long-term patterns can be illustrated more fully with examples drawn from a study of another Head Start class of 17 children in a semirural area in the northeastern United States conducted during the 1997–1998 school year (Nicolopoulou, 2002). These children came from backgrounds of poverty combined, in most cases, with family difficulty or instability. The teacher introduced the storytelling and story-acting practice into the classroom that year with my assistance. In addition to monitoring its operation, for a 2-day period each month an assistant and I conducted systematic observations of other classroom activities, including the children's unstructured free play.

The children in this class began the school year with significantly weaker narrative skills than corresponding middle-class children or even children in some other Head Start classes I have observed. For example, they showed less familiarity with the basic conventions for telling a freestanding, self-contextualized story—such as marking beginnings and endings, explicitly relating events in temporal sequence, and constructing a complete narrative scenario—and less mastery of the relevant language skills. Their narrative skills improved significantly during the year, but even in the spring these were still less advanced than those of equivalent-aged children in middle-class preschools I have studied. Early in the school year, the children's pretend play was also rather limited and fragmentary—generally restricted to a small range of stereotyped roles, with minimal scenarios and very little play-related communication. Both the quantity and quality of their pretend play increased during the school year but, again, these remained relatively weak in most cases.

Thus, although the children immediately displayed great enthusiasm for telling stories, at first they had some difficulty doing this effectively. In their early attempts at storytelling, they simply listed a string of characters (and sometimes mentioned other potentially relevant elements), usually without providing actions, descriptions, or plots. After several weeks of this proto-narrative groping, one child, April, produced a story that met the minimal standards for a freestanding fictional story:

> Wedding girl and wedding boy, and then there was a baby. And then there was the person that brought out the flowers. And then there was some animal that wrecked the house, the church house that people were getting married in. And a person was listening to a wedding tape. And that's all.
> *(April, 5;1)*

This story was not very complex, but it did include a relatively coherent and explicit scenario, a set of interrelated characters, and a sketchy but readily discernible plot. It also introduced and combined a set of organizing themes that were to prove to be powerfully appealing to other children in the class: (a) a wedding, featuring the two linked characters of wedding girl and wedding boy and (b) animal aggression.

The dynamics of the storytelling and story-acting practice then set in motion a process of narrative borrowing and mutual cross-fertilization. A few weeks later, another child, Anton, who had acted as the wedding boy in April's story, composed a story using these themes and adding his own elaborations. In Anton's story, the wedding couple got married and then went on to have children (an event that, incidentally, happens very rarely in boys' stories). Shortly afterward, April told a slightly reworked version of her story. Over time, this story paradigm was gradually taken up and reused, with variations and elaborations, by other children in the class until it became pervasive in the children's storytelling. By the spring, all the children in the class had told at least some stories that included this bundle of themes, and more than half of them had used it in most of their stories. This narrative paradigm became a cultural tool that was shared and elaborated on by the classroom peer group as a whole (for more details, see Nicolopoulou, 2002).

Given the extent to which this cluster of themes captured the children's attention and imagination and the enthusiasm with which different children appropriated it for their own storytelling, one might have expected these themes to appear

Children's Pretend Play and Storytelling **23**

in their pretend play as well. However, this was not the case for most of the year. In fact, not until May did we observe a play episode in which three girls, who had used these themes profusely in their stories, enacted a wedding girl and wedding boy scenario. The classroom teacher confirmed that this was the first time she had noticed the children using these themes in their play, although the same girls subsequently used them in a few more play episodes. Nor did the characteristic themes in the children's play appear in their stories.

In short, even at the end of the school year there was a striking disjunction between the rapid and pervasive thematic cross-fertilization between the children's stories and the relative lack of thematic cross-fertilization between their storytelling and their pretend play narratives. The contrast in this respect between the pattern in this Head Start class and those in the middle-class preschools suggests that the children in this class, despite their developmental advances over the course of the year, had still not reached a level of narrative proficiency that would facilitate effective integration and flexible cross-fertilization between their pretend play and storytelling.

Concluding Remarks

In this chapter I have not really presented firm conclusions. Instead, I have tried to propose an orienting perspective and some working hypotheses that I hope can provide useful food for thought. So let me close by summing these up.

Children's pretend play and narrative should not be artificially separated and studied in mutual isolation. Instead, they should be viewed as closely related and often intertwined forms of socially situated symbolic action. A key point of intersection between them is that pretend play itself has an important narrative dimension, since it centers on the enactment of narrative scenarios. In fact, for a number of purposes, it is appropriate and illuminating to see children's pretend play and storytelling—more precisely, their production and comprehension of stories—as complementary modes of their narrative activity on a continuum ranging from the discursive exposition of narratives in storytelling to their enactment in pretend play. Furthermore, the active interplay and cross-fertilization between pretend play and storytelling can significantly promote children's learning and development in a range of domains, including language, cognition, and imagination.

However, young children's ability to engage flexibly and fruitfully in this active interplay is neither automatic nor simply given. It is a developmental achievement that requires a certain amount of time and effort to accomplish. It can then serve, in turn, as a foundation and impetus for further development. Thus, I propose that we should regard children's pretend play and storytelling as initially parallel and complementary modes of their narrative activity, with at least partly distinct origins and developmental pathways, which young children are gradually able to integrate effectively. To put it another way, there are

24 Ageliki Nicolopoulou

good reasons to see the developmental relationship between young children's pretend play and storytelling as one that moves from narrative complementarity to convergence.

I have also suggested, a bit more speculatively, that at least part of the explanation for this pattern of initial disjunction and gradual integration is that, especially in their early phases, young children's pretend play and storytelling require and promote partly distinctive but ultimately complementary clusters of narrative-related skills. This complementary relationship between the two activities is an important reason why their coordination and cross-fertilization can be beneficial, but it also helps explain why integrating them requires time and effort to accomplish.

To the extent that this proposed model can be successfully followed up and refined, I think it can have significant and useful implications for both research and practice. In terms of research, it can help guide and enrich our understanding of the dynamics of young children's development. And, in practical terms, one key implication is that the successful integration of these two forms of young children's narrative activity—play and story—can create a powerful matrix for learning and development. So we need to identify, support, facilitate, and/or design the kinds of social contexts and practices that can most effectively help children achieve this narrative convergence and cross-fertilization and benefit from them.

Notes

1 To avoid cumbersome formulations and repetitions, I will sometimes simply say *storytelling* to cover story production and comprehension. And where the word *play* appears unmodified, it usually refers to pretend play. Meanings should be clear from context.
2 For non-U.S. readers: Head Start is a federally funded preschool program serving children from low-income families.
3 Pseudonyms have been assigned to all children discussed in this chapter.

References

Astington, J. W., & Jenkins, J. M. (1995). Theory of mind development and social understanding. *Social Cognition and Emotion, 9,* 151–165.

Bamberg, M. (Ed.). (1997). *Narrative development: Six approaches.* Mahwah, NJ: Erlbaum.

Benson, M. S. (1993). The structure of four- and five-year-olds' narratives in pretend play and storytelling. *First Language, 13,* 203–223.

Berman, R., & Slobin, D. I. (Eds.). (1994). *Relating events in narrative: A crosslinguistic developmental study.* Hillsdale, NJ: Erlbaum.

Boyd, B. (2009). *On the origins of stories: Evolution, cognition, and fiction.* Cambridge, MA: Harvard University Press.

Bruner, J. (1986). *Actual minds, possible worlds.* Cambridge, MA: Harvard University Press.

Bruner, J. (1992). The narrative construction of reality. In H. Beilin & P. Pufall (Eds.), *Piaget's theory: Prospects and possibilities* (pp. 229–248). Hillsdale, NJ: Erlbaum.

Children's Pretend Play and Storytelling **25**

Cohen, D., & MacKeith, S. A. (1991). *The development of imagination: The private worlds of childhood.* New York, NY: Routledge.

Cooper, P. M. (2005). Literacy learning and pedagogical purpose in Vivian Paley's "storytelling curriculum." *Journal of Early Childhood Literacy, 5,* 229–251.

Cooper, P. M. (2009). *The classrooms all young children need: Lessons in teaching from Vivian Paley.* Chicago, IL: University of Chicago Press.

Eckler, A., & Weininger, O. (1989). Structural parallels between pretend play and narratives. *Developmental Psychology, 25,* 736–743.

Farver, J. M. (1992). Communicating shared meaning in social pretend play. *Early Childhood Research Quarterly, 7,* 501–516.

Fein, G. G. (1987). Pretend play: Creativity and consciousness. In D. Gorlitz & J. Wohlwill (Eds.), *Curiosity, imagination, and play* (pp. 282–304). Hillsdale, NJ: Erlbaum.

Fein, G. G. (1995). Toys and stories. In A. D. Pellegrini (Ed.), *The future of play theory* (pp. 151–164). Albany: State University of New York Press.

Feldman, C., Bruner, J., Kalmar, D., & Renderer, B. (1993). Plot, plight, and dramatism: Interpretation at three ages. *Human Development, 36,* 327–342.

Fireman, G. D., McVay, T. E., & Flanagan, O. J. (2003). *Narrative and consciousness.* New York, NY: Oxford University Press.

Galda, L. (1984). Narrative competence: Play, storytelling, and story comprehension. In A. D. Pellegrini & T. D. Yawkey (Eds.), *The development of oral and written language in social context* (pp. 105–117). Norwood, NJ: Ablex.

Glaubman, R., Kashi, G., & Koresh, R. (2001). Facilitating the narrative quality of sociodramatic play. In A. Göncü & E. L. Klein (Eds.), *Children in play, story, and school* (pp. 132–157). New York, NY: Guilford Press.

Goldman, L. R. (1998). *Child's play: Myth, mimesis and make-believe.* New York, NY: Berg.

Göncü, A. (1993a). Development of intersubjectivity in the dyadic play of preschoolers. *Early Childhood Research Quarterly, 8,* 99–116.

Göncü, A. (1993b). Development of intersubjectivity in social pretend play. *Human Development, 36,* 185–198.

Harris, P. (2000). *The work of the imagination.* Malden, MA: Blackwell.

Hart, B., & Risley, T. R. (1995). *Meaningful differences in the everyday experience of young American children.* Baltimore, MD: Brookes.

Hoff, E. (2006). How social contexts support and shape language development. *Developmental Review, 26,* 55–88.

Howes, C., Unger, O., & Matheson, C. C. (1992). *The collaborative construction of pretend: Social pretend play functions.* Albany: State University of New York Press.

Ilgaz, H., & Aksu-Koç, A. (2005). Episodic development in preschool children's play-prompted and direct-elicited narratives. *Cognitive Development, 20,* 526–544.

Kavanaugh, R. D. (2006a). Pretend play and theory of mind. In L. Balter & C. S. Tamis-LeMonda (Eds.), *Child psychology: A handbook of contemporary issues* (Vol. 2, pp. 153–166). Philadelphia, PA: Psychology Press.

Kavanaugh, R. D. (2006b). Pretend play. In B. Spodek & O. Saracho (Eds.), *Handbook of research on the education of young children* (2nd edition, pp. 269–278). Mahwah, NJ: Erlbaum.

Kavanaugh, R. D., & Engel, S. (1998). The development of pretense and narrative in early childhood. In O. N. Saracho & B. Spodek (Eds.), *Multiple perspectives on play in early childhood education* (pp. 80–99). Albany: State University of New York Press.

McCabe, A., & Bliss, L. S. (2003). *Patterns of narrative discourse: A multicultural, lifespan approach.* Boston, MA: Allyn & Bacon.

26 Ageliki Nicolopoulou

McNamee, G. D. (1987). The social origins of narrative skills. In M. Hickmann (Ed.), *Social and functional approaches to language and thought* (pp. 287–304). Orlando, FL: Academic Press.

McNamee, G. D., McLane, J. B., Cooper, P. M., & Kerwin, S. M. (1985). Cognition and affect in early literacy development. *Early Child Development and Care, 20,* 229–244.

Miller, P. J., Hengst, J., Alexander, K., & Sperry, L. (2000). Versions of personal storytelling/ versions of experience: Genres as tools for creating alternate realities. In K. S. Rosengren, C. N. Johnson, & P. L. Harris (Eds.), *Imagining the impossible: Magical, scientific, and religious thinking in children* (pp. 212–246). New York, NY: Cambridge University Press.

Miller, P. J., Hoogstra, L., Mintz, J., Fung, H., & Williams, K. (1993). Troubles in the garden and how they get resolved: A young child's transformation of his favorite story. In C. A. Nelson (Ed.), *Memory and affect in development: The Minnesota symposia on child psychology* (Vol. 26, pp. 87–114). Hillsdale, NJ: Erlbaum.

Nicolopoulou, A. (1993). Play, cognitive development, and the social world: Piaget, Vygotsky, and beyond. *Human Development, 36,* 1–23.

Nicolopoulou, A. (1996). Narrative development in social context. In D. I. Slobin, J. Gerhardt, J. Guo, & A. Kyratzis (Eds.), *Social interaction, social context, and language: Essays in honor of Susan Ervin-Tripp* (pp. 369–390). Mahwah, NJ: Erlbaum.

Nicolopoulou, A. (1997a). Children and narratives: Toward an interpretive and sociocultural approach. In M. Bamberg (Ed.), *Narrative development: Six approaches* (pp. 179–215). Mahwah, NJ: Erlbaum.

Nicolopoulou, A. (1997b). Worldmaking and identity formation in children's narrative play-acting. In B. D. Cox & C. Lightfoot (Eds.), *Sociogenetic perspectives on internalization* (pp. 157–187). Mahwah, NJ: Erlbaum.

Nicolopoulou, A. (2002). Peer-group culture and narrative development. In S. Blum-Kulka & C. E. Snow (Eds.), *Talking to adults: The contribution of multiparty discourse to language acquisition* (pp. 117–152). Mahwah, NJ: Erlbaum.

Nicolopoulou, A. (2005). Play and narrative in the process of development: Commonalities, differences, and interrelations. *Cognitive Development, 20,* 495–502.

Nicolopoulou, A. (2007). The interplay of play and narrative in children's development: Theoretical reflections and concrete examples. In A. Göncü & S. Gaskins (Eds.), *Play and development: Evolutionary, sociocultural, and functional perspectives* (pp. 247–273). Mahwah, NJ: Erlbaum.

Nicolopoulou, A., Brockmeyer, C., de Sá, A., & Ilgaz, H. (2014). Narrative performance, peer-group culture, and narrative development in a preschool classroom. In A. Cekaite, S. Blum-Kulka, V. Aukrust, & E. Teubal (Eds.), *Children's peer talk: Learning from each other* (pp. 42–62). New York, NY: Cambridge University Press.

Nicolopoulou, A., Cortina, K. S., Ilgaz, H., Cates, C. B., & de Sá, A. B. (2015). Using a narrative- and play-based activity to promote low-income preschoolers' oral narrative, emergent literacy, and social competence. *Early Childhood Research Quarterly, 31,* 147–162.

Nicolopoulou, A., de Sá, A., Ilgaz, H., & Brockmeyer, C. (2010). Using the transformative power of play to educate hearts and minds: From Vygotsky to Vivian Paley. *Mind, Culture, and Activity, 5,* 61–71.

Nicolopoulou, A., & Ilgaz, H. (2013). What do we know about pretend play and narrative development? A response to Lillard, Lerner, Hopkins, Dore, Smith, and Palmquist on "The impact of pretend play on children's development: A review of the evidence." *American Journal of Play, 6,* 55–80.

Nicolopoulou, A., McDowell, J., & Brockmeyer, C. (2006). Narrative play and emergent literacy: Storytelling and story-acting meet journal writing. In D. Singer, R. Golinkoff, & K. Hirsh-Pasek (Eds.), *Play = learning: How play motivates and enhances children's cognitive and social-emotional growth* (pp. 124–144). New York, NY: Oxford University Press.

Nicolopoulou, A., & Richner, E. S. (2007). From actors to agents to persons: The development of character representation in young children's narratives. *Child Development, 78,* 412–429.

Nicolopoulou, A., Scales, B., & Weintraub, J. (1994). Gender differences and symbolic imagination in the stories of four-year-olds. In A. H. Dyson & C. Genishi (Eds.), *The need for story: Cultural diversity in classroom and community* (pp. 102–123). Urbana, IL: National Council of Teachers of English (NCTE).

Paley, V. G. (1986). *Mollie is three: Growing up in school.* Chicago, IL: University of Chicago Press.

Paley, V. G. (1988). *Bad guys don't have birthdays: Fantasy play at four.* Chicago, IL: University of Chicago Press.

Paley, V. G. (1990). *The boy who would be a helicopter: The uses of storytelling in the classroom.* Cambridge, MA: Harvard University Press.

Pellegrini, A. D. (1985). The narrative organization of children's fantasy play: The effects of age and context. *Educational Psychology, 5,* 17–25.

Peterson, C. (1994). Narrative skills and social class. *Canadian Journal of Education, 19,* 251–269.

Reese, E. (2013). Culture, narrative, and imagination. In M. Taylor (Ed.), *The Oxford handbook of the development of imagination* (pp. 196–211). New York, NY: Oxford University Press.

Richner, E. S., & Nicolopoulou, A. (2001). The narrative construction of differing conceptions of the person in the development of young children's social understanding. *Early Education and Development, 12,* 393–432.

Roskos, K. A., & Christie, J. F. (Eds.). (2000). *Play and literacy in early childhood.* Mahwah, NJ: Erlbaum.

Rowe, D. W. (1998). The literate potentials of book-related dramatic play. *Reading Research Quarterly, 33,* 10–35.

Rowe, D. W. (2000). Bringing books to life: The role of book-related dramatic play in young children's literacy learning. In K. A. Roskos & J. F. Christie (Eds.), *Play and literacy in early childhood: Research from multiple perspectives* (pp. 3–25). Mahwah, NJ: Erlbaum.

Sachs, J., Goldman, J., & Chaille, C. (1984). Planning in pretend play: Using language to coordinate narrative development. In A. D. Pellegrini & T. D. Yawkey (Eds.), *The development of oral and written language in social context* (pp. 119–128). Norwood, NJ: Ablex.

Sachs, J., Goldman, J., & Chaille, C. (1985). Narratives in preschoolers' sociodramatic play: The role of knowledge and communicative competence. In A. Pellegrini & L. Galda (Eds.), *Play, language, and stories: The development of children's literate behavior* (pp. 45–61). Norwood, NJ: Ablex.

Saracho, O. N. (2012). *An integrated play-based curriculum for young children.* New York, NY: Routledge.

Saracho, O. N., & Spodek, B. (Eds.). (2003). *Contemporary perspectives on play in early childhood education.* Charlotte, NC: Information Age.

Sawyer, R. K. (1997). *Pretend play as improvisation: Conversation in the preschool classroom.* Mahwah, NJ: Erlbaum.

Schwebel, D. C., Rosen, C. S., & Singer, J. L. (1999). Preschoolers' pretend play and theory of mind: The role of jointly constructed pretense. *British Journal of Developmental Psychology, 17,* 333–348.

Singer, D., Golinkoff, R., & Hirsh-Pasek, K. (Eds.). (2006). *Play = learning: How play motivates and enhances children's cognitive and social-emotional growth.* New York, NY: Oxford University Press.

Tabors, P. O., Snow, C. E., & Dickinson, D. K. (2001). Homes and schools together: Supporting language and literacy development. In D. K. Dickinson & P. O. Tabors (Eds.), *Beginning literacy with language: Young children learning at home and school* (pp. 313–334). Baltimore, MD: Brookes.

Taylor, M., & Carlson, S. M. (1997). The relation between individual differences in fantasy and theory of mind. *Child Development, 68,* 436–455.

Trawick-Smith, J. (1998). A qualitative analysis of metaplay in the preschool years. *Early Childhood Research Quarterly, 13,* 433–452.

Vygotsky, L. S. (1967). Play and its role in the mental development of the child. *Soviet Psychology, 12,* 6–18. Translation of a stenographic record of a lecture given in Russian in 1933.

Wells, G. (1986). *The meaning makers: Children learning language and using language to learn.* Portsmouth, NH: Heinemann.

Wolf, D. P., Rygh, J., & Altshuler, J. (1984). Agency and experience: Actions and states in play narratives. In I. Bretherton (Ed.), *Symbolic play: The development of social understanding* (pp. 195–217). Orlando, FL: Academic Press.

Wolf, S. A., & Heath, S. B. (1992). *The braid of literature: Children's worlds of reading.* Cambridge, MA: Harvard University Press.

Youngblade, L. M., & Dunn, J. (1995). Individual differences in young children's pretend play with mother and siblings: Links to relationships and understanding other people's feelings and beliefs. *Child Development, 66,* 1472–1492.

PART I

Pretense and Storytelling in Autism Spectrum Disorder

2

PRETEND PLAY IN CHILDREN WITH AUTISM SPECTRUM DISORDERS

A Review of the Literature

Mahwish Chaudry and Cheryl Dissanayake

The development of pretend play has attracted much research attention over many decades, as its emergence provides one of the earliest windows into the child's mental life. The failure to develop pretense has similarly attracted empirical and clinical attention, as its absence is an early marker of atypical development. A disorder that has traditionally been characterized by the absence of pretense is autism spectrum disorder (ASD; Sigman & Capps, 1997). ASD refers to a group of neurodevelopmental disorders marked by impairments in social communication and a restricted range of repetitive and stereotyped behaviours and interests (*Diagnostic and Statistical Manual of Mental Disorders*; 5th ed.; *DSM–5*; American Psychiatric Association [APA], 2013). In previous versions of the *DSM* (4th ed., text rev.; *DSM–IV–TR*; APA, 2000), autistic disorder (commonly known as *autism*), Asperger's disorder, and pervasive developmental disorder not otherwise specified were treated as separate but related entities. Deficits in pretense or imagination has been included as one of the diagnostic criteria for autism in this and earlier versions of the *DSM*, with the *DSM–5* being the first edition to exclude references to pretense or imaginary deficits in ASD.

Studies have shown that markers of ASD are present during early stages of childhood and manifest as deficits in social attention and communication, including joint attention, imitation, emotional expression, and language. Pretense, which usually develops within the second year of life, has been identified as one of the early markers, with deficits in this ability concurrently linked with a diagnosis of ASD at 24 months (Barbaro & Dissanayake, 2013). In this chapter, we will review studies of pretense in ASD and the theoretical accounts that have been proposed to explain difficulties in pretense that manifest in ASD. In so doing, we will present an update on our current understanding of pretense in ASD.

Pretend Play in Typical Development

Pretend or symbolic play refers to the symbolic use of an object or action and can be described as having an "as if" quality. According to Leslie (1987), pretend play may manifest as (a) object substitution: using one object in place of another (e.g., using a wooden block as a car), (b) attribution of absent or false properties (e.g., pretending that a bed is a swimming pool), and (c) imaginary object present (e.g., pretending that empty plates have food). Symbolic play may also include attribution of animacy (e.g., moving a doll's legs as though she is walking; Harris, Kavanaugh, Wellman, & Hickling, 1993; Lillard, 1993) and role-play (e.g., a child pretending to be a teacher; Brown, Prescott, Rickards, & Paterson, 1997; Nielsen & Dissanayake, 2000). Symbolic play has been distinguished from *functional* play, which involves the literal use of an object (e.g., moving a toy car along the floor; Fein, 1981). However, these boundaries are not always clear as functional play gives way to pretense.

Typically developing children initially engage in functional play (Ungerer, Zelazo, Kearsley, & O'Leary, 1981), and during the second year of life, they begin to display basic symbolic play (Lowe, 1975; Nielsen & Dissanayake, 2004). Their pretense skills increase in complexity and frequency during toddlerhood, reaching their peak during the late preschool years (Fein, 1981). The frequency of symbolic play begins to decline at around six years of age, when pretense and creativity begin to manifest in areas other than play (Harris, 2000).

There is strong evidence to suggest that symbolic play in children is universal and appears to follow specific developmental trends, including:

*   Decentration: A shift from using the self as the agent to using another object as an agent of play (e.g., teddy bear; Lowe, 1975).
*   Decontextualisation: Using objects with fewer perceptual and functional similarities with the symbolic object (e.g., using a straw as a pencil; Ungerer et al., 1981).
*   Integration: The ability to combine individual pretend play acts to form sequences in play (McCune-Nicolich, 1981).

The presence of similar developmental trends in symbolic play across cultures suggests a biological basis to its development (Harris, 1994). Indeed, there is a strong body of research that supports the role of symbolic play in the development of various cognitive and social skills. Connolly and Doyle (1984) found that the amount and complexity of pretend play engaged in significantly predicted a child's popularity, affective role taking, and teacher ratings of peer social skills. Symbolic play has also been found to be associated with language development (Lewis, Boucher, Lupton, & Watson, 2000; McCune-Nicolich, 1981). Furthermore, it seems to have a strong association with theory of mind (Lillard, 1993; Nielsen & Dissanayake, 2000), creativity (Dansky, 1980), and executive functioning (Jarrold,

Boucher, & Smith, 1994; Kelly, Dissanayake, Hammond, & Ihsen, 2011). Given the positive benefits of pretend play in early development, it is important to understand the reported pretend play deficits in children with ASD.

Pretend Play in Children With ASD

There is a considerable body of research charting pretend play deficits in children with ASD (see reviews in Jarrold, 2003; Jarrold, Boucher, & Smith, 1993). However, there are conflicting views on the nature of these impairments. Studies have found deficits in these children's ability to produce pretend play under unstructured or spontaneous conditions (Charman et al., 1997; Libby, Powell, Messer, & Jordan, 1998), whereas some studies have found intact pretense in children with ASD under structured or adult-assisted conditions (Charman & Baron-Cohen, 1997; Lewis & Boucher, 1988). Moreover, a few studies have also found that children with ASD can comprehend pretense acts as well as typically developing children (Jarrold, Smith, Boucher, & Harris, 1994; Kavanaugh & Harris, 1994). This disparity in findings may be a result of methodological differences between studies that need to be considered when interpreting the research findings.

Studies Supporting Pretend Play Deficits in ASD

Wing, Gould, Yeates, and Brierly (1977) conducted one of the first studies of symbolic play in children with autism. They recruited a sample of 108 children, aged 60 to 168 months, and included children with autism, "autistic-like" children, and children with intellectual disabilities. They observed children's free play and conducted interviews with their parents and teachers about their symbolic activities. The children were classified as either showing symbolic play, stereotyped symbolic play (symbolic play that is repetitive and unvarying), or no symbolic play. On the basis of their findings, Wing et al. (1977) concluded that there is a link between symbolic play deficits and early childhood autism. Atlas (1990) replicated these findings by comparing the play behaviour of 26 children with autism and 22 children with schizophrenia (mean chronological age of 114 months). Symbolic play was found to be a powerful discriminator between the two groups, with the children with autism showing major deficits in pretense. However, in both these studies, a proportion of children with ASD showed stereotyped symbolic play, leading Wing et al. (1977) to conclude that children with autism are capable of some form of symbolic play, albeit of a repetitive nature.

It should be noted that Wing et al. (1977) and Atlas (1990) used an inadequate definition of pretend play, which included a "lively discussion of past experiences." This seems to be more of an indicator of children's memory as opposed to their pretend play abilities. Moreover, stereotyped symbolic play measured by Wing et al. (1977) included instances of functional play as well as a narrow range of repetitive behaviours with no reference to pretense (e.g., preoccupation with space). Jarrold et al. (1993) have argued that stereotyped symbolic play should not be considered an example of pretense, as any play that is repetitive indicates a learned routine. In addition, the participant groups in both studies were not formally matched on chronological age (CA) or mental age (MA). Moreover, Wing et al. (1977) combined children with autism, children with psychosis, and children with severe language disorder together in a single group.

Stone, Lemanek, Fishel, Fernandez, and Altemeier (1990) studied the play behaviour of 91 children between the ages of 36 and 72 months. The performance of 22 children with autism was compared with that of 15 hearing-impaired, 15 intellectually disabled, 19 language-impaired, and 20 typically developing children. They observed children's spontaneous play and found that although there was no significant difference in the rate of symbolic play acts between groups, more children with autism failed to show any symbolic play at all compared to children in the other groups. Although the groups were matched on CA, the autism group had lower IQ and verbal scores than the other groups, which makes it difficult to interpret these findings. Given the relationship between pretense and verbal abilities, the children in the autism group with lower verbal scores might have been at a disadvantage compared to those in the control groups (Jarrold et al., 1993).

Ungerer and Sigman (1981) were the first to investigate pretend play in children with ASD under both an unstructured and a structured or adult-assisted condition. They suggested that a structured play environment may produce more diverse and sophisticated pretend play as compared to spontaneous or unstructured situations and thus may be more conducive to engagement in pretend play. Their study included 16 children with autism (aged 39 to 74 months; mean CA = 51.7 months; mean MA = 24.8 months), which was later expanded to include control groups of intellectually disabled (aged 32 to 80 months; mean CA = 50.7 months; mean MA = 26.6 months) and typically developing children (aged 16 to 25 months; mean CA = 20.8 months; mean MA = 24.6 months; Sigman & Ungerer, 1984). In the structured condition, pretend play was elicited if not produced spontaneously by the child. The experimenter verbally instructed the child to carry out the pretense act (e.g., feed the baby with the bottle), and if that did not work, she modelled the act for the child. Children with ASD were found to be deficient in pretend play under both structured and unstructured conditions. However, the number of symbolic play acts demonstrated by the autism group increased when play was elicited. This study has been criticised for modelling the pretend play acts for the children, as any resultant play produced may be imitation on the part of the child rather than a symbolic play act (Jarrold et al., 1993). It should, however, be noted that there is some evidence supporting a developmental link between imitation and pretend play in typical development (Nielsen & Dissanayake, 2004). Therefore, the pretend play produced after modelling may indicate an underlying symbolic ability, albeit at a very basic level. Mundy, Sigman, Ungerer, and Sherman (1986) examined the structured and spontaneous symbolic play of 18 children with autism (mean CA = 53.3 months; mean MA = 25.7 months), 18 children with intellectual disabilities (mean CA = 50.2 months; mean MA = 26 months), and 18 typically developing children (mean CA = 22.2 months; mean MA = 25 months). They found that children with autism showed fewer symbolic play acts compared to both control groups, although this difference was only significant in the structured condition. However, this study has also been criticised for failing to determine whether the children with autism spent less time than controls engaged in symbolic play in either condition. Jarrold et al. (1993) argued that as children with autism have problems with generation, they could not be expected to show a great number of novel acts. Therefore, the amount of time spent in symbolic play would have more accurately demonstrated differences between the groups. Moreover, both the Mundy et al. (1986) study and the Ungerer and Sigman studies (Sigman & Ungerer, 1984; Ungerer & Sigman, 1981) matched groups for general MA instead of verbal MA. Jarrold et al. (1993) argued that verbal abilities should be used for matching groups when investigating symbolic abilities given the strong relationship between language and symbolic play (Jarrold, Boucher, & Russell, 1997).

Baron-Cohen (1987) addressed some of the limitations in previous studies investigating pretend play in children with ASD by matching control groups on verbal mental age (VMA) and carefully differentiating pretense from other categories of play (sensorimotor, ordering, functional). He examined pretend play in 10 children with autism (aged 42.2 to 148.8 months; mean CA = 49.2 months; mean VMA = 30 months), 10 children with Down syndrome (aged 30 to 146.4 months; mean CA = 90 months; mean VMA = 30 months), and 10 typically developing children (aged 36 to 61.2 months; mean CA = 49.2 months; no VMA measured). Significantly fewer children with autism showed pretend play as compared to the other two groups, and pretend play was evident in nonautistic children with intellectual disabilities relative to their MAs. However, this study used the British Vocabulary Picture (BVP) Scale to measure VMA (Lewis & Boucher, 1988), which is a measure of vocabulary, and children with ASD often have a more advanced vocabulary as compared to other language abilities (Paul, 1987). Thus, this scale may have overestimated their VMAs, placing them at a disadvantage compared to controls, which could explain the pretense deficits observed in the children with autism.

Charman et al. (1997) compared pretend play behaviour under spontaneous and elicited conditions in very young children: an autism group comprising 12 children (CA = 20.7 months; verbal comprehension [VC] = 4.8), a developmentally delayed group comprising 18 children (CA = 21.1 months; VC = 6.67), and a typically developing group comprising 18 children (CA = 20.3 months; VC = 13.8). Children in both the developmentally delayed and ASD groups showed significantly less spontaneous and elicited pretend play as compared to children in the typically developing group. The developmentally delayed group, nevertheless, was significantly better at elicited pretend play than the ASD group. These findings suggest that pretend play deficits are apparent from a very young age in children with autism.

Libby et al. (1998) investigated spontaneous pretend play in children with autism, children with Down syndrome, and typically developing children matched on verbal abilities. They found that the children with autism produced significantly fewer symbolic play acts than those without autism. However, upon closer examination of the symbolic play acts, they found no significant difference among the three groups on pretend play classified as object substitution. The difference, however, remained significant for other categories of pretend play; that is, attribution of false properties and reference to an absent object. This finding supports the argument that children with autism have some capacity to engage in symbolic play. As object substitutions are the first form of symbolic play to emerge in typical development, it is possible that the development of pretense in children with autism is delayed (Corrigan, 1987).

Studies Supporting Intact Pretend Play in Children With ASD

A number of studies have found no differences between the pretend play of children with ASD and other control groups under structured (elicited or instructed) play conditions. Lewis and Boucher (1988) measured spontaneous and elicited pretend play in children with ASD (mean CA = 132 months), children diagnosed with moderate learning difficulties (mean CA = 98 months), and a group of typically developing children (mean CA = 55 months), matched on expressive language abilities. They found that when pretend play was elicited, there was no difference in the quality and duration of pretend play between the groups. However, this study has been criticised for using the Renfrew Action Picture Test to match the groups, which underestimates comprehension ability (including vocabulary and comprehension of grammar; Jarrold et al., 1993). Therefore, the ASD group may have had an advantage over the control groups, affecting the results (Jarrold et al., 1997).

Jarrold, Boucher, and Smith (1996) compared the symbolic play abilities of 14 children with ASD with 14 children with moderate learning difficulties, matched on CA and VMA. The children were examined under spontaneous, elicited, and instructed conditions. The frequency of symbolic play in children with autism was found to increase when pretense was elicited (e.g., "Show me what you can pretend to do with this"). However, these children spent less time engaged in pretend play in both spontaneous and elicited conditions as compared to the control group. In contrast, when the children were instructed to perform pretend play acts (e.g., "Feed the cake to the doll"), no significant differences were found between the groups. These results were replicated by Charman and Baron-Cohen (1997) in school-age and adolescent children. They investigated spontaneous and instructed pretend play in children with autism (CA = 140.3 months; VMA = 46.2 months) and children with intellectual disabilities (CA = 149.0 months; VMA = 37.6 months) and found that when instructed to produce an object substitution, children with ASD did not differ from controls. However, they found that the ASD group produced fewer novel and spontaneous pretend play acts as compared to the controls. This study also showed that children with ASD with a VMA of 4 years were able to produce very basic object substitutions at a level seen in typically developing children in the latter half of the second year of life (Fein, 1981). Therefore, Charman and Baron-Cohen (1997) argued that the pretense difficulties evident in children with ASD are a result of developmental delays as opposed to a specific deficit.

Further support for intact pretense in children with ASD comes from studies exploring their comprehension of pretense. Kavanaugh and Harris (1994) compared pretense comprehension in a sample of 12 children with autism (mean CA = 118.8 months) and 12 children with intellectual disabilities (mean CA = 116.4 months), matched on verbal ability. The children were shown toy animals, and the experimenter acted out pouring a pretend substance over the animals (e.g., pouring tea over the teddy bear). When children were asked to choose a picture that depicted the outcome of the pretend transformation, the children with autism performed as well as the controls in identifying the correct picture. Jarrold, Smith, et al. (1994) replicated these findings using a similar methodology and a larger sample of 24 children with autism (mean CA = 112.8 months; mean VMA = 55.2 months), 24 children with moderate learning difficulties (mean CA = 111.6 months; mean VMA = 54 months), and 24 typically developing children (mean CA = 60 months; mean VMA = 55.2 months). They, too, found no significant differences between the three groups, suggesting that, like the typically developing children, children with autism were able to understand pretend play.

A number of unpublished doctoral studies undertaken at La Trobe University have also found intact pretense under *both* structured and unstructured conditions in young, high-functioning children with ASD (full-scale IQ of greater than 70) between 4 and 7 years of age. Prescott (2003) studied pretend play in children with autistic disorder, Asperger's disorder, and typically developing children using a tea party scenario that measured different types of pretense with varying degrees of complexity. She found that both the structured and unstructured pretend play of children with ASD (both autistic disorder and Asperger's disorder) was comparable to that of the typically developing controls with the exception of object substitutions. Children with autistic disorder showed some difficulty engaging in object substitution (e.g., using a wooden cylinder as an airplane) as compared to the typically developing children. Nonetheless, object substitution was the most frequently observed play type in all groups.

Kelly (2007) replicated Prescott's (2003) finding using a standardised task to measure pretend play (test of pretend play [ToPP]; Lewis & Boucher, 1997). With the exception of object substitution, she also found that the overall symbolic play abilities of children with high-functioning autism were comparable to those of typically developing children. More recently, Mifsud (2011) investigated the production and comprehension of object substitution in children with high-functioning autism. She found that the children with autism and the typically developing children were not differentiated on either the production or comprehension of object substitution. However, children in the ASD group took longer to produce instructed pretense acts as compared to typically developing children.

In undertaking their studies, the La Trobe researchers (Kelly, 2007; Mifsud, 2011; Prescott, 2003) addressed some of the limitations of previous research by controlling for the age of the participants (ages of 48 to 84 months), their level of functioning (including only high-functioning children with ASD), and matching the groups on VMA and overall MA. Each of these studies consistently found that these preschool to early-school-age children with ASD were not pervasively impaired in their pretend play abilities as previously suggested. However, a recent study from the same laboratory found that deficits in pretend play at 24 months are highly predictive of an ASD diagnosis at 24 months of age in a very young mixed-abilities sample of children (Barbaro & Dissanayake, 2013).

The Social Attention and Communication Study (SACS) focused on the prospective identification of ASD using repeated and routine monitoring of social attention and communication behaviours in infants and toddlers within the community-based Victorian Maternal and Child Health Services. Barbaro and Dissanayake (2013) compared the presence or absence of behavioural markers between children with ASD and children with developmental and/or language delays (DD–LD) at 12, 18, and 24 months. Pretend play was found to be one of the most important concurrent markers for a diagnostic classification of autism at 24 months (but not at 18 months). They found that at 18 months, the ASD group and the DD–LD group demonstrated comparable levels of pretend play. The children with DD–LD improved their pretend play considerably (deficits in pretend play declined from 57% to 8%) between 18 and 24 months, unlike children in the ASD group. However, the researchers in this study did find that children with ASD demonstrated some ability to engage in pretend play.

The studies discussed previously (Kelly, 2007; Mifsud, 2011; Prescott, 2003) that have found comparable pretend play performance in children with ASD as compared to typically developing children investigated older children aged between 48 and 84 months. One possible explanation for these disparate findings could be that children with ASD, as noted previously, are delayed in their development of pretense and show improvements in pretend play at later ages as compared to children without ASD (Charman & Baron-Cohen, 1997; Hobson, 2008; Mifsud,

2011). Longitudinal studies are needed to test this hypothesis, charting the emergence of pretend play at different developmental time points in young children with ASD compared to children without ASD.

Very few longitudinal studies have investigated pretend play in children with ASD. Sigman (Sigman, 1998; Sigman & Ruskin, 1999) conducted a comprehensive study of 70 children with autism, 59 with developmental delays, 93 with Down syndrome, and 108 typically developing children. The children were first tested when they were between 24 and 60 months old and then tested again around eight to twelve years later. Pretend play was investigated as an early indicator of later verbal and social abilities, but no attention was given to how pretend play developed with age in these children.

To date, the only published study to investigate pretend play in children with ASD over time was conducted by Rutherford, Young, Hepburn, and Rogers (2007). They measured pretense under both adult-assisted and spontaneous play conditions in 28 children with autism (mean CA = 33.65 months), 18 children with other developmental disorders (mean CA = 35 months), and 27 typically developing children (mean CA = 19.67 months). The groups were matched on overall MA and VMA at the first assessment and the follow-up assessment (24 months later for the clinical groups and 12 months later for the typically developing children). The children with autism showed deficits in both adult-assisted and spontaneous pretend play at both time points as compared to the two control groups.

Rutherford et al.'s (2007) findings are inconsistent with previous findings of intact spontaneous (Kelly, 2007; Prescott, 2003), adult-assisted (Jarrold et al., 1996; Lewis & Boucher, 1988), and elicited (Mifsud, 2011) pretense in children with ASD. One possible explanation for the inconsistency may be the measure used by Rutherford et al. (2007) to assess pretend play. They used the Fewell Play Scale (Fewell & Rich, 1987) to measure pretend play abilities in both conditions, which is an experimental scale with only minimal information available on its validity and reliability. Moreover, this scale was designed to measure play abilities in children aged between 5 and 30 months. In the Rutherford et al. (2007) study, this scale was used in the follow-up assessment for the ASD and DD–LD groups, despite both groups exceeding 30 months of age. Lastly, the scale involves the examiner presenting the child with a set of toys and observing and scoring the child at play. Although the toy sets are changed several times during the assessment to capture a wide range of play skills, this might not be the optimal way to assess pretend play in children with ASD. As these children have been found to have deficits in cognitive flexibility (Liss et al., 2001), they might find it difficult to adapt to the changes in toy sets and play themes within the assessment. Considering these factors, the findings of this study need to be interpreted with caution.

Hobson, Lee, and Hobson (2009) focused on the "playfulness" of pretend play in order to identify why the pretense observed in children with ASD may be of poorer quality and may lack the creativity and flexibility typically seen in children. They proposed that while the mechanics of pretend play may be equivalent between children with ASD and typically developing children, there is a lack of investment and pleasure in the play that amounts to a deficit in what they term *playful pretense*. However, using a slightly modified version of the Hobson et al. (2009) coding scheme, we found no differences in the playfulness of pretense in comparing groups of high-functioning children with autism and typically developing children (Mifsud, 2011).

Theoretical Accounts of Pretend Play Deficits in Children With ASD

Several theories have been proposed to explain the pretend play deficits in children with ASD (Jarrold, 2003; Jarrold et al., 1993; Lillard et al., 2013; Rutherford et al., 2007). This review will focus on the metarepresentational hypothesis, the executive functioning hypothesis, and the general cognitive development hypothesis.

Metarepresentational Hypothesis

The metarepresentational theory is one of the most prominent in the field and has received a lot of attention over the past years. According to this theory, engaging in symbolic play requires the child to "decouple" an object's primary representation (e.g., a banana) from its symbolic representation (e.g., a telephone). Leslie (1987) attributed pretend play deficits in children with autism to an inability to metarepresent (representation of a representation). This ability to metarepresent or decouple was also proposed to be related to *theory of mind*, where the child must decouple his or her own thoughts from those of another and understand the distinction between them. Leslie (1987) argued that children with ASD demonstrate deficits in both symbolic play and theory of mind due to an underlying inability to form and process metarepresentations (Leslie & Frith, 1990).

There is some evidence supporting this metarepresentational account. Taylor and Carlson (1997) found that typically developing children with better theory of mind scores were more likely to create imaginary friends and have more active imaginations. Astington and Jenkins (1995) also found that children who performed better on a theory of mind task engaged in more pretend play (see also Nielsen & Dissanayake, 2004). Children with autism have well-established difficulties in their theory of mind (Baron-Cohen, Leslie, & Frith, 1985; Russell, Mauthner, Sharpe, & Tidswell, 1991).

However, there are numerous problems with the metarepresentational theory. As discussed previously, many studies have shown that children with ASD can engage in pretend play under elicited or instructed play conditions (Jarrold, 2003; Kelly, 2007; Lewis & Boucher, 1988), and even those who failed theory of mind tasks have been found to engage in spontaneous pretend play (Prescott, 2003). There is also evidence that children with ASD are comparable to typically developing children in understanding pretense (Jarrold, Smith, et al., 1994; Mifsud, 2011). Since the metarepresentational hypothesis proposes symbolic deficits under all conditions, it cannot adequately account for these findings.

Executive Functioning Hypothesis

Another prominent model, the executive functioning hypothesis, proposes that difficulties with executive control and planning abilities underlie pretend play deficits in children with ASD (Jarrold et al., 1993; Rutherford & Rogers, 2003). Executive functioning involves planning, inhibitory control, ability to generate novel behaviour, working memory, shifting attention, and carrying out goal-directed behaviours. Pretend play has been linked with executive functioning, as it requires disengagement from the real world (inhibition), creating new pretend play acts (generativity), and shifting attention from interpretation of one object to another (set shifting; Kelly et al., 2011; Rutherford & Rogers, 2003).

Numerous studies have found deficits in executive functioning in children with ASD (Lewis & Boucher, 1995; Ozonoff, Pennington, & Rogers, 1991). Ozonoff et al. (1991) found that children with autism performed worse on tasks requiring planning and flexibility as compared to a learning-disabled control group. Lewis and Boucher (1995) suggested that children with autism show impaired spontaneous pretend play and intact structured pretend play due to difficulties in accessing play schemas and information from their knowledge base, which results in impaired generativity.

There have only been a few studies that have investigated the relationship between executive functioning and pretend play in children with ASD, and the findings from these studies have been inconsistent. Kelly (2007) investigated the relationship between pretend play and the executive functioning abilities of generativity and inhibition in children with ASD (mean CA = 64.50 months) and typically developing children (mean CA = 58.65 months), matched on VMA and MA. Inhibition was measured by using a variation of the Stroop task that required children to respond *sun* when shown a picture of the moon and vice versa. Generativity was measured by using a semantic fluency task in which the children were asked to name as many animals as possible in 60 s in one trial and as many things to eat or drink within 60 s in the second trial. The results indicated that pretend play in children with ASD was associated with both of these executive functioning measures.

Rutherford and Rogers (2003) found that pretend play skills in young children with ASD (mean CA = 33.93 months) were associated with generativity but not with set shifting, another executive functioning measure that they investigated. Generativity was measured by assessing the child's ability to generate novel play schemes (independent of pretend play) using a particular set of toys. Set shifting was measured using a spatial reversal task that assessed the child's ability to change his or her search strategy when the spatial location of a reward changed. Another study investigating the executive functioning hypothesis (Lam & Yeung, 2012) also failed to find a relationship between symbolic play and set-shifting abilities in children with ASD (mean CA = 73.32 months). They used the standard Wisconsin Card Sorting Test to measure set-shifting abilities.

On the basis of the studies reviewed previously, there does appear to be a relationship between pretend play and specific executive functioning abilities in children with ASD, despite the use of different experimental tasks to measure these abilities. Generativity has been found to be positively associated with symbolic play abilities in children with ASD (Kelly, 2007; Rutherford & Rogers, 2003), but no such relationship has been found for set shifting (Lam & Yeung, 2012; Rutherford & Rogers, 2003; Rutherford et al., 2007). Since executive functioning comprises a complex set of abilities (including generativity, inhibition, goal-directed behaviour, working memory, and attentional control), it is possible that each of these different abilities has a specific relationship with pretend play in children with ASD (Rutherford et al., 2007). Therefore, to properly investigate the executive functioning hypothesis, there is a need to systematically investigate the relationship between pretend play and the different types of executive functioning abilities in children with and without ASD. To date, this work remains outstanding.

General Cognitive Development Hypothesis

The general cognitive development hypothesis proposes that pretend play develops as children mature cognitively (Rutherford et al., 2007). It is argued that since pretend play, language, and other cognitive abilities emerge in children at around the same age, there might be a strong relationship between these processes (Bergen, 2002). There is some empirical evidence supporting the proposed link between general cognitive development and pretend play (see Lillard et al., 2013). Stanley and Konstantareas (2007) found a reciprocal relationship between cognitive ability and pretense, where development in one facilitates development in the other.

Pretend Play and Verbal Cognition

It is suggested that language and symbolic play are related because they both depend on symbolization (Lewis, 2003). The relationship between language and pretend play in typically developing children is well established. Lewis et al. (2000) used standardised assessments of children aged 12 to 72 months and found symbolic play to be related to both language production and comprehension. McCune

(1995) found evidence that the relationship between symbolic play and language varied with age. Studying typically developing children between 8 and 24 months, he found a significant relationship between the onset of symbolic play and initial word production, between sequences of symbolic play and word combinations, and between planned symbolic play and multiword utterances.

Pretend play and language abilities have also been found to be related in children with ASD. Sigman and Ungerer (1984) investigated the relationship between play and cognitive abilities in 16 children with ASD (mean CA = 51.7 months), 16 children with intellectual disabilities (mean CA = 50.7 months), and 16 typically developing children (mean CA = 20.8 months). They assessed receptive and expressive language skills in these children by getting an independent linguist to conduct a clinical language evaluation. Both receptive and expressive language abilities were related to symbolic play in their sample of children with autism. However, only receptive language was found to be related to pretend play in the two control groups. Sigman and Ruskin (1999) also investigated the relationship between language and symbolic play in 69 children with ASD aged between 36 and 72 months. They found significant correlations between mean language age, based on receptive and expressive language ages, and the frequency of pretend play instances in these children.

In contrast, Stanley and Konstantareas (2007) found expressive language, but not receptive language, to be related with symbolic play in children with ASD. They investigated the relationship between symbolic play with verbal and non-verbal cognitive abilities in a cross-sectional sample of 101 children, aged between 24 and 216 months. The Peabody Picture Vocabulary Test—Revised (PPVT–R) was used to measure receptive language (Dunn & Dunn, 1981), and the Reynell Developmental Language Scale (RDLS) was used to measure receptive and expressive language (Reynell & Curwen, 1977). However, these measures might not have accurately captured the verbal abilities of these children. As children with ASD have been found to have a more advanced vocabulary than other components of language (Paul, 1987), the PPVT–R may have overestimated their receptive language skills. Second, the researchers used the first edition of the RDLS to measure verbal abilities instead of the revised scale (Edwards & Reynell, 1997). The previous scale is outdated and not reflective of current knowledge regarding language development in children (Edwards, Garman, Hughes, Letts, & Sinka, 1999). Therefore, the findings from this study need to be interpreted with caution.

To date, there have been no published studies investigating the relationship between language and symbolic play in children with ASD across different developmental periods. Mifsud (2011) suggests that the influence of language abilities on pretense may be different for children with ASD as compared to typically developing children. This further supports the argument that there may be a different developmental pathway for pretend play in ASD, once again supporting the need for longitudinal studies. This would allow the relationship between pretend play and both expressive and receptive language to be investigated in children with ASD at different ages and contrasted in children without ASD.

Pretend Play and Nonverbal Cognition

Nonverbal cognitive abilities may also influence the development of symbolic play. For example, motor skills are needed to form sequences of actions necessary for symbolic play. It is suggested that typically developing children progress through different stages of play as they mature cognitively (Piaget, 1962). Indeed, Baron-Cohen (1987) found that children with ASD who demonstrated symbolic play had significantly higher nonverbal MAs than those that did not. In contrast, other studies have shown that symbolic play in children with ASD is even more delayed than would be predicted from their nonverbal mental abilities (Power & Radcliffe, 1989; Riguet, Taylor, Benaroya, & Klein, 1982). However, there have been only a few studies that have directly investigated the relationship between nonverbal cognitive abilities and pretend play in children with ASD.

A recent study by Thiemann-Bourque, Brady, and Fleming (2012) investigated this relationship in 35 children with ASD (mean CA = 49.2 months) and 38 children with developmental delays (mean CA = 49.7 months). Nonverbal abilities were assessed using the Mullen Scales of Early Learning (MSEL; Mullen, 1995). A significant correlation was found between pretend play and nonverbal abilities in the children with ASD. These results are consistent with the findings of Stanley and Konstantareas (2007), who investigated the relationship between pretend play and social development, ASD symptomatology, and verbal and nonverbal cognitive abilities (mean CA = 91 months). Nonverbal abilities were measured with the Leiter International Performance Scale—Arthur Adaptation (Arthur, 1980), which is ideal for use with children with ASD, as it does not require the use of expressive or receptive language (Shah & Holmes, 1985). The Object Permanence test was utilised as a measure of nonverbal abilities for very low-functioning children who found the Leiter test challenging. The scores from this test were positively and significantly correlated to the scores from the Leiter task, validating their use in place of the Leiter scores (Stanley & Konstantareas, 2007). The results showed that nonverbal cognitive abilities were a unique predictor of pretend play even after controlling for all the other variables (verbal ability, social development, and ASD symptomatology).

Rutherford and Rogers (2003) failed to find a positive correlation between nonverbal MA and pretend play in children with ASD (mean CA = 33.93 months) in contrast to the relationship found in typically developing children (mean CA = 19.46 months) and children with developmental delays (mean CA = 34.83 months). They suggested that nonverbal cognitive abilities correlate highly with general developmental level in typical development, whereas in ASD, general cognitive development does not account for different skills, and the developmental

Discussion

On the basis of the literature reviewed here, it is clear that the theoretical frameworks proposed to date are inadequate to explain what we know about pretense in ASD. Clearly, deficits in pretense in ASD are not pervasive, with some children, particularly those with good cognitive abilities, able to engage in spontaneous as well as elicited or instructed symbolic play. However, there remain considerable unknowns in the area of pretense and ASD.

In the new *DSM–5* (APA, 2013), pretend play is no longer included as a diagnostic criterion for ASD, although this omission has not been argued for. We presume that this change reflects the mixed outcomes of existing research on pretend play in children with ASD and the lack of a theoretical account of pretense abilities and disabilities in this population, highlighting the need for deeper investigation into this key aspect of children's development.

The empirical literature indicates a gap in our understanding of how pretense develops in children with ASD. There is a clear need to undertake comparative longitudinal studies to investigate pretend play across different developmental time points in young children with and without ASD. The correlates of this important developmental milestone also need to be better understood.

A question of interest regarding the general cognitive development hypothesis is whether the relationship between pretend play and cognition is bidirectional or unidirectional. A bidirectional relationship between these variables would imply that pretense, language, and nonverbal cognition are part of an integrated, reciprocally developing system. In contrast, a unidirectional relationship would imply a cause-and-effect relationship; that is, pretense having a causal effect on the development of nonverbal and verbal abilities or vice versa (Bergen, 2002). Stanley and Konstantareas (2007) argued that the relationship between pretend play and cognitive ability is reciprocal, with development in one facilitating improvement in the other. However, to our knowledge, there is no longitudinal research that has directly investigated this assumption.

Furthermore, research on collaborative social pretend play—looking specifically at the degree to which children with autism are able to engage in shared pretense in interactive contexts—is less common (cf. Douglas & Stirling, this volume). We do know that children with autism find spontaneous social play, especially that which includes imaginative play, very difficult (Jordan, 2003; Schuler & Fletcher, 2002; Sigman & Ruskin, 1999; Wolfberg, 2009). Moreover, the majority of studies to date have included adults as play partners, with a lack of attention to pretend play among peers. In a paper reviewing definitions of pretend play and the implications for autism, Jarrold, Carruthers, Smith, and Boucher (1994) observed that investigation into the ability of children with autism to produce and comprehend complex social pretend play is an important yet missing piece of the puzzle.

In addition to the need for longitudinal studies of pretense, we also need to further explore the executive functioning hypothesis. Research on executive functions and play needs to focus on specific executive abilities to systematically explore their relationship with the capacity for pretend play, as it appears that different executive functioning skills possibly influence pretense differently. Furthermore, studies of collaborative pretense with peers are needed to understand the contributions that children with autism are able to make to sustain play in socially demanding contexts. In particular, a focus on their metacommunicative abilities in the context of pretense may provide deeper understanding of their play. It is only through such detailed study that we will begin to more fully understand both the abilities and weaknesses of children with autism in terms of their capacity for pretense.

References

American Psychiatric Association. (2000). *Diagnostic and statistical manual of mental disorders* (4th ed., text rev.). Washington, DC: Author.

American Psychiatric Association. (2013). *Diagnostic and statistical manual of mental disorders* (5th ed.). Washington, DC: Author.

Arthur, G. (1980). *Instruction manual: Arthur adaptation of the Leiter International Performance Scale*. Chicago, IL: Stoelting.

Astington, J.W., & Jenkins, J.M. (1995). Theory of mind development and social understanding. *Cognition & Emotion, 9*(2–3), 151–165.

Atlas, J.A. (1990). Play in assessment and intervention in the childhood psychoses. *Child Psychiatry & Human Development, 21*(2), 119–133.

Barbaro, J., & Dissanayake, C. (2013). Early markers of autism spectrum disorders in infants and toddlers prospectively identified in the social attention and communication study (SACS). *Autism, 17*(1), 64–86.

Baron-Cohen, S. (1987). Autism and symbolic play. *British Journal of Developmental Psychology, 5*(2), 139–148.

Baron-Cohen, S., Leslie, A. M., & Frith, U. (1985). Does the autistic child have a "theory of mind"? *Cognition, 21*(1), 37–46.

Bergen, D. (2002). The role of pretend play in children as cognitive development. *Early Childhood Research and Practice, 4*(1), 2–15.

Brown, P. M., Prescott, S.J., Rickards, F.W., & Paterson, M.M. (1997). Communicating about pretend play: A comparison of the utterances of 4-year-old normally hearing and deaf or hard-of-hearing children in an integrated kindergarten. *Volta Review, 99* (1), 5–17.

Charman, T., & Baron-Cohen, S. (1997). Brief report: Prompted pretend play in autism. *Journal of Autism and Developmental Disorders, 27*(3), 325–332.

Charman, T., Swettenham, J., Baron-Cohen, S., Cox, A., Baird, G., & Drew, A. (1997). Infants with autism: An investigation of empathy, pretend play, joint attention, and imitation. *Developmental Psychology, 33*(5), 781–789.

Connolly, J.A., & Doyle, A.B. (1984). Relation of social fantasy play to social competence in preschoolers. *Developmental Psychology, 20*(5), 797–806.

Corrigan, R. (1987). A developmental sequence of actor-object pretend play in young children. *Merrill-Palmer Quarterly, 33,* 87–106.

Dansky, J.L. (1980). Make-believe: A mediator of the relationship between play and associative fluency. *Child Development, 51,* 576–579.

Dunn, L.M., & Dunn, L.M. (1981). *Peabody Picture Vocabulary Test: Forms L and M.* Circle Pines, MN: American Guidance Service.

Edwards, S., Garman, M., Hughes, A., Letts, C., & Sinka, I. (1999). Assessing the comprehension and production of language in young children: An account of the Reynell Developmental Language Scales III. *International Journal of Language & Communication Disorders, 34*(2), 151–171.

Edwards, S., & Reynell, J. (1997). *Reynell Developmental Language Scales III.* Windsor, UK: NFER-Nelson Health & Social Care.

Fein, G.G. (1981). Pretend play in childhood: An integrative review. *Child Development, 52,* 1095–1118.

Fewell, R.R., & Rich, J.S. (1987). Play assessment as a procedure for examining cognitive, communication, and social skills in multihandicapped children. *Journal of Psychoeducational Assessment, 5*(2), 107–118.

Harris, P.L. (1994). Understanding pretence. In C. Lewis & P. Mitchell (Eds.), *Children's early understanding of mind: Origins and development.* (pp. 235–259). Hillsdale, NJ: Erlbaum.

Harris, P. L. (2000). *The work of the imagination.* Malden, MA: Blackwell.

Harris, P.L., Kavanaugh, R.D., Wellman, H.M., & Hickling, A.K. (1993). Young children's understanding of pretense. *Monographs of the Society for Research in Child Development, 58,* i–107.

Hobson, R.P. (2008). Interpersonally situated cognition. *International Journal of Philosophical Studies, 16*(3), 377–397. http://dx.doi.org/10.1080/09672550802113300

Hobson, R. P., Lee, A., & Hobson, J. (2009). Qualities of symbolic play among children with autism: A social-developmental perspective. *Journal of Autism and Developmental Disorders, 39,* 12–22.

Jarrold, C. (2003). A review of research into pretend play in autism. *Autism, 7*(4), 379–390.

Jarrold, C., Boucher, J., & Russell, J. (1997). Language profiles in children with autism. *Autism, 1*(1), 57–76.

Jarrold, C., Boucher, J., & Smith, P. (1993). Symbolic play in autism: A review. *Journal of Autism and Developmental Disorders, 23*(2), 281–307.

Jarrold, C., Boucher, J., & Smith, P.K. (1994). Executive function deficits and the pretend play of children with autism: A research note. *Journal of Child Psychology and Psychiatry, 35*(8), 1473–1482.

Jarrold, C., Boucher, J., & Smith, P.K. (1996). Generativity deficits in pretend play in autism. *British Journal of Developmental Psychology, 14*(3), 275–300.

Jarrold, C., Carruthers, P., Smith, P., & Boucher, J. (1994). Pretend play: Is it metarepresentational? *Mind and Language, 9,* 445–468.

Jarrold, C., Smith, P., Boucher, J., & Harris, P. (1994). Comprehension of pretense in children with autism. *Journal of Autism and Developmental Disorders, 24*(4), 433–455.

Jordan, R. (2003). Social play and autistic spectrum disorders. *Autism, 7,* 347–360.

Kavanaugh, R.D., & Harris, P.L. (1994). Imagining the outcome of pretend transformations: Assessing the competence of normal children and children with autism. *Developmental Psychology, 30*(6), 847–854.

Kelly, R.C. (2007). *An exploration of the role of executive functions in the symbolic play of children with high functioning autism, children with Asperger's disorder, and typically developing children* (Unpublished doctoral dissertation). La Trobe University, Melbourne, VIC, Australia.

Kelly, R., Dissanayake, C., Hammond, S., & Ihsen, E. (2011). An investigation of the relationship between symbolic play and executive function in young children. *Australasian Journal of Early Childhood, 36,* 21–27.

Lam, Y.G., & Yeung, S.S. (2012). Cognitive deficits and symbolic play in preschoolers with autism. *Research in Autism Spectrum Disorders, 6*(1), 560–564.

Leslie, A. M. (1987). Pretense and representation: The origins of "theory of mind." *Psychological Review, 94*(4), 412–426.

Leslie, A. M., & Frith, U. (1990). Prospects for a cognitive neuropsychology of autism: Hobson's choice. *Psychological Review, 97,* 122–131.

Lewis, V. (2003). Play and language in children with autism. *Autism, 7*(4), 391–399. http://dx.doi.org/10.1177/1362361303007004005

Lewis, V., & Boucher, J. (1988). Spontaneous, instructed and elicited play in relatively able autistic children. *British Journal of Developmental Psychology, 6*(4), 325–339.

Lewis, V., & Boucher, J. (1995). Generativity in the play of young people with autism. *Journal of Autism and Developmental Disorders, 25*(2), 105–121.

Lewis, V., & Boucher, J. (1997). *The test of pretend play.* London, UK: Psychological Corporation.

Lewis, V., Boucher, J., Lupton, L., & Watson, S. (2000). Relationships between symbolic play, functional play, verbal and non-verbal ability in young children. *International Journal of Language & Communication Disorders, 35*(1), 117–127.

Libby, S., Powell, S., Messer, D., & Jordan, R. (1998). Spontaneous play in children with autism: A reappraisal. *Journal of Autism and Developmental Disorders, 28*(6), 487–497.

Lillard, A.S. (1993). Young children's conceptualization of pretense: Action or mental representational state? *Child Development, 64*(2), 372–386.

Lillard, A.S., Lerner, M.D., Hopkins, E.J., Dore, R.A., Smith, E.D., & Palmquist, C.M. (2013). The impact of pretend play on children's development: A review of the evidence. *Psychological Bulletin, 139*(1), 1–34. http://dx.doi.org/10.1037/a0029321

Liss, M., Fein, D., Allen, D., Dunn, M., Feinstein, C., Morris, R. . . . Rapin, I. (2001). Executive functioning in high-functioning children with autism. *Journal of Child Psychology and Psychiatry, 42*(2), 261–270.

Lowe, M. (1975). Trends in the development of representational play in infants from one to three years. *Journal of Child Psychology and Psychiatry, 16*(1), 33–47.

McCune, L. (1995). A normative study of representational play in the transition to language. *Developmental Psychology, 31*(2), 198–206.

McCune-Nicolich, L. (1981). Toward symbolic functioning: Structure of early pretend games and potential parallels with language. *Child Development, 52*(3), 785–797.

Mifsud, J. (2011). *A comparative investigation of symbolic play competency in children with high-functioning autism* (Unpublished doctoral dissertation). La Trobe University, Melbourne, VIC, Australia.

Mullen, E.M. (1995). *Mullen Scales of Early Learning.* Circle Pines, MN: American Guidance Service.

Mundy, P., Sigman, M., Ungerer, J., & Sherman, T. (1986). Defining the social deficits of autism: The contribution of nonverbal communication measures. *Journal of Child Psychology and Psychiatry, 27*(5), 657–669.

Nielsen, M., & Dissanayake, C. (2000). An investigation of pretend play, mental state terms, and false belief understanding: In search of a metarepresentational link. *British Journal of Developmental Psychology, 18,* 609–624.

Nielsen, M., & Dissanayake, C. (2004). Imitation, pretend play and mirror self-recognition: A longitudinal investigation through the second year. *Infant Behavior & Development, 27,* 342–365.

Ozonoff, S., Pennington, B.F., & Rogers, S.J. (1991). Executive function deficits in high-functioning autistic individuals: Relationship to theory of mind. *Journal of Child Psychology and Psychiatry, 32*(7), 1081–1105.

Paul, R. (1987). Communication. In D.J. Cohen & A. Donnellan (Eds.), *Handbook of autism and pervasive developmental disorders* (pp. 61–84). New York, NY: Wiley.

Piaget, J. (1962). *Play, dreams and imitation* (Vol. 24). New York, NY: Norton.

Power, T.J., & Radcliffe, J. (1989). The relationship of play behavior to cognitive ability in developmentally disabled preschoolers. *Journal of Autism and Developmental Disorders, 19*(1), 97–107.

Prescott, S. (2003). *An investigation of the symbolic play abilities of children with high-functioning autism, children with Asperger's disorder and typically developing children* (Unpublished doctoral dissertation). La Trobe University, Melbourne, VIC, Australia.

Reynell, J., & Curwen, M.P. (1977). *Manual for the Reynell Developmental Language Scales (Revised).* Windsor, England: NFER (National Educational Research).

Riguet, C.B., Taylor, N.D., Benaroya, S., & Klein, L.S. (1982). Symbolic play in autistic, Down's, and normal children of equivalent mental age. *Journal of Autism and Developmental Disorders, 11*(4), 439–448.

Russell, J., Mauthner, N., Sharpe, S., & Tidswell, T. (1991). The "windows task" as a measure of strategic deception in preschoolers and autistic subjects. *British Journal of Developmental Psychology, 9*(2), 331–349.

Rutherford, M., & Rogers, S.J. (2003). Cognitive underpinnings of pretend play in autism. *Journal of Autism and Developmental Disorders, 33*(3), 289–302.

Rutherford, M., Young, G.S., Hepburn, S., & Rogers, S.J. (2007). A longitudinal study of pretend play in autism. *Journal of Autism and Developmental Disorders, 37*(6), 1024–1039. http://dx.doi.org/10.1007/s10803-006-0240-9

Schuler, A., & Fletcher, C. (2002). Making communication meaningful: Cracking the language interaction code. In R. Gabriels & D. Hill (Eds.), *Autism: From research to individualized practice* (pp. 41–52). London, UK: Jessica Kingsley.

Shah, A., & Holmes, N. (1985). Brief report: The use of the Leiter International Performance Scale with autistic children. *Journal of Autism and Developmental Disorders, 15,* 195–203.

Sigman, M. (1998). The Emanuel Miller Memorial Lecture 1997: Change and continuity in the development of children with autism. *Journal of Child Psychology and Psychiatry, 39*(6), 817–827.

Sigman, M., & Capps, L. (1997). *Children with autism: A developmental perspective.* Cambridge, MA: Harvard University Press.

Sigman, M., & Ruskin, E. (1999). Continuity and change in the social competence of children with autism, Down syndrome, and developmental delays. *Monographs of the Society for Research in Child Development, 64*(1), 109–113.

Sigman, M., & Ungerer, J.A. (1984). Cognitive and language skills in autistic, mentally retarded, and normal children. *Developmental Psychology, 20*(2), 293–302.

Stanley, G.C., & Konstantareas, M.M. (2007). Symbolic play in children with autism spectrum disorder. *Journal of Autism and Developmental Disorders, 37*(7), 1215–1223. http://dx.doi.org/10.1007/s10803-006-0263-2

Stone, W.L., Lemanek, K.L., Fishel, P.T., Fernandez, M.C., & Altemeier, W.A. (1990). Play and imitation skills in the diagnosis of autism in young children. *Pediatrics, 86*(2), 267–272.

Taylor, M., & Carlson, S.M. (1997). The relation between individual differences in fantasy and theory of mind. *Child Development, 68*(3), 436–455.

Thiemann-Bourque, K.S., Brady, N.C., & Fleming, K.K. (2012). Symbolic play of preschoolers with severe communication impairments with autism and other developmental delays: More similarities than differences. *Journal of Autism and Developmental Disorders, 42*(5), 863–873.

Ungerer, J.A., & Sigman, M. (1981). Symbolic play and language comprehension in autistic children. *Journal of the American Academy of Child Psychiatry, 20*(2), 318–337.

Ungerer, J.A., Zelazo, P.R., Kearsley, R.B., & O'Leary, K. (1981). Developmental changes in the representation of objects in symbolic play from 18 to 34 months of age. *Child Development, 52*(1), 186–195.

Wing, L., Gould, J., Yeates, S.R., & Brierly, L.M. (1977). Symbolic play in severely mentally retarded and in autistic children. *Journal of Child Psychology and Psychiatry, 18*(2), 167–178.

Wolfberg, P. (2009). *Play and imagination in children with autism* (2nd ed.). New York, NY: Teachers College Press.

3

PLAY, NARRATIVE, AND CHILDREN WITH AUTISM

Karen Stagnitti

Introduction

In 1991, Westby stated that "to be truly competent in the world children must be able to do more than repeat a string of facts. . . . To exist successfully within the world requires an understanding of people . . ." (p. 131). Understanding people within their social and cultural contexts, "reading" the emotional intention of interactions of others, understanding the roles that people take on, and perceiving when social situations change all contribute to a person's social perception, integration, and acceptance within their social group and culture. Understanding the intentions of others' motivations and beliefs was coined as *theory of mind* in 1978 and defined as "the ability to impute mental states to self and to others" (Hughes & Leekam, 2004, p. 591). In 1987, Leslie put forward the idea of a cognitive model for pretend play based on information processing and introduced the concept of metarepresentation, which referred to representations of representations. A primary representation would be a child using a box for storage (that is, the literal use of the object), and metarepresentation would be the child using the box as a car (the child imposes meaning on the object so that it represents something else, also called *symbols in play* or *object substitution*). Leslie argued that pretense was an early manifestation of children's developing understanding of mental states. He argued that key cognitive skills in children's understanding of others' pretense were the child's ability to use symbols, attribute properties, and develop concepts with absent objects (for example, the "invisible man," Leslie, 1987, p. 420, in a play scene would be a reference to a person with an absent physical presence) and that these cognitive abilities were also evidence of comprehending and conceptualising mental states. Mental state terms are words such as *know*, *think*, *believe*, and *wonder*.

Children with autism spectrum disorder (ASD) have difficulty with mental state verbs such as "he thinks that" rather than verbs such as "he says that" (Hughes & Leekam, 2004; Leslie, 1987), and these mental state verbs are early competencies involved in social–perceptual theory of mind and social interactions (Hughes & Leekam, 2004). Leslie (1987) argued that for children with autism, the low ability in pretend play, particularly metarepresentation, underpinned the low ability in theory of mind. Since Leslie (1987) wrote his theory, the concept of theory of mind has widened to include a "range of mental states from perception to intention, cognition and emotion" (Hughes & Leekam, 2004, p. 591). Hughes and Leekam (2004) summarised four theories or positions within theory of mind, which were (a) the nativistic position, where children's developing theory of mind is influenced by social environments and pretend play is understood to be a manifestation of theory of mind; (b) the *theory theory* position, where social environments determine the richness of a child's theory of mind while the child interprets these influences; (c) the simulation theory, where a child's theory of mind depends on self-awareness and capacity for pretense and influence of social play partners; and (d) the executive function position, where the individual's development of theory of mind is related to underlying goal-directed behaviour, and social situations impoverish or enhance executive function ability. Influences on theory of mind, then, have been shown to include the impact of culture, genetics, family structure, relationship with a secure attachment figure, the child's play with others, and the child's cognitive and linguistic development (see Hughes & Leekam, 2004). The position argued by Leslie (1987) of theory of mind being underpinned by metarepresentation has been weakened, with further research showing that multiple factors impact theory of mind and that high-functioning children with autism do have the ability to produce symbols in play (metarepresentation) and be playful in pretend play (see Chaudry & Dissanayake, this volume). However, a deeper understanding has also been gained about the complexity of pretend play with symbols being part of this complexity.

Children's interactions within their social world and their development in pretense and theory of mind can be traced from infancy to older childhood. From 2 months of age, children pick up emotional cues from others by watching the eyes and mouth of the person who is speaking and responding to these interactions (Baron-Cohen, 1996; Sunderland, 2007; Ting Wang, Lee, Sigman, & Dapretto, 2006). For example, an infant in an environment with loud, angry shouting will cry. An infant's recognition of actions as intentional and joint visual attention contribute to developing theory of mind and social interactions (Baron-Cohen, 1996; Hughes & Leekam, 2004). Indeed, infants' responses to the singsong speech of adults "suggests that infants . . . are drawn to the types of vocal interplay that they experience as more meaningful and recognisable" (Edwards, 2011, p. 192). This suggests that infants have communicative intent within social interaction with others. In toddlerhood, emotional self-regulation, increasing ability in language, and a growing realisation of other's emotions (for example, comforting a younger sibling) contribute to the toddler's social awareness and understanding of mental states (Hughes & Leekam, 2004). Early forms of social–perceptual theory of mind are manifested as joint attention, emotional recognition, and nonverbal forms of communication (Hughes & Leekam, 2004). This is supported in a longitudinal study by Brooks and Meltzoff (2015), who tested children at 10.5 months, 2.5 years, and 4.5 years. Gaze following (early social perception) at 10.5 months predicted use of mental state terms at 2.5 years, and use of mental state terms at 2.5 years predicted theory of mind at 4.5 years. These predictions remained significant after controlling for general language, maternal education, and nonsocial attention (Brooks & Meltzoff, 2015). During toddlerhood, children begin to understand that others can think the same things as themselves—for example, everybody loves red buses (Baron-Cohen, 1996). Toddlerhood is also the period when pretend play ability begins, and Rakoczy (2008a, 2008b) argued that children as young as 2 years do understand the intentionality of the pretend play act (for example, pouring "tea" into a cup and "drinking"). By at least 3 years of age, children understand that the play is occurring within a "context-specific normative structure of joint pretence" or "we-intentionality" (Rakoczy, 2008a, 2008b, pp. 510–511) and that joint social pretend play sets up the context between the "we," with the implicit rules reflecting conventions within the child's cultural context. In other words, children show understanding of mental states of others through their pretend play. By preschool age, children have developed an understanding that people may show different emotions to what they really feel and that their emotions are influenced by mood or past events (Hughes & Leekam, 2004). They understand that others can have different beliefs than themselves, can sustain a conversation with peers, show ability to negotiate and cooperate in play, and have longer sequences in elaborate pretend play (Hughes & Leekam, 2004; Stagnitti, 2007). By school age, children's theory of mind understanding includes multiple mental states such as moral dilemmas, ambiguity of truths, beliefs about beliefs, bluffing, and influence of bias on beliefs (Hughes & Leekam, 2004).

Concepts of mental states are required for conversational exchanges with others (Peterson, Garnett, Kelly, & Attwood, 2009). The characteristics of language involved in conversational exchanges that relate to mental states include syntactic ability; pragmatic understanding of the task questions; and discourse skills, which include understanding mutual beliefs, knowledge, and assumptions (Hughes & Leekam, 2004). Children create joint shared meanings in their pretend play through conversational exchanges, which include extending the ideas of others, introducing a new idea, adding in new props, and showing acceptance or rejection of peers' ideas through verbal and nonverbal communication (Whittington & Floyd, 2009). Children create shared meaning in the play through conversing with each other about the play. What is not clear is if it is the conversation itself

54 Karen Stagnitti

or the verbal and nonverbal interactions during play that is the crucial factor in the understanding of mental states. Conversation exchanges can include narratives and involve the co-construction of ideas from one person to another. Children also co-construct (the we-intentionality of Racokzy, 2008a, 2008b) in social pretend play. The next sections consider narrative and pretend play in relation to children with ASD, and these are followed by a case study of a child who increased his ability in pretend play and personal narrative.

Narrative

Narrative is understood similarly to Stirling, Douglas, Leekam, and Carey (2014) "as a genre, or type of discourse, involving the relation of a sequence of events" (p. 172) within a story structure. It is further conceptualised as a "cognitive activity inseparable from its pragmatic and social dimensions" (Goldman, 2008, p. 1982). To be able to produce and comprehend a narrative presupposes that individuals have differing beliefs and viewpoints. Narrative is a complex cognitive task and involves social–perceptual theory of mind. For example, producing a narrative involves relating a set of events that are sequentially organised in time and space and have cause and effect; an evaluative point; global structure; different perspectives of characters and psychological states; and, for some narratives, a narrator's voice (Stirling et al., 2014). We construct our world through narrative, as it is "a key component of personal identity and social functioning in all human communities" (Stirling et al., 2014, p. 173). Personal narratives are the retelling of our personal experiences (Goldman, 2008) and contribute to our understanding of who we are.

Goldman (2008) stated that personal narratives pose unusual challenges for children with high-functioning autism (HFA), as these children are less attuned to emotional cues and may not be aware of the social value of the narrative. Their stories may be affected by a limited ability to take another's point of view. Goldman (2008) introduced sharing personal memories to 38 children who were grouped into children with autism, typically developing children, and children with developmental language disorders. The children were encouraged to converse with Goldman across eight topics using a story stem technique. Results showed that children with autism produced fewer proper narratives and that their narratives lacked high points and coherence, with fewer characters and resolution elements than the narratives of the children in the other two groups (Goldman, 2008). The children with HFA relied more on lists of facts, and their stories had few interpretations of the behaviours of characters, which would have given insight into the social meaning of the narrative (Goldman, 2008). Conversational narrative (narrative occurring within conversational exchanges) often involves personal narratives, which presupposes that a person can coordinate turn-taking ability, control the sequential relevance of contributions, maintain a topic, and shift and coordinate the conversation in response to the interlocutor (Stirling et al., 2014).

For children with ASD, there are contradictory and mixed results from previous research across all aspects of narrative production except for a consistent finding that children with ASD have difficulty with the establishment of a global coherence of narrative through use of causal language (see Stirling et al., 2014, for an excellent overview of the research on narrative understanding for children with autism). Compared to other groups, people with ASD have significant differences in narrative production in the following areas: focus on minor details or problem with global coherence, ability to shift perspectives, range of evaluative devices, accuracy of story recall, bizarre language, perseveration, and use of nongrammatical phrases (Stirling et al., 2014). Taking different perspectives in a narrative and moving between perspectives is an indication of theory of mind and was poorly done by children with ASD (Stirling et al., 2014).

Pretend Play

Pretend play (also called *imaginative play*, *make-believe play*, *representational play*, or *fantasy play*) occurs when children engage in play scenarios that extend beyond the literal meaning of the props in the play. For example, a child is literally playing with a large box, a small box, and two sticks, but as the child becomes immersed in a play scenario that is set on a body of water where there are plenty of fish to catch, the large box becomes a boat, the small box becomes the motor, and the two sticks become fishing rods. If a second child comes to join the play, the children create shared meaning that enables the continuation of the play (Rakoczy, 2008a; Whittington & Floyd, 2009). Creating shared meanings within social play requires children to generate increasingly complex narratives by extending on the ideas of others, imposing implicit rules within the context of their play, and showing understanding of the intention of the narrative structure that reflects and represents their real or fictional world (Feldman, 2005; Peter, 2003; Rakoczy, 2008a; see also Nicolopoulou, Barbosa de Sá, & Brockmeyer, 2010). Creating shared meaning requires a child to have awareness of mental states and theory of mind as the play narrative unfolds in consideration of others' perspectives (either psychologically or spatially). Roby and Kidd (2008) found that children who had invisible imaginary friends were superior at explaining a situation from the viewpoint of their interlocutor. They argued that the active construction of pretense between the child and his or her imaginary friend meant that the child was continually monitoring the state of mind of his or her imaginary friend.

Pretend play is a complex ability, influenced by a child's social and cultural milieu, which involves more than metarepresentation. First, a child must be able to initiate a play idea ("What will I play?"), plan what they need for the play (for example, "Do I need a spoon or a box?"), logically sequence their play actions, interact with peers, engage in metarepresentation (use symbols, attribute properties, refer to absent objects), play in reference to something or someone outside of themselves, and problem solve within a play script or narrative (for example, the baby is sick or the truck is out of petrol; Lewis, Boucher, & Astell, 1992; Stagnitti, 2010). When engaged in pretend play, children are recreating and learning about social situations, integrating emotional understanding of their world, and using metacognitive play skills (such as use of symbols in play—object substitution, attributing properties, referring to absent objects, and logical sequential play actions; Stagnitti, 2007; Whitebread, Coltman, Jameso, & Lander, 2009).

Children create narratives in their pretend play that increase in complexity as they produce problems, integrate characters, and use symbols (Peter, 2003; Stagnitti, 2009a). Whitehead, Marchant, Craik, and Frith (2009) found that when adults were engaged in pretend play, a vast amount of the brain was activated, particularly the areas of the brain concerned with narrative. The results of Whitehead et al. (2009) were consistent with "the proposal that pretend play is a form of communicative narrative, associated with the ability to mentalize" (p. 369). Nicolopoulou (2005; this volume) argued that narratives were the discursive exposition of stories and that pretend play was the enactment of story.

The development of pretend play and narrative in typical children occurs in parallel (Stagnitti & Jellie, 2006). For example, when children are 2 years of age, their play has short logical sequences of play actions, and their play scripts are about their life experiences. At this age, children tell stories about themselves, and they do this before they read. From 2 to 3 years of age, children begin to tell fictional stories and, in play, children begin to integrate characters and scenes from books, TV, or media (Stagnitti & Jellie, 2006). By school age, children can link events to form a story script; temporally sequence events to solve a problem; sequence events in a logical, sequential manner using characters; and embed characters, symbols, and problems within their play scripts (Stagnitti & Jellie, 2006). When children can logically sequence their play actions into a narrative and extend their play with peers, they are showing the ability to "think forward" about what will happen next. To carry out a complex play narrative, children require an understanding of the characters in the play scenario, an understanding of the play context, what props are needed in the play, and where the play script is likely to develop (Stagnitti, 2009b; Westby, 1991). The ability to logically sequence play actions, build a narrative, and think forward is often lacking or limited in the play of children with ASD.

Children with ASD have been reported to play with fewer objects, become intensely preoccupied with parts of an object or toy, spend less time playing, be more functional than symbolic in their play, be repetitive in their play, have fewer functional play actions, and experience difficulties with spontaneous, self-initiated pretend play (Charman & Baron-Cohen, 1997; Naber et al., 2008). Children with ASD are also known to have difficulties in social interaction and play with peers

Play, Narrative, and Children With ASD **57**

(Naber et al., 2008). Charman and Baron-Cohen (1997), through a structured experimental research design, found that novel object substitutions and novel play actions with toys were not performed by the children with ASD. However, Maclean (this volume) and Chaudry and Dissanayake (this volume) both report on children with autism engaging in symbolic play and play scenes.

In my own work with children with ASD, I have found that children can spontaneously use symbols in play, but this is often isolated and not linked within a play scene or script. Some children with autism may reproduce scripts from TV, movies, or their favourite book, but the reproduction does not always include their own spontaneous additions. Children with higher functioning autism can substitute objects in their play, but this occurs with one pretend play action (Stagnitti, 1998)—for example, crossing two sticks and "flying" them into the air.

Peter (2003), through the play drama intervention, found that children with severe and complex learning needs could begin to develop spontaneous initiation of pretend play. Sherratt (2002) reported on a 4-month intervention in a classroom with five children with ASD that explored teaching the children to use symbolic pretend play. He used an approach that involved structure, affect, and repetition with modelling, prompting, and eliciting play actions by others. He found that a child's emotional engagement in the play was effective in eliciting spontaneous symbolic play. The Learn to Play program (Stagnitti, 1998, 2009b) also aims to develop in children with developmental issues the ability to spontaneously initiate pretend play. I have become interested in whether building the capacity of a child with ASD to spontaneously initiate pretend play would parallel an inherent understanding of narrative. Peter (2003) linked pretend play, narrative, and social competence and found that a play-drama intervention was effective with children with severe and complex learning needs in increasing their engagement and understanding of narrative. This chapter now turns to a case study of a child diagnosed with ASD and his progress in developing the ability to spontaneously initiate pretend play and an understanding of narrative. Before the case study, an explanation of the Learn to Play program is given.

Learn to Play Program

The Learn to Play program (Stagnitti, 1998) is a developmentally based program that focuses on the following pretend play skills: scripts in play; logical, sequential actions in play; object substitution; social interaction; role-play; and doll or teddy play. The program is a dynamic program in which the therapist is constantly responding to the child within the play context.

The program is suitable for children with a developmental play age of 12 to 18 months and with at least one meaningful word or gesture. The Learn to Play program is not suitable for children who have no language or meaningful gestures, as the child is not ready for the cognitive demands of pretend play. It has been found that nonverbal children do not generalise imitation to novel play actions (Ingersoll & Schreibman, 2006), and this has been confirmed in the Learn to Play program. Many children with ASD who enter the program do so with pretend play ability at the 18-month developmental play level, regardless of chronological age. That is, the children come with functional understanding of the use of objects; no ability to logically sequence play actions; and poor ability in social interaction, role-play, and doll or teddy play. Play scripts could either reflect strong interests such as dinosaurs or characters from multimedia or no scripts at all. Most children with ASD who have come into the program have missed earlier personal play scripts such as pretending to have a drink. All children who have been part of the program have had difficulties with social interaction with peers and delays in language.

The principles of the Learn to Play program are:

1. Gain the child's focused attention towards the play materials. If the child is not focused or there is no shared attention, then the intervention is not neurologically effective (Doidge, 2010). Shared attention is often lacking in children with ASD (Ingersoll & Schreibman, 2006), and a key principle of the Learn to Play program is to gain shared attention or focused attention. To do this, the therapist uses his or her voice, face, and body to show enthusiasm for the play. The therapist is enthusiastic about playing, making noises with objects, and modelling the play action and works to gain the child's interest.

2. Start simple (Doidge, 2010), meaning that the program begins where the child is developmentally. Children with delayed pretend play only understand the play context at the level at which they are currently playing. If you begin to engage with a child in play at a higher level, they will not join you in the play because they do not understand what you are doing.

3. Repetition with variation (Doidge, 2010) helps the child to build their understanding of the play context. For example, you don't just pretend to have one cup of tea; you may need to have 50 cups of tea in playing "tea parties" with the child. In the play context of tea parties, you put the cup to your lips and you offer a cup to the teddy or others who are also joining in the play. You vary how you have your cup of tea—for example, you drink it, you blow on it as if it is hot, you stir your tea, you offer a cup to the child, and so on. It is the repetition with variation while the child is engaged that gives time for the child to understand what the play narrative demands.

4. Pretend play, language, and social skills "fire together" (Doidge, 2010). While the adult is modelling the play to the child, the adult is talking about the play (*metaplay*; see Pellegrini & Galda, 1993) and socially interacting with the child while introducing pretend play skills.

5. Pretend play involves the use of symbols in play. Pretend play engages the child in higher level thinking, as representation is a unique aspect of pretend play (Leslie, 1987).
6. Play with the child involves the emotional enjoyment of playing. Stagnitti and Casey (2011) found that the more emotionally involved the child was in the play, the deeper the child's learning in the play, which transferred to increased ability to add novel actions to the play and generalise their play skills to early childhood settings. Sherratt (2002) also found that the emotional engagement of the child in the play was associated with spontaneous changes in the play, as opposed to just showing the child the play actions.
7. Child-initiated play brings with it a deeper understanding of the context of play. Whitebread et al. (2009) reported that the ability to undertake the task for oneself resulted in a deeper understanding of the task.

Figure 3.1 shows the model of the Learn to Play program. First, an understanding of the child's developmental play level is ascertained. Then, the therapist chooses developmentally appropriate play activities for that child. The therapist models the play action(s) with consideration for the amount of play materials and prepares a variety of play scenes for the child's level of play. Repetition with variation is used in the early sessions until the child begins to initiate their own play actions. There is emotional engagement with the therapist using voice, tone, face, and body to express emotions, and the therapist is constantly responding to the child, either allowing time for the child to imitate or initiate or repeating play actions if the child has focused attention. The therapist challenges the child as the child increases in play ability by either

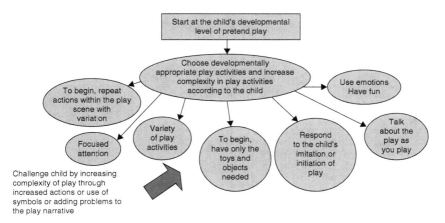

FIGURE 3.1 Overview of the Learn to Play program.

adding more actions to a play sequence or introducing object substitution to the play in increasing complexity.

For children with ASD, the following additional aspects are also used in the Learn to Play program:

- Begin with **structure**, with the therapist only having exactly the play materials needed and the therapist modelling the play actions while ensuring that the child has focused attention.
- During the play, the therapist **shifts the child's attention** by interrupting and/or challenging the play (for example, the therapist moves the child's car out of the line).
- The therapist uses **protodeclarative pointing** (that is, if the toy is "over there," you point to it as you name it) during the play and in particular to bring the child back to the play context.
- The key play ability focus is on developing **logical, sequential sequences** of play actions. This relates to the level of complexity and narrative in the play.
- Only use **play scripts** where the child has had some life experience. The beginning play scripts are either a reflection of the child's life experiences or a reflection of their interests.
- As you are developing a child's ability to spontaneously play, it is important not to rote teach; therefore, you should use a **variety of play scenes** from **the same developmental level.**
- **Remove structure** as the child begins to initiate play; step back and follow the child by modelling what the child is doing, talking about what the child is playing, and suggesting changes to the child's play as they increase in their ability to play.

The following is a case study of a child who was involved in the Learn to Play program from 2010 to 2012. This case study highlights the child's increase in pretend play ability and his understanding of narrative. A pseudonym is used for the child's name in the case study.

Henry

Henry was 3 years old and had been diagnosed with ASD by the local specialist team who worked with children with ASD. He first met me when I assessed his pretend play ability at his home. His parents had prepared him for the assessment and assured him that he would be safe. This was to decrease his anxiety. The assessment was the 3-year-old version of the Child-Initiated Pretend Play Assessment (Stagnitti, 2007), which is carried out on the floor in front of a "cubby" house that is made of a sheet thrown over two adult chairs. As Henry and I sat on the floor, a set of toys was offered to Henry, and he was invited to do whatever he

Play, Narrative, and Children With ASD **61**

would like with the materials. At first, Henry sat beside me and sang a little song quietly to himself. I was quiet and made no other demands of him. Once Henry's anxiety levels decreased, he began to look at the toys, and he spontaneously fed one of the small dolls with a spoon. No other spontaneous actions were observed apart from manipulation of the play materials. The second set of play materials is a set of unstructured play materials. Henry manipulated the objects with no object substitution noted and did not play for very long. The result of his assessment showed that he had one spontaneous action (feeding the doll), which was a single action that he repeated. This was a play script to do with the body (feeding) and also reflected a domestic narrative. He had no object substitution and did not show any interest in social interaction with me. He did not show any interest in role-play, and his parents reported that he did not engage in role-play at home. Henry did imitate actions of characters from movies, such as *WALL-E*, where he would move in a certain way. At these times, the action was a single action and was scripted directly from the movie. There were no additional spontaneous actions. The Learn to Play program for Henry, then, began on the 12- to 18-month level of pretend play development, which meant body-based play stories with one repeated action and no object substitutions.

For the first 3 months, Henry was seen every 3 weeks at home for play sessions; then, in the following year his parents brought Henry to a play room at the local university, as they had consented to be part of the research program investigating the Parent Learn to Play outcomes for children with ASD. The sessions were once a fortnight for 9 months, with the parent participating with their child in the play sessions facilitated by the therapist. The play sessions began with me modelling single play actions repeatedly, working on gaining focused attention (joint attention), and pacing the sessions so that Henry could join in the play when ready. Examples of the play scenes enacted at this stage were feeding the teddy, racing horses across the floor, drinking cups of tea, throwing the ball to a large doll and the doll throwing it back to Henry, pushing a truck around the room, and then adding the teddy bear to ride in the truck. In these early sessions, Henry could be difficult to engage or become distracted by noises or other extraneous events, so there were many occasions when his joint attention would need to be refocused on the play. One of the early sessions that showed a shift in Henry's play was a play scene where Henry, myself, and the teddy were having a tea party. We were "drinking" from the empty cups, and I would repeat the play action of drinking from the cup with variations such as blowing on the cup as if it were hot, offering the cup to the teddy to drink, having a drink myself, stirring in the cup, and drinking. Henry was engaged and watching—then he saw that I had left a small object with a *P* on it (the pepper shaker) in the tea set bag. He started to move the pepper shaker in the air. I responded by sneezing. I sneezed and sneezed and sneezed. He looked at me and smiled and continued to shake the pepper shaker, having made the connection between his shaking of the object and my sneezing.

62 Karen Stagnitti

I got tired of sneezing and because Henry had focused attention, I made the teddy sneeze. Henry looked directly at the teddy—complete focus—and continued to shake the pepper shaker. The teddy sneezed and sneezed and sneezed. The teddy sneezed so much that it started to do somersaults (repetition with variation). We had been playing for about 15 minutes. Henry continued to shake the pepper shaker, and teddy continued to sneeze. Then, Henry picked up the teddy, placed the pepper shaker to the teddy's nose, and said Ahchoo, Ahchoo as he made the teddy move in his hands as if it were sneezing. Then, Henry pressed the teddy to his shoulder and said all right in order to comfort the teddy (that is, recognising teddy's emotion; this was Henry's first indication during the play sessions of his understanding of mental states). He repeated placing the pepper to the teddy's nose, with sneezing and comforting four more times before he began to lose interest and we moved on to another play scene. This example of the teddy sneezing showed that Henry was decentering in his play by imposing on teddy different actions to himself. He also demonstrated that he understood the emotional context of the scene and had imposed a mental state on the teddy.

Henry's family requested another year in the program. Henry had now developed in his play to where he could spontaneously initiate four play actions in a logical sequence. Throughout his 2 years in the program, Henry stayed at this level of logical sequences for 12 months. During his second year in the program, Henry was externally assessed by another organisation as being intellectually disabled and then 6 months later as not being intellectually disabled. It was a tumultuous year for the family. However, during this time, other aspects of his play ability were beginning to develop. He could now use objects as symbols in play, such as a box for a car or a bed, a block as a mobile phone, and paper for a blanket for the teddy. When introducing symbols in play to children with ASD, there are many times when I need to demonstrate exactly what to do, as the idea of using an object in a nonliteral way is beyond their comprehension at first. For example, one of the first objects I usually introduce as a symbol in play is a small block to be used as a mobile phone. Children often respond with, "It's a block." I reply, "Yes, I know, but today we are going to use it as a phone." Some children have told me that they will show me how to use it properly if I give them another block. I then instruct the child on exactly what to do such as, "You put the block to your face and talk to the block like this." After more than three repetitions of pretending to talk on the phone to myself, to their mother or father, and to the teddy, most children with HFA are able to make the shift to understanding the symbolic meaning of the block as a phone (Leslie's metarepresentation).

After 15 months, Henry's spontaneous play scenes in the Learn to Play sessions had extended to cooking dinner, playing doctor to fix the hurt teddy, teddies going on adventures over mountains (with the mountains being chairs with pieces of cloth covering them) and climbing through caves (the caves being under the chairs under the cloth), going on train rides, and playing out scenes on a large car mat that also included a zoo corner. These play scenes with Henry were now extending to stories beyond his everyday experience, and Henry understood the intentions of the pretense within the context of the play scenes.

There were many times when Henry was difficult to engage in play scenes. It was as if he were living in a bubble, and to get into the bubble to engage Henry in a play scene meant ensuring that the play scenes were of interest to him and constantly pacing the session to match his responses. At times, the Learn to Play sessions would include his strong interests and be reenactments of stories from his favourite movies or books, such as reenacting *Lightning McQueen* and *Ben 10* scenes. This is similar to Oscar (Maclean, this volume), who engaged in plots from his favourite films, cartoons, and games, and this pretend play was a way for Oscar and his father to connect and enjoy social interaction with each other. For Henry, the Learn to Play session enacting scenes from *Lightning McQueen* involved making cars from cardboard boxes that Henry and his father could stand in and pull up to their waists so that they could "drive" and "race" the cars. In *Lightning McQueen*, there is a large truck, and in the play this truck was represented by two adult chairs with a cloth thrown over the top (symbolic of a large truck). Henry, with his car around his waist, could sit in the "truck" with the cloth over his head while the chair was rocked as if the truck were moving. This play scene allowed for repetition of racing cars, going in the large truck, and sleeping. For this play session, Henry was engaged for 50 minutes.

In the second year, other changes in his play were observed, such as embedding a problem in the story like a bird hurting its wing, with Henry providing a resolution to the problem by taking it to the "hospital" to fix the wing. In this scene, he took on the role of the doctor and put on a doctor's coat. During this time, Henry's spontaneous play action sequence still remained at four to five spontaneous actions. Even so, Henry could now attribute properties to objects, refer to absent objects in the play scene, substitute objects in the play, add problems and resolutions, and extend play action sequences after prompting or the modelling of further logical actions—the latter being a challenge to extend the play.

By the last sessions, it was clear that Henry understood the play narrative by his spontaneous logical additions of play actions to the play scene. As Henry's play became more complex, he could engage in higher level play skills, such as spontaneous extension of play sequences, using symbols in play, imposing meaning within the context of the play scene, and using characters in the play, and he could manage a cohesive narrative in the play that included all these elements. The longer the sequence of play actions, the more complex the play scene can become, because more problems can be added within the play narrative and more characters can be introduced into the play scenes. In Henry's last play session, he was interacting with characters in the play (that is, the teddy and puppets) as if they were alive. He was talking to them and laughing and joking with them. He took over the play session and had a spontaneity in his play scenes that had not

64 Karen Stagnitti

been present earlier when he seemed to be stuck in a bubble. He carried out a magic show, laughing and joking with the play characters, and followed through with additions to the play scenes that were logical and sequential and that resolved problems he was embedding in the play.

Henry's Written Narratives

Two months after Henry had finished the Learn to Play program, his mother rang and said that he had spontaneously begun to write books. She said that I would appreciate what he had done, as narrative and play had been emphasised and embedded through the program. His books were a series of pictures, and he had asked his mother to write the words below the pictures. She wrote exactly what he dictated. He had not yet begun his first year of school. His books contained spontaneous stories that showed a story structure—beginning, middle, and end. They contained emotions and humour and reflected Henry's life experiences, as well as fictional stories (for example, farting robots) that he had created. An example of two of his stories is below. Because Henry's narratives were based on personal experiences, his written narratives are analysed using narrative analysis approaches by Goldman (2008) and Bamburg and Damrad-Frye (1991). Following Goldman (2008), the written narratives are first analysed in terms of narrative conventional elements (opening, setting, action, obstacle, resolutions, and ending) and then in terms of narrative style (evaluation, coherence [reference tracking, use of time and tense, causal relations between elements in the story], goal direction, high points [linguistic highlighting of parts of the story], and story type). The narratives are then analysed using the five categories of the lexical items of Bamburg and Damrad-Frye (1991): frames of mind (ability to present a perspective), character speech, distancing devices, negative statements, and causal connectors and motivations of characters. The titles of the written narratives are given for convenience. Henry did not title his narratives.

Narrative 1: Popping an Idea

Henry looks at the time *[picture of a clock with a person underneath the clock looking up and holding his hands to his head]*
He makes a card for *[sister's name]*
He writes her name *[picture of the card Henry made with the name and a heart]*
His brain popped a great idea *[picture of Henry smiling with a lightbulb above his head]*
He goes to the beach and sits on the sand and drinks a blue drink with a straw *[picture of smiling person sitting on a lounge chair with a blue glass and a straw to his mouth]*
He sees a little red bird in a tree *[picture of a tree with a red bird at the top]*

Play, Narrative, and Children With ASD   **65**

[picture of a rainbow]

Henry digs in the sand [picture of smiling person digging with one arm, sun in the sky]

He flies his kite at the beach [picture of a smiling person holding a kite]

He's happy [see Figure 3.2]

He dives into the water [see Figure 3.2]

He yawns [picture of yawning person sitting on a bed]

Then he goes to sleep and snores [picture of person under the blankets on a bed with z'z'z'z]

In the written narrative "Popping an Idea," Henry begins with actions—"looks at the time and makes a card." The picture sequence begins with a detailed picture of a clock. This engages the audience with the indication that something is going to happen. It also sets the scene a little but does not indicate where it takes place or who *Henry* is. However, given that this is a personal narrative he is dictating to his mother, it doesn't matter as much. It is interesting that he introduces the character as Henry first, then continues using the pronoun *he* to refer to the character. He has a picture of the card he made for his sister (in reality, Henry did make the card). The picture of the card indicates emotion with the picture of a heart. The heart

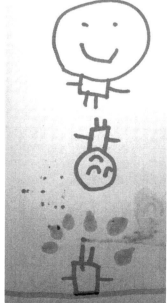

FIGURE 3.2 Pages from Henry's written narrative "Popping an Idea" showing emotion and sequence.

symbol is interpreted as Henry's awareness of the purpose of a card, as it addresses the receiver of the card. He also shows emotions, as the picture of Henry is happy. There is an obstacle—"his brain popped a great idea"—as this event interrupts the card making and contributes to the story plot. The event of his brain popping an idea leads to a series of events that resolve and have a final point with Henry sleeping and snoring. When Henry's brain pops an idea, he again shows happiness by a picture of Henry smiling, indicating a causal link between the idea and the emotion. There is coherence with respect to the use of tense change. Henry shows evaluation throughout his written narrative, as he has a "great" idea and is happy during his activities on the beach, which made him tired (he yawns, sleeps, and snores). However, his story is action oriented, with his narrative being coherent from the view that it starts with activities at home, then out at the beach, and then home again to sleep. The seeming interruption to the plot—"He sees a little red bird in a tree"—with the accompanying picture appears to move his story out of the beach story. An alternative explanation, however, is that this event is part of the story—that is, he saw a bird in a tree while sitting on the beach having a drink. There are no explicit links between sitting on the beach and seeing the bird, as there are no connectors to know how or why this links to the narrative. Complexity of the picture of diving (see Figure 3.2) is evident, with the sequence of events showing the opening of eyes and a happy face prior to the dive, eyes closed as he dives (and he is still happy), and then no head to show that he has successfully dived into the water. The written narrative has no causal markers or goals such as linking Henry being tired from all the activities at the beach to going home and sleeping, but the use of *then* in the last line is a link between events at the beach and at home. The high point is early in the story when his brain popped an idea.

Henry used frames of mind in his story—"happy." There is no character speech; rather, the narrative is in the third person, and there are no hedges or negative connectors. Overall, details are present, although the more specific details that link the sequences of events are quite simple. With the written narrative, some of these links may be omitted because he is retelling the story to his mother; therefore, it could move into the genre of recount.

Narrative 2: It Rained

> The moon was in the sky *[picture of a moon]*
> Then the sun came up *[picture of sun behind a green mound]*
> *[picture of the sun full in the sky]*
> Henry watched some TV *[picture of TV with TV scene of happy person]*
> The traffic light stopped *[traffic light—red, yellow, green]*
> *[picture of a person stopped]*
> Then Henry slid down the slide *[person "sliding" down a wiggly diagonal line]*
> It was sunny *[picture of a sun]*

Then a rain cloud came *[grey cloud]*
And Henry said "Oh, no" *[see Figure 3.3]*
Then the rain came *[five large raindrops above a sad person]*
[picture of a grey cloud]
Then the sun came out *[picture of a sun]*
And it made a rainbow *[picture of a rainbow]*
And Henry was happy *[smiling person]*
The sun made Henry warm *[person with wide smile showing teeth, hands behind head]*
And Henry cleaned his teeth with lots of bubbles *[picture of person cleaning teeth]*
Then he read a book *[picture of a book]*
And he went to sleep *[person snoring z'z'z'z in bed]*
Then he jumped on the trampoline *[person jumping on trampoline]*
Then he ate an oval biscuit *[picture of head and shoulders with arms stretched out with an oval shape and dots on it]*

In Written Narrative 2, Henry sets the scene—the moon was in the sky, the sun came up. The day was beginning. Action occurs when Henry watches TV. There is an understanding of time and sequence. An obstacle comes in the form of a rain cloud with the evaluation "Oh, no" and the picture showing a sad face with arms touching his head (see Figure 3.3). The resolution is the sun

FIGURE 3.3 A drawing from "It Rained" showing emotion ("Oh, no").

68 Karen Stagnitti

coming out, and it warms Henry. This makes Henry happy (his pictures go from a smiling person to a person smiling showing teeth). This illustrates his emotional awareness of degrees of happiness. (Could this be related to the development of emotive language—oral and written—which equates to *happy, very happy*, and *ecstatic?*) He elaborates his mental state through pictures. There is some violation to the logical sequence of events as Henry goes from watching TV to traffic lights and then later abruptly goes from being warm in the sun to cleaning his teeth. There are no hedges, but there are many connections such as *then* and *and*. The logical sequence is from inside the home to being outside, then going inside, outside on the trampoline, then eating. The story is not constructed around a motive or goal, and the high point centres on the "Oh, no" which, as in Narrative 1, is earlier in the story.

His narrative is again action based, with frames of mind referred to such as distress or sadness when the rain came and then smiling faces (denoting happiness) when the sun came out and made him warm. There is character speech in this narrative—"Oh, no"—which is direct personal speech. There is no ending to this narrative compared with the first narrative.

Both stories have one problem and a resolution. The first narrative uses a combination of present and past tense. The second narrative is in past tense. Again, this may be because he is narrating his story to his mother so that it could become more of a recount, which requires the use of past tense.

Throughout the Learn to Play program, Henry's parents had been involved at each step. When Henry started school (this was a month after Henry had written his narratives), his mother e-mailed to say that Henry "slipped right in" to the school context. He understood the context of the classroom and the role of the teacher and of himself as the student. He knew what to do—he understood the narrative or discourse requirements of school.

Conclusion

For children to pretend in play, they are required to logically sequence their play actions, incorporate another's point of view, use symbols, and impose meaning. From the beginning of pretend play, children are creating stories in their play. By 5 years of age, they are able to play out scenarios with peers over 2 to 3 weeks, embed and resolve problems in the play, and understand cause and effect. The longer the play sequences, the longer the narrative, and the longer the narrative, the more complexity that is embedded through events, use of props, and imposing mental states on characters. The case study of Henry illustrates his pretend play ability developing to show spontaneity in extension of play actions and use of symbols in play. He drew and dictated written narratives that illustrated an understanding of mental states.

When children understand pretend play scenarios, they also understand the context of what is happening. They understand which characters are part of the context, what those characters say and do, and what props and scenes are needed that fit with the context. For children with ASD, there has been debate about how to work with these children so that they are able to add novel, spontaneous actions and events into their play and understand the pretense. The Learn to Play program, like Peter's (2003) and Sherratt's (2002) play intervention, combines pretend play ability with emotional engagement and a child's interest to build complex play abilities as much as possible for children with complex learning needs. Advances in neuroscience have shown that areas of the brain associated with narrative and theory of mind are activated when people are engaged in pretend play (Whitehead et al., 2009). The power to play out a story provides children with the experience of narrative by being involved in developing a logical sequence of events and understanding pretense in characters and play partners.

References

Anderson, D. (Producer), Lasseter, J., & Ranft, J. (Co-Directors). (2006). *Cars* [Motion picture]. United States: Pixar.

Bamburg, M., & Damrad-Frye, R. (1991). On the ability to provide evaluative comments: Further explorations of children's narrative competencies. *Journal of Child Language, 18,* 689–710.

Baron-Cohen, S. (1996). *Mindblindness. An essay on autism and theory of mind.* London, UK: MIT Press.

Brooks, R., & Meltzoff, A. (2015). Connecting the dots from infancy to childhood: A longitudinal study connecting gaze following, language, and explicit theory of mind. *Journal of Experimental Child Psychology, 130,* 67–78.

Charman, T., & Baron-Cohen, S. (1997). Brief report: Prompted pretend play in autism. *Journal of Autism and Developmental Disorders, 27*(3), 325–332.

Doidge, D. (2010). *The brain that changes itself.* Melbourne, VIC, Australia: Scribe.

Edwards, J. (2011). The use of music therapy to promote attachment between parents and infants. *The Arts in Psychotherapy, 38*(3), 190–195.

Feldman, C. (2005). Memesis: Where play and narrative meet. *Cognitive Development, 20,* 503–513.

Goldman, S. (2008). Brief report: Narratives of personal events in children with autism and developmental language disorders: Unshared memories. *Journal of Autism and Developmental Disorders, 38,* 1982–1988.

Hughes, C., & Leekam, S. (2004). What are the links between theory of mind and social links? Review, reflections and new directions for studies of typical and atypical development. *Social Development, 13,* 590–691.

Ingersoll, B., & Schreibman, L. (2006). Teaching reciprocal imitation skills to young children with autism using a naturalistic behavioural approach: Effects on language, pretend play, and joint attention. *Journal of Autism and Developmental Disorders, 36*(4), 487–505.

Leslie, A. M. (1987). Pretense and representation: The origins of "theory of mind." *Psychological Review, 94,* 412–426.

Lewis, V., Boucher, J., & Astell, A. (1992). The assessment of symbolic play in young children: A prototype test. *European Journal of Disorders of Communications, 27,* 231–245.

Man of Action (Writers). (2005–2008). *Ben-10* [Television series]. In Cartoon Network Studios (Producer). Burbank, CA: Cartoon Network Studios.

Morris, J. (Producer), & Stanton, A. (Director). (2008). *WALL-E* [Motion picture]. United States: Pixar.

Naber, F. B. A., Bakermans-Kranenburg, M.J., van IJzendoorn, M.H., Swinkels, S. H. N., Buitelaar, J. K., Dietz, C. . . . van Engeland, H. (2008). Play behavior and attachment in toddlers with autism. *Journal of Autism and Developmental Disorders, 38,* 857–866.

Nicolopoulou, A. (2005). Play and narrative in the process of development: Commonalities, differences, and interrelations. *Cognitive Development, 20,* 495–502.

Nicolopoulou, A., Barbosa de Sá, A., & Brockmeyer, C. (2010). Using the transformative power of play to educate hearts and minds: From Vygotsky to Vivian Paley and beyond. *Mind, Culture, and Activity, 17,* 42–58.

Pellegrini, A., & Galda, L. (1993). Ten years after: A re-examination of symbolic play and literacy research. *Reading Research Quarterly, 28,* 163–175.

Peter, M. (2003). Drama, narrative and early learning. *British Journal of Special Education, 30*(1), 21–27.

Peterson, C.C., Garnett, M., Kelly, A., & Attwood, T. (2009). Everyday social and conversation applications of theory-of-mind understanding by children with autism-spectrum disorders or typical development. *European Child Adolescent Psychiatry, 18,* 105–115.

Rakoczy, H. (2008a). Pretense as individual and collective intentionality. *Mind & Language, 23*(5), 499–517.

Rakoczy, H. (2008b). Taking fiction seriously: Young children understand the normative structure of joint pretence games. *Developmental Psychology, 44,* 1195–1201.

Roby, A., & Kidd, E. (2008). The referential communication skills of children with imaginary companions. *Developmental Science, 11,* 531–540.

Sherratt, D. (2002). Developing pretend play in children with autism: A case study. *Autism, 6,* 169–179.

Stagnitti, K. (1998). *Learn to play: A practical program to develop a child's imaginative play.* Melbourne, VIC, Australia: Coordinates.

Stagnitti, K. (2007). *Child-initiated pretend play assessment.* Melbourne, VIC, Australia: Coordinates.

Stagnitti, K. (2009a). Children and pretend play. In K. Stagnitti and R. Cooper (Eds.), *Play as therapy: Assessment and therapeutic interventions* (pp. 59–69). London, UK: Kingsley.

Stagnitti, K. (2009b). Play intervention: The Learn to Play program. In K. Stagnitti and R. Cooper (Eds.), *Play as therapy: Assessment and therapeutic interventions* (pp. 176–186). London, UK: Kingsley.

Stagnitti, K. (2010). Helping kindergarten teachers foster play in the classroom. In A. Drewes and C. Schaefer (Eds.), *School-based play therapy* (pp. 145–161). New York, NY: Wiley.

Stagnitti, K., & Casey, S. (2011). Il programma Learn to Play con bambini con autismo: Considerazioni pratiche e evidenze. *Autismo Oggi, 20,* 8–13.

Stagnitti, K., & Jellie, L. (2006). *Play to learn: Building literacy in the early years.* Melbourne, VIC, Australia: Curriculum Press.

Stirling, L., Douglas, S., Leekam, S., & Carey, L. (2014). The use of narrative in studying communication in autism spectrum disorders. In J. Arciuli and J. Brock (Eds.), *Communication in autism* (pp. 171–215). New York, NY: Benjamins.

Sunderland, M. (2007). *What every parent needs to know.* London, UK: DK Books.

Ting Wang, A., Lee, S. S., Sigman, M., & Dapretto, M. (2006). Developmental changes in the neural basis of interpreting communicative intent. *Social Cognitive and Affective Neuroscience, 1,* 107–121.

Westby, C. (1991). A scale for assessing development of children's play. In C. Schaefer, K. Gitlin-Weiner, & A. Sandgrund (Eds.), *Play diagnosis and assessment* (pp. 131–161). New York, NY: Wiley.

Whitebread, D., Coltman, P., Jameso, H., & Lander, R. (2009). Play, cognition and self-regulation: What exactly are children learning when they learn through play? *Educational & Child Psychology, 26,* 40–52.

Whitehead, C., Marchant, J. L., Craik, D., & Frith, C. D. (2009). Neural correlates of observing pretend play in which one object is represented as another. *Social Cognitive and Affective Neuroscience, 4,* 369–378.

Whittington, V., & Floyd, I. (2009). Creating intersubjectivity during socio-dramatic play at an Australian kindergarten. *Early Child Development and Care, 179,* 143–156.

4

DEVELOPING RECIPROCITY WITH TECHNOLOGY AND STORYTELLING

The Design of an Authorable Virtual Peer for Children With Autism Spectrum Disorder

Andrea Tartaro and Justine Cassell

Introduction

Storytelling and pretend play characterize many children's interactions with their peers and are integral to children's development. While these interactions are natural for typically developing children, difficulties with social communication directly affect the kinds of interaction children with autism spectrum and related disorders (ASD) have with their peers, as well as their use of storytelling and pretend play (Douglas & Stirling, this volume). Children's play and storytelling rely on reciprocity—language that engages another person in an interactive exchange. Children with autism have difficulty engaging in reciprocal social interactions (American Psychiatric Association, 2013), and these difficulties could be a component of the trouble they have telling stories and playing with peers.

Our research looks at how technology, specifically a virtual peer, could be used to support children with ASD in engaging in storytelling and other peer interactions (Tartaro & Cassell, 2008; Tartaro, Cassell, Ratz, Lira, & Nanclares-Nogués, 2015). A virtual peer is a computer-animated child that is projected life sized on a screen and interacts with children by telling stories (Cassell et al., 2000). Our previous research suggested that children with ASD increased their use of specific forms of language used in interactive exchanges over the course of an interaction telling stories with a virtual peer but not with their human peers (Tartaro & Cassell, 2008). This chapter asks: How can we leverage this ability to interact with a virtual peer to design tasks and a technology system for learning about reciprocity?[1]

To address this question, we apply constructionist theory in education, which suggests that building artifacts supports learning by engaging metacognitive skills, including planning, taking the perspective of others, and reflection (Bers & Cassell, 1998; Robertson & Nicholson, 2007). We describe how we applied constructionist theory to learning about social interaction by developing constructionist tasks for virtual peer technology. Our goal is to create tools that allow children to create stories and social behaviors for a virtual peer and then operate the virtual peer in the manner of a puppet while it interacts with another person. We argue that these tasks, which we call *authoring* the virtual peer, engage metacognitive skills, including planning, monitoring, and revising a social interaction. We illustrate that authoring encourages children to employ targeted reciprocity skills and reveals behaviors that may be affecting those skills.

The research presented here is part of a multiple-phase project to develop and evaluate a social group–based intervention incorporating technology that targets the difficulties children with ASD have with peer social interaction (Tartaro, 2011; Tartaro & Cassell, 2008; Tartaro et al., 2015). This chapter specifically describes the design stage of the project. While our goal is to design technology that supports children in developing reciprocity skills they can use in interactions with peers, both the theoretical basis of the research and the technology design process could be applied to the design of technologies and interventions for other skills. In what follows, we first provide background on ASD, research on interventions for autism that motivates our approach, and details of the theories and methods this work is based on. We then describe the study we conducted to design the intervention tasks and technology, including methods for working with children with ASD. We conclude by discussing knowledge gained about the social behaviors of children with ASD, as suggested by their use of the system.

Background

ASD is a developmental disorder characterized by two main features: (a) "persistent deficits in social communication and social interaction" and (b) "restrictive, repetitive patterns of behavior, interests, or activities" (American Psychiatric Association, 2013, p. 50). Language ability varies widely: Some individuals with ASD have little to no intelligible speech; others can only speak in simple sentences, while others can communicate in full sentences (American Psychiatric Association, 2013). Even for those with functional language, social communication difficulties translate to a number of specific deficits in reciprocity affecting peer interactions, such as "failure to initiate or respond to social interactions," "difficulties sharing in imaginative play," and "absence of interest in peers" (American Psychiatric Association, 2013, p. 50). Given that successful interactions rely on these reciprocity components, increasing children's ability to effectively use reciprocal language forms, such as asking and responding to questions or initiating and expanding on topics of conversation, may improve their ability to engage with peers.

Intervention Approaches and Innovative Technologies for Autism

Numerous interventions are currently used to support children with ASD in developing social communication skills. Our research builds on the success of three approaches that are used to address reciprocity skills and peer interaction: social skills groups, narrative approaches, and technological approaches. Social skills groups are an evidence-based approach (Reichow & Volkmar, 2010), where groups of individuals with autism learn and practice social interaction skills. Groups are frequently comprised of children of similar ages and abilities to facilitate age-appropriate interactions. Group programs often include didactic instruction on specific social skills; modeling of social skills by therapists or typically developing group participants; role-play exercises where participants practice new skills; and unstructured activities, such as board games, where contextualized use of social skills can be practiced as appropriate situations arise (e.g., Baker, 2003; Jackson, Jackson, Bennett, Bynum, & Faryna, 1991; McGinnis & Goldstein, 1984, 1990; Webb, Miller, Pierce, Strawser, & Jones, 2004). While recent studies and metareviews support the efficacy of social skills groups (Cappadocia & Weiss, 2011; Reichow & Volkmar, 2010; Wang & Spillane, 2009), limitations exist. For example, conversational skills are difficult to target (Barry et al., 2003), and many evaluations demonstrate limited generalization of skills outside the group setting (e.g., Barry et al., 2003; Castorina & Negri, 2011; White, Koenig, & Scahill, 2010). Thus, additional research is needed to address these limitations.

Another common approach uses narrative and pictures to illustrate social situations and appropriate responses—for example, Social Stories (Gray, 1994b), comic strip conversations (Gray, 1994a), and social skills picture stories (Baker, 2001). Across these approaches, stories describe and illustrate social situations and contrast inappropriate behaviors with acceptable responses. These stories are typically individualized to the situations and behaviors that a particular child faces. Research offers evidence of the effectiveness of Social Stories and related approaches (e.g., Adams, Gouvousis, VanLue, & Waldron, 2004; Barry & Burlew, 2004), which are often used in conjunction with other therapies (Reichow & Volkmar, 2010).

Recent research is demonstrating that a variety of technological solutions, including personal computers, the Internet, video and multimedia, mobile devices, shared active surfaces, virtual and augmented reality, sensors and wearables, robotics, and natural inputs (e.g., speech, eye tracking, etc.; Kientz, Goodwin, Hayes, & Abowd, 2014) can provide unique opportunities for enhancing intervention, increasing our understanding of autism, and improving the diagnosis of autism. Kientz et al. (2014) provide a review of different technologies for autism to date, along with a classification scheme useful for understanding the different approaches. In our own work, we found that the technology of virtual peers—life-sized, computer-animated children that interact using speech and gestures (Cassell et al., 2000)—may provide a context for developing social interaction skills (Tartaro & Cassell, 2008) by using technology to combine and build on the benefits of peer and narrative interventions. A virtual peer is projected on a large screen, as illustrated in Figure 4.1. Children have physical toys, a dollhouse, and various figurines to play with, and the virtual peer has virtual counterparts

FIGURE 4.1 Virtual peer displayed life sized.

to these toys. The intention of this setup is to create a "shared reality" space in the physical world rather than a virtual reality on the screen (Cassell et al., 2000). Children work together with the virtual peer to develop a story—the virtual peer starts the story and then takes turns with the child to finish the story. Behind the scenes, an experimenter is watching the interaction and selecting prerecorded story continuations when it is the virtual peer's turn. The interaction is based on how children collaborate to tell stories, and the virtual peer's speech acts and behaviors are designed to follow a detailed model of those that children use in interactions with each other (Wang & Cassell, 2003).

This collaborative narrative task requires those same reciprocity skills that are difficult for children with ASD. To tell stories together, children must listen and respond to their peer's story contributions and add to the development of the story. We conducted a study to examine how specific social skills are used when children with ASD co-construct a narrative during peer social interactions and how these behaviors manifest in interactions with virtual peers (Tartaro & Cassell, 2008). Using a within-subjects, counterbalanced design, we compared the stories children with ASD told with the virtual peer to those they told with a same-aged, typically developing peer using the same toys and environment. Our findings suggest that when children interacted with virtual peers, their appropriate use of language forms that maintain a conversation increased. This increase did not occur with their typically developing peers. In addition, the content of their utterances was more appropriate overall in interactions with the virtual peer versus their typically developing peer. We concluded that these findings, taken together with the availability and willingness of virtual peers to engage in interactions, support the use of collaborative narratives with a virtual peer as a context for developing social interaction skills. However, the study does not provide the mechanisms through which learning reciprocity skills occur—we do not know how children can use the virtual peer to learn these skills in a way that translates to them using the skills in interaction with their (human) peers.

Constructionism and Metalinguistic Reflection

To help children develop reciprocity skills that transfer to interactions with their peers, our research proposes that we can apply an educational theory of learning through building artifacts, called *constructionism* (Harel & Papert, 1991), to virtual peer technology. In learning environments based on constructionist theory, children design and build artifacts, such as computer games, and through these tasks build an understanding of disciplines such as math (e.g., Kafai, 1995) or creative writing (Howland, Good, & Robertson, 2007; Kafai, 1995). Theorists believe that by constructing artifacts, children reflect on what they are learning in new ways (Kafai, 1995) to become better learners (Resnick, Bruckman, & Martin, 1996; Resnick & Silverman, 2005) and use metacognitive skills, including planning,

Developing Reciprocity With Technology **77**

taking the perspective of others, and reflection (Bers & Cassell, 1998; Robertson & Nicholson, 2007). For example, Steiner, Kaplan, & Moulthrop (2006) specifically looked at how reflecting on others' experiences affected children's design of artifacts in a study that asked children to create games. Their findings suggest that testing creations with players led children to restructure their games and focus more on their audience's experiences rather than their own stories (Steiner et al., 2006). Similarly, Bers and Cassell (1998) found that story-authoring interactions on their system, SAGE, allowed children to both explore their own identities and engaged them in *decentering*—taking the point of view of others. Our research focuses on developing language and social interaction skills; therefore, our goal is to engage children in metacognitive activities related to language. We call metacognitive skills related to language, such as reflecting on or monitoring language use, *metalinguistic skills* (Gombert, 1992).

Design-Based Research

Thus, our goal is to design a system based on virtual peer technology that supports children with ASD in developing peer social interaction skills by engaging constructionist learning mechanisms of planning, reflecting, and taking the perspective of others. We used a research method called design-based research (DBR) that develops and tests theories on how learning occurs in its natural context. Design-based researchers iteratively develop and evaluate a system focused on *embodying* and testing *conjectures* on mechanisms of learning (Sandoval, 2004). In other words, the design-based researcher develops a conjecture (Sandoval, 2004) about how learning occurs and designs a system that reflects that idea so that the theory behind the conjecture is built into the design of the system. That theory is then evaluated by testing and refining the system in the educational context in which it will be used (Sandoval, 2004). This iterative process involves continually testing and refining a design (Barab & Squire, 2004). Designers create a learning tool, test it, determine what works and what doesn't, revise the tool, and test it again.

DBR emphasizes the theoretical contributions made possible by the methodology. Barab and Squire (2004) argue that:

> Design-based research requires more than simply showing a particular design works but demands that the research move beyond a particular design exemplar to generate evidence-based claims about learning that address contemporary theoretical issues and further the theoretical knowledge in the field.
>
> *(pp. 5–6)*

In other words, a DBR project is aimed at not only achieving the intervention goals of the project but also at exploring theories of learning.

Design Study

In this study, we focus on designing an interface and tasks that children with ASD can use to develop peer social interaction. We specifically aim at designing a system that encourages children with ASD to develop reciprocity skills through metalinguistic reflection.

The Design Conjecture

Following the DBR methods described previously, we designed a system by developing a design conjecture (Sandoval, 2004) about the potential mechanisms of a virtual peer intervention. The conjecture is based on principles of constructionist theory and mechanisms of learning that occur by engaging metacognitive skills, including planning, reflection, and perspective taking (Bers & Cassell, 1998; Robertson & Nicholson, 2007). The conjecture we propose is:

Constructing (planning), reflecting on (engaging in and observing), and revising storytelling interactions will increase use of reciprocity skills in children with ASD.

Method

DBR often requires that learners expose their thinking through visual and verbal descriptions of ideas (Collins, Joseph, & Bielaczyc, 2004). A design research method called participatory design (PD) is often used to support this process, where end users and developers collaborate throughout the design process. While PD has been used with children (Druin, 2002) as well as individuals with disabilities (Cohene, Baecker, & Marziali, 2005; Cole, Dehdashti, Petti, & Angert, 1994; Fischer & Sullivan, 2002; McGrenere et al., 2003; Moffatt, McGrenere, Purves, & Klawe, 2004; Wu, Richards, & Baecker, 2004), PD with children with social impairments poses new challenges. Specifically, (a) children with ASD have difficulty communicating the types of feedback needed for PD and (b) the diverse abilities of children with ASD challenge generalization from one child to the next. Using typical evaluation tools, such as questionnaires and interview questions, with children with ASD may not yield reliable results. For example, topics or stories that appeal to a child's interests may increase engagement with the system. However, when we asked one child, "What else would you like Sam [the virtual peer] to talk about?" he simply repeated back the things the virtual peer could already say. However, while using the system, the same child developed new stories that were only tangentially related to things the virtual peer could already say. Thus, applying methods for drawing themes from observational data is particularly important with this population. In addition, specific language abilities and other skills vary. Therefore, working with this population requires careful planning and the application of design methods. We developed a three-step process to address these challenges.

Developing Reciprocity With Technology **79**

1. Individual design sessions with familiar children: Prior to beginning this study, we worked with the children in a weekly social skills group for approximately a year and a half. Children with autism have unique means of communicating their likes and dislikes, when they are frustrated, etc. Thus, getting to know the individual children was critical. Focusing on a familiar child independently allowed us to adapt to the child's needs in terms of the pace of the session, the kinds of questions we asked, and the behaviors that suggest emotions such as engagement or dislike.

2. Iterative sessions and introduction of participants: Children with autism are a challenging population to work with because diverse abilities within the population are combined with limited access to researchers (particularly for researchers who do not work in a clinical setting). To address this challenge, we used a process of iterative sessions with individual children and iterative introduction of new participants to the study as details were ironed out with each child. The study began as individual case studies and eventually developed into three phases of research: (a) developing the task, (b) designing the interface, and (c) generalizing with children of varying abilities. The phases are described below.

3. Assessment of relevant abilities to inform generalization: Finally, a diagnosis of autism or other social impairment provides very little information about the abilities and challenges an individual child has. To choose and evaluate successful interventions, it is critical to understand specific behaviors of individual children. Therefore, assessing relevant abilities, along with narrative descriptions of participants, is critical for discussion of generalization and estimating children for whom virtual peers may be beneficial. Relevant characteristics for the virtual peer tasks include expressive and receptive language and the severity of social impairment. The measures we chose by which to evaluate these abilities are described below. Finally, narrative descriptions of the participants demonstrate the diversity of behaviors in children with high-functioning autism, such as echolalia, shyness, verbosity in nonreciprocal interactions, etc.

Because the iterative nature of DBR differs from traditional experimental processes, Collins et al. (2004) propose that reports present a study in five sections: (a) design goals, (b) setting of the study, (c) description of each phase, (d) outcomes found, and (e) lessons learned.

Design Goals

Based on the design conjecture above, our design goal is to create technology tools for

- planning and creating storytelling interactions;
- engaging in storytelling interactions in ways that enable children to take on the perspective of others and reflect on the interaction; and
- revising the interactions.

These tools aim to allow children to not only engage in face-to-face storytelling with a virtual peer, as in our previous studies, but to also create new behaviors and stories for the virtual peer and use the virtual peer as a puppet while it interacts with another person by selecting the stories and behaviors they created. We call these latter activities authoring the virtual peer.

Setting and Participants

The research was conducted at a local after-school social skills program for children with ASD. We worked with two classes: six children from one class and one from another class. The study lasted approximately eight months, though holidays and other conflicts (such as children's absences) meant that the study did not occur every week. The classes each met once a week for 1.5 hours and began with children practicing greeting each other and some group discussion. The group discussion was usually focused around a monthly theme, such as back to school in September or holidays in December. During this time, the group leader would encourage participation from the children by asking questions about the topic, such as "Who is your teacher this year?" The group then broke into smaller group "table activities" such as games or art projects. Children practiced social interactions and turn taking during these activities. The group also included several "buddies"—typically developing children or teens who helped facilitate interaction with the children with ASD.

Participants With ASD[2]

Seven children aged 8–12 with existing ASD diagnoses participated in the study. Table 4.1 summarizes the basic characteristics of the participants and provides a brief description of each.

We administered several tests to characterize the language abilities and severity of social impairment of the participants:

- Test of Nonverbal Intelligence—3 (TONI–3; Brown, Sherbenou, & Johnsen, 1997). The TONI–3 is a brief screening of nonverbal IQ that is administered without the use of any language. It was used to screen participants for a nonverbal intelligence score of 75 or above.
- Peabody Picture Vocabulary Test—IV (PPVT–IV; Dunn & Dunn, 2007). The PPVT–IV is a language ability scale that measures children's receptive

TABLE 4.1 Summary of Participants

Fictional name	Gender	Age (start of study)	Grade in school	Description
Mikey	Male	9	4	Mikey is very verbal and interacts well with adults. However, he seems shy and uninterested around his friends. His language ability appears to be at the middle level of the group, which is reflected in his Peabody Picture Vocabulary Test—IV (PPVT–IV) and Expressive Vocabulary Test (EVT–2) scores. One of Mikey's autistic behaviors is that he doesn't like change in routine, which made scheduling research sessions with him difficult.
Cindy	Female	9	4	Cindy has good expressive and receptive language skills and is often talkative. However, her interactions are often nonreciprocal—she enjoys sharing with the group during greeting time, for example, but often does not engage other children by asking questions.
Chris	Male	8	3	Chris uses the least amount of expressive language of the group. Although he is capable of phrase speech, he rarely says anything complex. His contributions to both conversations in the group program and in the intervention storytelling tasks are often echolaic and noncontingent.
Peter	Male	9	4	Peter is often outgoing and affectionate with adults and older "buddies." Although he uses a lot of language, his expressive and receptive language are at a kindergarten level according to PPVT and EVT scores. Peter's stories were all retellings of various fairy tales that he insisted go the way he knew the stories.
Tony	Male	10	4	Tony is very high functioning and interacts well with adults. He is also particularly friendly with another boy in the group, Chuck. However, like all children with social impairments, their interactions with each other are often awkward. Tony was selected as the first user for the system. Though mainly

(Continued)

82 Andrea Tartaro and Justine Cassell

TABLE 4.1 (Continued)

Fictional name	Gender	Age (start of study)	Grade in school	Description
				selected as the first participant because he was one of the higher functioning children available, he made a particularly good first user because he was able to understand not only the task but also his role as someone using the system to help make it better for others to use. He understood, for example, not to talk to other children about the virtual peer (VP) and often asked if Chuck had met the VP yet.
Paul	Male	11	6	Paul is clearly bright and in many ways advanced for his age (his expressive and receptive language skills are above his chronological age), and he, too, interacts well with adults. However, his speech is hard to understand, and he has a clear tendency to focus on particular topics. For example, Paul was very interested in scary stories; thus, his stories often carried this theme. Interestingly, Paul was also very creative in his storytelling. He seemed to come up with original ideas and was able to expand on them. One particular problem he had was eliciting and incorporating information from others.
Chuck	Male	10	4	Although Chuck comes across as shy, sometimes speaks very softly, and avoids eye contact, he has good receptive and expressive language skills. He is often interested in engaging with peers despite his challenges with it. He is particularly friendly with Tony.

language. Children's standardized scores ranged from 70 to 104, with age equivalents ranging from 6 years 2 months to 12 years 11 months.

- Expressive Vocabulary Test (EVT–2; Williams, 2007). The EVT–2 is a language ability scale that measures children's expressive language. Children's standardized scores ranged from 74 to 112, with age equivalents ranging from 5 years 7 months to 12 years 5 months. Language ability (receptive and expressive) will be discussed with regards to qualitative performance with the authorable virtual peer.

- Social Responsiveness Scale (SRS; Constantino & Gruber, 2005). The SRS is a measure of the severity of autistic social impairment that yields an overall standardized (T) score as well as scores on five treatment subscales: social awareness, social cognition, social communication, social motivation, and autistic mannerisms. The test is used to characterize the severity of social impairment in each of the children. All T scores were clinically significant: in the moderate range (60–75) for three children and severe range (above 75) for four children. Scores in the moderate range "indicate deficiencies in reciprocal behavior that are clinically significant and are resulting in mild to moderate interference in everyday social interactions." Scores in the severe range are "strongly associated with a clinical diagnosis of" ASD and "suggest a severe interference in everyday social interactions" (Constantino & Gruber, 2005, Score Form). The SRS is particularly well suited for this research because of its focus on reciprocity skills.

Table 4.2 summarizes the characteristics of the children. Chronological ages are included, as well as age equivalents on the language measures.

Typically Developing Participants

This study also included nine typically developing children, ages 8–12. One child was a buddy in the clinical social group—the only one in the group within the age range of participants in the study. He occasionally participated in the technology design sessions with a child with autism. The other eight typically developing participants were used to model typical behavior on a new narrative task developed for the system (described below).

TABLE 4.2 Participant Characteristics

Fictional name	Gender	Age[a]	TONI–3 standard score	PPVT–IV standard score	EVT–2 standard score	SRS T score
Mikey	Male	9	91	80	97	117
Cindy	Female	9	105	99	112	72
Chris	Male	8	97	88	75	78
Peter	Male	9	88	70	74	61
Tony	Male	10	96	101	97	65
Paul	Male	11	118	104	102	78
Chuck	Male	10	100	78	92	78

[a]At start of study.

Research Phases

The design study evolved in three main phases: (a) task development, (b) designing the interface, and (c) generalizing with children of varying abilities. This section will describe each phase.

Phase 1: Task Development

To implement the design conjecture, we hypothesized that we could make a virtual peer that could not only engage in face-to-face storytelling, as in our previous studies, but also be authorable by the children, as described in the design goals above. Using this authorable virtual peer (AVP), users should be able to create new behaviors and stories for the virtual peer and use the virtual peer in the manner of a puppet while it interacts with another person by selecting prerecorded story segments. We developed an initial system composed of four tasks in author mode: (a) select buttons that represent speech and nonverbal actions, (b) organize the buttons into groups so as to allow actions to be quickly located, (c) provide a name for each group, and (d) order the groups on the panel. We conducted an initial evaluation of this system with typically developing children that suggests that children employ metalinguistic skills while authoring and operating the AVP (Tartaro, 2011). However, it is not clear whether the single panel of groups is ideal for children to find utterances they need during an interaction and that the concept of creating meaningful groups is intuitive. Moreover, feedback on previous studies from researchers and caretakers of children with ASD indicated that there were doubts about the age and gender appropriateness of the storytelling task, which asked children to make up a story using a dollhouse and figures. This task also may not be ideal for targeting reciprocity skills. Finally, the existing task required the virtual peer to take a long turn to set up the context of the story—we needed a task that was more interactive and required shorter turns on the part of the child and virtual peer. In what follows, we describe the requirements, process, and results for developing a new task.

Task Requirements

The task requirements include:

1. Narrative: The narrative aspect of the intervention is motivated by previous interventions using narrative.
2. Age- and gender-appropriate: The task needs to be appropriate for children 8–12 years old and take into account the gender ratio of autism, which affects boys 4 times more often than girls.
3. Dyadic and collaborative: The task should encourage the virtual peer and child to work together cooperatively.

Developing Reciprocity With Technology **85**

4. Interactive: The task should provide a lot of opportunity for back and forth in short turns.
5. Reveals a number of relevant skills: The task should apply to situations beyond the current skills focus (reciprocity) so it can be applied in future research on skills such as turn taking, initiating an interaction, imaginative use of objects, functional use of objects, and creativity.
6. Physical objects: The task should incorporate physical objects to encourage interaction and increase the sense of a shared reality with the virtual peer. Physical objects can also be used to target nonverbal behaviors such as shared attention.
7. Narrow context: To allow for prerecorded responses, the context should be narrow enough to predict possible things to say. This is particularly important since children create the stories.

Task Development Process

In DBR, not only is the final solution important, but also the initial, unsuccessful approaches, as well as why they were not chosen, are valuable (Collins et al., 2004) and can provide guidance for others designing interventions. Therefore, in this section we describe different tasks we considered leading up to the final task.

Our first attempt at developing a new task modified the dollhouse into a school. The motivation behind this change was threefold: (a) The physical setup could remain essentially the same, with a house that extends into the virtual peer's space, and only the furniture needed to change; (b) the organizing theme of the social skills group when the study was initiated was back to school, so this would integrate with the group program; and (c) the school theme could be used to elicit personal narratives of the children's day. Moreover, the context was controlled, and short contributions from the virtual peer could yield somewhat predictable responses—for example, talking about a project in art class.

We found that this task had several drawbacks: It did not seem to elicit functional or imaginative play with the props, it involved little creativity on the part of the children and limited application of the data to future projects because of the narrow scope of the props, and it did not apply any existent research on autism.

To make the task more applicable to current research in children with ASD, we turned to the tasks used in a standardized autism observation test, the Autism Diagnostic Observation Schedule (ADOS; Lord, Rutter, DiLavore, & Risi, 2002). Several tasks on the ADOS incorporate similar skills to those targeted by this intervention: the free play task; telling a story from a wordless picture book; repeating back the story in a cartoon; and the "make a story" task. In the free play task, children are given dolls or figurines and other toys and given the opportunity to play with them. At some point, the examiner tries to join in the play. However, this task is typically used with younger children and did not seem age appropriate for our target users. Furthermore, it did not include a specific prompt that could easily be adopted for a dyad task. In the cartoon task, children are asked to study a six-frame cartoon and then tell the story portrayed in the cartoon back to the examiner. One of the main goals of this task is to elicit gestures. However, the cartoons are short and would not provide much opportunity for turn taking and interaction. This left storytelling from a wordless picture book, where children narrate a story while going through the book, and the make a story task, where children tell an imaginative story using selected objects in the story.

We tried both these tasks with the children with ASD, matched together in dyads. The storytelling from a wordless picture book did not translate well to a dyad task because it was not clear how the children should take turns and did not easily hold the children's attention. The make a story task, however, successfully provided a structure for the interaction. This task, and how it fulfills the task requirements, is described in detail below. In addition to children with ASD performing the task in dyads, typically developing children (four dyads) performed the task in dyads as models of typical behavior and for designing stories for the virtual peer.

Final Task Description

The make a story task from the ADOS is used in Modules 3 and 4 (for verbally fluent children and adults) as an opportunity "to observe creativity in a play-like situation that is appropriate for adolescents and adults" (Lord et al., 2002, p. 86). The child selects five objects from a bag—some of the objects have a clear narrative purpose, such as a pair of miniature glasses, while others are more abstract, such as a piece of string. Children are asked to make a story using all five of their objects.

We modified this task to be dyadic. We collected a number of objects similar to those used in the ADOS and divided them into two bins—one for the objects with a clear narrative purpose and one for more abstract objects. Since we were collecting a larger number of objects than provided in the ADOS, we wanted to ensure that children had some of each type of object. While this was not critical for the current goal of developing reciprocity, it makes the task relevant to a broader range of skills, such as creativity, imaginative use of objects, and functional use of objects. Children were then asked to select an object from each box and then one more object from either box (with two children, they took turns selecting the fifth object). Thus, in dyads, the children had five objects to share, or with the virtual peer, the child had three objects and the virtual peer had two objects in the virtual world. The children, or child with the virtual peer, were then asked to make up a story together using all five of the objects. By working together to tell a story, children had to negotiate turn taking and use reciprocal discourse to engage

Developing Reciprocity With Technology **87**

their partners. We compared dyads of typically developing children completing this task to dyads of children with ASD and found very different performances.

Typically Developing Children Performing the Task Together

When typically developing children performed the task, they used skills that fit the task requirements. Consider the following transcript of a typical interaction:

TD1: This is the drive-thru *[setting a plain wooden block in the center of the table]*. OK, my bus and then your lamb, and then my skateboard.
[coordinated play with one boy driving the bus up to the drive-thru, and the other boy driving his toy—a rocking horse figurine—up to the drive-thru as well]
TD2: I'm going first. Hey!
TD1: Hey!
TD2: Hey!
TD1: Beep beep!
TD2: I was here first!
TD1: Fine.
TD2: Excuse me. I'd like one Double Whopper, two orders of large fries, and a Diet Coke, please.

Child 1 initiates a story based on a common script of a drive-thru, but not a retelling of an existing story. He quickly establishes the context for the story and uses a plain wooden block as a drive-thru, demonstrating imaginative use of objects. He uses eye gaze to confirm that his friend agrees to the context. He also drives his bus up to the drive-thru, demonstrating functional use of objects. The two boys coordinate their play and seamlessly demonstrate reciprocity throughout the interaction.

Children With ASD Performing the Task Together

In stark contrast, when two children with ASD engage in the task, a number of behaviors characteristic of autism are revealed. Consider the following interaction:

ASD1: *[holding a bear figurine on the table]* Once upon a time there was a little girl named Goldilocks. Suddenly, her mother says to her, be careful, don't get lost in the woods. And finally she went outside to the backyard. And then she saw three little bears, and then she went into a pretty house . . . *[unintelligible] [puts head down on the table mumbling]*
[ASD2 is turned away from ASD1 and is engaging in stereotyped play with the toy bus by spinning the wheels]

In contrast to the first typically developing child, the first child with ASD does not attempt to establish a common context with his partner. His interaction is not reciprocal, and in fact by the end he is speaking too quietly to be intelligible. Furthermore, his story is a simple retelling of a common fairy tale, with no creative contributions. The second child with ASD shows no signs of interest in the task or his partner. Instead, he demonstrates some behaviors, including stereotyped play with one of the toys, self-stimulating behaviors, and lack of eye contact.

Thus, the task appears to provide opportunities to engage in the targeted reciprocity skills of the intervention, and in fact the typically developing children do so with no problem. However, when the children with ASD perform the task, their challenges with reciprocity (and other) skills are evident, thus providing intervention opportunities.

Implementation in the Virtual Peer

Based on one of the stories told by the typically developing children, we wrote several short turns for the virtual peer (one to three utterances long) that included story expansions and questions. We also included backchannel feedback utterances, utterances to fix mistakes, and utterances to start and end the interaction. This story was then used to introduce children to the authoring system. As children became familiar with the system, they modified this story and created new stories.

Phase 2: Development of Authoring Interface

The authoring tools aim to give children control of the virtual peer's behaviors while it interacts with another person, allow them to plan the pieces of a story they will need, and create new story segments for the virtual peer.

Interface Requirements

The tools had to fulfill several requirements:

1. Make certain reciprocity skills explicit:
   - Expanding on what someone said
   - Asking questions
   - Providing backchannel feedback
   - Fixing mistakes
2. Enable children to plan a conversation
3. Enable revisions
4. Be specific to the targeted skills (reciprocity) but flexible to extend to future skills

Final Interface Description

The final interface consists of two separate types of functionality for operating the virtual peer while it interacts with another person and authoring the interaction by creating stories.

Operation Functionality

The tools to operate the virtual peer are designed as a series of panels. At the top of each panel is a navigation bar of all the panels in the system. Below is a collection of buttons. Each button, when pressed, launches a script for the virtual peer to perform and then displays a specified panel in the system.

Each panel contains buttons for a skill related to reciprocity: expanding on what someone else says (called *Add to Story*), asking questions (called *Ask a Question*), providing backchannel feedback (called *Show Interest*), and fixing mistakes (called *Fix*). Two additional panels include buttons for starting and ending a story. These specific panels could be changed for future studies depending on the specific skills targeted.

Authoring Functionality

In authoring mode, buttons on panels can be selected and modified or removed. The system includes three author mode functions: (a) *Add*, (b) *Change*, and (c) *Remove*. Adding a new button allows users to select and edit a button from a larger library of buttons or create a new button. When users create a new button, they specify a label for their new button, record the audio, and select the next panel. To select an appropriate next panel, children must think about the structure of a reciprocal conversation. The final version of the system also allows children to select some basic gestures, such as waving or pointing. The Change function enables the user to modify any of the content of the button, including the audio (by making a new recording) and text, and what button panel will appear next. The final functionality is illustrated in Figure 4.2.

Phase 3: Generalizing With Children of Varying Abilities

The final phase of the research introduced new participants with more diverse abilities as users of the authoring system. The children with higher levels of receptive and expressive language—Cindy, Mikey, and Chuck—were able to use the tools similarly to Paul and Tony to create and revise story interactions. However, Chris and Peter had more difficulty. They had more trouble understanding the concept of selecting an appropriate response for the virtual peer based on what the interlocutor said. Future work could investigate if a more scripted system for

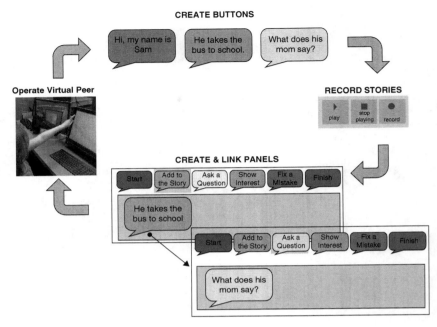

FIGURE 4.2 Authoring a virtual peer.

controlling the virtual peer could help children with language ability below a first- or second-grade level develop more basic skills of turn taking that occurs during social interaction. The system could include one turn per panel, labeled with simple icons (such as a question mark for questions), instead of the text of the utterance.

Outcomes

The goals of a DBR project are twofold: (a) develop an intervention tool that is theoretically motivated and (b) increase our understanding of learning by embodying theories in the design of a system and evaluating the theories by evaluating the system (Sandoval, 2004). Toward the first goal, we developed an AVP system motivated by constructionist theory of learning by building artifacts (Harel & Papert, 1991). With the system, children can build social interactions.

Toward the second goal, the three phases of design research suggest the following about ASD, storytelling, and play:

1. *AVPs can help us identify behaviors that may be affecting reciprocity in ASD or different ways in which children are not reciprocal.* Some of the children, when

recording new utterances for the virtual peer, would record long story segments that did not provide opportunities for input from the other person. For example, while some children's interactions lack reciprocity because they do not ask questions, others do not wait for responses from their interaction partner. The difficulty one child had waiting for responses was evident in one of the utterances he authored for the virtual peer, "Wanna hear a scary story? Well, if you said yes, that's good. If you said no, then too bad, 'cause I'm about to tell one. One day . . ." *[continues on with the story]*.

2. *AVPs can help children with ASD employ the targeted reciprocity skills, including adding to what someone has said, asking questions, listening, and providing backchannel feedback.* The authoring tools are designed to make each skill explicit both when using the system to operate the virtual peer and when authoring new utterances for the virtual peer. Children categorize utterances by skill during the authoring tasks and use these skill categories to find buttons while operating. The authoring task of specifying what panel should come next makes explicit how these skills come together in interactions with a partner.

3. *Using the AVP, children with ASD can employ metalinguistic skills to monitor and modify social behavior.* Perhaps most importantly, and relevant to the design conjecture, children showed evidence of monitoring and revising their interactions. In general, children tended to talk out loud while they were operating the virtual peer and either suggested things they couldn't say or pointed out that a relevant utterance was not available. They also indicated afterward that they did not make the virtual peer say something they should have. For example, from the very first session, Tony showed evidence of monitoring the interaction between the virtual peer and the research assistant by noticing things he wanted to say but which were not available. When the person interacting with the virtual peer asked about a grade on an assignment, the participant said, "I don't know. There really isn't a grade that I can tell." Later in the session, he reflects on this, "Well, when you were [asking] some things, I didn't really get a chance to answer them because they weren't on the computer." In a later session, he reflects on one of the interactions, comments that he should have used more question buttons, and asks to repeat the interaction. Children also modified their own recordings, expanding on their stories after an interaction. They also previewed new utterances while creating them (before an interaction) and changed them when they did not like them.

Lessons Learned and Conclusion

This chapter set out to answer the question: How we can leverage the ability of children with ASD to make contingent contributions in interactions with a virtual peer to design tasks and a technology system for learning about reciprocity? Using an iterative, DBR method, we developed a system that encourages children to monitor and reflect on reciprocity by making explicit the components of reciprocity (e.g., expanding on what someone has said, asking questions) and how they are sequenced. We present evidence that suggests that children can use the AVP tools to plan and construct storytelling interactions, monitor the limitations of their stories while controlling the virtual peer in an interaction with another person, and revise their stories. Furthermore, we suggest that virtual peers can help identify children's behaviors that may be affecting reciprocity and help children employ targeted skills by making them explicit.

In the process of designing the AVP, we developed techniques and tasks that can be applied to the design of future interventions and studies for understanding storytelling and play in children with ASD. First, we developed three techniques to maximize the participation of children in the design of the system: (a) conduct individual design sessions with familiar children to allow for monitoring and responding to individual needs, (b) use a process of iterative sessions with individual children and iterative introduction of new participants to capture as many problems as possible before using a new participant, and (c) assess relevant abilities to inform generalization. In addition, we developed a task that is well suited for our goals but that could also be applied to other skills such as turn taking, initiating an interaction, imaginative use of objects, functional use of objects, and creativity. We adapted the make a story task for the ADOS so that children tell a story together using objects. Since this task is from the ADOS, it is relevant to current research on ASD.

Although children's use of the virtual peer authoring system suggests that the tasks and technology developed in this study support children's use of reciprocity skills and that children employ metalinguistic skills for planning, reflecting on, and revising their use of language while authoring, this study does not evaluate transfer of children's use of the targeted skills to face-to-face interactions with peers. Furthermore, although this research was carried out in the context of a clinical social group program, the system was not part of a comprehensive intervention. These are the goals of another study that suggests that the system can be incorporated as a component of a group social skills program and that interactions with the AVP support children's use of reciprocity during interactions with peers (Tartaro et al., 2015).

Acknowledgments

The authors would like to thank Autism Speaks, the Spencer Foundation, the Northwestern Alumnae Association, Kris Johnsen, and Melanie Johnsen for their funding and support.

Notes

1 This book chapter is a portion of a doctoral dissertation, *Authorable Virtual Peers: Technology as an Intervention for Difficulties with Peer Social Interaction in Children with Autism Spectrum and Related Disorders* (Tartaro, 2011).
2 All participants have been assigned a pseudonym.

References

Adams, L., Gouvousis, A., VanLue, M., & Waldron, C. (2004). Social Story intervention: Improving communication skills in a child with an autism spectrum disorder. *Focus on Autism and Other Developmental Disabilities, 19*(2), 87–94.

American Psychiatric Association. (2013). *Diagnostic and statistical manual of mental disorders* (5th ed.). Washington, DC: Author.

Baker, J.E. (2001). *The social skills picture book.* Arlington, TX: Future Horizons.

Baker, J.E. (2003). *Social skills training for children and adolescents with Asperger syndrome and social-communication problems.* Shawnee Mission, KS: Autism Asperger Publishing.

Barab, S., & Squire, K. (2004). Design-based research: Putting a stake in the ground. *Journal of the Learning Sciences, 13*(1), 1–14.

Barry, L.M., & Burlew, S.B. (2004). Using Social Stories to teach choice and play skills to children with autism. *Focus on Autism and Other Developmental Disabilities, 19*(1), 45–51.

Barry, T.D., Klinger, L.G., Lee, J.M., Palardy, N., Gilmore, T., & Bodin, S.D. (2003). Examining the effectiveness of an outpatient clinic-based social skills group for high-functioning children with autism. *Journal of Autism and Developmental Disorders, 33*(6), 685–701.

Bers, M. U., & Cassell, J. (1998). Interactive storytelling systems for children: Using technology to explore language and identity. *Journal of Interactive Learning Research, 9*(2), 183–214.

Brown, L., Sherbenou, R. J., & Johnsen, S. K. (1997). *Test of Nonverbal Intelligence* (3rd ed.). Austin, TX: PRO-ED.

Cappadocia, M.C., & Weiss, J.A. (2011). Review of social skills training groups for youth with Asperger syndrome and high functioning autism. *Research in Autism Spectrum Disorders, 5,* 70–78.

Cassell, J., Ananny, M., Basu, A., Bickmore, T., Chong, P., Mellis, D. . . . Yan, H. (2000, April 1–6). *Shared reality: Physical collaboration with a virtual peer.* Paper presented at the Association for Computing Machinery (ACM) Special Interest Group on Computer-Human Interaction (SIGCHI) Conference on Human Factors in Computing Systems, Amsterdam, Netherlands.

Castorina, L.L., & Negri, L.M. (2011). The inclusion of siblings in social skills training groups for boys with Asperger syndrome. *Journal of Autism and Developmental Disorders, 41,* 73–81.

Cohene, T., Baecker, R., & Marziali, E. (2005, April). *Designing interactive life story multimedia for a family affected by Alzheimer's disease: A case study.* Paper presented at the Association for Computing Machinery (ACM) Special Interest Group on Computer-Human Interaction (SIGCHI) Conference on Human Factors in Computing Systems, Portland, OR.

Cole, E., Dehdashti, P., Petti, L., & Angert, M. (1994, April 26–27). *Participatory design for sensitive interface parameters: Contributions of traumatic brain injury patients to their prosthetic software.* Paper presented at the Association for Computing Machinery (ACM) Special

Interest Group on Computer-Human Interaction (SIGCHI) Conference on Human Factors in Computing Systems, Boston, MA.

Collins, A., Joseph, D., & Bielaczyc, K. (2004). Design research: Theoretical and methodological issues. *Journal of the Learning Sciences, 13*(1), 15–42.

Constantino, J. M., & Gruber, C. P. (2005). *Social Responsiveness Scale.* Los Angeles, CA: Western Psychological Services.

Druin, A. (2002). The role of children in the design of new technology. *Behaviour & Information Technology, 21*(1), 1–25.

Dunn, L. M., & Dunn, D. M. (2007). *Peabody Picture Vocabulary Test* (4th ed.). San Antonio, TX: Pearson.

Fischer, G., & Sullivan, J. F. (2002, June). *Human-centered public transportation systems for persons with cognitive disabilities: Challenges and insights for participatory design.* Paper presented at the Participatory Design Conference, Malmo, Sweden.

Gombert, J.E. (1992). *Metalinguistic development.* Chicago, IL: University of Chicago Press.

Gray, C. (1994a). *Comic strip conversations: Colorful, illustrated interactions with students with autism and related disorders.* Arlington, TX: Future Horizons.

Gray, C. (1994b). *The new social story book.* Arlington, TX: Future Horizons.

Harel, I., and Papert, S. (1991). *Constructionism.* Norwood, NJ: Ablex.

Howland, K., Good, J., & Robertson, J. (2007, June). *A learner-centered design approach to developing a visual language for interactive storytelling.* Paper presented at the Interaction Design and Children Conference (IDC 2007), Aalborg, Denmark.

Jackson, D.A., Jackson, N.F., Bennett, M.L., Bynum, B.M., & Faryna, E. (1991). *Learning to get along: Social effectiveness training for people with developmental disabilities.* Champaign, IL: Research Press.

Kafai, Y.B. (1995). *Minds in play: Computer game design as a context for children's learning.* Hillsdale, NJ: Erlbaum.

Kientz, J.A., Goodwin, M. S., Hayes, G. R., & Abowd, G. D. (2014). *Interactive technologies for autism.* San Rafael, CA: Morgan & Claypool.

Lord, C., Rutter, M., DiLavore, P.C., & Risi, S. (2002). *Autism Diagnostic Observation Schedule.* Los Angeles, CA: Western Psychological Services.

McGinnis, E., & Goldstein, A.P. (1984). *Skillstreaming the elementary school child.* Champaign, IL: Research Press.

McGinnis, E., & Goldstein, A.P. (1990). *Skillstreaming in early childhood.* Champaign, IL: Research Press.

McGrenere, J., Davies, R., Findlater, L., Graf, P., Klawe, M., Moffatt, K. . . . Yang, S. (2003, November 10–11). *Insights from the aphasia project: Designing technology for and with people who have aphasia.* Paper presented at the Association for Computing Machinery (ACM) Special Interest Group on Computer-Human Interaction (SIGCHI) Conference on Universal Usability, Vancouver, BC, Canada.

Moffatt, K., McGrenere, J., Purves, B., & Klawe, M. (2004, April 24–29). *The participatory design of a sound and image enhanced daily planner for people with aphasia.* Paper presented at the Association for Computing Machinery (ACM) Special Interest Group on Computer-Human Interaction (SIGCHI) Conference on Human Factors in Computing Systems, Vienna, Austria.

Reichow, B., & Volkmar, F.R. (2010). Social skills interventions for individuals with autism: Evaluation for evidence-based practices within a best evidence synthesis framework. *Journal of Autism and Developmental Disorders, 40,* 149–166.

Resnick, M., Bruckman, A., & Martin, F. (1996). Pianos not stereos: Creating computational construction kits. *Interactions, 3*(5), 40–50.

Resnick, M., & Silverman, B. (2005). *Some reflections on designing construction kits for kids.* Paper presented at the Interaction Design and Children Conference (IDC 2005), Boulder, CO.

Robertson, J., & Nicholson, K. (2007). *Adventure author: A learning environment to support creative design.* Paper presented at the Interaction Design and Children Conference (IDC 2007), Aalborg, Denmark.

Sandoval, W.A. (2004). Developing learning theory by refining conjectures embodied in educational designs. *Educational Psychologist, 39*(4), 213–223.

Steiner, B., Kaplan, N., & Moulthrop, S. (2006). *When play works: Turning game-playing into learning.* Paper presented at the Interaction Design and Children Conference (IDC 2006), Tampere, Finland.

Tartaro, A. (2006). *Storytelling with a virtual peer as an intervention for children with autism.* Paper presented at the Association for Computing Machinery (ACM) Special Interest Group on Computer-Human Interaction (SIGCHI) Conference on Accessibility and Computing, Portland, OR.

Tartaro, A. (2011). *Authorable virtual peers: Technology as an intervention for difficulties with peer social interaction in children with autism spectrum and related disorders* (Unpublished doctoral dissertation). Northwestern University, Evanston, IL.

Tartaro, A., & Cassell, J. (2008). *Playing with virtual peers: Bootstrapping contingent discourse in children with autism.* Paper presented at the International Conference of the Learning Sciences, Utrecht, Netherlands.

Tartaro, A., Cassell, J., Ratz, C., Lira, J., & Nanclares-Nogués, V. (2015). Accessing peer social interaction: Using authorable virtual peer technology as a component of a group social skills intervention program. *ACM Transactions on Accessible Computing, 6*(1), 2:2–2:29.

Wang, A., & Cassell, J. (2003, June). *Co-authoring, corroborating, criticizing: Collaborative storytelling between virtual and real children.* Paper presented at the Workshop of Educational Agents: More Than Virtual Tutors, Vienna, Austria.

Wang, P., & Spillane, A. (2009). Evidence-based social skills interventions for children with autism: A meta-analysis. *Education and Training in Developmental Disabilities, 44*(3), 318–342.

Webb, B.J., Miller, S.P., Pierce, T.B., Strawser, S., & Jones, W.P. (2004). Effects of social skill instruction for high-functioning adolescents with autism spectrum disorders. *Focus on Autism and Other Developmental Disabilities, 19*(1), 53–62.

White, S.W., Koenig, K., & Scahill, L. (2010). Group social skills instruction for adolescents with high-functioning autism spectrum disorders. *Focus on Autism and Other Developmental Disabilities, 25*(4), 209–219.

Williams, K. T. (2007). *Expressive Vocabulary Test* (2nd ed.). San Antonio, TX: Pearson.

Wu, M., Richards, B., & Baecker, R. (2004, July 27–31). *Participatory design with individuals who have amnesia.* Paper presented at the Participatory Design Conference, Toronto, ON, Canada.

5

SOCIAL ROBOTS AS STORYTELLERS

Can a Social Robot Encourage Children With Autism Spectrum Disorder to Ask Questions During Playtime?

Ramona Simut, Cristina Costescu, Johan Vanderfaeillie, Daniel David, and Bram Vanderborght

Introduction

Profound impairment in social interaction is considered to be the most important deficit that children diagnosed with an autism spectrum disorder (ASD) experience during their life span (Nikopoulos & Keenan, 2003; Scattone, 2007) and the most challenging area for treatment (Weiss & Harris, 2001). Undesirable social behaviors, such as poor eye contact or a lack of awareness of others, may hinder children with ASD from actively participating in simple social play or games (American Psychiatric Association, 2000). Since play is considered the catalyst for social integration and since play enhances language development, social skills, and general cognitive functioning (Dauphin, Kinney, Stromer, & Koegel, 2004; Tsao & Odom, 2006), failure to appropriately interact during playtime can result in children with ASD remaining socially isolated and marginalized. It is generally known that children with ASD rarely engage in creative, spontaneous play activities and do not tend to initiate social contact or play interactively with typically developing peers. On the contrary, they have a preference for repetitive and ritualistic actions with toys (Williams, Higgins, & Brayne, 2006). Limitations in creative pretend play among children with autism relate to their restricted interpersonal communication and engagement (Hobson, Hobson, Malik, Bargiota, & Calo, 2013). On the other hand, more recent studies have shown that children with ASD can learn how to engage appropriately in play situations (Koegel, Vernon, Koegel, Koegel, & Paullin, 2012; Stagnitti, O'Connor, & Sheppard, 2012). And, moreover, there are an increasing number of studies that agree on the fact that children with ASD have both an understanding of pretense and a capacity for pretend play (Chaudry & Dissanayake, this volume; Douglas & Stirling, this volume; Jarrold, 2003; Maclean, this volume).

Several options are being examined for improving the capacity of children with ASD in social interaction and communication. The evidence-based treatments include Applied Behavior Analysis (ABA), peer-mediated training, video modeling, and Social Story intervention (Bass & Mulick, 2007; Matson, Matson, & Rivet, 2007; Nikopoulos & Keenan, 2003; Scattone, 2007; Stagnitti et al., 2011; Tsao & Odom, 2006). However, there is still demand for studies of effectiveness (i.e., how these interventions work in real clinical practice) and efficacy (i.e., how they work in controlled clinical conditions; Reichow & Volkmar, 2010; Wang & Spillane, 2009). The common limitation of the majority of social skills treatments is the lack of generalization and maintenance of the intervention effects and also a lack of motivation and engagement of children in the learning process (Karkhaneh et al., 2010).

The lack of generalization and maintenance could be related to the strict behavioral approach of most of the treatments (see, for example, ABA). Thus, some children with ASD may learn new behaviors, but they could have difficulties in generalizing them in other contexts. Therefore, an adjunctive cognitive component is needed that could provide more flexibility to the learned skills. The lack of motivation and engagement can be explained by the empathizing–systemizing theory (Baron-Cohen, 2009) that describes individuals with ASD as having a preference for systems that change in highly lawful or predictable ways and as becoming disabled when faced with systems characterized by less lawful change, such as the social world. Accordingly, in several studies it has been hypothesized that if social information is presented in an attractive manner that is easily understood and clearly identifies the expected behaviors, individuals with ASD engage more successfully in social interactions (Koegel et al., 2012; Quirmbach, Lincoln, Feinberg-Gizzo, Ingersoll, & Andrews, 2009).

Consequently, there is growing demand for researchers to investigate how to improve and develop techniques that can offer a suitable approach for children with ASD in order to engage them better in social situations. In line with this demand, two directions are described below: Social Stories and robot-assisted interventions. The aim of the current study is to use the strengths of robot interventions to increase the efficiency of Social Story interventions in order to improve the social skills of children with ASD.

Social Story Intervention

Social Stories are individualized short scripts that help children with ASD develop appropriate behaviors in social interactions and interpersonal relationships by teaching them the relevant components of social situations (Gray, 2004; Kuoch & Mirenda, 2003). An increasing number of studies support the potential of Social Stories for addressing inappropriate behaviors and for teaching social skills to individuals with ASD (Karkhaneh et al., 2010). Over the last decade, several authors have argued for the effectiveness of Social Stories at the level of increasing desirable behaviors, such as greeting and sharing toys (Swaggart et al., 1995), choice and play behavior (Barry & Burlew, 2004), and appropriate social interaction (Scattone, Tingstrom, & Wilczynski, 2006).

Some preliminary data support the efficiency of this type of intervention for improving social abilities in individuals with ASD. Although there is not yet a definitive consensus, Social Stories are one of the most used social skills treatments for children with ASD (Green et al., 2006; Kokina & Kern, 2010), because it is a relatively inexpensive treatment and relatively easy to implement, which is based on the strengths of children with ASD: Social Stories are visual, situation specific, offer explicit information, and tend to have short learning intervals with immediate effects (Andrews, 2004; Smith, 2001). There are several ways to implement Social Stories: They can be read by the therapist or presented using audio equipment, computer-based programs (Pop et al., 2013), or videotapes (Bernad-Ripoll, 2007; Mandasari, Lu, & Theng, 2011; Xin & Sutman, 2011). Based on technological advancements, this study presents an innovative manner of delivering a Social Story by using a social robot as a storytelling agent.

Robot-Assisted Therapy

A growing number of studies have been investigating the application of advanced interactive technologies to address core deficits related to autism—namely, computer technology (Bernard-Opitz, Sriram, & Nakhoda-Sapuan, 2001), virtual reality environments (Mitchell, Parsons, & Leonard, 2007), virtual peers (Tartaro & Cassell, this volume), and robotic systems (Dautenhahn & Werry, 2004; Kim et al., 2013; Kozima & Nakagawa, 2006; Scassellati, Admoni, & Matarić, 2012). These technology-based applications, especially in the area of robotics, offer great possibilities for innovation in social skills treatment for children with ASD. Technical advances have enabled robots to perform human-like functions, and they are deployed in robot-assisted therapy (RAT). Robotic systems have been used to investigate if it is possible to create a learning environment to improve social skills (understanding and interaction) of children with ASD (Diehl, Schmitt, Villano, & Crowell, 2012). The RAT research field is an innovative one that proposes not to create new interventions in autism but to use the technological development (i.e., social robots) in the already-existing evidence-based treatments for ASD. The idea is that by using robots as adjunctive to the classical treatments, their efficacy and/ or effectiveness will be increased.

Based on the empathizing–systemizing theory of Baron-Cohen (2009), robots can be described as predictable and lawful systems, which are very easy for children with ASD to cope with. On the other hand, human behavior, despite being the best model for imitation and social skills development, is complex and subtle, so it is hardly possible to be understood and imitated by children with ASD (Happé, 2005). Social situations contain an incredible amount of information, which can be very difficult for the child to systemize and therefore understand. Robots might have the potential to be used in ASD therapies due to several advantages: (a) the anthropomorphic embodiment of the robot offers human-like social cues and at the same time retains object-like simplicity; (b) robots can be programmed to gradually increase the complexity of the tasks by presenting solely relevant information; moreover, information can be repeated in the same format, without trainer fatigue; (c) robots are predictable and therefore controllable, enable errors to be made safely, and provide possibilities to train a wide range of social and communication behaviors to prepare for real-life exposition; and (d) children with ASD are known to be more responsive to feedback, even social feedback, when it is administered via technology rather than a human (Ozonoff, 1995).

An increasing number of research groups have examined the response of children with ASD to robots. Several studies suggest that some children with ASD prefer interactive robots compared to passive toys (Dautenhahn et al., 2009; Diehl et al., 2014). Also, it has often been found that some children with ASD prefer robot-like characteristics over human-like characteristics in social interactions (Kim et al., 2013; Robins, Dautenhahn, Boekhorst, & Billard, 2005; Vanderborght et al., 2012) and respond faster when cued by robotic movement compared to human movement (Bird, Leighton, Press, & Heyes, 2007; Pierno, Mari, Lusher, & Castiello, 2008).

Different types of social robots have been investigated in emerging research showing that children with ASD proactively approach the robots (Kim et al., 2013; Kozima, Michalowski, & Nakagawa, 2009) and that robots can act as mediators between the child and the therapist (Pradel & Giannopulu, 2010). In addition, social robots have also been explored for triggering or teaching different types of social behaviors, such as play skills (Francois, Powell, & Dautenhahn, 2009; Wainer, Dautenhahn, Robins, & Amirabdollahian, 2010), imitation skills (Duquette, Michaud, & Mercier, 2008; Tapus et al., 2012), and joint attention (Kozima et al., 2009; Robins, Dickerson, Stribling, & Dautenhahn, 2004). Even if the majority of these studies were exploratory, often declaring mixed results, each of them stated that robots generate a high degree of motivation and engagement in children and that children with different levels of symptom severity did not manifest difficulties in understanding and interacting with a robot (Diehl et al., 2012; Scassellati et al., 2012). Different studies suggested that the social impairment of children with ASD would improve if more of their general interests were incorporated into the learning activities (Koegel et al., 2012; Quirmbach et al., 2009). Therefore, due to the intrinsic appeal of technology to children with ASD, social robots can become potential peers to exercise social behaviors during playtime. Based on their strengths, social robots could be used in therapies as a "social crutch" (Goodrich et al., 2012; Ricks & Colton,

2010; Robins, Dautenhahn, & Dickerson, 2009) that engages children, teaches them social skills, and assists them in the transfer of this knowledge to interactions with humans.

The results of our previous research in this area are in line with the outcomes described previously. We investigated a social robot as a storyteller agent

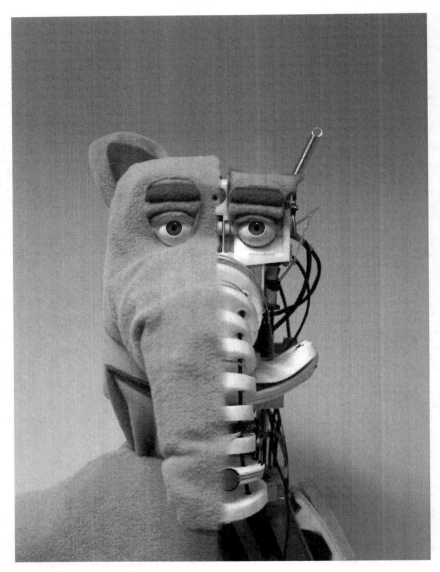

FIGURE 5.1 The huggable robot Probo: a section view.

for teaching abilities like sharing toys, greeting, and asking for help (Pop et al., 2013; Vanderborght et al., 2012). In Vanderborght et al. (2012), it was shown that a Social Story intervention conducted by a robot was more motivating and led to a lower level of prompting to perform the targeted social skill compared to an intervention conducted with a therapist. Pop et al. (2013) investigated whether Social Stories presented by a social robot have a greater effect than those presented on a computer display on the expression of the independent social abilities of children with ASD. In order to test this hypothesis, 20 children with ASD were involved in the study (seven in the control group, six in the computer-presented Social Stories group, and seven in the RAT group). Figure 5.1 shows the social robot used in the study. The results showed that using the social robot to implement a Social Story intervention was more effective for improving the independence of expression of social abilities for the participants than the computer screen. The study presented here continues to explore the use of the social robot as a storyteller in order to further explore the stability and generalization of our obtained outcomes. We hypothesized that the robot-assisted Social Story intervention would significantly improve the target behavior (i.e., asking questions during playtime).

Method

Participants

Six children (two girls and four boys) diagnosed with ASD were recruited from a Romanian daily care center for children with ASD (the Autism Transylvania Association). The chronological age of the participants was between 5 and 9 years old, and all of them used simple sentences. The children were diagnosed according to the criteria for autism given in the *Diagnostic and Statistical Manual of Mental Disorders* (4th ed., text rev.; *DSM–IV–TR*; American Psychiatric Association, 2000). The ASD diagnosis was verified for each of the participants by a clinical psychologist using the Autism Diagnostic Observation Schedule (Lord et al., 2000), Module 2, all obtaining a score above the cutoff.

Setting

The study took place at the center in a therapy room (about 20 m²), where children were used to taking part in therapeutic activities. The room was divided into two halves by a fake wall (see Figure 5.2): one half contained a small table with the robot affixed to it, a moveable table for toys, and two chairs in front of the robot (one for the child and one for the therapist); the other half was the control room for the operator of the robot. No toys or pictures on the walls were exposed in the experimental room in order to help the children focus their attention on the task.

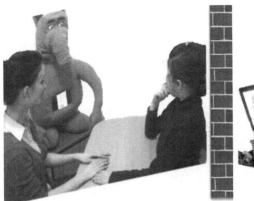

FIGURE 5.2 Overview of Probo, the child, the experimenter, and the operator in the room where the study took place.

Materials

The Social Robot Probo as a Storytelling Agent

The robot Probo has been developed to study human–robot interaction and to develop RAT with a special focus on children. The social interaction for Probo is predefined to focus on verbal and nonverbal communication and, as such, is designed to act as a social interface by employing human-like social cues and interactive communication modalities (Goris, Saldien, Vanderborght, & Lefeber, 2011). With 20 degrees of freedom in the head, the robot is able to express attention and emotions via its gaze and facial expressions (Simut et al., 2012). A user-friendly robot control center (RCC) enables the operator to control the robot in an intuitive way in a Wizard of Oz (WoZ) setting (Wilson & Rosenberg, 1988). WoZ refers to a person who remotely operates the robot, controlling a number of elements along the autonomy spectrum, from fully autonomous to fully teleoperated, as well as mixed-initiative interaction (Riek, 2012). This is a well-known design paradigm in the human–robot interaction field and is used to elicit participants' beliefs that the robot is behaving and responding autonomously. For this study, the WoZ paradigm was used in real time, with the operator hidden behind the false wall dividing the experiment room in two (see Figure 5.2). Through the video camera inside the robot head, the operator is able to see inside the therapy room. With a game pad and a mouse, he is able to make the robot show different emotions, control the gaze of the head and eyes, start animations (sleeping, nodding *yes* and *no*, eye blinking), and start the preprogrammed social story. A lip-synch module allows the lips to move according to the robot's recorded human voice.

FIGURE 5.3 The safe and huggable design of Probo allows for both cognitive and physical interaction.

To guarantee safe physical interaction between the robot and the children, compliant actuation systems and a layered form structured with foam and fabric are implemented (Simut et al., 2012). These elements contribute to the aspect of safe, soft, and "huggable" interaction (Simut et al., 2011), which is in contrast with other robots used for ASD therapies that are usually very rigid and are covered with hard plastic shells. During the interactions, we noticed that the children were very spontaneous in physically touching the robot (see Figure 5.3).

Asking Questions Social Story

The Social Story used in this intervention aimed to teach children with ASD how to ask questions in a spontaneous way during playtime with the therapist. The Social Story was written with regard to the children's comprehension level (Gray, 2000a; Gray & Garand, 1993) and included *descriptive, directive, perspective*, and *affirmative* sentences (Gray, 2004). Appendix B provides an English version of the Social Story used, translated from the Romanian version. The Social Story was visually supported by illustrations appropriate to the child's skills in terms of reading images, attention span, and cognitive ability. The illustrations and content of the Social Story were selected from the book *The New Social Story Book: Illustrated Edition* (Gray, 2000b) and shown on the belly screen of the robot (see Figure 5.4).[1]

FIGURE 5.4 Using the social robot Probo as a social storytelling agent for children with ASD (with a close-up showing the screen on the robot's belly).

Research Design

A time series design was used. This type of design decreases the effects of natural variation between participants on the results. This design controls for several potential risks to internal validity, such as maturation. It was unlikely that maturation would be a confounding factor if the scores were found to be consistently low before treatment and consistently high after treatment (Mertens, 2009).

Procedure

Each participant had seven standardized sessions (one for a baseline measurement and six for the intervention sessions), lasting 15–20 minutes per day and conducted by a clinical psychologist trained by the experimenter (first author). After permission was granted by parental signed consent, all sessions were videotaped for further analysis.

Baseline Measurement

First, all the participants were assessed during a baseline phase, in which a standardized play task was organized (with an average duration of 7–10 min). Three opportunities for asking questions were created by the therapist in each game (e.g., the therapist hid the toy that the child wanted for play in order to elicit the question *Where is the toy?*). The child was assessed as to whether he or she was able to spontaneously ask questions related to the game actions and what level of prompting he or she needed to manifest the target behavior. The target skill was known clinically to be a challenging one for each participant, and the baseline measurements confirmed clinical records as to the level of prompting needed to elicit the behavior at the commencement of the study. There were no major differences between the children's performance during the baseline phase (see Figure 5.5).

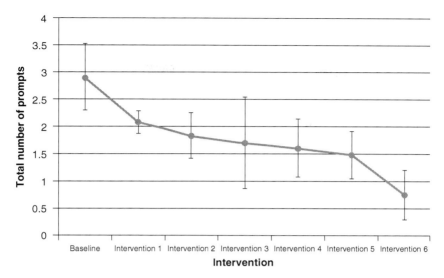

FIGURE 5.5 The evolution of the level of prompting needed to elicit questions from children with ASD.

Intervention Sessions

In the intervention sessions, the play task was identical to the one used in the baseline measurement but was performed after the habituation, story listening, and comprehension questions phases, as detailed below. The child was invited to play a standardized construction game with the therapist with the same number of opportunities set for asking questions. The questions were taken as a target behavior if they were asked appropriately (i.e., the question had to be produced by the child in the specific moment when it was triggered by the opportunity created by the therapist). The level of prompting (needed for the child to produce the targeted questions) was assessed in both the baseline and intervention sessions, as detailed below.

Habituation With the Robot

Before the first intervention session, a habituation period with the robot was provided for all the participants, with an average duration of 3–5 minutes. This habituation phase was conducted by the therapist, and the aim was to let the child interact with Probo in order to become familiar with it (i.e., the child was saying hello and asking questions and the robot was answering verbally and by showing different emotions and animations, such as falling asleep, nodding *yes* and *no*, blinking its eyes, singing).

Story Listening

The habituation phase was followed by hearing the story told by the robot. The session began in an identical way for every child. When the child and the therapist entered the room, the therapist announced to the child that the Social Story would start, and then the robot started to tell the story. During this phase, Probo also expressed happy and sad emotions that were included in the story (see Appendix B) and moved his head, eyes, and trunk. The average length of this phase was 2 minutes.

Comprehension Questions

The Social Story listening was followed by a list of comprehension questions assessing the participants' understanding of the story (i.e., "How do you ask when you want to play with a toy that is missing?" "What do you say to someone who is playing with the toy that you want to play with?" "How do people you play with feel when you ask them questions during your game?"). The questions were supposed to be answered with 100% accuracy. If the participant did not respond correctly, the therapist repeated the correct answer until the child was able to offer an accurate answer without any prompting. This phase lasted a maximum of 5 minutes.

The structure of the story was always the same (see Appendix B), but the play tasks and the toys used in the game varied from one session to another. Therefore, the learning process also implied generalized learning.

Response Measurement

The dependent variable for all the participants in the study was the level of prompting needed to be offered by the therapist to the child in order for the child to perform the target skill in an appropriate way. The prompting was offered in three different manners: (a) verbal manner (i.e., the therapist provides the first letter from one word or the first word from one sentence), (b) gestural manner (i.e., the therapist indicates with his or her finger, head, or hands specific elements of interest); and (c) physical manner (i.e., the therapist uses gentle movements to direct the child's head or hands toward specific elements of the therapeutic environment).

The level of prompting needed to perform the target skill (i.e., asking questions during play) was assessed using a 7-point scale as follows:

0 = *occurrence of the target behavior without any prompting*
1 = *occurrence of the target behavior with gestural prompting (e.g., when the therapist had to point toward the specific toy relevant to the question or point in the direction of the event relevant to the question and raise his or her shoulders)*
2 = *occurrence of the target behavior with physical prompting (e.g., when the therapist had to touch the child's chin to remind him or her to ask the required question)*
3 = *occurrence of the target behavior with gestural and verbal prompting (e.g., when the therapist, over and above the gestural prompting, pronounced the first syllable or the first word from the required question)*

4 = *occurrence of the target behavior with physical and verbal prompting*
5 = *occurrence of the target behavior with gestural, verbal, and physical prompting*
6 = *no occurrence of the target behavior*

The level of prompting for the targeted skill (i.e., asking questions; see the Procedure section) was assessed at the end of each intervention session. The 7-point scale was developed based on the 5-point scale of Barry and Burlew (2004) used for defining decision-making behavior. The therapist was trained in the ABA method to provide the minimal level of prompting needed and gradually increase the level if required. Both the therapist and the coders were blind to the research questions of the study.

Interobserver Agreement

Two psychologists, trained by the experimenter, independently assessed the level of prompting used by the participants to perform the target behavior (i.e., asking questions) based on the video recordings of the therapy sessions. Interobserver agreement was calculated for 40% of the sessions. Cohen's kappa was higher than 0.80 in all cases.

Treatment Integrity

The trained observers also checked the integrity of treatment implementation for each session and for each participant. A checklist containing the correct procedural steps in implementation was used to assess treatment integrity for each session. On the checklist, the observers indicated, for example, whether an introduction to the Social Story was provided to the child and whether correct answers to the comprehension questions were provided as needed. The checklist is summarized in Appendix A. The mean value of treatment integrity across all sessions was 89%.

Results

Data Analysis

The analysis was done at two different levels. First, our analysis focused on the group as a whole. A nonparametric Friedman test was used to investigate the differences between the data recorded at different moments of the study. Second, analysis was conducted at an individual level. Patterns of evolution from baseline to the sixth intervention for each of the participants are described as well as the similarities and differences between the participants.

Group-Level Analysis

The mean and standard deviation values of the level of prompting needed to get the ASD children to ask questions are presented below (see Table 5.1 and Figure 5.5). The graph in Figure 5.5 shows a continuous descending trend in the help needed for asking questions. This evolution is more accelerated in the first interval

108 Ramona Simut et al.

TABLE 5.1 Group Means and Standard Deviations Showing the Level of Prompting Needed to Elicit Questions by the Group With ASD Across the Sessions

	Mean	Standard deviation
Baseline	2.90	.60
Intervention 1	2.08	.20
Intervention 2	1.83	.41
Intervention 3	1.70	.84
Intervention 4	1.61	.53
Intervention 5	1.48	.44
Intervention 6	0.75	.46

(baseline to Intervention 1) than in the subsequent interventions. A similar pattern of evolution is visible for each of the participants taken as individuals (see Figure 5.6). A nonparametric Friedman test was used to test if there were significant differences between the measurements recorded at different moments. The analysis indicates significant overall differences, $\chi^2(6, N = 6) = 23.55, p < 0.001$. The overall effect size (calculated as the difference of the means between the baseline and the sixth intervention and divided by the standard deviation of the score differences) proved to be large (corrected Hedges' $g = 2.06$).

In order to investigate the degree of change between pairs of temporal intervals, we used the Wilcoxon test for consecutive measurements. The differences were statistically significant or marginally statistically significant for the interval from baseline to Intervention 1 ($Z = -2.20, p = 0.027$) with a large effect size ($g = 1.32$) and for the interval from Intervention 5 to Intervention 6 ($Z = -1.75$, $p < 0.08$), also with a large effect size ($g = 0.90$; Cohen, 1988). The differences between other intervals were not statistically significant.

Individual-Level Analysis

The graphs in Figure 5.6 depict the children's individual patterns of change from baseline to the sixth intervention session. The patterns of evolution are very similar, proving a rather low variability of the effect at the individual level. The magnitude of the effect of the intervention was different for the children. Three participants (Participants 1, 2, and 4) succeeded in asking questions in a play task with a minimum level of prompting by Intervention 6. Participants 3, 5, and 6 needed a higher level of prompting to perform the targeted behavior at Intervention 6.

Conclusions and Future Directions

In this work, we focused on improving the social ability of asking questions for children with ASD by using social robots in a Social Story intervention. This study

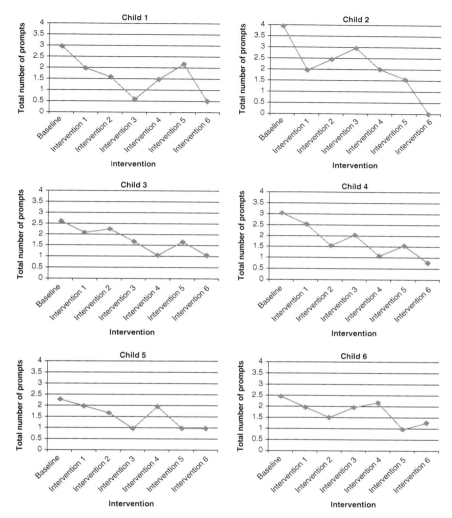

FIGURE 5.6 The evolution of each participant from baseline to the last intervention session.

Note. The *y*-axis indicates the values of the level of prompting needed by each of the participants to perform the target behavior to ask questions, and the *x*-axis indicates the number of sessions during the baseline and intervention phases.

investigated whether using the known preference of children with ASD for robotic toys improves the effectiveness of Social Story intervention in increasing the level of social interaction of six preschoolers diagnosed with ASD. Our aim was not to replace the therapist but to use the robot as an adjunct to the classical Social Story intervention. Based on our results, it can be concluded that the mixed-methods intervention tested here helped the children to increase their level of independence in asking questions; more specifically, the Social Story intervention conducted by the robot Probo was efficient for all the participants. Moreover, in all cases, we can see that the intervention with Probo proved to be effective from the first session.

We hypothesized that the robot-assisted Social Story intervention would significantly improve the target behavior (i.e., asking questions during playtime). The outcomes of the current study support this hypothesis. This suggests that social robots have the potential to be used as adjuncts to the classical social skills treatments for children with ASD (i.e., Social Story intervention) in order to increase the efficacy and/or effectiveness of these treatments. This is in line with our earlier studies (see the Introduction to this chapter), which showed that the use of a social robot to present Social Stories resulted in greater benefits than presentation of the stories on a computer screen (Pop et al., 2013) or than a Social Story intervention conducted by a therapist (Vanderborght et al., 2012).

Future research should test this technique over a longer time period and on a larger scale to be able to monitor any potential long-term effects. The aim of this study was to increase interactivity between the child and the therapist during playtime (through increases in the child spontaneously asking questions), but it will be interesting for future studies to explore if the effects of a Social Story intervention delivered through a social robot are maintained outside the therapy room during play with other children or adults. Taking as a reference point the data at an individual level, future research should focus on identifying what specific category of children with ASD (age, verbal development, IQ, etc.) from the autism spectrum may gain more benefits from a robot-assisted Social Story intervention.

Nevertheless, this type of exploratory study has clinical relevance for practitioners or caregivers of individuals with ASD. Even though this study has several methodological limitations (e.g., a small sample size, the lack of a control group, and the short length of the intervention), it provides an important contribution to both ASD therapies and human–robot interaction research fields and further supports the findings from our earlier research on combining interventions using social robots and Social Stories. To conclude, the results can potentially contribute to the search for a better and more tailored robotic design that will help children with ASD improve their social abilities and maintain those improvements in daily life.

Acknowledgments

The authors first thank the children and their families and also thank the Autism Transylvania Association for their hospitality in performing the experiments. This work has been supported by Consiliul National de Cercetare (CNCS)–Bucharest; Romania project PN-II-IDPCE-2011-3-0484, "Exploring Robot-Assisted Therapy for Children with ASD"; the EU project Dynamizing Research and Education for All through Mobility in ACP (DREAM); and Innovatie door Wetenschap en Technologie (IWT) SB Grant 121591.

Note

1 An anonymous reviewer suggested that the story used is more in the nature of a social script rather than a strictly interpreted social story. As we note, the story was in fact based on Gray (2000a, 2000b, 2004).

References

American Psychiatric Association. (2000). *Diagnostic and statistical manual of mental disorders* (4th ed., text rev.). Washington, DC: Author.

Andrews, S. (2004). *Using Social Stories to increase reciprocal social interactions and social comprehension in school aged children diagnosed with autism* (Unpublished doctoral dissertation). California School of Professional Psychology, San Diego, CA.

Baron-Cohen, S. (2009). Autism: The empathizing–systemizing (E-S) theory. *Annals of the New York Academy of Sciences, 1156,* 68–80. http://dx.doi.org/10.1111/j.1749-6632.2009.04467.x

Barry, L.M., & Burlew, S.B. (2004). Using social stories to teach choice and play skills to children with autism. *Focus on Autism and Other Developmental Disabilities, 19*(1), 45–51.

Bass, J.D., & Mulick, J.A. (2007). Social play skill enhancement of children with autism using peers and siblings as therapists. *Psychology in the Schools, 44*(7), 727–735.

Bernad-Ripoll, S. (2007). Using a self-as-model video combined with Social Stories™ to help a child with Asperger syndrome understand emotions. *Focus on Autism and Other Developmental Disabilities, 22,* 100–106.

Bernard-Opitz, V., Sriram, N., & Nakhoda-Sapuan, S. (2001). Enhancing social problem solving in children with autism and normal children through computer-assisted instruction. *Journal of Autism and Developmental Disorders, 31*(4), 377–384.

Bird, G., Leighton, J., Press, C., & Heyes, C. (2007). Intact automatic imitation of human and robot actions in autism spectrum disorders. *Proceedings of the Royal Society of London B: Biological Sciences, 274*(1628), 3027–3031.

Cohen, J. (1988). *Statistical power analysis for the behavioral sciences.* Hillsdale, NJ: Routledge Academic.

Dauphin, M., Kinney, E., Stromer, R., & Koegel, R. (2004). Using video-enhanced activity and matrix training to teach socio-dramatic play to a child with autism. *Journal of Positive Behavior Interventions, 6*(4), 238–250.

Dautenhahn, K., Nehaniv, C., Walters, M., Robins, B., Kose-Bagci, H., Mirza, N., & Blow M. (2009). KASPAR—A minimally expressive humanoid robot for human–robot interaction research. *Applied Bionics and Biomechanics, 6*(3), 369–397.

Dautenhahn, K., & Werry, I. (2004). Towards interactive robots in autism therapy: Background, motivation and challenges. *Pragmatics Cognition, 12,* 1–35.

Diehl, J.J., Crowell, C.R., Villano, M., Wier, K., Tang, K., & Riek, L.D. (2014). Clinical applications of robots in autism spectrum disorder diagnosis and treatment. In V. Patel, V. Preedy, & C. Martin (Eds.), *Comprehensive guide to autism* (pp. 411–422). New York, NY: Springer.

Diehl, J.J., Schmitt, L.M., Villano, M., & Crowell, C.R. (2012). The clinical use of robots for individuals with autism spectrum disorders: A critical review. *Research in Autism Spectrum Disorders, 6*(1), 249–262.

Duquette, A., Michaud, F., & Mercier, H. (2008). Exploring the use of a mobile robot as an imitation agent with children with low-functioning autism. *Autonomous Robots, 24*(2), 147–157.

Francois, D., Powell, S., & Dautenhahn, K. (2009). A long-term study of children with autism playing with a robotic pet: Taking inspirations from non-directive play therapy to encourage children's proactivity and initiative taking. *Interaction Studies, 10*(3), 324–373.

Goodrich, M.A., Colton, M., Brinton, B., Fujiki, M., Atherton, J., Robinson, L. . . . Acerson, A. (2012). Incorporating a robot into an autism therapy team. *IEEE Intelligent Systems, 27*(2), 52–59.

Goris, K., Saldien, J., Vanderborght, B., & Lefeber, D. (2011). Mechanical design of the huggable robot Probo. *International Journal of Humanoid Robotics, 8*(3), 481–511.

Gray, C. (2000a). *The new social story book*. Arlington, TX: Future Horizons.

Gray, C. (2000b). *The new social story book: Illustrated edition*. Arlington, TX: Future Horizons.

Gray, C. (2004). Social Stories 10.0: The new defining criteria & guidelines. *Jenison Autism Journal, 15*(4), 2–18.

Gray, C., & Garand, J.D. (1993). Social stories: Improving responses of students with autism with accurate social information. *Focus on Autistic Behavior, 8*(1), 1–10.

Green, V., Pituch, K., Itchon, J., Choi, A., O'Reilly, M., & Sigafoos, J. (2006). Internet survey of treatments used by parents of children with autism. *Research in Developmental Disabilities, 27*(1), 70–84.

Happé, F. (2005). The weak central coherence account of autism. In F.R. Volkmar, R. Paul, A. Klin, & D. Cohen (Eds.), *Handbook of autism and pervasive developmental disorders* (pp. 640–649). Hoboken, NJ: Wiley.

Hobson, J.A., Hobson, R.P., Malik, S., Bargiota, K., & Calo, S. (2013). The relation between social engagement and pretend play in autism. *British Journal of Developmental Psychology, 31*(1), 114–127.

Jarrold, C. (2003). A review of research into pretend play in autism. *Autism, 7*(4), 379–390.

Karkhaneh, M., Clark, B., Ospina, M.B., Seida, J.C., Smith, V., & Hartling, L. (2010). Social Stories™ to improve social skills in children with autism spectrum disorder: A systematic review. *Autism, 14*(6), 641–662.

Kim, E.S., Berkovits, L.D., Bernier, E.P., Leyzberg, D., Shic, F., Paul, R., & Scassellati, B. (2013). Social robots as embedded reinforcers of social behavior in children with autism. *Journal of Autism and Developmental Disorders, 43*, 1038–1049.

Koegel, L.K., Vernon, T.W., Koegel, R.L., Koegel, B.L., & Paullin, A.W. (2012). Improving social engagement and initiations between children with autism spectrum disorder and their peers in inclusive settings. *Journal of Positive Behavior Interventions, 14*(4), 220–227.

Kokina, A., & Kern, L. (2010). Social Story™ interventions for students with autism spectrum disorders: A meta-analysis. *Journal of Autism and Developmental Disorders, 40*(7), 812–826.

Kozima, H., Michalowski, M., & Nakagawa, C. (2009). Keepon: A playful robot for research, therapy, and entertainment. *International Journal of Social Robotics, 1*, 3–18.

Kozima, H., & Nakagawa, C. (2006). Interactive robots as facilitators of children's social development. In A. Lazinica (Ed.), *Mobile robots towards new applications* (pp. 269–286). Mammendorf, Germany: Verlag.

Kuoch, H. & Mirenda, P. (2003). Social Story interventions for young children with autism spectrum disorders. *Focus on Autism and Other Developmental Disabilities, 18*(4), 219–227.

Lord, C., Risi, S., Lambrecht, L., Cook, E.H., Jr., Leventhal, B.L., & DiLavore, P.C. (2000). The Autism Diagnostic Observation Schedule-Generic: A standard measure of social and communication deficits associated with the spectrum of autism. *Journal of Autism and Developmental Disorders, 30*, 205–223.

Mandasari, V., Lu, M.V., & Theng, L.B. (2011). 2D animated social story for assisting social skills learning of children with autism spectrum disorder. In L.B. Theng (Ed.), *Assistive and augmentive communication for the disabled: Intelligent technologies for communication, learning and teaching* (pp. 1–24). New York, NY: Information Science Reference.

Matson, J.L., Matson, M.L., & Rivet, T.T. (2007). Social-skills treatments for children with autism spectrum disorders: An overview. *Behavior Modification, 31*(5), 682–707.

Mertens, D.M. (2009). *Research and evaluation in education and psychology: Integrating diversity with quantitative, qualitative, and mixed methods.* Thousand Oaks, CA: SAGE.

Mitchell, P., Parsons, S., & Leonard, A. (2007). Using virtual environments for teaching social understanding to 6 adolescents with autistic spectrum disorders. *Journal of Autism and Developmental Disorders, 37*(3), 589–600.

Nikopoulos, C.K., & Keenan, M. (2003). Promoting social initiation in children with autism using video modeling. *Behavioral Interventions, 18*(2), 87–108.

Ozonoff, S. (1995). Reliability and validity of the Wisconsin Card Sorting Test in studies of autism. *Neuropsychology, 9*(4), 491–500.

Pierno, A.C., Mari, M., Lusher, D., & Castiello, U. (2008). Robotic movement elicits visuomotor priming in children with autism. *Neuropsychologia, 46*(2), 448–454.

Pop, C.A., Simut, R.E., Pintea, S., Saldien, J., Rusu, A.S., Vanderfaeillie, J. . . . Vanderborght, B. (2013). Social robots vs. computer display: Does the way social stories are delivered make a difference for their effectiveness on ASD children? *Journal of Educational Computing Research, 49*(3), 381–401.

Pradel, G., & Giannopulu, I. (2010). Multimodal interactions in free game play of children with autism and a mobile robot. *Neurorehabilitation, 27,* 305–311.

Quirmbach, L.M., Lincoln, A.J., Feinberg-Gizzo, M.J., Ingersoll, B.R., & Andrews, S.M. (2009). Social stories: Mechanisms of effectiveness in increasing game play skills in children diagnosed with autism spectrum disorder using a pretest posttest repeated measures randomized control group design. *Journal of Autism Developmental Disorders, 39,* 299–321.

Reichow, B., & Volkmar, F.R. (2010). Social skills interventions for individuals with autism: Evaluation for evidence-based practices within a best evidence synthesis framework. *Journal of Autism and Developmental Disorders, 40*(2), 149–166.

Ricks, D.J., & Colton, M.B. (2010, May 3–7). *Trends and considerations in robot-assisted autism therapy.* Paper presented at the 2010 IEEE International Conference on Robotics and Automation (ICRA), Anchorage, AK.

Riek, L.D. (2012). Wizard of Oz studies in HRI: A systematic review and new reporting guidelines. *Journal of Human-Robot Interaction, 1*(1), 119–136.

Robins, B., Dautenhahn, K., Boekhorst, R., & Billard, A. (2005). Robotic assistants in therapy and education of children with autism: Can a small humanoid robot help encourage social interaction skills? *Universal Access in the Information Society, 4*(2), 105–120.

Robins, B., Dautenhahn, K., & Dickerson, P. (2009, February 1–7). *From isolation to communication: A case study evaluation of robot assisted play for children with autism with a minimally expressive humanoid robot.* Paper presented at the 2009 Second International Conference on Advances in Computer-Human Interactions.

Robins, B., Dickerson, P., Stribling, P., & Dautenhahn, K. (2004). Robot-mediated joint attention in children with autism: A case study in robot-human interaction. *Interaction Studies, 5,* 161–198.

Scassellati, B., Admoni, H., & Matarić, M. (2012). Robots for use in autism research. *Annual Review of Biomedical Engineering, 14,* 275–294.

Scattone, D. (2007). Social skills interventions for children with autism. *Psychology in Schools, 44*(7), 717–726.

Scattone, D., Tingstrom, D.H., & Wilczynski, S.M. (2006). Increasing appropriate social interactions of children with autism spectrum disorders using social stories. *Focus on Autism and Other Developmental Disabilities, 21*(4), 211–222.

Simut, R., Pop, C., Saldien, J., Rusu, A., Pintea, S., Vanderfaeillie, J. . . . Vanderborght, B. (2012, March 5–8). *Is the social robot Probo an added value for Social Story intervention for children with autism spectrum disorders?* Paper presented at the Seventh Annual Association for Computing Machinery (ACM)/Institute of Electrical and Electronics Engineers (IEEE) International Conference on Human-Robot Interaction, Boston, MA.

Simut, R., Pop, C., Vanderborght, B., Saldien, J., Rusu, A., Pintea, S. . . . David, D. (2011, November). *The huggable social robot Probo for social story telling for robot assisted therapy with ASD children.* Paper presented at the International Conference on Informatics Engineering and Information Science, ICIEIS 2011, Kuala Lumpur, Malaysia.

Smith, C. (2001). Using social stories to enhance behavior in children with autistic spectrum difficulties. *Educational Psychology in Practice, 17,* 337–345.

Stagnitti, K., Kenna, R., Malakellis, M., Kershaw, B., Hoare, M., & de Silva-Sanigorski, A. (2011). Evaluating the feasibility, effectiveness and acceptability of an active play intervention for disadvantaged preschool children: A pilot study. *Australasian Journal of Early Childhood, 36*(3), 66–72.

Stagnitti, K., O'Connor, C., & Sheppard, L. (2012). Impact of the Learn to Play program on play, social competence and language for children aged 5–8 years who attend a specialist school. *Australian Occupational Therapy Journal, 59*(4), 302–311.

Swaggart, B., Gagnon, E., Bock, S.J., Earles, T.L., Quinn, C., Myles, B.S., & Simpson, R.L. (1995). Using social stories to teach social and behavioral skills to children with autism. *Focus on Autistic Behavior, 10,* 1–16.

Tapus, A., Peca, A., Aly, A., Pop, C., Jisa, L., Pintea, S. . . . David, D.O. (2012). Children with autism social engagement in interaction with Nao, an imitative robot: A series of single case experiments. *Interaction Studies, 13*(3), 315–347.

Tsao, L., & Odom, S. (2006). Sibling-mediated social interaction intervention for young children with autism. *Topics in Early Childhood Special Education, 26*(2), 106–123.

Vanderborght, B., Simut, R., Saldien, J., Pop, C., Rusu, A.S., Pintea, S. . . . David, D.O. (2012). Using the social robot Probo as a social story telling agent for children with ASD. *Interaction Studies, 13*(3), 348–372.

Wainer, J., Dautenhahn, K., Robins, B., & Amirabdollahian, F. (2010, December 6–8). *Collaborating with Kaspar: Using an autonomous humanoid robot to foster cooperative dyadic play among children with autism.* Paper presented at the 2010 Institute of Electrical and Electronics Engineers (IEEE)-Robotics and Automation Society (RAS) International Conference on Humanoid Robots, Nashville, TN.

Wang, P., & Spillane, A. (2009). Evidence-based social skills interventions for children with autism: A meta-analysis. *Education and Training in Developmental Disabilities, 44*(3), 318–342.

Weiss, M., & Harris, S.L. (2001). Teaching social skills to people with autism. *Behavior Modification, 25*(5), 785–802.

Williams, J., Higgins, J., & Brayne, C. (2006). Systematic review of prevalence studies of autism spectrum disorders. *Archives of Disease in Childhood, 91*(1), 8–15.

Wilson, J., & Rosenberg, D. (1988). Rapid prototyping for user interface design. In M. Helander (Ed.), *Handbook of human-computer interaction* (pp. 859–873). Amsterdam, Netherlands: North Holland.

Xin, J.F., & Sutman, F.X. (2011). Using the smart board in teaching social stories to students with autism. *TEACHING Exceptional Children, 43*(4), 18–24.

Appendix A

THE CHECKLIST FOR TREATMENT INTEGRITY

Dear Observer,

Please write down an X when you consider the answer to be *yes* near the number that corresponds to the intervention step that was respected by the experimenter and write down an O when you believe that the intervention step was not respected.

1. Triggering the beginning of the Social Story (using verbal expressions such as *The story starts now!* or *Let's listen to the story!* or *Pay attention to Probo, the story is starting!*).
2. Ensuring that the participant has all the necessary conditions in order to follow the story by checking if the child has the **correct body position**, oriented to the robot; stopping the story when the child cannot focus his or her attention on the story; or offering prompts, such as a **verbal prompt** (*Pay attention to the story!*), an **indicative prompt** (pointing with an index finger to the robot), or a **physical prompt** (slow orientation of the child's head to the robot).
3. Asking the three comprehension questions immediately after the story ends.
4. Implementing the task in a naturalistic way (to create the game's opportunities for the child in a spontaneous and playful manner).
5. Offering a prompt to the child for the child to give the correct answers (i.e., the experimenter offers a prompt when the child cannot independently manifest the target behavior).
6. Offering feedback to the participant (in order to correct wrong answers or to give a reward for the correct answers).

Appendix B

THE TRANSLATED VERSION (FROM ROMANIAN TO ENGLISH) OF THE SOCIAL STORY *HOW DO I ASK QUESTIONS WHEN I PLAY WITH OTHERS?* WITH THE EMOTIONS TO BE DEMONSTRATED BY THE ROBOT INCLUDED

When I play with someone else, I ask questions. It's good to ask questions *[happy emotion]*.

If a toy is missing, I may ask, "Where is it?"

After I ask something, I may wait for the other person to answer.

If I want to know what is happening in the game, I may ask: "What is the car doing?" or "What is the doll doing?"

After I ask something, I wait for an answer.

If I want a toy, I may ask, "Can I play with that toy?"

After I ask for the toy, I may wait for the other person to give me the toy.

If I ask questions when I play with other people, they are happy *[happy emotion]* and they like to play with me.

People are happy *[happy emotion]* when I ask them questions. It's nice to ask questions when I play with someone else.

6

THE INTERSECTION OF PRETENSE AND STORYTELLING IN CHILDREN WITH AUTISM SPECTRUM DISORDER

Susan Douglas and Lesley Stirling

Introduction

The production and articulation of story within pretend play is a complex cognitive task. In some cases, play may encode or enact stories that are, in some sense, preexisting. In others, the stories emerge as part of play and necessitate online and often collaborative production of the plot. Narrating pretend play also requires the storyteller to manage multiple roles such as those of the narrator, the different characters, and possibly even the role of director if the pretend play is collaborative. Children need to manage the manipulation of props to set the scene for the narrative and act out the story as it unfolds—all while simultaneously producing the articulated narrative. Thus, narrative within pretend play is a unique mode of storytelling with important features to consider when undertaking analysis.

The term *autism spectrum disorder* (ASD) refers to a spectrum of pervasive developmental disorders for which the diagnostic criteria refer to impairments in social communication and the presence of restricted and repetitive interests and behaviours (*Diagnostic and Statistical Manual of Mental Disorders*; 5th ed.; *DSM–5*; American Psychiatric Association [APA], 2013). Children with ASD are considered to show hallmark deficits in pretend play thought to be related to their social and cognitive difficulties (see Chaudry & Dissanayake, this volume; Stagnitti, this volume). Studies of oral narrative in children with ASD have tended to focus on production tasks in controlled settings using wordless picture books (cf. Stirling, Douglas, Leekam, & Carey, 2014, for a review of narrative methodologies in ASD), although there are studies that have examined narratives in ASD in naturalistic settings (e.g., Capps, Kehres, & Sigman, 1998; Solomon, 2004; Stirling & Barrington, 2007). While the parallels between pretend play and narrative have long been acknowledged in the developmental literature (e.g.,

118 Susan Douglas and Lesley Stirling

Galda, 1984; Galda & Pellegrini, 2007; Garvey, 1990; Göncü & Klein, 2001; Harris, 2000; Kavanaugh & Engel, 1998; Nicolopoulou, 2007; Roskos & Christie, 2000), few studies have examined the structural and linguistic characteristics of narratives constructed as part of pretend play, even in typical development (cf. Benson, 1993).

Stories that emerge as part of pretend play present a unique context in which to consider how children with ASD manage a multidimensional approach to the real and the imaginary. In this chapter, we first articulate a conceptual framework for investigating story within pretend play by delineating the concept of the *pretend play narrative* and discussing whether and how we can investigate its structural and imaginal qualities as part of the broader narrative genre. We then address the question of whether or not children with ASD engage in this type of storytelling within pretend play produced as part of naturalistic interaction with an adult and, if they do, what structural and imaginal qualities their pretend play narratives exhibit and how sophisticated their pretend play narratives are. We make use of three analytic approaches in addressing these questions: (a) a structural overview of the presence and complexity of pretend play and narrative in the children's interactions, (b) Applebee's (1978) model of structural development in children's narratives, and (c) Glaubman & Fein's (n.d.) Realistic–Imaginal Scale (RIS).

The Intersection of Storytelling and Pretense

The inclusion of pretend play storytelling in the narrative genre is not without precedent. Since early work by Piaget (1962) and Vygotsky (1978), the significance of pretend play for children's development has been extensively studied, and a range of published work has reported correlations between pretend play ability and language abilities, including narrative ability, along with other aspects of cognitive development (cf. Kasari, Chang, & Patterson, 2013; Lillard et al., 2013, Nicolopoulou & Ilgaz, 2013). Researchers have also focused more narrowly on the relationship between play and story. Paley (1990) makes the strong claim that "play . . . [is] story in action, just as storytelling is play put into narrative form" (p. 4), and Nicolopoulou in particular has been concerned with teasing out both the similarities and differences and the potential developmental cross-fertilisation between these two types of childhood activity (e.g., Nicolopoulou, 2005, 2007, this volume). Nicolopoulou finds it useful to speak of "narrative scenarios" as an aspect of children's symbolic thought independent of their manifestation, as in the following diagram (Figure 6.1).

Similarly, Glaubman, Kashi, and Koresh (2001) conceptualise children's sociodramatic play as a kind of narrative. However, they identify important differences that distinguish sociodramatic play from narrative, such as the use of objects in play and the minimum requirement of at least two participants.

FIGURE 6.1 Nicolopoulou's (2005, 2007) two types of encoding of narrative scenarios.

Extensive attention has been paid within relevant literatures in linguistics, narratology, and related fields to the defining criteria for a stretch of language to count as a narrative. Labov (Labov, 1972; Labov & Waletzky, 1967) provided both a maximal and a minimal characterisation of the kinds of prototypical, personal experience, "extraordinary event" narratives he worked with: Minimally, a narrative must involve at least two clauses describing sequentially ordered events, and prototypically, narratives are taken to include some combination of the functional components he labelled *abstract, orientation, resolution, evaluation*, and *coda* in addition to this *complicating action*. Labov is not unique in recognising the key importance of temporal sequencing to narrative, although others have highlighted a notion of global connectedness—coherence/cohesion or causal relation—as an important additional feature of prototypical narratives (e.g., Stein & Glenn, 1979; Toolan, 1988; Trabasso, Secco, & Van den Broek, 1984). The concept of a key concern, complication, or problem that is to be resolved is also a traditional aspect of the idea of story.

However, others have pointed out that many discourse segments that one might want to analyse as narrative depart from this model. Ochs and Capps (2001) identified a number of dimensions relevant to narrative and suggested that each of these should be viewed as a cline, with the prototypical narratives of the Labov kind situated at one end of the cline: monologic, very "tellable" with a clear point and moral, and clearly set off from the surrounding discourse. In contrast, conversational narratives may be fragmentary, evocative, and dynamically co-constructed by conversational partners (Norrick, 2000). There are strong parallels between conversational narratives and pretend play narratives, which we will discuss further.

When children engage in pretend play with a play partner, they frequently enact stories that may encode generic sociocultural scripts and/or may have a fictional flavour. These involve characters either role-played by the children or in the form of toys or figurines that they animate. The events of the story unfold in a dynamic fashion as the play proceeds. Background information or orientation is often provided and may be the focus of significant effort as a scene and props are set up. Most importantly, the children are seen to be creating an encapsulated projected world, just as they do in more prototypical storytelling. In their play, as in their storytelling, children draw on a range of material, from their own experience on the one hand, to the stories they are exposed to in various media on the other (storybooks, TV, and other visual media, as well as stories from other children). The stories of pretend play probably lie on a continuum from more planned or inter-textual (acting out something that has been previously seen, experienced, or acted out) to stories that are more novel, serendipitous, and dynamically constructed.

From a linguistic and discourse analytic perspective, the primary question to be asked is whether and how episodes of pretend play can be seen as relating in any direct way to the genre of narrative discourse. Do these "stories" constitute narratives in any interesting sense and, if so, how can we analyse them so as to gain an understanding of the way in which they relate to more prototypical narrative productions? An initial caveat is that not all episodes of pretend play should be seen as enacting a story. A child who performs a single instance of pretend pouring of tea from a plastic teapot or pretend brushing of teeth with a toy carrot is indeed engaged in pretense, but at best the act alludes to a scenario that might be developed as a narrative. There is clearly a cline from this minimal and isolated type of instance to fully fledged enactment of stories—and this is similar to the cline we may assume exists within adult conversational narrative, as indicated previously.

Second, it is important to note that children engaged in pretend play frequently include in their discourse explicit accounts or descriptions of a narrative kind. Thus, in Nicolopoulou's (2005, 2007, this volume) terms, they may mix *discursive* narrative and *enacted* narrative. These discursive elements may accompany pretend play acts and provide an explanatory gloss for them, or they may provide background material that supports the developing play. These accounts are often a kind of simultaneous narration (Polanyi, 1989)—and are nonstereotypical in that they need not be in the past tense. For this reason, Giffin (1984), in her work on metacommunication, identified narrative contributions as one type of metacommunication: Play partners use what she terms *storytelling* as a way to introduce more elaborate plots to the pretend play while still being engaged in play. She notes that these narrative contributions are delivered with rising intonation at the end of phrases which typically begin with *and*, as in the following example in which a child describes dying and coming alive again: "and I was crying in heaven . . . and I got back alive. . . . And I was crying" (Giffin, 1984, p. 85). In Giffin's (1984) own words, "[the cadence] cues other players to hear the message as a narrative, about the play world but not of it" (p. 85; also see Trawick-Smith, 1998, among others, on narrative elements of pretend play interactions).

Third, regardless of the degree of commentary provided, these interactions involve a sequence of enacted events that can be seen as composing a story. If there were no verbal interaction at all, we could still see the sequence of events as constituting a story (although in the minimal case where we have a child engaged in solitary and silent pretend play, it may be more difficult to see the child as actively engaged in the production of a story). However, there normally *is* interaction of two major kinds: metacommunicative remarks relevant to and developing the play and dialogic interactions between characters.

In this context, it may be relevant to consider the well-established distinction made in the literature on narrative between an abstract notion of story as a set of component events and their organisation with respect to one another and the way these are presented as a concrete manifestation in an actual discursive event or text. The Russian formalists distinguished *fabula* and *syuzhet*; the French structuralists made a distinction between *histoire* and *discours*; and Bruner distinguished *story* as the abstract set of events from *discourse* as the text in which the story is manifest and *telling*, which is the communicative act of narration (cf. Bruner, 1986; Pier, 2003). Just as Norrick (2000) points out that, for conversational narratives, a storyline may be constructable, even if narrative clauses are not present, ordered, or contributed by a single speaker, so for pretend play narratives, a *story* in the Bruner sense may be determinable, even if the *discourse* is fragmentary and the *telling* is largely via enactment rather than linguistic acts.

Pretend play narratives probably most resemble enacted stories within dramatical contexts: Drama will generally involve a script that constitutes a fully planned out and completed story in advance of the performance. Pretend play narratives also bear a relationship to multimodal or performed stories of a more prototypical kind (e.g., Bauman, 1986; Glaubman et al., 2001).

Finally, pretend play narratives share some of the characteristics of conversational narratives more generally. Conversational narratives are known to be more complex in their structure than prototypical monologic narratives: They may be interrupted, there may be simultaneous conversations going on, and they may be repetitive or may require several attempts to complete. Many are what Norrick (2000) calls *diffuse*, in the sense that they may lack overt presentation of a clear sequence of events (Nicolopoulou, 2007, talks of this in terms of pretend play involving "a cluster of loosely connected themes" [p. 254]). They are often co-constructed by the participants, and this can mean that they change in somewhat unplanned-for ways if there is negotiation over the content between the participants.

In summary, there is considerable evidence as to why we might want to view pretend play stories as "narratives". First, they are often not purely enacted: There is usually some degree of metacomment or descriptive narration on the part of the participants. They also display the creation of a projected story world, and they exhibit some of the functional components considered to be part of narratives: They have beginnings, characters, orientation, and a sequence of narrative events. They may also include evaluation, resolution, and codas—but if they don't, we cannot in all conscience refuse to call them narratives given that more standard kinds of storytelling may lack these features, especially among children's discourse.

Pretense and Storytelling in Autism Spectrum Disorder

Previously published research on pretend play and ASD has revealed mixed findings. Historically, children with ASD have been considered to show characteristic deficits in pretend play related to their social and cognitive difficulties and, until the publication of the *DSM–5*, difficulty with pretend play was one of the diagnostic criteria for autism (*Diagnostic and Statistical Manual of Mental Disorders*; 4th ed., text rev.; *DSM–IV–TR*; APA, 2000). However, there is now a growing body of research that shows that children with ASD can engage in pretend play comparable to typically developing controls when prompted (Jarrold, Boucher, & Smith, 1996; Lewis & Boucher, 1988) or even spontaneously (Kelly, 2007; Mifsud, 2011; Mifsud, Kelly, Dissanayake, & Leekam, 2009; Prescott, 2003; see Chaudry & Dissanayake, this volume, for an overview of the research in this area). Research focused on children's understanding of pretense has shown that children with ASD demonstrate good comprehension of pretend acts, suggesting that when difficulty in participating in pretend play occurs, it is not due to a limited capacity to make sense of nonliteral behaviours (Jarrold, Smith, Boucher, & Harris, 1994; Kavanaugh & Harris, 1994). Hobson, Lee, and Hobson (2009) focused on a different aspect of pretend play in an attempt to identify why the pretense observed in children with ASD may be of poor quality and may lack the creativity and flexibility seen in typical children (see also Hobson, Hobson, Malik, Bargiota, & Calo, 2013). They proposed that while the mechanics of pretend play are equivalent between high-functioning children with ASD and neurotypical children, there is a lack of investment and pleasure in the play, which amounts to a deficit in what they term *playful pretense*. However, using a modified version of the Hobson et al. (2013) coding scheme, Dissanayake and colleagues found no differences in the playfulness of pretend play between a group of high-functioning children with autism and typically developing children (Mifsud, 2011; Mifsud et al., 2009).

Research looking specifically at the degree to which children with ASD are able to engage in *shared* or *negotiated* pretense in *interactive* contexts in the form of collaborative social pretend play is scarce (Prendeville, Prelock, & Unwin, 2006; Wolfberg, Bottema-Beutel, & DeWitt, 2012). Children with ASD are known to find spontaneous social play very difficult (Jordan, 2003; Schuler & Fletcher, 2002; Sigman & Ruskin, 1999), and Wolfberg (2009) noted that social play that includes imaginative play is particularly challenging for these children. Furthermore, research taking a discourse analytic approach to communication and metacommunication within pretend play interactions in ASD is restricted to a small study by Wolfberg and Schuler (1999), recent work by Freeman and Kasari (2013), and Douglas and Stirling (2012a, 2012b).

The substantial body of research on narrative in ASD has also yielded somewhat mixed results (Stirling et al., 2014). Matched-group experimental studies investigating the production of oral narratives in children with ASD have reported a wide range of results that present a complex profile. While some studies found that children with ASD produced narratives that were shorter and less complex than those of the control groups (e.g., Capps, Losh, & Thurber, 2000; Klin, 2000; Tager-Flusberg, 1995), other studies found no difference (e.g., Diehl, Bennetto, & Young, 2006; Losh & Capps, 2003; Norbury & Bishop, 2003). Similarly, results have varied in terms of group differences on measures of coherence (e.g., Colle, Baron-Cohen, Wheelwright, & van der Lely, 2008; Diehl et al., 2006; Norbury & Bishop, 2003) and the use of psychological state terms and evaluation (e.g., Begeer, Malle, Nieuwland, & Keysar, 2010; Capps et al., 2000; Norbury & Bishop, 2003; Tager-Flusberg & Sullivan, 1995). However, some children with ASD can produce narratives that are similar to those of neurotypical children in terms of characteristics such as length, complexity, structure, and features that draw on mental state understanding such as psychological state terms and evaluation. Recent work by Stirling, Barrington, Douglas, and Delves (in press) indicates that despite differences in their approach to a story retelling task, children with ASD attending mainstream primary schools demonstrated an understanding of what it means to retell a story and that many were able to creatively work within a prescribed story schema to produce a new version of the stimulus story. Research into play and storytelling is particularly understudied in children with ASD and so there is not, as yet, a clear picture of the storytelling capabilities of children with ASD in the context of pretend play.

Method

The data considered in this study were collected as part of a previous language study investigating verb acquisition (Douglas, 2012). The spontaneous interaction of children with ASD and their mothers and/or the researcher was recorded during six hour-long visits to each child's home over a period of 3 months.

These data were revisited for the current study to consider the extent to which pretend play narratives were incorporated into the interactions in this comparatively naturalistic setting. The aims of this study were to ascertain whether or not children with ASD engaged in pretend play episodes that encapsulated enacted and/or discursive narratives—that is, pretend play that involved production of story; to analyse the coherence of the narrative structure of these pretend play stories from a developmental perspective; and to analyse the narrative competence in terms of the child's ability to transition from utilising realistic objects and conventional roles and activities to engage with imaginative elements (Glaubman & Fein, n.d.). In this section, we outline the methodology under the headings of Participants, Procedure, and Analysis.

Participants

Five Australian children with ASD aged between 3.6 and 7.2 years participated in the original study. They had each received a formal diagnosis based on *DSM–IV* criteria (APA, 1994) by a team of assessors from a recognised child mental health service. The Wechsler Preschool and Primary Scale of Intelligence (WPPSI–R or WPPSI–III) was used to assess performance IQ; 4 of the 5 children scored in the Low Normal to Normal range, and one child scored Below Normal. As part of their formal assessment, the children were also scored on the Childhood Autism Rating Scale (CARS; Schopler, Reichler, & Renner, 1988). This is a diagnostic assessment with good psychometric properties used to observe and subjectively rate 15 items of child behaviour on a 4-point scale ranging from normal to severe, which then yields a composite score. Four children received scores that indicated mild autism (30–36.5), and one child received a score that indicated moderate to severe autism (37–40). All of the children were monolingual speakers of English, and language ability was measured on a corpus of 100 utterances for each child (taken from Session 1) using mean length of utterance (MLU) at the level of the morpheme and the Index of Productive Syntax (IPSyn). IPSyn counts the occurrences of 56 syntactic and morphological forms, yielding subscores evaluating the developmental stage and sophistication of children's use of noun phrases, verb phrases, questions or negations, and sentence structures that combine into a total score for grammatical complexity of the child's language (Scarborough, 1990). Both MLU and IPSyn scores indicated that all the children had quite productive language, despite evidence of expressive language delay (between 6 and 24 months). The children were enrolled in special schools, mainstream primary schools, kindergartens, or early intervention programs, and the socioeconomic status of the families based on parental occupation ranged from lower middle to middle class. The ages and abilities of the children are summarised in Table 6.1; pseudonyms are used to refer to the children.

TABLE 6.1 Participant Details

Child	Age (years)	CARS	IQ	MLU[a]	IPSyn[b]	No. of sessions
David	3.6	31	100	3.18 (3)	57 (~2.6)	6
Peter	4.6	34	76	4.19 (3.9)	80 (~3.6)	6
Liam	5.6	41	75	5.5 (5)	95 (≥4)	6
Kevin	6.7	35	84	4.9 (4.6)	82 (~3.9)	6
Joseph	7.2	30	66	6.23 (N/A)	95 (≥4)	6

[a]Figures in parentheses indicate the average age at which typically developing children attain the same MLU (Miller & Chapman, 1981). [b]Figures in parentheses indicate the approximate age at which typically developing children achieve equivalent scores of grammatical complexity.

Procedure

The first author visited the home of each child for each of the six sessions. Prior to the original study, the researcher was not familiar with any of the participants, who were recruited via advertisements with autism associations and parent groups. Each visit consisted of the videotaping of child-led spontaneous conversation and activities with the mother, the researcher, or both, depending on the preferences of the children (all five children were keen to interact with the researcher and frequently directed their attention towards her). Gifts consisting of toys (e.g., farm sets, cars, miniature furniture) and activities (e.g., sticker books) were given to the children at the beginning of each session to facilitate interaction (with the intention of eliciting category labels and verbs of action), although many children preferred to play with their own toys. As play was not the focus of the original study, there was no deliberate introduction of play or conscious modelling of play by the researcher or the mothers, nor were the narratives elicited.

Analysis

The corpus consisted of 30 video-recorded interactions, including six sessions per child, each lasting approximately one hour. Transcripts were prepared using the min-CHAT version of the Codes for the Human Analysis of Transcripts (CHAT) system from the Child Language Data Exchange System (CHILDES; Mac-Whinney, 2000). All occurrences of pretend play were identified in the recorded interactions. Pretend play was operationally defined as any thematically cohesive instance of play that included one or more of the following acts (Nielsen & Dissanayake, 2000): object substitution (e.g., pretending a stick is a toothbrush); attribution of imaginary properties (e.g., pretending a doll has a dirty face); imaginative play involving absent objects or imaginary characters (e.g., pretending to use an imaginary hammer); attribution of animacy (e.g., making a doll walk); and role-play (e.g., playing the part of a vet or a teacher). Pretend play sequences were not required to consist of continuous stretches of the discourse, as they could be interrupted by extraneous activities in ways to be described below. Pretend play sequences were identified by the first author and then cross checked with the second author. There was unanimous agreement on the number of play sequences, and the small number of disagreements regarding the boundaries of the play sequences were resolved through discussion.

From the initial set of pretend play instances, pretend play narratives were identified for analysis on the basis of two criteria. First, the narrative had to be initiated and maintained by the child—that is, the child began the story arc and was primarily responsible for the construction of the narrative. Second, these story sequences were judged as narratives if they contained a temporally ordered sequence of events (cf. Labov & Waletzky, 1967; Stein & Glenn, 1982).

This sequence of events could be as minimal as two temporally ordered *complicating action* clauses (Labov, 1972) without necessarily including *orientation* (providing background and setting information) or *evaluation* (the narrator's views on the events). This type of "skeleton" narrative was selected as the minimum structure, primarily because of the context in which pretend play narratives are produced; often they emerge organically as part of play sequences where objects, settings, and roles are already established, and so the orientation is essentially already known to the participants and any audience. This embedded quality is also true more generally of conversational narratives, as described previously.

The narratives were then divided into episodes, where episodes were considered to be discourse-semantic units within the narrative. These units usually contained a sequence of more than one proposition and were characterised by an overarching theme or topic and a coherent sequence of events involving consistency in characters and/or temporal and spatial location (cf. Ji, 2002; Longacre, 1979; Tomlin, 1987; van Dijk, 1982).

For each child, we considered the degree to which they included narratives as defined previously in their pretend play and the complexity of these narratives, measured by their length in number of propositions, number of episodes, and number of characters included. We also assessed the developmental stage and sophistication of the pretend play narratives using two existing metrics: a modification of Applebee's (1978) model of narrative forms (Glaubman et al., 2001) and a scale of narrative competence developed by Glaubman and Fein (n.d.) called the Realistic-Imaginal Scale (RIS).

Applebee's (1978) model of narrative forms is based on earlier studies of concept development by Bruner and colleagues (Bruner, Goodnow, & Austin, 1956; Bruner, Olver, & Greenfield, 1966) and Vygotsky (1962). His model captures the organisation and complexity of children's narratives by treating plots of stories as series of elements that each have their own attributes (e.g., characters, actions, settings, themes). Based on his analysis of stories told by typically developing children aged between 2 and 5, Applebee found six basic types of structures that occurred in a specific developmental progression, represented in Figure 6.2.

The most basic narrative type he termed *heaps*. These stories have a series of events that have very few connecting links. The next level is *sequences*, in which the story elements are linked together because of similarities to a common core of the story, but with no causal connections. Level 3 stories are termed *primitive narratives*, which differ from *sequences* in that the story elements are complementary events organised around a central situation. Level 4 stories contain chained events that are causally related, but there is no overarching theme bringing the elements together into a cohesive narrative—hence the name *unfocused chains*. *Focused chains* are the next level of narrative, and they differ from unfocused chains in that there is a central protagonist who participates in a series of causally linked events. The final level is *narratives* where, as the name suggests, children produce stories that

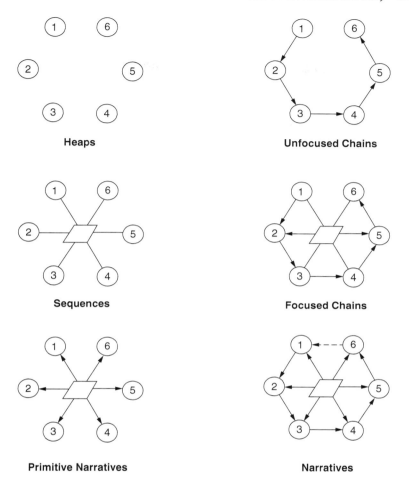

FIGURE 6.2 The six basic structures of children's stories (Applebee, 1978, p. 58; reprinted with permission of publisher).

are organised around a central theme and that contain causal links between the elements.

The second analytical protocol applied was the RIS. Designed to apply to both play and story, it is derived from the work of Bruner (1990) and Fein (1989) and is based on the theory that social pretend play and storytelling are two types of narrative forms in which children must manage a "two tier mental state" (Glaubman & Fein, n.d., p. 2). That is, children shift between the real world—in which the play (or story) is anchored in both the use of physical space and/or cultural conventions (e.g., a tea party script) and in the negotiations that take place about the development of the pretense or story—and the imaginary world in which the characters engage with internal states and fantastical events can occur. The scale is composed of 17 items designed to identify behaviours that demonstrate children's ability to shift between the realistic (i.e., real-world objects, ordinary events, and normative cultural conventions) and the imaginary (e.g., extraordinary events, cognitive and emotional states). These 17 items are arranged into four categories that capture different properties of the connections between the child, the real-world environment, and the world of the play or story. The scale showing the 17 items grouped in the four categories is detailed in tabular form in the Appendix.

The first category is the physical world and includes Items 1 to 4: **objects**, **actions**, **events**, and **locale-spatial**. This category captures children's ability to disengage with the realistic properties of objects (e.g., pretend a pencil is a toothbrush), to ascribe agency to toys (e.g., pretend that a teddy bear has thoughts and feelings), and to imagine events that are not constrained by current place or time of the speech event (e.g., pretend to be in a different place such as the park).

The second category addresses social–cultural content and includes Items 5 to 7: **themes**, **cultural norms**, and **social relations**. These items capture different ways in which children's play or storytelling can reflect or diverge from cultural conventions and social scripts. Children may engage with themes directly borrowed from reality (e.g., family meal time) that involve ordinary activities (e.g., meal preparation) and typical relationships (e.g., parent and child), or they may have fantasy themes involving exceptional events and social relations such as dragons who wish to become Barbie dolls.

The third category deals with inter- and intrapersonal relations and incorporates Items 8 to 12: **roles**, **speech/language**, **affect attribution**, **cognitive attribution**, and **social–cognitive**. This category captures children's portrayal of characters; that is, how grounded in reality are these characters (roles), are they enacted with linguistic mannerisms that are different from those of the child (speech/language), and are these characters presented as experiencing emotions (affect attribution) and mental states (cognitive attribution) and as engaging with the internal states of other characters. Item 12 (social–cognitive) encodes the degree to which the play or story is co-constructed, from simple exchange of dialogue between characters through to extension of each player's contribution.

The final category considers the structural features of play or stories in Items 13 to 17: **action-event frame**, **event structure**, **time reference**, **play/story communicate**, and **cognitive functioning**. The first item (action-event frame) addresses whether children can expand the story structure to include actions or events that enlarge the original story frame or even integrate new events. The next two items encode the complexity of the event structure (e.g., is it a simple, single episode or a series of integrated episodes) and the use of time (e.g., are there specific mentions of time or linguistic encoding of time in the use of tense, or is time indefinite). Item 16 evaluates the ability of children to integrate the multiple roles of the director or narrator with the player or character by "stepping out" of the playframe—the imagined world—in order to explicitly negotiate the direction of the play or story (cf. Giffin's, 1984, work on metacommunication in pretend play). Item 17 (cognitive functioning) is about the ability of children (while in character) to recognise the thoughts and beliefs of their fellow characters and to integrate this in the play or story—for example, explicit statements such as "I think you're sick" through to inferencing such as recognising illness and offering treatment when someone says "I am very hot."

The items are also specified for three levels on the realistic–imaginative continuum, identified as *realistic*, *transitional*, and *imaginal*. Items 6 (cultural relations) and 17 (cognitive functioning) can be coded as realistic or imaginal but not transitional. The distinction is binary for these items since play can only adhere to or deviate from cultural conventions and players' contributions, and responses regarding thoughts and beliefs can only be direct (representational) or inferred (metarepresentational).

For each of the analyses undertaken, the data were double coded by the first author and a second coder. They reached a high level of agreement (between 92% and 94%), and all disparities were resolved through discussion.

Results

Overview of Data

From a total of 66 instances of pretend play in the corpus, 34 pretend play narratives were identified across the five participants. Thirty-three pretend play narratives were included for analysis, and one narrative had to be excluded. A summary of the pretend play narratives is presented in Table 6.2.

David had only one pretend play narrative, which is not surprising given that he was only 3½ years of age. Peter was a prolific storyteller who produced almost three pretend play narratives per session. He was also the only child to produce co-constructed narratives—a point to which we will return later. Liam had only five instances of pretend play, which included only three pretend play narratives; however, he had an interesting approach to storytelling, which explains why there are not more. His approach will be discussed further below. Kevin had a total of five narratives, and Joseph had eight. As Table 6.2 reveals, all of Kevin's and almost all of Joseph's pretend play involved storytelling. Some of the stories are quite long (up to 12 episodes for Peter), and others consist of only a single episode. All of the children include multiple characters in their pretend play narratives, with at least two and as many as eight. As Table 6.2 reveals, the mean length of the pretend play narratives in episodes is around two to three episodes.

130   Susan Douglas and Lesley Stirling

TABLE 6.2 Summary Characteristics of Pretend Play Narratives

	Total instances of pretend play	Total pretend play narratives in play corpus	Mean no. of propositions (length) of narratives	Mean no. of characters in narratives	Mean no. of episodes in narratives
David	25	1	17	2	2
Peter	22	17	28	3	3.5
Liam	5	3[a]	75	4	3.5
Kevin	5	5	23	4	3
Joseph	9	8	30	3	3
Total	66	34			

[a]One story could not be analysed, as it was only partially captured on video.

We see evidence in the pretend play narratives of both enacted narrative and discursive narrative (Nicolopoulou, 2005, 2007). Most often, the children switch between the two modes within single narratives, creating a complex interplay of narrative forms. Table 6.3 illustrates the complex relationship between discursive and enacted narrative within the stories we examined. It identifies and exemplifies at least four possible types of relationships between enacted events and linguistically described or narrated events within the sequential organisation of the play or discursive interaction.[1]

Peter's narratives are often enacted narratives with rich dialogic interactions between characters. However, all of the children include discursive elements that provide a simultaneous narration of the enacted play. As illustrated in Table 6.3, the tense of these discursive elements varies, determined by their relationship to the action but also by the children's verbal abilities and their stylistic choices in expressing their stories. The use of narrative present tense is a well-described phenomenon in adult stories and, as noted previously, "simultaneous narration" (Polanyi, 1989) is more likely to evoke use of the present tense; we find past tense used comparatively little in the event clauses in our corpus.

Narrative Coherence—Applebee (1978) Analysis

The pretend play narratives were individually evaluated using an adaptation of Applebee's (1978) six-level developmental cline of narrative ability in typical development. The different levels of structural sophistication of the children's pretend play narratives are detailed in Table 6.4.

David's single story is sequential in its structure. It is more complicated than a set of unconnected events but has only associative concrete links. According to Applebee (1978), this type of story structure is common for typically developing

TABLE 6.3 Relationships Between Enacted and Discursive Narrative

	Action	Relation	Description
Type 1	Player action	Precedes	Description
Example	Liam makes the toy dragon stomp across the floor.		Liam says, "He's stomping."
Example	Peter and the researcher are making the toy animals chase one another, and the pretend fence breaks.		Peter says, "Oh no, it broke."
Type 2	Player action	Occurs simultaneously with	Description
Example	Peter makes the feet walk across the floor.		Peter says, "Look at my feet! My feet is walking."
Example	David is pretending to eat pretend grapes.		David says, "I eat it a grapes."
Example	Liam makes the toy dragon go inside the doll's house.		Liam says, "And she went back inside."
Type 3	Description as plan or stated intention	Precedes	Player action
Example	Peter says to adult: "You have to make the hippopotamus go up there and get the ball down."		Adult makes the toy hippo go up and get the ball down.
Example	Liam says, in the voice of the Barbie speaking to the dragon, "I'll twist you around."		Liam makes the Barbie twist the dragon and makes the dragon say, "Ow."
Type 4[a]	Player enactment of events	Occurs independent of and interspersed with or linking	Description of other events not enacted
Example	Liam has just finished enacting a dialogue between the dragon and the Barbie, in which the Barbie tells off the dragon for taking her bikini.		Liam says, "And then Barbie went back to sleep."
Example	Prior to this contribution, Liam is producing represented speech, and after it he is trying to take a dress off the toy dragon and discussing this with the researcher.		Liam says, "And then she went back to bed and she pulled off her clothes and she pretended it was a dragon's get married."

[a]Our examples of this type come primarily from the most discursive narrative in our corpus, the "Dragon Barbie" story by Liam. Liam even distinguishes prosodically between the narrated clauses and other linguistic contributions that include represented speech by the characters and asides to the researcher.

132 Susan Douglas and Lesley Stirling

TABLE 6.4 Applebee (1978) Scores for Structural Complexity of Pretend Play Narratives

Child	Applebee scores						Total
	Level 1: Heaps	Level 2: Sequences	Level 3: Primitive narratives	Level 4: Unfocused chains	Level 5: Focused chains	Level 6: Narratives	
David	0	1	0	0	0	0	1
Peter	0	2	4	7	4	0	17
Liam	0	0	0	1	0	1	2
Kevin	0	2	0	1	2	0	5
Joseph	0	0	2	2	4	0	8
Total	0	5	6	11	10	1	33

2-year-olds and is still present in the narratives of 3-year-olds. Peter's stories are predominantly between Levels 3 and 5, with most at Level 4—unfocused chains. At this stage of development (typically occurring at age 3), children often shift from one episode to the next without any real continuity or central theme. This type of narrative is not unexpected in the context of pretend play because of the dynamic nature of the play and the spontaneous evolution of the plot and hence the narrative. Despite having only two analysable stories, Liam is the only child to produce a Level 6 narrative—that is, a narrative with a fully developed theme that is central to all of the causally linked episodes. In typical development, Level 6 narratives begin to appear at age 3 and are more prevalent by age 5, although focused chains are still more common. Kevin's pretend play narratives range from sequences (Level 2) to focused chains (Level 5), where the episodes are causally linked, but there is no central theme. Interestingly, Applebee (1978) notes that this type of narrative structure is typical of adventure stories, which is the predominant pretend play narrative genre of Kevin's stories. The majority of Joseph's stories are also Level 5, with no examples of Applebee's narratives category. However, they are more sophisticated in other ways, which we will discuss next.

Narrative Sophistication—Realistic–Imaginal Scale

The pretend play narratives were also analysed using the RIS (Glaubman & Fein, n.d.), which measures narratives on a continuum from those involving concrete characters and events grounded in the children's own sphere through to those containing story elements that are displaced from children's observable reality. As detailed previously, the scale includes 17 items grouped into four categories, which (excluding Items 6 and 17) can be cross coded as realistic, transitional, or imaginal. While the scale was originally developed to analyse both storytelling and social pretend play, we used it in this study to analyse the sophistication of the pretend play narratives produced by the children with ASD.

Each episode within the 33 analysable pretend play narratives was coded as realistic, transitional, or imaginal across the four subcategories. The scores for all episodes for each child's pretend play narratives were combined to produce an average score for that child. Given the small number of children studied and the well-known heterogeneity of the population of children with ASD, we discuss the profile for each child in turn. The graphs in Figures 6.3–6.7 show the proportional distribution over the three levels of the RIS—realistic, transitional, and imaginal—for each of the four subcategories for each child.

David's data show that his single pretend play narrative is very much grounded in reality: that is, realistic events with typical social–cultural content. The setting is a toy car park with a petrol station, and the action involves parking a car and then filling the petrol tank. Transitional elements appear in the categories of inter- and intrapersonal relations and structural features where he plays a character other than himself (the driver of the car) in the pretend play narrative, and the structure is a chain of events.

For Peter's pretend play narratives, the physical worlds and social–cultural content are most frequently transitional to imaginal, where object use is regularly symbolic (e.g., sticks become hammers), and there is considerable make-believe (e.g., the action takes place in remote imaginative settings such as parks). For the inter- and intrapersonal relations, modality, character roles, and character speech are highly imaginative, including anthropomorphised trains that walk on legs and a hippopotamus as a doctor. There is some attribution of psychological states in Peter's pretend play narratives, such as when the miniature toy lion (controlled by Peter) tells the miniature toy hippopotamus (controlled by the researcher): "Hey, I'm scared of the monster." However, it is often absent. Structurally, the narratives tend to be simple

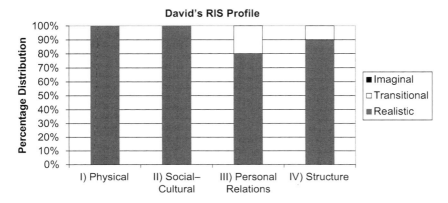

FIGURE 6.3 Realistic–Imaginal Scale profile for David.

134 Susan Douglas and Lesley Stirling

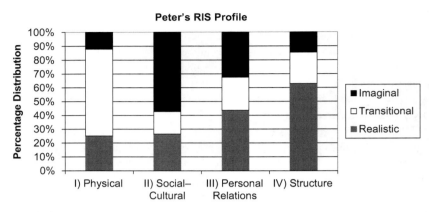

FIGURE 6.4 Realistic–Imaginal Scale profile for Peter.

event chains, but Peter does demonstrate good metacommunicative competence in the construction of the pretend play narratives; he is able to switch from playing a character to directing the researcher, as demonstrated in the exchange in Example 1.

1. Child and researcher are playing with miniature animals and a toy fire station that includes a petrol pump. Child addresses researcher.

Child: You have to hold the hippopotamus.
[Child addresses the hippopotamus, now held by the researcher]
Child: Hippopotamus, you have to fix the petrol.
Researcher: What's wrong with the petrol?
Child: It needs fixing to fix.
Researcher: It needs fixing.
[Researcher makes the hippopotamus try to fix the petrol pump]

(P4: 1427–1432)

As well as demonstrating a high level of narrative ability on Applebee's developmental cline, the sophistication of Liam's pretend play narratives is also evident in the high proportions of transitional and imaginal elements across all four categories of the RIS. The fantastical themes of Liam's narratives and the counter-conventional cultural norms and social relations are indicated in Figure 6.4 in the very high proportion *of imaginal* elements in the social–cultural content. In Liam's pretend play narratives, dragons break into Barbies' houses and steal their bikinis. Similarly, high proportions of imaginal and transitional elements are present in the inter- and intrapersonal relations in terms of the character roles and representations of psychological states, as shown in Example 2.

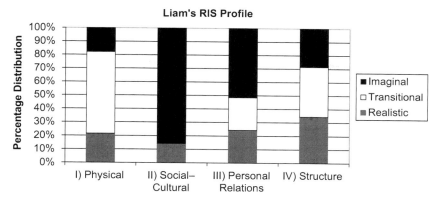

FIGURE 6.5 Realistic–Imaginal Scale profile for Liam.

2. Child pretends that the dragon (who he has just dressed up in a Barbie bikini) is talking.

Child: Oh look at me, I'm dragon Barbie.
Child: And she went back inside.
[The following is a dialogue between the dragon and a Barbie]
Child: Hello.
Child: A dragon Barbie?
Child: You're so little, Barbie.
Child: Are you too little?
Child: It's a dragon dressed up with my 'kini.
Child: You naughty dragon.

(L3: 742–751)

The structural features of Liam's pretend play narratives are also well developed, including complex event structures and explicit references to time. Liam also engaged in metacommunication and could shift easily between the roles of player and director.

Kevin's pretend play narratives are much more grounded in reality. The physical world is depicted in realistic actions and objects but with events played out in imaginary settings. The social–cultural content most frequently adheres to conventional themes, cultural norms, and social relations, while the inter- and intrapersonal relations include more imaginal elements such as less commonplace characters (e.g., fighter pilots) and the representation of character speech, as shown in Example 3.

3. The toy plane has been shot down, and a rescue mission is taking place. The child is talking to the researcher.

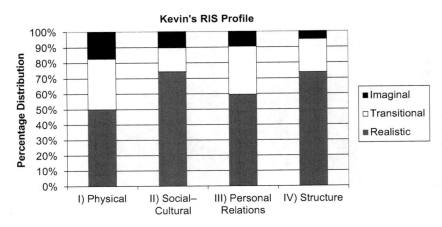

FIGURE 6.6 Realistic–Imaginal Scale profile for Kevin.

Child: The other planes are smashed.
Researcher: Yeah?
Child: The xxx one.
Child: I'm trying to get . . . get the guys out.
Researcher: Yeah, how are they gonna get them out?
Child: They're trying to get them out.
Researcher: Is it working?
Child: Yep.
Researcher: Excellent.
Child: And backwards and forwards.
[Child begins a dialogue between the imaginary drivers of the vehicles]
Child: What's happened to the aeroplane?
Child: Aeroplane got fire.
Child: It got smashed.

(K2: 2482–2495)

The structural features of Kevin's pretend play narratives also tend to be more grounded in reality, containing simple events without specific time references, and there is only infrequent engagement in metacommunication.

Joseph's pretend play narratives include a high proportion of imaginal elements in the physical world category. This reflects the fact that many of his pretend play narratives were constructed without the support of props because the setting, characters, and events are entirely imaginary. In contrast, the social–cultural content, the inter- and intrapersonal relations, and particularly the structural features were more realistic and transitional, as they typically included Joseph as himself or familiar figures, and there was little representation of character speech. However, Joseph did produce pretend play narratives that borrowed heavily from culture-specific fantasy

Intersection of Pretense and Story   **137**

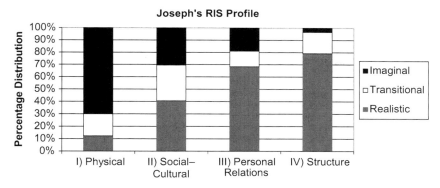

FIGURE 6.7 Realistic–Imaginal Scale profile for Joseph.

scripts such as a long narrative about secret conversations with Santa Claus and an interaction with Harry Potter (the boy wizard; Example 4).

4. *Child:* Um, at school today, me and ha- Harry Potter . . .
   Researcher: Mmm?
   Child: . . . was trying to do this.
   [Child mimicks the duelling scene from the movie Harry Potter and the Chamber of Secrets, holding up an imaginary wand in front of his body]
   Researcher: Yeah?
   Child: And we were trying to do this.
   [Child performs the same action]
   Researcher: Yeah?
   Child: Then, we walked.
   Researcher: Oh, you had a wizard's duel.
   Child: Then . . . and then . . .
   Researcher: Who won?
   Child: Then went back.
   Researcher: Yeah?
   Child: Then I said a spell.
   [Child makes crashing noises and waves his imaginary wand]
   (J4: 1352–1368)

Scoring of Individual Items

One of the features of the scoring system for the Realistic–Imaginal Scale is that items within each of the four categories may not necessarily be rated as present in the pretend play narratives, but this is not evident in the proportional distribution for each child presented in Figures 6.3–6.7. Given that many of the 17 items of the

RIS capture features that are noted in the literature as being challenging for children with ASD, we wanted to see how the children in our study profiled with respect to these specific items. Investigation of the raw data revealed that the children's pretend play narratives often did not contain items from the inter- and intrapersonal relations subcategory. The most often excluded item was affect attribution, which addresses the expression of emotion. This was the case for all participants except Liam. It was absent even from pretend play narratives where you might expect emotional expression or comment on the emotional state of the characters, such as Kevin's plane crash scenario and Joseph's duel with Harry Potter.

The second most excluded item was social–cognitive, which captures communication between the players or characters. The absence of this feature can be directly attributed to the fact that the majority of pretend play narratives were produced by the children with little scope for creative input from others—a point to which we will return below. The final item excluded only sometimes was cognitive attribution, which ascribes physical perceptions at the realistic level through to attribution of mental processes at the imaginal level. This is consistent with the cognitive profile of ASD. However, typically developing children often leave out these elements in a story until around the age of 9 (Bamberg & Damrad-Frye, 1991). Since the oldest child in this group was only 7 years of age, it is not possible to comment in this study beyond noting the absence of this item.

Additional Characteristics of the Children's Pretend Play Narratives

One quality of the pretend play narratives that is not captured by either the Applebee (1978) scale or the RIS but that demonstrates an unexpected skill level in the children was that, irrespective of the complexity of the structure or the sophistication of the narratives, all of the children demonstrated a surprising capacity for maintaining a story schema. This is reflected in the ability of the children to come back to the story, even after long periods of interruption between episodes. These interruptions could take the form of negotiations about how the story should proceed or a shift in attention to activities or topics outside the story before returning for another episode. An extension of this phenomenon is found in one of Kevin's stories in which the story structure, represented schematically in Figure 6.8, includes two uninterrupted episodes followed by a short break, two more episodes followed by a long break, and a summary of the story so far before continuation to a final episode.

A final feature we want to consider is an interesting phenomenon we have labelled *storyboarding*. This where the children spend a lot of time setting up a pretend play narrative—constructing an orientation—but no actual narrative eventuates. There are examples of this in Peter's data, but it occurs most often in Liam's data. For example, Liam spends time preparing the physical space for play with a felt doll and a felt board: making a sun and a butterfly because it was going to be a sunny day in the park and deciding which of the felt doll's clothes would

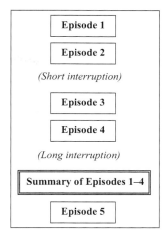

FIGURE 6.8 Schematic representation of a pretend play narrative by Kevin.

be most appropriate for a bike ride. Although Liam only produced three pretend play narratives, he spent a lot of time setting up pretend scenarios—often in great detail—only to abandon them for a new idea or a variation on the play theme. In one session, he spent approximately 30 min in continuous storyboarding.

Collaboration in Pretend Play Narratives

Researchers have commented on the challenge for children with ASD that engaging in social play presents (e.g., Wolfberg, 2009). The question, then, of whether or not the children in this study collaborate in the construction of the pretend play narratives is worth considering in detail. The analysis from the RIS revealed that very few are collaborative to the extent that the child allowed the researcher (or mother) to co-construct the narratives. In other research, we have undertaken detailed analysis of the types of interactions between the adults and the children in the development of pretend play scenarios (Douglas & Stirling, 2012a, 2012b), but here we talk more generally about the nature of the engagement.

David's single pretend play narrative contains no initiations from him to include the adult play partner. However, questions and comments from the adults about the plot and the scene setting are positively acknowledged, indicating that he is still engaged with the adults and that minimal creative input is accepted. Most frequently, David's interaction indicates that the adult is positioned as the audience.

Peter allows the adult play partner to participate in the pretend play narratives in a number of ways: Sometimes the adult is situated as the audience, but he also invites the adult play partner to take on character roles—there are nine instances of this in the data. The character assignments are achieved in sometimes quite subtle ways

140 Susan Douglas and Lesley Stirling

(e.g., he will pass the researcher a toy and address the toy, or he will keep talking to a toy until the researcher takes on the role of that toy and responds appropriately). Evidence of co-construction in Peter's pretend play narratives is also found in the nature of the negotiations between Peter and the researcher, which occur outside the narrative: Contributions from the researcher regarding plot development, introduction of characters, and scene setting are sometimes accepted. This suggests that, on occasion, the adult is permitted to participate in the creative story construction process.

Liam's pretend play narratives suggest a misalignment of expectations between him and the researcher regarding participant roles. He does not accommodate the researcher's attempts to participate in the co-construction of the pretend play narratives, but he does actively recruit the researcher to be the audience; although the researcher does successfully offer input on two occasions, contributions that recognise Liam's creative control are more likely to be successful. Liam's storytelling is highly engaged with the adult play partner, even if the adult's role is predominantly designated as the audience.

Similar to Liam, Kevin also actively engages the adult as the audience for his narratives. We see evidence of this in his frequent use of vocatives in invitations such as "Something's inside that, Sarah" (K2: 2457). Moreover, contributions that are rejected by Kevin include attempts at co-construction such as new plot elements and suggestions for pretend play narratives. Contributions from the researcher are predominantly about extending or confirming Kevin's established plots, indicating that the audience role is often accepted.

Joseph also frequently positions the researcher as the audience in his pretend play narratives. The interaction includes many successful attempts to engage the adult as the audience, such as the use of vocatives and questions such as "You heard that?" (J5: 728). However, endeavours by the researcher to participate in the development of the narrative are most likely to be unsuccessful.

Discussion and Conclusion

The pretend play narratives we analysed as part of the current study provide further evidence that pretense and storytelling are indeed closely intertwined activities. Nicolopoulou (2005, 2007, this volume) describes pretend play and storytelling as distinct but complementary modes of children's narrative activity in early development that may overlap (cf. also Stagnitti, this volume). We found that the children in our study would switch between discursive narrative (prototypical storytelling) and enacted narrative (acting out of pretend play scripts) within pretend play narratives. Most frequently, we found that children would use discursive elements to provide an explanatory gloss for the enacted play, creating simultaneous narration.

Researchers have argued that in pretend play, the role-play dimension means that young children are focused on character development with particular reference to connecting people's actions with intentions, desires, and beliefs about the world (see Kavanaugh & Engel, 1998). Nicolopoulou (2005, 2007) suggested that the nature of pretend play emphasises this focus, whereas the development of early narrative skills outside the context of play is centred on plot structure. Interestingly, we found that, with the exception of Liam, the children in our study did not appear to be focused on the internal states of characters. The analysis using the RIS revealed that there was often little representation of the affective and cognitive states of characters, and even when the children were storyboarding, the focus of the planning was on plot development and the necessary scene setting. However, our results are consistent with the deficits in social–emotional reciprocity that are a diagnostic feature of ASD (APA, 2013).

Recent research on pretend play and ASD has found that children can participate in elicited pretense, engage in spontaneous pretense, and even derive pleasure from the experience (Chaudry & Dissanayake, this volume; Douglas & Stirling, 2012a, 2012b; Kelly, 2007; Mifsud et al., 2009; Prescott, 2003). Our analyses in the current study reveal that not only can children with ASD engage in acts of pretense, they can also construct pretend scenarios with sequences of narrative events that can be classified as pretend play narratives. While there is variation in the structural coherence and the sophistication of the pretend play narratives, all of the children produce at least one narrative—including the youngest child at 3½ years of age. The coding according to the Applebee (1978) scheme of narrative coherence revealed that the children most often produced narratives that were structured around a central theme—sometimes with but often without causal connections—or unfocused chains of events. This is consistent with other studies that have found that narratives produced by children with ASD are not as structurally sophisticated as the narratives of typically developing children of comparable ages (Diehl et al., 2006; Losh & Capps, 2003). However, the structure of pretend play narratives, in general, is less like prototypical monologic narratives and more closely resembles conversational narratives (Norrick, 2000). As Norrick has stated, conversational narratives may lack a clear sequence of events and may not have a definitive resolution. We found similar features in the pretend play narratives produced by the children. Further parallels we identified in the data include interruptions, repetitions, and negotiations over content.

The RIS rated the pretend play narratives in terms of narrative sophistication with a focus on the ability of the children to shift between the realistic elements and the more abstract and imaginary elements. We found that the pretend play narratives of Liam and, to a lesser extent, Peter reflected a stronger separation from reality than those of the other children across the three subcategories of the physical world, social–cultural content, and personal relations. Liam in particular engaged with highly imaginative concepts with unusual themes and strong character development that incorporated internal mental processes. In contrast, David's and Kevin's stories were more closely connected to realistic depictions of actions, objects, and events with characters that were outside their personal experience but not highly imaginative. For Joseph, the story structure and content were grounded in reality but separated from the physical world in the imaginative depiction of objects, actions, and events. The RIS also revealed that very few of the pretend play narratives were collaborative to the extent that the child and the researcher (or mother) co-constructed the narratives. While there was communication about the plots, characters, and settings between the children and the adults, what this metacommunication reflected was a strong preference for most of the children to control the development of the pretend play narratives (cf. also Douglas & Stirling, 2012a). The nature of the interaction is that the children did engage the adult play partner in their pretend play narratives, but this varied from the adult as the audience through to clearer attempts to establish collective intentionality and to act jointly in the pursuit of a collaboratively produced pretend play narrative.

In summary, the children in our study (particularly Peter and Liam) demonstrated an encouraging capacity for engaging with the complex cognitive task of pretend play narrative production. The social communication difficulties children on the spectrum experience mean that they face unique challenges to successful peer interaction in the domain of social imaginary play. The preliminary findings of this original research detail the strengths and weaknesses of pretend play narrative abilities in a small group of children with ASD and highlight areas for potential interventions that would promote successful peer engagement in social pretense. To build on these preliminary findings, future research should be conducted with a larger group of children with ASD in order to provide a stronger profile of their capacity to engage in pretense and storytelling. Further studies should also include a comparison group of typically developing children and extend the research to analyse narrative and pretense in children with ASD engaged in peer group play.

Acknowledgements

We are grateful to the children and their families for their participation in this research. We also thank two anonymous reviewers and Artin Göncü for their comments. Material in this chapter was presented at the Autism Victoria Research Forum in 2009, and we also thank members of the audience for their feedback.

Note

1   We do not address the full range of complexities here. In particular, instances vary between whether the narration consists of simultaneous description of ongoing actions or whether it is of a more prototypical kind and hence could appear as a narrative clause in an oral narrative told independent of play. All examples here are from the child; we leave to one side contributions by the adult.

References

American Psychiatric Association. (1994). *Diagnostic and statistical manual of mental disorders* (4th ed.). Washington, DC: Author.
American Psychiatric Association. (2000). *Diagnostic and statistical manual of mental disorders* (4th ed., text rev.). Washington, DC: Author.

American Psychiatric Association. (2013). *Diagnostic and statistical manual of mental disorders* (5th ed.). Washington, DC: Author.

Applebee, A. (1978). *The child's concept of story: Ages two to seventeen*. Chicago, IL: University of Chicago Press.

Bamberg, M., & Damrad-Frye, R. (1991). On the ability to provide evaluative comments: Further explorations of children's narrative competencies. *Journal of Child Language, 18,* 689–710.

Bauman, R. (1986). *Story, performance, and event: Contextual studies of oral narrative*. Cambridge, UK: Cambridge University Press.

Begeer, S., Malle, B., Nieuwland, M., & Keysar, B. (2010). Using theory of mind to represent and take part in social interactions: Comparing individuals with high-functioning autism and typically developing controls. *European Journal of Developmental Psychology, 7*(1), 104–122.

Benson, M. (1993). The structure of four- and five-year-olds' narratives in pretend play and storytelling. *First Language, 13,* 203–223.

Bruner, E. (1986). Ethnography as narrative. In V. Turner & E. Bruner (Eds.), *The anthropology of experience* (pp. 139–155). Champaign: University of Illinois Press.

Bruner, J. (1990). *Acts of meaning*. Cambridge, MA: Harvard University Press.

Bruner, J., Goodnow, J., & Austin, G. (1956). *A study of thinking*. New York, NY: Wiley.

Bruner, J., Olver, R., & Greenfield, P. (1966). *Studies in cognitive growth: A collaboration at the Center for Cognitive Studies*. New York, NY: Wiley.

Capps, L., Kehres, J., & Sigman, M. (1998). Conversational abilities among children with autism and children with developmental delays. *Autism, 2*(4), 325–344.

Capps, L., Losh, M., & Thurber, C. (2000). "The frog ate the bug and made his mouth sad": Narrative competence in children with autism. *Journal of Abnormal Child Psychology, 28*(2), 193–204.

Colle, L., Baron-Cohen, S., Wheelwright, S., & van der Lely, H. (2008). Narrative discourse in adults with high-functioning autism or Asperger syndrome. *Journal of Autism and Developmental Disorders, 38,* 28–40.

Diehl, J., Bennetto, L., & Young, E. (2006). Story recall and narrative coherence of high-functioning children with autism spectrum disorders. *Journal of Abnormal Child Psychology, 34*(1), 87–102.

Douglas, S. (2012). *Understanding actions, states, and events: Verb learning in children with autism*. Berlin, Germany: de Gruyter.

Douglas, S., & Stirling, L. (2012a). Metacommunication, social pretend play and children with autism. *Australasian Journal of Early Childhood, 37*(4), 34–43.

Douglas, S., & Stirling, L. (2012b). *Social pretend play in autism: Negotiated shared pretence and collective intentionality*. Unpublished manuscript.

Fein, G. (1989). Mind, meaning, and affect: Proposals for a theory of pretense. *Developmental Review, 9,* 345–363.

Freeman, S., & Kasari, C. (2013). Parent-child interaction in autism: Characteristics of play. *Autism, 17,* 147–161.

Galda, L. (1984). Narrative competence: Play, storytelling, and story comprehension. In A. Pellegrini & T. Yawkey (Eds.), *The development of oral and written language in social contexts* (pp. 105–117). Norwood, NJ: Ablex.

Galda, L., & Pellegrini, A. (Eds.). (2007). *Play, language, and stories* (2nd ed.). Norwood, NJ: Ablex.

Garvey, C. (1990). *Play*. Cambridge, MA: Harvard University Press.

Giffin, H. (1984). The coordination of meaning in the creation of a shared make-believe reality. In I. Bretherton (Ed.), *Symbolic play: The development of social understanding* (pp. 73–100). Orlando, FL: Academic Press.

Glaubman, R., & Fein, G. (n.d.). *Narrative competence in pretense play and stories*. Unpublished manuscript.

Glaubman, R., Kashi, G., & Koresh, R. (2001). Facilitating the narrative quality of sociodramatic play. In A. Göncü & E. Klein (Eds.), *Children in play, story, and school* (pp. 132–157). New York, NY: Guilford Press.

Göncü, A., & Klein, E. (Eds). (2001). *Children in play, story, and school*. New York, NY: Guilford Press.

Harris, P. (2000). *The work of the imagination*. Oxford, UK: Wiley-Blackwell.

Hobson, J., Hobson, P., Malik, S., Bargiota, K., & Calo, S. (2013). The relation between social engagement and pretend play in autism. *British Journal of Developmental Psychology, 31,* 114–127.

Hobson, R., Lee, A., & Hobson, J. (2009). Qualities of symbolic play among children with autism. *Journal of Autism and Developmental Disorders, 39,* 12–22.

Jarrold, C., Boucher, J., & Smith, P. (1996). Generativity deficits in pretend play in autism. *British Journal of Developmental Psychology, 14,* 275–300.

Jarrold, C., Smith, P., Boucher, J., & Harris, P. (1994). Comprehension of pretense in children with autism. *Journal of Autism and Developmental Disorders, 24,* 433–455.

Ji, S. (2002). Identifying episode transitions. *Journal of Pragmatics, 34,* 1257–1271.

Jordan, R. (2003). Social play and autistic spectrum disorders. *Autism, 7,* 347–360.

Kasari, C., Chang, Y.-C., & Patterson, S. (2013). Pretending to play or playing to pretend. *American Journal of Play, 6,* 124–135.

Kavanaugh, R., & Engel, S. (1998). The development of pretense and narrative in early childhood. In O.N. Saracho & B. Spodek (Eds.), *Multiple perspectives on play in early childhood education* (pp. 80–99). Albany: State University of New York Press.

Kavanaugh, R.D., & Harris, P.L. (1994). Imagining the outcome of pretend transformations: Assessing the competence of normal and autistic children. *Developmental Psychology, 30,* 847–854.

Kelly, R. (2007). *The role of executive functions in the pretend play of children with high-functioning autism* (Unpublished doctoral dissertation). La Trobe University, Melbourne, VIC, Australia.

Klin, A. (2000). Attributing social meaning to ambiguous visual stimuli in higher-functioning autism and Asperger syndrome: The Social Attribution Task. *Journal of Child Psychology and Psychiatry, 41*(7), 831–846.

Labov, W. (1972). The transformation of experience in narrative syntax. In W. Labov (Ed.), *Language in the inner city: Studies in the black English vernacular* (pp. 354–396). Philadelphia: University of Pennsylvania Press.

Labov, W., & Waletzky, J. (1967). Narrative analysis: Oral versions of personal experience. In J. Helm (Ed.), *Essays on the verbal and visual arts* (pp. 12–44). Seattle: University of Washington Press.

Lewis, V., & Boucher, J. (1988). Spontaneous, instructed and elicited play in relatively able autistic children. *British Journal of Developmental Psychology, 6,* 325–339.

Lillard, A., Lerner, M., Hopkins, E., Dore, R., Smith, E., & Palmquist, C. (2013). The impact of pretend play on children's development: A review of the evidence. *Psychological Bulletin, 139*(1), 1–34.

Longacre, R. (1979). The paragraph as a grammatical unit. In T. Givón (Ed.), *Syntax and Semantics 12: Discourse and syntax* (pp. 311–335). New York, NY: Academic Press.

Losh, M., & Capps, L. (2003). Narrative ability in high-functioning children with autism or Asperger's syndrome. *Journal of Autism and Developmental Disorders, 33*(3), 239–251.

MacWhinney, B. (2000). *The CHILDES Project: Tools for analyzing talk*. Mahwah, NJ: Erlbaum.

Mifsud, J. (2011). *A further investigation of the symbolic play of children with HFA and TD children* (Unpublished doctoral dissertation). La Trobe University, Melbourne, VIC, Australia.

Mifsud, J., Kelly, R., Dissanayake, C., & Leekam, S. (2009, May). *Symbolic play in high-functioning autism: How "playful" is their play?* Poster session presented at the International Meeting for Autism Research, Chicago, IL.

Miller, J., & Chapman, R. (1981). The relations between age and mean length of utterance. *Journal of Speech and Hearing Research, 24,* 154–161.

Nicolopoulou, A. (2005). Play and narrative in the process of development: Commonalities, differences, and interrelations. *Cognitive Development, 20,* 495–502.

Nicolopoulou, A. (2007). The interplay of play and narrative in children's development: Theoretical reflections and concrete examples. In A. Göncü & S. Gaskins (Eds.), *Play and development: Evolutionary, sociocultural and functional perspectives* (pp. 247–273). Mahwah, NJ: Erlbaum.

Nicolopoulou, A., & Ilgaz, H. (2013). What do we know about pretend play and narrative development? A response to Lillard, Lerne, Hopkins, Dore, Smith, and Palmquist on "The impact of pretend play on children's development: A review of the evidence." *American Journal of Play, 6*(1), 55–81.

Nielsen, M., & Dissanayake, C. (2000). An investigation of pretend play, mental state terms, and false belief understanding: In search of a metarepresentational link. *British Journal of Developmental Psychology, 18,* 609–624.

Norbury, C., & Bishop, D. (2003). Narrative skills of children with communication impairments. *International Journal of Language & Communication Disorders, 38*(3), 287–313.

Norrick, N. (2000). *Conversational narrative: Storytelling in everyday talk.* Amsterdam, Netherlands: Benjamins.

Ochs, E., & Capps, L. (2001). Living narrative: Creating lives in everyday storytelling. *Language in Society, 34,* 470–474.

Paley, V. (1990). *The boy who would be a helicopter: The uses of storytelling in the classroom.* Cambridge, MA: Harvard University Press.

Piaget, J. (1962). *Play, dreams and imitation in childhood.* New York, NY: de Gruyter.

Pier, J. (2003). On the semiotic parameters of narrative: A critique of story and discourse. In T. Kindt & H.-H. Müller (Eds.), *What is narratology? Questions and answers regarding the status of a theory* (pp. 73–97). Berlin, Germany: de Gruyter.

Polanyi, L. (1989). *Telling the American story: A structural and cultural analysis of conversational storytelling.* Cambridge, MA: MIT Press.

Prendeville, J., Prelock, P., & Unwin, G. (2006). Peer play interventions to support the social competence of children with autism spectrum disorders. *Seminars in Speech and Language, 27,* 32–46.

Prescott, S. (2003). *An investigation of the symbolic play abilities of children with high functioning autism, children with Asperger's disorder and typically developing children* (Unpublished doctoral dissertation). La Trobe University, Melbourne, VIC, Australia.

Roskos, K., & Christie, J. (Eds.). (2000). *Play and literacy in early childhood.* Mahwah, NJ: Erlbaum.

Scarborough, H.S. (1990). Index of Productive Syntax. *Applied Psycholinguistics, 11,* 1–22.

Schopler, E., Reichler, R., & Renner, B. (1988). *The Childhood Autism Rating Scale (CARS).* Los Angeles, CA: Western Psychological Services.

Schuler, A., & Fletcher, C. (2002). Making communication meaningful: Cracking the language interaction code. In R. Gabriels & D. Hill (Eds.), *Autism: From research to individualized practice* (pp. 41–52). London, UK: Kingsley.

Sigman, M., & Ruskin, E. (1999). Continuity and change in the social competence of children with autism, Down syndrome, and developmental delays. *Monographs of the Society for Research in Child Development, 64,* 1–114.

Solomon, O. (2004). Narrative introductions: Discourse competence of children with autistic spectrum disorders. *Discourse Studies, 6*(2), 253–276.

Stein, N., & Glenn, C. (1979). An analysis of story comprehension in elementary school children. In R.O. Freedle (Ed.), *New directions in discourse processing: Advances in discourse processing* (Vol. 2, pp. 53–120). Norwood, NJ: Ablex.

Stirling, L., & Barrington, G. (2007). "Then I'll huff and I'll puff or I'll go on the roff!" thinks the wolf: Spontaneous written narratives by a child with autism. In A. Schalley & D. Khlentzos (Eds.), *Mental states: Language and cognitive structure* (Vol. 2, pp. 133–171). Amsterdam, Netherlands: Benjamins.

Stirling, L., Barrington, G., Douglas, S., & Delves, K. (in press). "I'll blow your house down by your cinie cin chin": Recall, structure, and complexity in written story retellings by typically developing children and children with Autism Spectrum Disorders. In L. Naigles (Ed.), *Innovative investigations of language in autism spectrum disorder.* Washington, DC: APA Books.

Stirling, L., Douglas, S., Leekam, S., & Carey, L. (2014). The use of narrative in studying communication in Autism Spectrum Disorders: A review of methodologies and findings. In J. Arciuli & J. Brock (Eds.), *Communication in autism* (pp. 171–216). Amsterdam, Netherlands: Benjamins.

Tager-Flusberg, H. (1995). "Once upon a ribbit": Stories narrated by autistic children. *British Journal of Developmental Psychology, 13*(1), 45–59.

Tager-Flusberg, H., & Sullivan, K. (1995). Attributing mental states to story characters: A comparison of narratives produced by autistic and mentally retarded individuals. *Applied Psycholinguistics, 16*(3), 241–256.

Tomlin, R. (1987). Linguistic reflections of cognitive events. In R. Tomlin (Ed.), *Coherence and grounding in discourse* (pp. 455–479). Amsterdam, Netherlands: Benjamins.

Toolan, M. (1988). *Narrative: A critical linguistic introduction.* London, UK: Routledge.

Trabasso, T., Secco, T., & Van den Broek, P. (1984). Causal cohesion and story coherence. In H. Mandle, N. Stein, & T. Trabasso (Eds.), *Learning and comprehension of text* (pp. 83–111). Hillsdale, NJ: Erlbaum.

Trawick-Smith, J. (1998). A qualitative analysis of metaplay in the preschool years. *Early Childhood Research Quarterly, 13*(3), 433–452.

van Dijk, T. (1982). Episodes as units of discourse analysis. In D. Tannen (Ed.), *Analyzing discourse: Text and talk* (pp. 177–195). Washington, DC: Georgetown University Press.

Vygotsky, L. (1962). *Thought and language.* Cambridge, MA: MIT Press.

Vygotsky, L. (1978). *Mind in society.* Cambridge, MA: Harvard University Press.

Wechsler, D. (1989). *Wechsler Preschool and Primary Scale of Intelligence—Revised.* San Antonio, TX: Psychological Corporation.

Wechsler, D. (2002). *Wechsler Primary and Preschool Scale of Intelligence—Third Edition (WPPSI–III).* San Antonio, TX: Harcourt Assessment.

Wolfberg, P. (2009). *Play and imagination in children with autism* (2nd ed.). New York, NY: Teachers College Press.

Wolfberg, P., Bottema-Beutel, K., & DeWitt, M. (2012). Including children with autism in social and imaginary play with typical peers: Integrated Play Groups model. *American Journal of Play, 5,* 55–80.

Wolfberg, P., & Schuler, A. (1999). Fostering peer interaction, imaginative play and spontaneous language in children with autism. *Child Language Teaching and Therapy, 15,* 41–52.

Appendix

ITEMS FROM THE REALISTIC–IMAGINAL SCALE (AFTER GLAUBMAN & FEIN, N.D.)

I. The Physical World

	Realistic	*Transitional*	*Imaginal*
1. Objects	Realistic	Substitutional	No actual object
2. Actions	Realistic	Imitative make-believe	No actual action
3. Events	"As if" contextualised events	Restructured pretend events	"What if" events Remote or novel combinations
4. Locale-spatial	Compatible with props	Not typical of props	Remote imaginative setting

II. Social–Cultural Content

	Realistic	*Transitional*	*Imaginal*
5. Themes	Mundane activity	Special occasions	Unusual or fantastic
6. Cultural norms	Conventional	—	Exceptional or counterconventional
7. Social relations	In keeping with role status	Irregular	Deviant

III. Inter- and Intrapersonal Relations

	Realistic	*Transitional*	*Imaginal*
8. Roles	As a child, resembling player	Familiar figure	Fantasy, remote figure
9. Speech/language	Self-speech	Phrases, idioms	Speech of remote beings; rare adult terms
10. Affect attribution	Behavioural expression of emotion	Label of global state	Explicit attribution of emotion or mental state
11. Cognitive attribution	Ascribing physical perception and sensation	Attribution of indirect attention	Attribution of mental process
12. Social–cognitive	Verbal messages between players or characters	Reaction to others' message	Elaboration of others' message

IV. Structural Features

	Realistic	*Transitional*	*Imaginal*
13. Action-event frame	Maintain frame	Enrich, enlarge frame	External event integrated into episode
14. Event structure	Simple: one to two elements	Longer chain	Complex structure
15. Time reference	Indefinite, taken for granted	Time specifically mentioned in continuum with event	Time stated explicitly, remote from ongoing event
16. Play/story communicate	In-play, in-role enactment; director/ narrator roles	Metacommunication/ metaplay	Integration of player and director roles
17. Cognitive functioning	Representational	—	Metarepresentational/ Mental representation of other's representation

Reference

Glaubman, R., & Fein, G. (n.d.). *Narrative competence in pretense play and stories.* Unpublished manuscript.

7

DAD! YOU HAVE TO BE . . .

Autism, Narrative, and Family

Neil Maclean

Imagination is something that is different in each person. For me, it was making my lists, creating fictional genealogies of characters, planning imaginary ball games with players on baseball cards, creating different languages, and the list goes on. Each person is different and imagination is different for each person.

(Jean-Paul Bovee in Donnelly & Bovee, 2003, p. 476)

But the best school in the humanities for every man is in his own house.
(J.M. Baldwin, 1895, cited in Dunn, 1999, p. 240)

Introduction

I present an account of a form of interactive narrative play that my son, Leo,[1] demands of me and at which, over time, he has made me reasonably adept. Leo was formally diagnosed with autistic disorder at age 3 years 6 months, a probability that had been flagged by a developmental paediatrician a year earlier. He called our play *Pretend*.[2] "Dad! Can we play Pretend?"—but definitely in the imperative. The excerpts of Pretend around which this paper is built were recorded when he was 10 years old and in Grade 4 at his local primary school. We had been doing Pretend for at least 3 years. Three years further on, Leo is in Year 7 at his local high school and no longer refers to his narratives as Pretend but rather announces that he has an idea for a game, a novel, or just an idea. While the tropes have changed, the basic structure of our interaction and the energy with which Leo drives it have been continuous.

150 Neil Maclean

Research into the capacity for pretense and pretend play, and difficulties with social play, have formed sustained themes of the literature on autism (Jarrold, 2003; Jordan, 2003). The evidence for difficulties with social play has been consistent. Research into the capacity for pretense has proved more complex. As Jarrold (2003) remarks, "in practical terms, judging whether an individual is truly pretending is surprisingly difficult" (p. 385). Nevertheless, there is an emerging agreement that children diagnosed with autism have both an understanding of pretense and a capacity for pretend play (Chaudry & Dissanayake, this volume; Douglas & Stirling, this volume; Jarrold, 2003). Their difficulties lie with developing that capacity through social relationships, particularly with their peers. Play, then, has also been treated as a window on developmental processes. Researchers have been able to talk about the ways in which social, cognitive, affective, and symbolic capacities feed off each other and the ways in which those feedback relationships may break down (Hobson, 2012; Jarrold, 2003; Jordan, 2003, pp. 349–350; Lewis & Boucher, 1995; Stagnitti, this volume). It is with this in mind that Williams, Costall, and Reddy (1999) insist on the "reciprocal nature of the interactions between the child, other people, and objects" (p. 367). This developmental quality of play has, in turn, made it a site for therapeutic intervention, with the aim of changing or strengthening these feedback processes (Greenspan & Wieder, 1998; Jordan, 2003; Stagnitti, this volume; Wolfberg, 2009).

In this chapter, I am concerned with the ways in which narrative and interactive dynamics feed off each other to sustain Pretend, often over a period of an hour or more. I will be documenting the specific narrative devices that Leo employs and the ways in which they demand my participation. As Douglas and Stirling (this volume) have pointed out, research on both storytelling and interactive play involving children diagnosed with autism is limited. This is particularly the case for older children. It is important, then, to add to our understanding of the quality and mechanics of such play through an extended single case study.

I will also be concerned with the developmental consequences of Pretend. It is striking that it remains one of the few interests to motivate Leo to actively seek out other people and to explore their capabilities. I will describe Pretend as both grounded in family relationships but also as a key means through which Leo actively develops his most immediate social relationships. Pretend has, in the process, become integral to our sense of what family is. In this way, Leo both consolidates and extends an environment that supports the development of his capabilities and interests. The term *prosthetic environment* has been used to describe the role of autism specific therapy and education in providing such support (Eyal, Hart, Onculer, Oren, & Rossi, 2010, pp. 36, 263–269; Hart, 2014; Holmes, 1990). In this chapter, I will be arguing that we should reverse the direction of that argument and understand Leo as building his own prosthetic environment.

Method

As a range of researchers have recognised (Dunn, 1999; Lord, 1993; Ochs, Kremer-Sadlik, Gainer Sirota, & Solomon, 2004; Silverman, 2012; Solomon, 2008, 2011; Wolfberg, 2009), attending to the actual development of the communicative and intentional practice of people diagnosed with autism has methodological as well as philosophical implications. Solomon makes this link explicit in describing the objectives of the Ethnography of Autism Project. Their goal was to

> examine language as it is used *in situ* by children with ASD [autism spectrum disorder] rather than seeing their language as a disembodied cognitive process awaiting remediation. Moreover, from the ethnographic perspective, children with ASD are seen as actively participating in the co-construction of their worlds through communication with others, rather than being acted upon by these others to be managed or treated.
>
> *(Solomon, 2008, pp. 150–151)*

Dunn's research similarly demonstrates the distinctive agency of such children within familial contexts:

> These findings are a challenge to the accounts based on experimental settings, and reinforce the argument that if at the end of the day we want to explain real-life behavior, we simply cannot ignore the reality of children's social behavior in situations that matter to them, or their interactive goals in their close relationships.
>
> *(Dunn, 1999, p. 236)*[3]

Parental anecdote repeatedly confirms Dunn's (1999) point that children diagnosed with autism respond far more positively and reciprocally in a familial context (see also Lord, 1993). Silverman, in turn, highlights love, both as a therapeutic technique and as the detailed implicated knowledge of a particular child, as the starting point of research (2012, Chapter 3). These are contexts in which both parents and children are intentionally committed.

In this study, I am concerned with the situatedness of language production in this study along three different axes. First, I locate the narrative production of Pretend within the relational and affective context of its enactment (Goffman, 1964). Second, I treat my chosen excerpts of Pretend as instances of a series with continuous, relational, affective, and thematic properties—a *type* of situation in Goffman's (1964) terms. Finally, I argue that Leo's reenactment and transformation of this type of situation over time has to be understood within the broader imperatives of the unfolding of a life driven by very distinctive interests and intentions.[4]

The ethnographic method also requires the participation of the researcher in the context of study, generally referred to as *participant observation* (Stocking, 1983).

It is important that the researcher be experientially and intentionally implicated, over a substantial period of time, in the same events and social context as the people being studied. In this way, they are enmeshed in relationships and chains of events as they unfold. They also develop an understanding of the replicable character of types of situations. Just as importantly, participant observation is also a form of learning. Elsewhere (Maclean, 2012), I have explored the similarities between such participant research and the dynamics of joint attention, specifically the conjoint understanding of meaning, intention, and use and the replicability of contexts of attention over time (Tomasello, 1995). In this project, I come to understand something of both Leo's and my own intentions through the ways in which he develops and recombines narratives and through the ways in which he demands my help in doing so.

Intentionality

Leo's Pretend is intentional in the foundational phenomenological sense of directedness to specific objects and goals in the world (Gurwitsch, 1966). In Schutz's (1967/1972, p. 59) terms, Leo has a project. He is engaged in the ongoing search of a wide range of media to build his ever-expanding bank of characters, superpowers, and scenarios. He is driven by an anticipated reworking of those resources into his own narrative combinations and developments—in other words, Pretend. I am not concerned with the question of Leo's recognition of the intentional states of others (Baron-Cohen, 1989, p. 226; Frith, 2003, pp. 131–133).[5] Leo's project is, however, grounded in a "[p]rimary embodied intersubjectivity ... [that] subtends the occasional and secondary intersubjective practices of explaining or predicting what other people believe, desire, or intend in the practice of their own minds" (Gallagher, 2001, cited in Zahavi, 2005, p. 214).[6] For me, Pretend is about my relationship to Leo, but I am not assuming that such a metalevel of relatedness has to be built into Leo's intentions.

The therapeutic logic of intervention programs such as Hanen (Sussman, 1999) and "floor time" (Greenspan & Wieder, 1998) is grounded in identifying the primary interests of the child. They then build on the intersubjective potential of the copresence of the parent or therapist and the child to develop interests into projects. These projects, in turn, extend those intersubjective dynamics.[7] The interests, however special, restricted, or otherwise, remain the drivers of the development, facilitated by these therapeutic interventions, and motivate the "compensatory" (Hobson, 2012, p. 16) skills established in the process. As such, the particular interests of a person diagnosed with autism remain at the core of their development.

Leo: A Case History

Leo's language acquisition was both delayed and disordered. He did not learn to talk until he was almost 4. I can remember dreaming that he had spoken, remarkable now given the almost unstoppable flow of propositions, demands, inventions, lists, and plot devices that pour out at the slightest opportunity. He was always, as his speech pathologist put it, "a determined communicator." Before he could speak, he recognised and used commercial logos to communicate, and we had begun to teach him sign language (see Lilley, 2009). At age 8, he still had not learned to read, and his teachers expressed doubts as to whether he ever would. His mother insisted that the motivation was there and embarked on an intensive teaching program.[8] By age 9, his reading was age appropriate, and by age 10 he had an eccentrically wide vocabulary.

Leo's drive to reenact, through gestures, scenes from his favourite videos dates from before he could speak. Commonly this would happen with his mother sitting up in bed or out on walks with me. Pretend as verbal interaction is the subsequent development of that drive. His immersion in narrative has always been both sympathetic and defensive. By sympathetic, I mean an intuitive response to the emotional quality of narrative rather than an empathetic engagement with a different point of view. His marked response to the emotional climaxes in *E. T. the Extra-Terrestrial* (ages 2–3) is an item of family lore. Very early on, he developed a detailed memory of moments in his children's videos that he did not wish to see again. Leo had always avoided signs of others' emotional distress, and most commonly these critical moments were to do with babies crying. As the moment approached, Leo would anxiously point to the fast-forward button. Months could have passed since the video had last been viewed and he would still pick the spot precisely.

I have come to understand Leo's impairments and strengths as intimately connected through this distinctive relationship to narrative. His specific language impairments are mirrored by the drive to communicate; his difficulties with remembering events, instructions, faces, and names, mirrored by a detailed archival memory of plot, scenario, and character; the social difficulties with play and interaction mirrored by an intuitive grasp of unfolding plot in films, cartoon episodes, and games. Even on a first viewing, he often anticipates plot shifts and twists that have not yet occurred to others.

This sustained realization of Leo's neurological difference through his engagement with the range of narrative resources in his immediate environment I propose, following Hacking (1999), to call *biolooping*.[9] I do so because it allows me to juxtapose this relatively closed developmental dynamic with the broader social process that Hacking calls *classificatory looping* (1999, pp. 114–115, 123–124). Hacking emphasises that, while recognising the transhistorical reality of autism as a neurological impairment,

> [i]n 1950 this [high-functioning autism] was not a way to be a person, people did not experience themselves in this way, they did not interact with their friends, their families, their employers, their counsellors, in this way; but in 2000 this was a way to be a person, to experience oneself, to live in society.
>
> *(Hacking, 2007, p. 303)*

154 Neil Maclean

With his diagnosis, Leo entered "autism world" (Eyal et al., 2010, p. 109). This is not a matter of his own consciousness of his classification. Rather, the argument is that his interactions now take place within the "larger matrix of institutions and practices surrounding this classification" (Hacking, 1999, p. 103). Over time, this has entailed speech therapy, a specialist paediatrician, assessments, occupational therapy, early intervention–oriented preschool, an anxiety clinic, autism-oriented special education, individual education plans in a mainstream school, and awareness raising, such as Carol Gray's "Sixth Sense" program.[10] Autism world is not a space of agreement on what autism is or on how to approach it (Lilley, 2011). Being recognised as an autistic person can be stigmatising (Lilley, 2013b). However, on balance, autism world has created a space in which Leo's difference is recognised and his project has had room to develop (see also Hart, 2014).

A key part of autism world is "autism parenting" (Eyal et al., 2010, p. 109), which mediates much of the initial uptake and impact of this institutional matrix. Parents, too, enter autism world and become part of "the wise" (Goffman, 1963; Lilley, 2013a). They search for services, read, attend support groups and information sessions, become activists and, of course, therapists (Eyal et al., 2010; Lilley, 2014; Silverman, 2012). Below I discuss my role as the "generous interlocutor" (Solomon, 2008) of Leo's Pretend. I am arguing that that "generosity" is not just an ethical position, although it is that, but that it is also a product of the choices we have made as a family about how to engage with autism world (Hart, 2014). For me, this entails the recognition of autism as a category and of Leo as a distinct, albeit always developing, kind of person. The attraction of Hacking's (1999, pp. 100–125) discussion of looping is that it allows me to draw the sociological and interpersonal levels of interpretation, also discussed in the Method section, together. Pretend, then, is the point at which biolooping and classificatory looping meet, and this chapter is an empirical response to Hacking's challenge to take on the "dynamics" rather than the "semantics" of classification (Hacking, 1999, p. 123; see also Hart, 2014, p. 287).

Pretend With Leo

Pretend can happen at any time. First thing on weekend mornings is common—as though the energy had been building overnight and now had to be expressed. Over one week, I recorded 10 hours, and that was not quite all.[11] Pretend motivates Leo's engagement with his family, with reading, and with toy and game play more generally. It can reconcile him to the anxiety of car trips. Leo, according to his own account, is "not a sporty guy" and has declared his need for a "stunt double" at school sport. However, while playing Pretend, Leo will follow me up and down the three flights of stairs in our house without thought.

Pretend is a dialogue in a proposition response form (see transcript excerpts below), but it is a closed dialogue. If it motivates Leo, it is also a way in which he takes possession of me. If his mother is around when we start playing, he will tell her to go away or shut the door. During the period when he was engaged with his mother comparing fantasy island homes (ages 7–8), he would exclude me. He will play Pretend with his grandfather in the room, but Leo's management of our interaction systematically excludes and irritates him. Within this closed dialogue, I am both the amanuensis of Leo's narrative project but also the source of new input and energy that keeps it from stalling.

The dramatis personae of Pretend are drawn from his wide knowledge of cartoon and action characters. I break the narrative sequences down into *orientation, complication*, and *resolution* (Labov & Waletzky, 1967/1997; see also Douglas & Stirling, this volume). The orientation often involves inserting his favourite characters into a scenario drawn from the video game he has just been playing or the cartoon he has just been watching. Complication can draw in any character from the full pantheon of programs and games he has accumulated, and involves devices such as superpowers, transformation, dimensional transfers, portals, and mind control. Resolution is the point at which the intention of my analysis parts company with that of Labov and Waletzky. For them, resolution is intimately linked to evaluation (1967/1997, p. 35) which, in turn, is closely tied to their focus on narratives of personal experience. My focus is on the intersubjective and performative dynamics of narration (Maclean, 1988). In this analysis, resolution is about the struggle over bringing Pretend to an end.

Leo's primary technique of narrative innovation is the *crossover*. This mirrors a common device in the cartoons and video games he loves: "when otherwise separated fictional characters, stories, settings, universes, or media in a video game meet and interact with each other."[12] He also uses the closely related technique of the mash-up, the overlay of content from different media and genres.

Orientation

Jefferson System[13] conventions have been used in the transcription of Narratives 1, 2, and 4. Narrative 3 was transcribed from memory after a car trip. Speaking as a character is in quotation marks. My clarifying comments are in brackets.

> **Narrative 1:** January 14, 2011, 9 a.m.
> **Start excerpt:** 45 s
> **End excerpt:** 2 min 54 s
> **Length of pretend:** 44 min

Nicktoons is both the ever-developing list of cartoons aired by the Nickelodeon channel but also a selection of characters from those cartoons that are joined as a group of heroes in a series of video games.[14] The games are crossovers. The Nicktoons' archenemies, the Syndicate, are villains drawn from the same series of cartoons. Annihilus, Blastaar, Crimson Dynamo, and Spiderman are characters drawn from the *Marvel Character Guide* (Cowsill, 2010). This Pretend is a mash-up of sources and scenarios.

156   Neil Maclean

4:   **Leo:**   Dad you have to be the Syndicate - they want to make an <u>alliance</u> with Ann↑ihilus.

5:   **Dad:**   Oh. Okay. The Syndicate's going to make an alliance with Annihilus.

[Throughout Lines 6 to 21, Leo is leafing through the Marvel Character Guide *selecting characters]*

6:   **L:**   And, a-, and - and - and ↑Blastaar.

7:   **D:**   And ↑who?

8:   **L:**   Blastaar. If he's (3)

9:   **D:**   Who's Blaster?

10:   **L:**   <u>Blastaar.</u>

11:   **D:**   <u>Blastaar.</u> Oh my god.

12:   **L:**   And (3)

13:   **D:**   Don't these guys look a bit tough for the Syndicate?

14:   **L:**   And - and the Crimson ↑Dynamo!

15:   **D:**   And the Crimson Dynamo.

16:   **L:**   With Dr <u>Doom</u>.

17:   **D:**   With Dr Doom as well? All right.

18:   **L:**   Dr ↑Voodoo-, Dor↑mammu.

19:   **D:**   Dormammu.

20:   **L:**   Dragon Man (6) Electro.

21:   **D:**   Electro. (3)

22:   **L:**   Dad can we start all over again?

23:   **D:**   Sure. Let's start all over again.

24:   **L:**   >Have to be Spiderman and wake up in a lab<

25:   **D:**   A:h.

26:   **L:**   [Spiderman's

27:   **D:**   ["How did I get here? What happened?"]

28:   **L:**   <u>No</u>, Spiderman's been here before.

29:   **D:**   Which lab is it?

30:   **L:**   Well, he's been to different <u>types</u> of labs. He <u>knows</u> what's going to happen next.

31:   **D:**   "Uh oh. <u>It's going to happen again.</u>"

32:   **L:**   [Have to be Spiderman

33:   **D:**   ["<u>Why do people keep doing this to me?</u>"]

34:   **L:**   Spiderman sees Ann↑ihilus in the - a container knocked out. >Have to be Annihilus and have swirly eyes in your container< - when you got knocked out.

35:   **D:**   "Wow he looks sick," says Spiderman. "I hope I'm not going to be merged with him."

The structure of Pretend is that propositions and statements require affirmation before the story can proceed (Line 5). If that affirmation is not forthcoming,

Leo will simply repeat the last proposal or imperative until he gets an answer. At Line 6, Leo has fallen into catalogue mode, sustained by leafing through the guide. Commonly this takes the form of a list of characters and a list of their powers. In this mode, I simply affirm each new character and power. Leo will generally ignore me if I attempt to switch to complication. Leo can be content to go on listing characters and powers for a long time.[15] In this case (Line 22), he changes the scenario himself and rapidly gets into complication. "Can we start all over again" is a common demand.

Narrative 2: March 17, 2011, 6 p.m.
Start excerpt: 0 min
End excerpt: 1 min 37 s
Length of pretend: 31 min

Jimmy Neutron (JN) is the leader of the Nicktoons. Other members include SpongeBob, Patrick, Timmy Turner, Danny Phantom, and Tak.

1:	**Dad:**	Jimmy Neutron's bored, is he?
2:	**Leo:**	Ye:s.
3:	**D:**	And why is he bored? Or where's he looking?
4:	**L:**	Jimmy Neutron's ↓bo:red, there's nothing to ↓do:.
5:	**D:**	There's <u>nothing</u> to <u>do</u>:?=
6:	**L:**	=Be Jimmy Neutron's ↑mu↓m.
7:	**D:**	"Jimmy Neu↑tron! What's the matter with you?"
8:	**L:**	Da:d
9:	**D:**	Mm?
10:	**L:**	You have to be Jimmy ↑Neu↓tron.
11:	**D:**	Yeah, I am Jimmy Neut↑ron. < "Well there's nothing to do ↑mum">.
12:	**L:**	And then do you know something-.
13:	**D:**	What's going-
14:	**L:**	When Jimmy ↑Neu↓tron's mum just <u>lea:ves</u> and Jimmy Neutron accidentally (.) presses the <u>delete</u> button and do you know what's going to ↑happen?
15:	**D:**	No, what's going to happen when he presses the delete button?
16:	**L:**	A huge vortex comes out of his (.) computer and then tries to suck him in, you have to be Jim↑my ↑Neu↓tron.
17:	**D:**	"<u>Ohhhhh:, I'm being sucked into the computer</u>".
18:	**L:**	And SpongeBob pressed the delete on this com↑puter ↑<u>too</u> ↓accidentally. And the same thing happened to Jimmy Neu-, and the same thing happened with ↑Sponge↓Bob.
19:	**D:**	"<u>Ahhhh, I'm being sucked into the computer.</u>"
20:	**L:**	The same thing happened to Patrick, Timmy (.) Turner, Danny Phantom, ↑and ↑T↓ak.
21:	**D:**	Wow, they all pressed delete and they all got ↑sucked ↑in.

158 Neil Maclean

22: **L:** No I mean, no I mean it's (.) trying to suck him in. You have to be (.) ↑Sponge↓Bob.

23: **D:** And what's SpongeBob doing, is he hanging onto something?

24: **L:** Ye:s.

25: **D:** And what's he hanging onto?

26: **L:** They're all gonna be sucked into (.) into cyberspace all at the same time and the (.) vortex is ↑clo↓sed. Be Jimmy Neutron's mum and try to find Jimmy ↑Neu↓tron.

As with Narrative 1, orientation establishes a cast of characters but in this case does not get stalled in list mode. The shift from mundane family situation (*I'm bored*) to the outer reaches of science and the universe is *the* device of the JN cartoons. However, here Leo has not appropriated an orientation from an existing JN episode and then developed his own complication (a tactic he does employ at times) but rather has pieced together the theme of boredom and the effect of hitting the delete key from two different episodes. In Stagnitti's terms (this volume), this is not simply "chunking."

Narrative 3: July 7, 2011; transcribed from memory after car trip

1: **Leo:** Have to be SpongeBob and Patrick getting hot dogs.

2: **Dad:** ((as Patrick)) "I'll have a hot dog with the lot!"

3: **L:** You mean he'll have it with everything.

4: **D:** That's what you say with fast food when you want everything – you say "the lot."

5: **L:** With "the lot." ((indistinct))

6: **D:** With "the lot."

7: **L:** With "the lot."

8: **D:** ((as SpongeBob)) "And I'll have a hot dog with pickles, cheese, and chili sauce but hold the onion."

9: **L:** And then

10: **D:** But really the hot dog seller was a mind control alien and the hot dogs were mind control devices.

11: **L:** Mmmm yes. No not really. The hot dog seller was a hologram.

12: **D:** Wow a hologram – and who controlled the hologram?

13: **L:** And the hot dog stand was a Decepticon.[16]

14: **D:** – a Decepticon?!

15: **L:** And the Decepticon shot flaming hot dogs at SpongeBob and Patrick.

16: **D:** And did SpongeBob and Patrick run or did they fight back?

17: **L:** SpongeBob used pickles as his rapid fire attack.

At Line 10, I propose a new direction that I think Leo will like. He thinks about it but rejects it. Sometimes he picks up a plot twist I propose, flapping his arms and humming with excitement. At Line 13, the crossover insertion of a Decepticon into a SpongeBob scenario moves the orientation into complication.

Complication

In Narrative 3, orientation develops very rapidly into complication. Here, Leo's sideways relationship to "telling" is evident. Leo's practice is to control the structural elements of orientation and resolution with complication distinctively dependent on an asymmetric structure of proposal and response. When I propose a development, Leo has the option of either running with it or vetoing it (e.g., Line 10). More often, Leo enjoins me to "be" a character, the device from which the title of this chapter stems. He may specify a plot development before such an injunction, and I am under instruction to enact it (Narrative 2, Line 16). He may simply tell me to be a particular character, in which case I have to invent a development that is in character, in an acceptable voice, and appropriate to the plot. Some developments lie between these two poles (Narrative 1, Line 34). In other sequences, the dependence on the scaffolding of injunction is abandoned (Narrative 3, Lines 11 to 17; Narrative 4 below, Lines 792 to 798). I return to the implications of this below. However, the premise of Pretend is that I am under instruction to enact and drive the narrative.

Marie Maclean identifies two aspects of the "energies unleashed" by narrative as oral performance:

> Narrative, like communication, involves negentropy, a marshalling of the resources of language against the seemingly random dispersion of our experience. Telling, because of its negentropic force, is one of the earliest creative formal skills we acquire.
>
> *(Maclean, 1988, p. 2)*

But with the pleasures of establishing the proper order and unfolding of the narrative comes the drive to control one's audience:

> In the teller-hearer relationship . . . just as redundancy is possibly the teller's most useful tool, so "noise," the hearer's emotional, ideological, physical, linguistic tendency towards non-cooperation, seems at first the greatest enemy. Yet at the same time it can be the greatest stimulus, constantly setting the challenge of winning the battle for control.
>
> *(Maclean, 1988, p. 3)*

Leo's telling is not only a struggle between teller and hearer. The narrative unfolds through continual swapping of the teller–hearer roles but with an underlying struggle over who will control its trajectory at any one point. Overall, Leo controls the trajectory. I, however, can insist on humorous detours in the way in which I propose, with no real expectation of acceptance. By introducing a

160   Neil Maclean

complication that he either accepts or has to propose an alternative to, I can also insist that Leo himself proposes if he wants to continue to control the narrative. This is my narrative therapeutic subterfuge. Leo's project is the instantiation of his story, but he can only realize this through the struggle for control over my voice.

Problems With Resolution

This struggle takes on a different form when I attempt to reassert control over the narrative trajectory and bring Pretend to a close.

> **Narrative 4:** March 22, 2011, 8 p.m.
> **Start excerpt:** 68 min
> **End excerpt:** 70 min
> **Length of pretend:** 70 min

Denzel Cracker is a member of the Syndicate, the archenemies of the Nicktoons. I'm not sure where the Crimson Dragon has been drawn from. The Navi are the autochthonous inhabitants of the planet invaded in the movie *Avatar*. Many of Batman's archenemies have been patients in the Arkham Asylum for the criminally insane. It is also a video game.

773: **Leo:**   When they spin around holding hands with each other ↑lau:↓ghi:ng.
774: **Dad:**   I see.
775: **L:**   (4) And then they le- (.) form the Crimson Dragon it↑sel:f. You have to (.) be Denzel Cracker and see it's a lot bigger than you. You have to be Denzel ↑Crack↓er:. (1) And gonna (--) do a little laugh a- a fake laugh and sound evil and >sound like a god at the same time< with that fake laugh and (.) and pretend something that you're not gonna ↑do:. (4).
776: **D:**   Mm↑mm. (.) [↑Ya ha ha.
777: **L:**   [You're not gonna do]. [Your fake laugh.
778: **D:**   [↑ Ha ha. Hoo (.) hoo hoo hoo (-) ha ha ha ha.] Oh. Ha ha ha ha. We can do that.
779: **L:**   And then the Crimson Dragon is gonna defeat them and >all the power comes out of Denzel Cracker and he looks< (.) extremely sorry and Denzel Cracker is still (1) and Denzel Cracker goes ↑cra↓zy: (.) and he says strange thi:ngs (.) and strange combinations of (1) of foo:d.
780: **D:**   {As a wailing noise} "Ohhh:hhh. (1) ↑Pickles (1) ↓Strawberry Jam".
781: **L:**   Be the Na:vi and think the (.) When he got [defeated the power came out of him.
782: **D:**   ["Buns, oysters!"]
783: **L:**   Then he gone cra:zy:.
784: **D:**   He's lost his mi:nd.
785: **L:**   And >then they're gonna< (.) bring him into Arkham A↑sylu:m.
786: **D:**   Oh okay.

Autism, Narrative, and Family **161**

787: **L:** He-ʾ (.) an- (.) but the other Syndicate members are gonna be put in the high secure ↑pri↓so:n (.) with no esca:pe.
788: **D:** That's right, with no escape. .Hhh all right.
789: **L:** You have to be the Nicktoo - You have to be the Navi (.) gonna thank the Nicktoons.
790: **D:** <↓ "We thank you Nicktoons for restoring our planet to us." >=
791: **L:** = "You may be on earth but you are (.) the goo:d".
792: **D:** Mm (1) .hh exactly. Okay.
793: **L:** "Here is our token of respect." >Have to be SpongeBob and not know what this small cute jellyfish thing is< (2)
794: **D:** It's a small cute jellyfish thing. ↑"Oh, how lovely," says SpongeBob.
795: **L:** Have to be Jimmy Neutron and touch it. (.) Have to be Patrick and touch and see it's not eletrica:l.
796: **D:** ↓"Yeah you didn't electrocute me, SpongeBob." That's it.
797: **L:** No, no, not yet. The- uh- (.) "<u>this</u> is our token of respect. Use it and you will (.) have good drea:ms."
798: **D:** Okay. Thank ↓you.

Leo understands the narrative structure of resolution (e.g., Lines 790 and 797). My most common device for wringing consent for ending Pretend from Leo is to frame it as the end of an episode: *to be continued*. However, Leo also resists resolution. He doesn't like transitions (they are genuinely upsetting). My sense is that at resolution, the energy of Pretend is simply turned back inwards.

Structurally, this is made clear in the tendency for resolution to simply become a new complication (Line 793) or a new orientation. It is also clear in the way energy picks up all the way through this narrative segment in the movement towards resolution. My rather desperate attempts, in the face of this energy, to bring this Pretend to an end after over an hour are apparent (Lines 788, 792, and 796). Haag, a psychoanalyst who has dealt extensively with children diagnosed with autism, captures the subjective impact of this energy on others in their orbit:

> For example when the child seems lost in his stereotypes, the therapist may feel herself liquefying to the extent of hardly being able to sit up, and of needing to use the arm rests of the chair, or to the sit on the floor with her back against the wall, in order to manage.
>
> *(Haag, 2005, p. 118)*

As is frequently the case with psychoanalysis, I want to both agree and disagree. I identify with that liquefying sensation of being caught in the detail and performative demands of Leo's imagination. This is a function of being subject to the narrative, the length of time over which it is sustained, and the resistance to closure. However, I reject the sense that Leo might simply be "lost in his stereotypes." If I get lost in anything, it is in Leo's tropes and the seemingly unstoppable quality of their inventive unfolding.

How Is Leo's Pretend Different?

At my first presentation of this paper,[17] I was asked how this differed from what typical boys of Leo's age do. It remains a good question. While narrative itself has been proposed as a core impairment of people diagnosed with autism (Bruner & Feldman, 1993), subsequent research has not identified replicable differences between the foundational narrative capacities of children with ASD and neurotypical children (Douglas & Stirling, this volume). There is, however, a recurrent theme of difficulties with producing and sustaining narratives (Bruner & Feldman, 1993; Diehl et al., 2006; Solomon, 2004). On the basis of an ethnographic study of discourse competence of children with ASD, Solomon concludes that:

> Fictional narrative introductions appeared to be well within the reach of children with lower verbal ability who competently and successfully used the procedurally stable practices afforded by the global pre-organization of these narratives by their modalities of expression (video-recording, printed text etc.). Narrative co-telling over the extended course of propositions, however, was more challenging, lending a degree of support to the theory of weak central coherence.
>
> *(Solomon, 2004, p. 271)[18]*

The key figure in accounts of the ways in which children diagnosed with autism do, nevertheless, develop both narrative and interactive competence is that of the generous interlocutor (Solomon, 2008), facilitator (Jordan, 2003, pp. 353ff), guide to participation (Wolfberg, 2009, Chapter 9), or radical translator (Hart, 2014). Generous interlocutors "design their talk and conduct to be comprehensible and interesting to children," "richly interpret the talk and conduct of the children," and "otherwise promote the child's social involvement" (Solomon, 2008, p. 159). I argue that it is my role as Leo's interlocutor in Pretend that is the key to the question of difference. I explore this difference through comparison with comparable data from a school-based study of a narrative project with 10-year-old boys.

Cross studies the ways in which "a group of 10-year-old boys mutually construct an evolving multilinear scenario whilst playing a storytelling game in class, borrowing from a number of genres and forms of engagement in ICT-mediated popular culture" (2005, p. 333).[19] Like Pretend, this storytelling game was a situation (Goffman, 1964) that was replicated and consolidated over time. Cross identifies the following *manoeuvres* that allow the game to develop: action sequence, speech or voice imitation, sound effects, sampling from popular culture, and incorporation of local school culture (Cross, 2005, p. 344). Leo has a comparable range. He draws characters and plot devices from cartoons and games rather than action sequences. He incorporates speech imitation, but whereas the boys Cross studies delight in their own prowess at voice imitation and sound effects (Cross, 2005, p. 347), Leo insists that I produce them (Narrative 4, Lines 775 and 776) and often that I repeat them until I get it

Autism, Narrative, and Family **163**

right.[20] Leo shows little inclination to extend speech imitation into sound effects. His sampling from popular culture is, however, very similar, particularly in drawing on blockbuster movies: *Jurassic Park* (Cross, 2005, p. 344), *Star Wars* (Cross, 2005, p. 348), and *Avatar* (Leo, Narrative 4). The biggest contrast in content is that Leo never draws on his life outside cartoons and popular culture as a narrative resource.

While there are differences, Leo clearly has identifiable "boy" cultural capital (Swain, 2004). He has a detailed knowledge of the highly textualized cartoon, film, and game terrain, with its action and fantasy tropes, that acts as a major point of reference for male teen and preteen performances of masculinity. He understands the pleasures of the mash-up (see Cross, 2005, p. 350) and of possessing an encyclopaedic knowledge of characters. He also has a detailed knowledge of the key plot elements of individual episodes and games. Like Leo, "[s]everal boys also reported that they aspired to be computer game designers" (Cross, 2005, p. 338). Leo's shared relationship to this textualized cultural space (along with a capacity to produce one-liners that routinely surprise and amuse both his classmates and teacher) has carved out for him an accepted social space in school. Cross's research allows one to understand how that might work.

There is, however, a tenuous quality to this space, and Leo spends a considerable amount of time on the margins of school activity. If one looks to the actual dynamics of the performance Cross (2005) is documenting, as opposed to its content, I propose that there are two immediate reasons Leo might have difficulty in participating in such a game. My original response to the question of what made Pretend different was to see in the rapid oscillation of the teller–hearer roles an index of the difficulty in sustaining narrative that Solomon (2004) describes. Cross's data, however, reveal a comparable pattern of turn taking. While some boys make more sustained contributions, there are as many who contribute only a single idea in any one turn.[21] The contrast lies, rather, with the scaffolding that Pretend requires to sustain this turn taking. In the narratives Cross records, there are no explicit instructions that mark turn taking itself. There are no comments on the adequacy of the contribution and no instructions on the voice required. One boy finishes, and the only cue is the handing over of the microphone. The way in which the boys themselves describe this process is telling. The interviewer puts it to them that their plays develop as if they could "read each others' minds." The boys respond:

> Chad: We look at each other's eyes, each other's EYES
> And we can see each others' minds
> And we can kinda do it in some way.
>
> *(Cross, 2005, p. 346)[22]*

It is the complete lack of scaffolding that distinguishes this from Leo's and my turn taking. To anyone familiar with the dominant tropes in the description of autism, the self-conscious recognition of empathy in references to "mind reading" and

164 Neil Maclean

looking in each others' "EYES" marks this off from our expectations of interaction with children diagnosed with autism.

The instructions with which Leo scaffolds Pretend reflect not only the need to explicitly manage turn taking but also the imperative control with which Leo drives his narratives. While there is a core of boys who dominate the games Cross follows through various forms of acknowledged performative expertise, there is no single voice that drives it (Cross, 2005, pp. 342–343). She describes, rather, a process of "autopoesis" (Cross, 2005, p. 343) in which the high points are improvised performative moves that gain recognition from the rest of the class. Leo's motivation is not performative. My dominant impression is rather of an inner idea that he needs to be given shape and to be enacted.

Implicit here is a contrast in the intentionality of narrative performance that Cross's conclusion makes explicit:

> Social networks were a priority and ICT was used as a means to an end around participation . . . The ICT tool most crucial to have was not a computer; instead, it was essential to have a mobile phone to keep up with the network of gossip primarily generated through their use.
>
> *(Cross, 2005, pp. 350–351)*

Leo's narrative experiments with a textualized virtual world do not provide a means to social ends. In many ways, the fact of his boy capital is incidental in that it is not driven by peer group recognition. Rather, he is primarily intentionally committed to developing his scenarios, and he makes claims on me in order to do so.

This is the interesting point. In pursuit of this end, Leo provides his own scaffolding. I have highlighted the imperative and directive nature of his participation and the micromanagement of plot development and character accent. It is in this scaffolding that I find evidence of both his impairment and the strategies he has developed to pursue his own special interest in narrative around that impairment.

I am an integral and necessary part of that strategy. In Hart's (2004) terms, the project is founded on "joint embodiment" (2014, p. 288). I can recognise myself in the description of the generous interlocutor, and indeed that has been the primary role set for me by the floor time (Greenspan & Wieder, 1998) model. Within this model, the interests of the child form the content of the interaction, but the directive subjectivity is that of the parent or therapist. My current view, however, is that, within the process of his development, Leo's has become the directive subjectivity within this carefully framed interaction and that the figure of generous interlocutor has been turned on its head. My key role is as his amanuensis.

Beyond Amanuensis

Sometimes Leo catches fire, and complication unfolds seamlessly, largely without the need for his directive scaffolding. If Leo does have an underlying difficulty in

Autism, Narrative, and Family **165**

sustaining narrative, at these moments the energy of his project, or his coherent anticipation of its direction, can transcend it.

Narrative 1 (continued): January 14, 2011, 9 a.m.
Start of excerpt: 27 min
End excerpt: 30 min 7 s
Length of pretend: 44 min

Summary of narrative between 5 and 27 minutes: Spiderman (SM) has been fused with the DNA of a range of villains and heroes and has acquired their powers. But SM is still in control of himself. The lab belonged to the Mad Thinker (MT). SM has freed himself from the control of the MT and wants him to reverse the process. The MT says that the process is irreversible. Dad proposes that SM should get one of the other superheroes to read the MT's mind to see what to do. Professor X does so and says, "It's true—the process is irreversible." Suddenly, SM says, "Something smells good!"

355: **Dad:** ((proposing alternatives)) Is he going to say, "<u>No! Not my spicy sausages</u>"? Or is he going to say, "I've still got spicy sausages there"?

356: **Leo:** ((as MT)) "I've still got spicy sausages." And then - then Spiderman is going to go up towards him and <u>eat one</u>.

357: **D:** Is that a mistake?

358: **L:** Yeah. And he's - and his mouth is so hot, he breaths <u>fire</u>.

359: **D:** "O:h! What was <u>that</u>?"

360: **L:** I added = Spiderman forgotten he was fused with Dragon Man. That means he can breathe <u>fire</u>. (2).

361: **D:** Oh. Does that mean he can eat spicy sausages too?

362: **L:** <u>Yes</u>.

363: **D:** Oh.

364: **L:** = The more spicy things he eats, the bigger his <u>flame is</u>.

365: **D:** "<u>Ha</u> ↑<u>ha</u>," says the Mad Thinker. "It's true. The experiment was a success. ↓Spiderman has dragon powers."

366: **L:** Have to be Spiderman and say, "So, the spicier the things are, the <u>bigger my flame is</u>?"

367: **D:** "That's correct, Spiderman."

368: **L:** Have to be Spiderman.

369: **D:** "Why did you do this, Mad Thinker?"

370: **L:** ((short run and hums to himself)) "Since - since I lost - since I - since I lost my pet gorillas and became super smart and been and had<u> super powers</u> I would say I would need a new assistant."

371: **D:** You lost your pet gorillas? How did that happen?

372: **L:** "Well, on the - when I was running ((from)) the Fantastic Four, I went into my - they rolled me into my ship and then my pet gorillas were left on the - on the - on the destroyed ↑space station,

166 Neil Maclean

		but it can still breed and they would never age."
373:	**D:**	And what happened to them?
374:	**L:**	"They turned it into a - I watched them every night and they turned it into a paradise without <u>me</u>."
375:	**D:**	Oh, no! The gorillas did?
376:	**L:**	"<u>Yes</u>."
377:	**D:**	So the gorillas don't want you anymore.
378:	**L:**	"<u>No</u>."
379:	**D:**	Oh dear! That's very sad.

From Line 370 to its rather poignant end, this segment develops naturally without the scaffolding of my turn taking under Leo's imperative. My sense is that, in conversation, an already-imagined story is being revealed. However, with my "Oh dear," Leo falls silent, and it is me who sets Pretend on a new direction with a question.

This momentary transcendence of the scaffolding is the mirror image of the structure of Narrative 4 in which, as Leo attempts to drive beyond resolution, my role as amanuensis also becomes redundant. However, in that case, my part in the conversation is simply overridden. Rather than the capacity to imaginatively sustain a narrative, in Narrative 4 it is the compulsion to keep going that is most evident.

In both cases, the fundamental contradiction of Leo's project remains. On the one hand, through Pretend he is expanding his interactive skills. On the other, it remains clear that the relationships he develops using those skills remain subordinated to his primary interest in his own narrative project. This interest is the ground on which his interactive skills are built but is also their limit.

Looping

While acknowledging this limit, it remains the case that, as the directive subjectivity, Leo now has the tools to generalize this model of narrative interaction to other generous interlocutors. Over time, he has developed specific styles of Pretend relationship, first with his mother and then with myself. He has recruited his aunt, who has a staying power almost matching his own, and who he now visits on a regular basis. He tests the capacities of his regular respite workers to see if they are worth engaging. He is starting to use his ideas as a technique for socialising at family dinner parties, marking a shift into more complex social contexts. Leo's imperative style has now extended into more sustained speeches that he delivers in class and, to our surprise, at family events.

Leo's content also changes. The Nicktoons and Spiderman have been replaced in his crossovers by a wide-ranging interest in mythology, pantheons of gods (Greek, Norse, Egyptian, Indian, Japanese), and the horror genre. History lessons and even science have more recently been a source of ideas.

Pretend is proving to be dynamic in both its social form and cognitive content. Leo is in the process of creating his own prosthetic environment (Eyal et al., 2010, p. 262) that is specifically responsive to his narrative interests. In doing so, he resocializes his most proximate interpersonal relationships to his own imperative interactive modality and recruits those persons to his project. He is also recognising the narrative elements he finds on YouTube and at school as resources for his narrative project. Leo's Pretend is a form of play in which there is a transactional feedback relationship between imagination, cognition, and sociality in the ongoing development of a specific kind of person. As he develops as this kind of person, he also changes the others in his orbit (Maclean, 2013).

Conclusion

In this chapter, I have described the intersubjective dynamics of Pretend and its techniques of innovation at a specific point of its development. At the same time, I have placed the characteristics of Pretend at that moment within a broader description of Leo's development understood from the perspective of his diagnosis of autism. I have argued for a link between the specific narrative dynamics that are revealed in the transcripts and the longer-term developmental transformation of Pretend as both Leo's project and as an interactive situation. I have framed this developmental process within the contemporary recognition of Leo as autistic, as a specific kind of person (Hacking, 2007), by many of the people he encounters in his family and school context. This recognition has provided the space for Leo to extend Pretend as a project. The elaboration of contemporary discourse about autism has also provided a language with which to think and talk about that difference (Hacking, 2009).

It is equally important to remember that, for Hacking (1999), looping is a two-way process. While classificatory looping provides a space for biolooping, the effects of biolooping can change our understanding of specific kinds of people. Eyal et al. (2010, pp. 262–263) similarly insist on the inside-out potential of the prosthetic environment. They argue that autism therapy works not only to change the child diagnosed with ASD but also works outwards to make the mainstream more diverse. In a particularly telling image, they argue that therapies "extend the perimeter of the prosthetic environment further into the mainstream" (Eyal et al., 2010, pp. 262–263; see also Hart, 2014, pp. 298–299). In this chapter, I have described, through the close analysis of interactive narrative, the kinds of mechanisms that might effect that extension.

However, in doing so, I have turned the therapeutic direction of the prosthetic environment narrative around. In his original essay, Asperger (1991) insists that "autistic individuals are distinguished from each other not only by the degree of contact disturbance and the degree of intellectual ability, but also by their personality and their special interests, which are often outstandingly varied and original" (p. 67).

If the recognition of Leo as autistic creates a space for him to develop, then it is Leo, with his distinctive interests, who fills that space and extends his prosthetic environment. He does so with an imperative intersubjectivity that appropriates others to his narrative project. Just as importantly, he fills that space with his own distinctive personality and a robust claim to recognition as both autistic and fully human.

Acknowledgements

My son's energy, enthusiasm, and inventiveness have inspired me to write this paper. My wife Rozanna Lilley has encouraged me to persist and has read many drafts, and my thinking has always developed in dialogue with her. Her own research with mothers of school-age children diagnosed with autism has given shape to my argument. Participants in the conference on Children's Play, Storytelling and Pretence were a generous audience to a tentative original version. Two clear-sighted anonymous referees, along with Susan Douglas and Lesley Stirling as editors, have provided good guidance for the final revision.

Notes

1 Leo is a pseudonym.
2 Capitalized hereafter when referring to our activity.
3 Bruner (1983, pp. 126–130) had already flagged the limitations of the experimental and quantitative bias of cognitive psychology as part of his own shift into narrative method.
4 Discussions of ethnography often treat this nesting of different levels of context in terms of the hermeneutics of part–whole relationships (Agar, 1980; Geertz, 1973; Thornton, 1988).
5 See Solomon (2011) for a close, phenomenologically informed description of the embodied aspects of communication and intersubjectivity in relationships involving children and teenagers diagnosed with autism.
6 See Zahavi (2005, Chapter 7) for a sustained critique of the *theory of mind* paradigm.
7 See Stagnitti (this volume) for a case study–based account of this style of therapy.
8 Using McGuiness and McGuiness (1998).
9 While Hacking references relatively closed *mind–body* dynamics such as yoga (Hacking, 1999, p. 109), I believe that my extension of the usage is in keeping with his discussion of "indifferent kinds" (Hacking, 1999, pp. 115–117).
10 http://www.autisminspiration.com/public/418.cfm?sd=15.
11 During this week, I responded to all bids for Pretend. I recorded 31 different episodes, missing some while walking to school. The frequency ranged from one to six episodes per day and lasted from 11 to 70 min. During this section and the following sections on orientation, complication, and problems with resolution, I describe Pretend as it happened during that week and in the period immediately around that. I use the present tense to capture the way the interaction unfolds. At other points in my analysis, I discuss the changing nature of Pretend over a longer period.
12 Wikipedia, Fictional crossovers in video games. Retrieved from http://en.wikipedia.org/wiki/Fictional_crossovers_in_video_games.

13 Jefferson System conventions can be found at http://homepages.lboro.ac.uk/~ssca1/notation.htm.
14 http://en.wikipedia.org/wiki/Nicktoons_Unite!
15 Compare with Douglas and Stirling (this volume) on *storyboarding* as satisfying in its own right—particularly in the case of Liam.
16 http://en.wikipedia.org/wiki/Decepticon.
17 This paper was first presented in 2011 at the conference on Children's Play, Storytelling and Pretence, University College, University of Melbourne, Melbourne, VIC, Australia.
18 Solomon explicitly refers here to children of "lower verbal ability." However, the implication of the generative claims of the diagnosis is that similar impairments can be found across the spectrum, while the trajectory of development and "compensation" varies.
19 ICT = information and communications technology.
20 Compare the seamless integration of accent or intonation into performance in the excerpt from Cross below with Leo (Narrative 4, Lines 775 and 776):

James:
Then the dragon didn't like the song
so he just
crushed em all
and he went
"Tragedy! I'm dead." *[really high voice; laughter off mic]*
"And I wish I could go on to bed!" (Cross, 2005, p. 341)

21 An example of a turn with a single idea would be:

Ian:
Then eventually
he started flyin
and someone shot him down (Cross, 2005, p. 341)

22 Line numbers on original removed.

References

Agar, M. (1980). Hermeneutics in anthropology: A review essay. *Ethos, 8*(3), 253–272. http://dx.doi.org/10.1525/eth.1980.8.3.02a00040

Asperger, H. (1991). "Autistic psychopathy" in childhood. (U. Frith, Trans.). In U. Frith (Ed.), *Autism and Asperger syndrome* (pp. 37–92). Cambridge, UK: Cambridge University Press.

Baron-Cohen, S. (1989). The autistic child's theory of mind: A case of specific developmental delay. *Journal of Child Psychology and Psychiatry, 30*(2), 285–297. http://dx.doi.org/10.1111/j.1469-7610.1989.tb00241.x

Bruner, J.S. (1983). *In search of mind: Essays in autobiography*. New York, NY: Harper & Row.

Bruner, J., & Feldman, C. (1993). Theories of mind and the problem of autism. In S. Baron-Cohen, H. Tager-Flusberg, & D. Cohen (Eds.), *Understanding other minds: Perspectives from autism* (pp. 267–291). Oxford, UK: Oxford University Press.

Cowsill, A. (2010). *Marvel: Earth's mightiest heroes the Avengers: The ultimate character guide*. London, UK: Dorling Kindersley.

170   Neil Maclean

Cross, B. (2005). Split frame thinking and multiple scenario awareness: How boys' game expertise reshapes possible structures of sense in a digital world. *Discourse: Studies in the Cultural Politics of Education, 26*(3), 333–353. http://dx.doi.org/10.1080/01596300500200086

Diehl, J., Bennetto, L., & Young, E. (2006). Story recall and narrative coherence of high-functioning children with autism spectrum disorders. *Journal of Abnormal Child Psychology, 34*(1), 87–102. http://dx.doi.org/10.1007/s10802-005-9003-x

Donnelly, J., & Bovee, J.-P. (2003). Reflections on play: Recollections from a mother and her son with Asperger syndrome. *Autism, 7*(4), 471–476. http://dx.doi.org/10.1177/1362361303007004011

Dunn, J. (1999). Making sense of the social world: Mindreading, emotion, and relationships. In P. Zelazo, J. Astington, & D. Olson (Eds.), *Developing theories of intention: Social understanding and self-control* (pp. 292–316). Mahwah, NJ: Erlbaum.

Eyal, G., Hart, B., Onculer, E., Oren, N., & Rossi, N. (2010). *The autism matrix: The social origins of the autism epidemic.* Cambridge, MA: Polity Press.

Frith, U. (2003). *Autism: Explaining the enigma.* Malden, MA: Blackwell.

Geertz, C. (1973). Thick description: Toward an interpretative theory of culture. In C. Geertz (Ed.), *The interpretation of cultures: Selected essays* (pp. 3–30). New York, NY: Basic Books.

Goffman, E. (1963). *Stigma: Notes on the management of spoiled identity.* Englewood Cliffs, NJ: Prentice Hall.

Goffman, E. (1964). The neglected situation. *American Anthropologist, 66,* 133–136. http://dx.doi.org/10.1525/aa.1964.66.suppl_3.02a00090

Greenspan, S., & Wieder, S. (1998). *The child with special needs.* Reading, MA: Perseus Books.

Gurwitsch, A. (1966). On the intentionality of consciousness. In J. Wild & J. Edie (Eds.), *Studies in phenomenology and psychology* (pp. 124–140). Evanston, IL: Northwestern University Press.

Haag, G. (2005). Conversation with Geneviève Haag. In D. Houzel & M. Rhode (Eds.), *Invisible boundaries: Psychosis and autism in children and adolescents* (pp. 107–122). London, UK: Karnac.

Hacking, I. (1999). *The social construction of what?* Cambridge, MA: Harvard University Press.

Hacking, I. (2007). Kinds of people: Moving targets. *Proceedings of the British Academy, 151,* 285–318. http://dx.doi.org/10.5871/bacad/9780197264249.001.0001

Hacking, I. (2009). Autistic autobiography. *Philosophical Transactions of the Royal Society B: Biological Sciences, 364,* 1467–1473. http://dx.doi.org/10.1098/rstb.2008.0329

Hart, B. (2014). Autism parents & neurodiversity: Radical translation, joint embodiment and the prosthetic environment. *BioSocieties, 9*(3), 284–303.

Hobson, R.P. (2012). Autism, literal language and concrete thinking: Some developmental considerations. *Metaphor and Symbol, 27*(1), 4–21. http://dx.doi.org/10.1080/1092648 8.2012.638814

Holmes, D.L. (1990). Community-based services for children and adults with autism: The Eden Family of Programs. *Journal of Autism and Developmental Disorders, 20*(3), 339–351. http://dx.doi.org/10.1007/BF02206546

Jarrold, C. (2003). A review of research into pretend play in autism. *Autism, 7*(4), 379–390. http://dx.doi.org/10.1177/1362361303007004004

Jordan, R. (2003). Social play and autistic spectrum disorders: A perspective on theory, implications and educational approaches. *Autism, 7,* 347–360. http://dx.doi.org/10.1177/1362361303007004002

Labov, W., & Waletzky, J. (1997). Narrative analysis: Oral versions of personal experience. *Journal of Narrative and Life History, 7*(1–4), 3–38. (Original work published 1967.)

Lewis, V., & Boucher, J. (1995). Generativity in the play of young people with autism. *Journal of Autism and Developmental Disorders, 25*(2), 105–121. http://dx.doi.org/10.1007/BF02178499

Lilley, R. (2009). Of angst and acceptance. *Melbourne's Child, 20*(7), 25–27. Retrieved from http://www.researchonline.mq.edu.au/vital/access/manager/Repository/mq:8450

Lilley, R. (2011). The ABCs of autism: Aspects of maternal pedagogy in Australia. *Social Analysis, 55*(1), 134–159. http://dx.doi.org/10.3167/sa.2011.550107

Lilley, R. (2013a). Crying in the park: Autism stigma, school entry and maternal subjectivity. *Studies in the Maternal, 5,* 1–28. Retrieved from http://www.mamsie.bbk.ac.uk/Lilley_SiM_5_2.html

Lilley, R. (2013b). It's an absolute nightmare: Maternal experiences of enrolling children diagnosed with autism in primary school in Sydney, Australia. *Disability & Society, 28*(4), 514–526. http://dx.doi.org/10.1080/09687599.2012.717882

Lilley, R. (2014). Professional guidance: Maternal negotiation of primary school placement for children diagnosed with autism. *Discourse: Studies in the Cultural Politics of Education, 35*(4), 513–526. http://dx.doi.org/10.1080/01596306.2013.871226

Lord, C. (1993). The complexity of social behaviour in autism. In S. Baron-Cohen, H. Tager-Flusberg, & D. Cohen (Eds.), *Understanding other minds: Perspectives from autism* (pp. 292–316). Oxford, UK: Oxford University Press.

Maclean, M. (1988). *Narrative as performance: The Baudelairean experiment.* London, UK: Routledge.

Maclean, N. (2012). On the road in Highlands Papua New Guinea: Intimacy and ethnographic method. *Qualitative Research, 12*(5), 575–587. http://dx.doi.org/10.1177/1468794112443475

Maclean, N. (2013). Living with disability: Care, rights and relational personhood. *Australian Journal of Human Rights, 19*(1), 133–153. Retrieved from https://www.academia.edu/4371853/Living_with_disability_care_rights_and_relational_personhood

McGuiness, C., & McGuiness, G. (1998). *Reading Reflex: The foolproof method for teaching your child to read.* London, UK: Penguin Books.

Ochs, E., Kremer-Sadlik, T., Gainer Sirota, K., & Solomon, O. (2004). Autism and the social world: An anthropological perspective. *Discourse Studies, 6*(2), 147–183. http://dx.doi.org/10.1177/1461445604041766

Schutz, A. (1972). *The phenomenology of the social world* (G. Walsh & F. Lehnert, Trans.). London, UK: Heinemann Educational Books. (Original work published 1967)

Silverman, C. (2012). *Understanding autism: Parents, doctors, and the history of a disorder.* Princeton, NJ: Princeton University Press.

Solomon, O. (2004). Narrative introductions: Discourse competence of children with autistic spectrum disorders. *Discourse Studies, 6*(2), 253–276. http://dx.doi.org/10.1177/1461445604041770

Solomon, O. (2008). Language, autism, and childhood: An ethnographic perspective. *Annual Review of Applied Linguistics, 28,* 150–169. http://dx.doi.org/10.1017/S0267190508080148

Solomon, O. (2011). Body in autism: A view from social interaction. In P. McPherron & V. Ramanathan (Eds.), *Language, body, and health* (pp. 105–144). Boston, MA: de Gruyter.

Stocking, G. W., Jr. (1983). The ethnographer's magic: Fieldwork in British anthropology from Tylor to Malinowski. In G. W. Stocking, Jr. (Ed.), *Observers observed: Essays on ethnographic fieldwork* (Vol. 1, pp. 70–120). Madison: University of Wisconsin Press.

Sussman, F. (1999). *More than words: Helping parents promote communication and social skills in children with autism spectrum disorder.* Toronto, ON, Canada: The Hanen Centre.

Swain, J. (2004). The resources and strategies that 10–11-year-old boys use to construct masculinities in the school setting. *British Education Research Journal, 30*(1), 167–185. http://dx.doi.org/10.1080/0141192031000163017

Thornton, R.J. (1988). The rhetoric of ethnographic holism. *Cultural Anthropology, 3*(3), 285–303. http://dx.doi.org/10.1525/can.1988.3.3.02a00050

Tomasello, M. (1995). Joint attention as social cognition. In C. Moree & P.J. Dunham (Eds.), *Joint attention: Its origins and role in development* (pp. 103–130). Hillsdale, NJ: Erlbaum.

Williams, E., Costall, A., & Reddy, V. (1999). Children with autism experience problems with both objects and people. *Journal of Autism and Developmental Disorders, 29*(5), 367–378. http://dx.doi.org/10.1023/A:1023026810619

Wolfberg, P. (2009). *Play and imagination in children with autism.* New York, NY: Teachers College Press.

Zahavi, D. (2005). *Subjectivity and selfhood: Investigating the first-person perspective.* Cambridge, MA: MIT Press.

PART II

Pretense and Storytelling in the Classroom

8

THE WRONGHEADED EXCLUSION OF IMAGINATIVE STORYTELLING FROM KINDERGARTEN WRITING INSTRUCTION

Patricia M. Cooper

Introduction

"I can fly," 5-year-old Gil announced upon being introduced to me at his home recently. "No kidding?" I responded. "I'm a superhero," he explained. "I made my own jetpack."

I wasn't surprised by Gil's declaration (all names of children and teachers are pseudonyms). In my former life as a kindergarten teacher in an early childhood center in Chicago, I lived with 4-, 5-, and 6-year-old superheroes on a daily basis. Princesses, runaway rabbits, and all sorts of villains—for superheroes to fight, of course—showed up a lot in the children's dramatic play (which in those days reigned freely for one hour daily). In time, following renowned early childhood educator Vivian Paley's (1981) lead, I learned to make room in the schedule for the children to dictate and dramatize their stories in a kind of spontaneous readers' theater. Soon I was knee deep in dictated narratives and dramatizations of Han Solo and Darth Vader, the boys' favorite topic in my first year as a scribe and makeshift theater director. The girls, too, produced their own casts of the good and the wicked—notably, Sleeping Beauty and Maleficent—but also endless variations on Mama Rabbit and the Bad Wolf. Similarly themed stories erupted in their drawings and attempts at independent writing. Just as importantly, outsized fantasies of real life, like receiving 1,000 birthday presents, or simply implausible ones, like falling down a hole on the way home from school (an inexplicable but regular strand in one of my kindergartens) also made themselves known.

All of this made sense to me as a young teacher, and still does. As Paley (1981) has frequently observed in her many books on classroom life, fantasy-inspired thoughts are the things young children refer to most often in their unsupervised moments of fantasy or imaginative play, also called *make-believe*, *pretend*, *dramatic*, and sometimes *story based*. (In this chapter, all of the aforementioned adjectives are used interchangeably to modify play.) Thus, how could their fantasies *not* spill over into the stories they wished to dictate and ultimately write independently?

The question under investigation in this chapter is twofold: What is the developmental and educational justification for encouraging young children's imagination-based written narratives in early writing instruction? Further, how is it supported or depressed by prevailing curriculum frameworks, standards, and teachers' practices?

In this analysis, I first provide the theoretical context and research base to view young children's imagination-based written narratives as what Paley (1981) called a "true extension of (imaginative) play" (p. 12), with benefits to overall development and academic achievement, particularly around the kindergarten year. Next, I argue that these benefits provide the educational rationale for promoting imaginative writing in the kindergarten curriculum. As I write, pedagogically, justification can be found in Dewey's theory of motivation in learning and the need to construct curriculum that is based on the child's present interests but is always led by the end goal (1902/1991).

The issue motivating this chapter is that imagination-based writing instruction is losing ground in American kindergartens, similar to the well-documented decline in opportunities for imaginative play (Pappano, 2010; Singer, Golinkoff, & Hirsh-Pasek, 2006). To give weight to the problem and its consequences, I describe two frameworks that currently exert considerable influence over early writing education in American schools today. The first is the writing workshop model promoted by Lucy Calkins, founder of the Teachers College Reading and Writing Workshop Project (TCRWP; Calkins, 1994, 2003, 2005, 2013). As I show, Calkins' writing workshop model aggressively steers children away from imaginative writing in kindergarten and first and second grades except in very specific and limited instances, driving them to write what she refers to as "*true* stories [emphasis added]." Findings from my investigation suggest that restricting young children's imagination in writing is a disturbing example of ideology trumping developmental and pedagogical theory in early childhood education.

Calkins' approach is easily contextualized within another and even more powerful influence over what will be taught in the American kindergarten writing curriculum in years ahead, the new Common Core State Standards Initiative (n.d.) for learning outcomes (hereafter referred to as *Common Core*). The Common Core is widely perceived as an effort to increase the academic learning of all children, so as to close achievement gaps among different ethnic, race, and socioeconomic groups, as well as to make American children as a single cohort more competitive worldwide. Although mandated adoption of the Common Core is still an ongoing debate in policy circles, 47 of the 50 states have adopted it as of this writing. Central to the purpose of this analysis is that the Common Core substandards for English Language Arts (ELA) do not include a call for imaginative writing in kindergarten or first or second grade. They do, however, include expectations for nonfiction writing.

Among other troubling aspects of these two trends is that research on language development suggests that depression of imaginative writing in the TCRWP and the Common Core frameworks is especially significant for those young children who rely on early schooling to bridge home–school differences in all areas that affect language and learning, including play and imagination (Dyson, 1997, 2003, 2006; Dyson & Genishi, 1993, 1994; McNamee, 2015).

Before I begin, I want to make clear that my analysis is not designed to critique all aspects of Calkins' writing workshop model or the value of asking children to write information-based or nonfiction text. Similarly, it does not seek to undermine all of the Common Core Standards or the standards movement writ large. My goal here is to question the educational and pedagogical wisdom in banning, discouraging, or effectively limiting kindergarteners' imagination-based written narratives. I argue that doing so grossly underserves the basic developmental needs of young children's psychosocial, language, or academic development. Hence, the sway of these two phenomena over kindergarten writing instruction must be reconsidered.

Method

This investigation employs instrumental case study methodology (Stake, 2005, 2010), which permits us to examine a phenomenon from a different perspective than its stated orientation in order to ask questions related to its ramifications. Stake (2005) writes: "The case . . . plays a supporting role, and it facilitates our understanding of something else" (p. 437). As noted, under examination is Calkins' mandate in writing workshop instruction that only true events are legitimate subject matter for children's story writing (1994, 2003, 2005, 2013). Also under study are the Common Core ELA Standards (n.d.) for the primary grades K–2. The focus grade level in this analysis is kindergarten.

Data Sources

Data sources were chosen to provide "thick description" (Geertz, 1973) of the problem, per the requirements of instrumental case study methodology (Stake, 2010). In addition to her published work, representative data on Calkins' approach include her commentary on a video of teacher–child interaction around story writing she rates as exemplary, as well as a description of what happens in the video itself. (Data related to Common Core Standards are provided from http://www.corestandards.org and http://www.corestandards.org/ELA-Literacy/).

Data Analysis

Analysis of the data proceeded thematically (Bogdan & Biklen, 2011) to generalize from the literature on socioconstructivist learning and pedagogy, the role of imagination in psychosocial and cognitive development, young children's interest in using imagination-based content when composing stories and, finally, writing instruction.

Socioconstructivist Learning

This analysis is informed by socioconstructivist theories of cognition, language, and child development, as well as research in play and emergent literacy (see, for example, Applebee, 1978; Bruner, 1986; Cooper, 1993, 2009; Cooper, Capo, Mathes, & Grey, 2007; Dyson, 2006; Genishi & Dyson, 2009; McNamee, 2015; Nicolopoulou, 2007; Piaget, 1945/1962; Rosenblatt, 2005; Singer et al., 2006; Snow, 1991;Vygotsky, 1978). In short, socioconstructivist theory enables us to perceive development across the domains as an ever-evolving confluence of internal tendencies and social contexts, from the psychosocial and cognitive to the physical, circumstantial, and cultural. In this view, adults, significant others, and, arguably, even significant events are said to "scaffold" children's learning in pivotal ways (Bodrova & Leong, 2007; Cooper, 2009; Rogoff, 1991;Vygotsky, 1978; Wertsch, 1991).

An essential byproduct of a socioconstructivist approach to education is its support for multimodal, multidimensional learning experiences across the ages, especially for young children (Copple & Bredekamp, 2009; Falk, 2012; Schwartz & Copeland, 2010). A prime example is the extensive benefits of imaginative play, which research shows advances young children's language development, imaginative thinking, purposeful action, and experimentation. Lev S. Vygotsky, Erik Erikson, Jean Piaget, and later theorists and researchers all recognize the rise and use of imaginative thinking and its action-based corollary, imaginative play, as a critical developmental achievement in the second half of early childhood (roughly three through seven years old).

Psychosocial Development

According to Vygotsky (1978), a child's ability to create an "imaginary, illusory world" or an "imaginary situation" is first seen in pretend play (action) sometime in the third year (all ages approximate). As a matter of social–emotional adaptation, he writes, pretend play allows young children to construct solutions related to real life problems or questions that provoke feelings of helplessness, unrealizable desires, or confusion (p. 93). Understanding young children's motivation to pretend or imagine in play is key to understanding the function of a given imagination-based episode. One familiar example is when children in this age group pretend that their dolls or stuffed animals have run away, only to be brought back home by a watchful grown-up. Another is when children send in the bad guys only so superheroes may be called to the rescue. Young children also use pretend play to practice rules they struggle with in the real world, such as being told not to hit others or to go to sleep.

Importantly, no developmental concern goes unexplored in imaginative play. Studies by Nicolopoulou (1996), Nicolopoulou, Scales, and Weintraub (1994), and Nicolopoulou and Richner (2004), for example, describe the way in which young children's imagination-based play and stories act as modes of inquiry into what it means to be a boy or a girl. Vygotskian theorists Bodrova and Leong (2006, 2007, 2008), along with Berk, Mann, and Ogan (2006), among others, further describe the link between imaginative play and social maturity in terms of its connection to self-regulation or executive function and state that imaginative thinking reaches its peak developmental potential somewhere in the sixth year. For most American children, this coincides with the kindergarten year, depending on the age of school entry.

The third stage of Erikson's (1950/1985) psychosocial theory of human development, initiative versus guilt, also illuminates the way in which pretend play and imaginative thinking provide 3- to 6-year-old children with tools that help them manage the psychosocial challenges in the years before leaving the home base for "big school" (for Erikson, first grade). Popularly referred to as the *am I good or am I bad stage*, its "danger," says Erikson (1950/1985), "is a sense of guilt over the goals contemplated and the acts initiated in one's exuberant enjoyment of new locomotor and mental power" (p. 255). Approval from significant others clears the path for children to separate from caregivers, cooperate with playmates, and act productively on their intentions, all of which prepares them to adapt to the multifaceted demands of later schooling.

Research on the value of imaginative play to young children's psychosocial development has attracted increasing attention in recent years with regard to its concomitant decrease in preschools and kindergartens, which traditionally designated it as a central component of the curriculum (Brown & Vaughn, 2009; Cooper, 2009; Paley, 2004; Pelligrini & Blatchford, 2002; Singer et al., 2006).

Symbolic Thought

According to Vygotsky (1978), the development of imaginative thinking as exemplified by imaginative play is fundamentally associated with the acquisition of symbolic function, meaning a child's successful substitutions of meaning for unrelated objects. This happens when blocks become cars and popsicle sticks become people. Vygotsky argues that symbolic play of this sort ultimately culminates in abstract thought and ultimately scientific concepts (p. 103).

180 Patricia M. Cooper

Piaget holds similar, though not duplicate, views to Vygotsky on the evolution and function of symbolic play in the posttoddler and premiddle childhood years, though he did not attribute as much impact as Vygotsky to pretend play as the precursor of abstract thought. To paraphrase, Piaget maintained that "the symbol concretizes and animates everything" for children below 7 because their "logico-verbal thought is still too inadequate and vague" (1945/1962, pp. 154–155). In essence, symbolic thought for the younger child is the ideal vehicle for exploration and experimentation of ideas and the physical world.

Language Development

The relationship between children's imaginative play and imaginative writing is foreshadowed in language development. Seminal language research (Britton, 1970; Halliday, 1975; Langer, 1967–1972; Weir, 1962/1970) reminds us that children typically learn to produce two types of language. One allows them to conduct "business" in the real world in real time (e.g., *bottle, I want more*). The other allows them to reflect on the real world in the past, present, or future tense (e.g., *One day, when I was little . . .*). Applebee (1978) refers to the former as *participant* language, which arrives first, and the latter as *spectator*, which surfaces sometime in the third year. However, according to Applebee, young children don't gain control over spectator-type language until well into the sixth year. The primary vehicle for the practice and production of spectator language during this period, he says, is the imaginative stories they hear and retell. He argues that telling imaginative stories actually helps young children distinguish fact from fiction and, in doing so, helps them "present alternatives, clarify dark corners, pose contradictions, and reconcile conflicts" (p. 134) in the real world, which clearly ties back to children's psychosocial development.

Related to Applebee's work is research on the dual nature of language development in early literacy acquisition, particularly around decontextualized and extended language use. Importantly, both are highly correlated with children's reading comprehension skills in the upper elementary grades (Dickinson & Porche, 2011; Heath, 1982; Snow, 1991; Snow, Burns, & Griffin, 1998). Of special consideration are the needs of children who may experience a disconnect between home and school expectations of language development. Although Dudley-Marling and Lucas (2009) rightly warn us against "pathologizing the language and culture of poor children," disparities between middle- and low-income children's performance on language-based measures relative to school expectations have been well documented. Dickinson and Sprague (2001), among many others, persuasively argue for the importance of early schooling in augmenting the language and literacy skills of young children from low-income families in culturally respectful and meaningful ways. Dyson (1997, 2003, 2006), Dyson and Genishi (1993, 1994, 2009), and McNamee's (2015) research on urban children's imaginative storytelling suggests that children are especially responsive to writing opportunities that invite personal interests. Other research (see Cooper et al., 2007; Nicolopoulou, Cortina, Ilgaz, Cates, & de Sá, 2015) shows that the vocabulary and literacy subskills of prekindergarten and kindergarten low-income and bilingual children significantly improve when they are given regular opportunities to dictate and dramatize original stories, the majority of which contain imagination-based content.

Socioconstructivist theory allows us to see the trajectory from language development to imaginative thinking to imaginative play and imaginative storytelling as a series of interrelated, scaffolded events. This view of narrative development in early childhood essentially redefines narrative writing as more than the mastery of subskills. Conceptually, it reflects a dynamic relationship between what children think about, what they are trying to understand, and what they need to practice (Nicolopoulou, 1996). Roskos and Christie's (2011) article on the *play–literacy nexus* reviews the research on the impact of imaginative play on literacy development and identifies ways to support the connection in practice.

Finally, Louise Rosenblatt (2005), whose work on transactional reading and writing is not invoked in discussions of young children's reading and writing education as often as it might be, sums up the inside and outside nature of young children's writing in this way:

> Writing is always an event in time, occurring at a particular moment in the writer's biography, in particular circumstances, under particular external as well as internal pressures. In short, the writer is always transacting with a personal, social, and cultural environment. Thus, the writing process must be seen as always embodying both personal and social, or individual and environmental factors.
>
> *(p. 17)*

Rosenblatt's (2005) view on the triangulated nature of the writing experience resonates with Paley's (1981) belief that kindergarten children write (or dictate) stories to tell each other what they are thinking about. They listen to each other's stories for the same reason. The question, then, is what *are* kindergarten children (often) thinking about? Whatever the topic, Paley tells us, there's a good chance its source is imagination based and driven (1981, 1986, 1988, 1990, 1992, 1997, 2004).

Encoding, Content, and Motivation to Learn

If theory and research related to young children's social–emotional development, language, literacy, and abstract thinking make the case for the role of imaginative stories in general development and later academic achievement, requiring children to write them down adds a practical wrinkle for young children and the teacher alike: the problem of encoding. Young children's physical and conceptual immaturity around encoding speaks directly to the issue of what content motivates them to learn and practice. The fact is, encoding depends on children's physical stamina and small muscle control as much as it does on their acquisition of phonemic awareness and sound and symbol correspondence, let alone the self-regulation required to attend.

Historically, both drawing and dictation were seen as prerequisites to independent writing (Bissex, 1980; Clay, 1975; Schickedanz & Collins, 2013; Van Allen, 1976). Space considerations make it impossible to include the ample evidence for young children's interest in dictating stories with imagination-based content that can be found in Paley's investigations into dictated stories (1981, 1990, 1992), as well as other research (Cooper, 1993, 2009; Dyson, 1997, 2003, 2006; Dyson & Genishi, 1993, 1994; Engel, 1995; Freeman & Sanders, 1989; Genishi & Dyson, 2009; Heath, 1982; Meier, 2009; Newkirk, 2007; Nicolopoulou, 1996, 2007; Nicolopoulou et al., 2015; Nicolopoulou, McDowell, & Brockmeyer, 2006). Suffice it to say that this interest runs deep.

Arguably, dictated stories with imagination-based content occupy a transitional space between oral storytelling and independent storytelling in and around the kindergarten year that cannot be ignored. I offer two short samples that elegantly illustrate the issue. The first (Box 8.1) is an e-mail I received that involves a story dictated by Natalia, a kindergartner, to Anne, her teacher. The second (Box 8.2) is a story Anne sent me that one of her students, Lucia, dictated to her.

Box 8.1

To: Patsy
From: Anne
Subject: Natalia's story

So today as Carly and Katie and Lauren gather around the story table with little Natalia and me, Natalia tells me another version of "Hansel and Gretel" . . . in which, instead of a witch, the villain is the [cartoon] character Sakemo from her last story—but this time Sakemo is half man and half woman(!). There are five kids instead of just Hansel and Gretel. In the end, Sakemo pushes the kids into the oven and they all die. At the end of the dramatization, the kids [audience to the actors] solemnly applauded the five little corpses. Oh, boy.

Box 8.2

Pocus Pocus
Dictated by Lucia to Anne

Once upon a time there was a little girl and a little boy and a big sister. They went to the woods. There were three witches. One was the witch mother and two were witch children. Then the witches saw the little boy, little girl, and the big sister. So the witches said, "You come here or else you'll be supper!" The children said, "No way!" Then the children found a bucket of water and they threw it at the three witches. Then the witches did not melt. The children ran. The witches ran after them. The witch got the little girl and the big sister said, "Give her back!" The witch said, "No way!" Then they got a magic book and they found a spell. Then the witches died. The end.

Characters/actors required for dramatization:
Little girl: Joanne
Little boy: Caleb
Big sister: Lucia
Mom witch: Flores
Other witches: Hannah, Tiana

Without a doubt, Lucia and Natalia's dictated stories represent the way in which imagination-based content can fuel young children's experimentation with symbols, psychosocial relationships, literacy skills, and language of all types, which can only be seen as foundational to later independent writing (of all types). This leads us to the question of children's motivation to write.

Dewey's classic analysis of the "problem of the child and the curriculum" provides a leading question for how to think about the inclusion or exclusion of imagination-based content in early writing instruction in terms of motivation to write. He asks: "Of what use, educationally speaking, is it to be able to see the end in the beginning?" (1902/1991, p. 192). Dewey is not directing us here to work backwards until we get to the lowest common denominator and, ipso facto, the curricular beginning. Rather, he is recommending the inverse interpretation. That is, the end—or at least a particular aspect of it—is foretold in the beginning. "Taken in this way," Dewey writes, "[the end] is no remote and distant result to be achieved, but a guiding method in dealing with the present" (1902/1991, p. 192).

The pedagogical problem is to distinguish which aspect of the end to cultivate. Dewey argues that it will be found in the "deeds," "acts," and "feelings" that represent the child's "culminating powers and interest" in the subject, which he contrasts with "waning" and "prophetic" powers and interest. According to Dewey, the former no longer require the teacher's attention, as the children's questions about them have been answered. And the latter need no attention yet, as the children have yet to pose questions of them.

In his review of the research on specific writing opportunities in the primary grades, Boscolo (2008) concludes that in addition to aiding young children's progress as encoders and constructors of narrative, effective writing instruction also promotes the child's "*positive attitude or disposition to writing* [emphasis added]" (p. 306).

For the purposes of this analysis, Vygotsky's work on the "Prehistory of Written Language" (1978) offers the definitive argument on the relationship between imagination, early writing, and the problem of encoding. He begins by establishing the link between symbolic function and imaginative play discussed previously, which paves the way for writing speech down. But this technical relationship between imaginative play and writing takes on psychosocial and cultural proportions when he turns to the problem of encoding by arguing against conflating children's efforts to write with their efforts to reproduce letters and words:

> Until now, writing has occupied too narrow a place in school practice as compared to the enormous role that it plays in children's cultural development. The teaching of writing has been conceived in narrowly practical terms. Children are taught to trace out letters and make words out of them, but they are not taught written language.
>
> *(Vygotsky, 1978, p. 105)*

Theorizing against a mechanistic view of writing, Vygotsky argues that kindergarten children should be given the opportunity to find writing "meaningful" and should be taught that writing is "necessary for something," a response to an "intrinsic need." In other words, that it is a "task that is necessary and relevant for life" (1978, p. 118). One can easily look to practical writing activities that might support the kindergarten child's discovery of writing in this way. Birthday invitations come to mind, as does labeling possessions.

In her many publications involving young children's dictated stories, Paley has called our attention to how imagination-based writing always draws on a mix of children's interests, popular culture, and home cultures (1981, 1986, 1988, 1990, 1992, 1997, 2004). Paley's experience fulfills Dewey's advice to look for a pedagogical starting point—a beginning—in the child's most intellectually active or culminating deeds, acts, and feelings around narrative. When talking about 4-, 5-, and 6-year-olds, all signs point to the rightness of imagination-based storytelling (Cooper, 2009; Dyson, 1997, 2003, 2006; Dyson & Genishi, 1993, 1994; McNamee, 2015).

Findings

Writing Workshop Curriculum

Calkins' workshop model is rooted in the tenets of writing process instruction. Pritchard and Honeycutt (2006) find that the definition of the writing process has evolved over time. As discussed here, a writing workshop directs the participant's construction of narrative through sequential and recursive steps involving prewriting, drafting, revision, editing, and sharing. (In *The Art of Teaching Writing*, 1994, Calkins expresses her preference for the terms *rehearsal, drafting, revision*, and *editing*.) Teachers in this model are expected to routinely conference with writers to aid growth and improvement. Peer-to-peer conferencing is often built in as well.

Calkins, a mentee of writing process curriculum developers Donald Graves and Donald Murray in the 1980s, first detailed her basic methodology for writing in her best-selling teacher's guide *The Art of Teaching Writing* (1994). She revised and amplified the approach in *Units of Study for Primary Writing: A Yearlong Curriculum* (2003), where she introduced what is known in the field as her *small moments* curriculum and effectively crystallized her exclusion of imagination-based stories. Her long-standing objective is for children to find writing topics in minor day-to-day events, like giving the dog a bath or walking to school. In those texts, fiction is included *only* as an optional unit for the end of the year.

Units of Study in Opinion, Information, and Narrative Writing, Grade K: A Common Core Workshop Curriculum (2013) is the most recent iteration of Calkins' workshop and, as its new title suggests, is designed to align closely with the Common Core. While much from the earlier series remains, fiction writing is no longer even an option for K–2. The "learning progressions" in the narrative writing units for kindergarten through second grade include lessons where children, again, "tell stories from their lives" and "everyday events." The unit for third grade continues this practice with a section on "crafting true stories." In an apparent nod to Common Core, it also introduces imaginative writing in the third grade by way of an additional unit on writing fairy tales.

Calkins disseminates her writing workshop methods through an extensive system of teacher education and professional development, as well as through her many best-selling publications and extensive program of teacher in-service. (The TCRWP website claims direct training of over 150,000 teachers, with Calkins' publications in 65% of American classrooms [http://readingandwritingproject.com/about/tcrwp.html]). Calkins has also recently adapted her approach to target Common Core Standards, as shown in two recent publications, *Pathways to the Common Core: Accelerating Achievement* (2012) and the aforementioned *Units of Study in Opinion, Information, and Narrative Writing, Grade K: A Common Core Workshop Curriculum* (2013).

186 Patricia M. Cooper

Although Calkins' work does not have the same political muscle behind it as Common Core, there is no denying its influence. Pritchard and Honeycutt (2006) note that, despite the scarcity of experimental research on her instructional methods, Calkins has had an "enormous impact on how the writing process approach is implemented in the early grades" (p. 281) around the nation. In New York City, the nation's largest school district, her writing workshop model has dominated early writing instruction for more than two decades. It has also spawned a large number of derivative models.

Calkins has been targeted for this analysis because she not only excludes imaginative writing from her curriculum but also directly rejects imaginative writing's role in young children's development as writers of narrative. Ironically, this is not to say that she doesn't recognize the children's interest in imagination-based content. In a somewhat puzzling twist, she acknowledges young children's "*urge* to write fiction [emphasis added]" and even says that, when allowed, it "is something to behold" (2005, p. 26). Yet, nonetheless, she mandates against it in her writing workshop curriculum through a signature requirement of the TCRWP K–2 writing workshop: that children write only "true" narratives. As defined by Calkins, a true narrative is something that has actually happened to the child, something the child has experienced firsthand. To this end, even kindergarteners are encouraged to write vignettes or what is known in the TCRWP approach as small moments. Calkins advises that if children "try to write fictional stories," they should be told, "[W]e are writing small moments of our lives." In other words, "we" are *not* writing moments of imagination. Calkins goes on to say that the teacher's job is to "lure [children] to find these vignettes [as] equally fascinating" as their fantasies (2005, p. vi).

Calkins' justification for "luring" young children away from their fantasy life is her apparent belief that the imagination-based content young children feel compelled to tell about betrays the low value they place on their real lives. In her breakthrough and best-selling *The Art of Teaching Writing* (1994), she observes:

> When we ask [children] to choose their own topics for writing, they often write about superheroes or retell television dramas. In word and deed, our children ask: Does my life really matter?
>
> When we help children know that their lives do matter, we are teaching writing.
>
> In the workshop children write about what is alive and vital and real for them . . .
>
> *(pp. 16–17)*

Calkins goes on to suggest that teaching writing is one and the same with rescuing children from their meaningless fantasies.

Criticism and research on Calkins' true narrative mandate are limited, though unequivocal in finding it unjustifiable, if not injurious (Cooper, 2009; Feinberg, 2005; Genishi & Dyson, 2009; Harwayne, 2001; Lensmire, 1994, 2000). In a recent

Exclusion of Imaginative Storytelling   **187**

publication, Dyson (2014) likens Calkins' refusal to entertain young children's desire to borrow content from the media (which Calkins refers to as "illegal") as a troubling tribute to "individualistic ideology" (p. 6) that works against children's need to connect with their peers and immediate culture. Similarly, in his work on the inanity of banning young boys' interest in writing about superheroes in a writing workshop, Newkirk (2007) asks: "By what standard can one claim that a young boy immersed in a Star Wars adventure is acting inauthentically?" (2007, p. 543).

To illustrate Calkins' ideology as it is actually practiced in the classroom, I turn now to sample text and action from a video produced and disseminated by Calkins and the TCRWP. Many more such descriptions and videos can be found in Calkins' collection of books and resources.

The video examined here, called *Providing and Then Withholding Scaffolding to Support one [sic] Child's Understanding of Narrative Structure* (http://vimeo. com/55954402), showcases a teacher–child conference designed to move a kindergarten child, Harold, from a reality-based fantasy to a "narrative structure," defined in the tagline as "writes events in sequence." The teacher's ostensible goal is getting Harold to write a true story.

Calkins herself introduces the video as "an old favorite" about a conference between a kindergarten teacher and a little boy named Harold. Though lengthy, I think her remarks are instructive to read in full.

> [W]atch how Harold's story gets so much better. You'll see that he came to Amanda [the teacher] with a story that didn't tell what happened first, next, and last. There really was no story sequence. And during the conference Amanda decided she needed to provide him with assisted support in writing and telling a story sequentially across pages. Amanda's helping Harold move towards the kindergarten standards for narrative writing, which say that students need to use a combination of drawing, dictating, and writing to narrate a single event or several closely linked events; to tell about the events in the order in which they occur; and to provide a reaction to what happened. Those are ambitious standards for narrative writing, in contrast, for example, to standards for opinion writing. Amanda gives Harold sequence words to help him do this—*first, next*, and so on. She could have been more explicit about what it means to tell a true story in sequence, but she made the decision instead to immerse Harold in the work so that he developed almost like a "felt sense" of what storytelling is like. Later she'll give him the support transferring what he was able to do in this piece to other pieces of writing. (http://vimeo.com/55954402)

When Calkins finishes, the screen shows a close-up of Harold's writing folder. We hear Amanda ask Harold if he can read us his story. Next we see Harold, a child of color of slight build who has not yet lost his baby teeth. He is reading to Amanda

188 Patricia M. Cooper

from his story pages. He points to different parts of the page, giggling repeatedly. He reads his story to Amanda. "First I was eating a hot dog. Then a burger. Then I ate a dollar. No, a cookie." He hesitates, and we see the written page, which features a page full of various-sized circular shapes inside of other shapes, some letters, and some hard-to-make-out figures. He points to one and adds, "A sausage."

Amanda acknowledges heartily that Harold has a "lot of things" on his paper and then asks what happens on the second page. Harold gestures at the page and says, giggling again, "I ate all the food." Amanda responds with exaggerated enthusiasm, "Oh, my gosh. What's it say?" Harold points to the letters $I L V F D$ he has enclosed in a rectangular shape. "I love food," he says, still giggling. Amanda again expresses her amazement at the story, finishing with, "Oh, my gosh. You must really love food. You ate a lot of food, Harold. Did you really eat all that food at one time?" Harold giggles some more.

Harold's story would read as in Box 8.3.

Box 8.3

I was eating a hot dog. Then a burger. Then I ate a cookie. And then I ate sausage. I ate all the food. I love food.

Amanda once again expresses her approval about Harold's story about eating all that food and then says, "You've got two pages here. First about eating all the food. And then how all the food was gone. That's a great story. I love how you wrote it across two pages. Just like a real writer does. In a real book." Amanda then asks Harold if he knows what his next story is going to be about. Harold nods. "It's going to be about this one," he says, pointing to something he has drawn on the original story. Amanda confirms that he is going to write one that is "kinda the same" as the first, and Harold nods, smiling. She says okay and then asks about the parts of the story across the pages: "Show me how it's gonna go." Harold says okay. "First . . . ," he starts off. Amanda interrupts. "But, Harold, look at me. Look at me. It's gotta be a *true* story about Harold."

Amanda quickly tells Harold that if she were telling a true story about Amanda, she would say something like how she went swimming with her friend Mary. "We went splashing into the water. A big wave came and pushed us down, under the water." She adds, "I got water up my nose." Harold whispers, "Okay," a few times as Amanda is speaking. When she finishes, she says, "I want you to try and tell your story like that. Go ahead, let me hear." Harold hesitates. "I can't tell my story like that," he protests a little. Amanda ignores this comment and repeats, "Oh, so let's try to think of a real true story that happened to Harold."

Five seconds pass. Harold looks away. "I don't know," he says. Amanda then tells him that when she wants to tell a story, she thinks about the things she does.

She asks what kinds of things Harold does. Suddenly Harold brightens. "Oh, I get dressed to go to school." Amanda responds highly encouragingly to this and asks what else he likes to do. He mentions going to the beach and going swimming (like Amanda). Amanda reacts similarly supportively. She asks him which story (of the two) he wants to tell. He chooses the one about getting dressed, finally producing the following story. Amanda asks him to repeat it as he moves his fingers across the blank pages of his writing book. Harold points at the place where words might go as Amanda turns the pages (see Box 8.4).

Box 8.4

First I wake up. Then I put on my shirt. Then I put on my pants. Then I put on my shoes. Then I walk to school.

Amanda asks, "And that's a true story, right? Did that really happen to you?" Harold nods. Then, with Amanda's help, he tells and retells his other story. The final version is given in Box 8.5.

Box 8.5

First I came to the beach. Then I ate lunch. Then I was swimming. With my mom. Then I ate snack. Then I left.

Amanda sends Harold off to commit his getting dressed story to paper by reminding him, "When you're doing your writing, Harold, I want you to be thinking about true stories from your life." Harold responds, "Alright."

Common Core State Standards in English Language Arts

The mission statement of the Common Core includes its aspiration to provide a "consistent, clear understanding of what students are expected to learn" (http://www.corestandards.org/). This is not to say that the Common Core is a source of curricular ideas, as noted in the Introduction to the key design consideration of the ELA standards, which emphasizes that the standards "focus on results rather than means" and spells out the intent not to recommend any one approach over another. The Introduction to the writing standards (http://www.corestandards.org/ELA-Literacy/W/introduction) reflects the call throughout the standards for increasing competency in a subject matter over time:

> The following standards for K-5 offer a focus for instruction each year to help ensure that students gain adequate mastery of a range of skills and

applications. Each year in their writing, students should demonstrate increasing sophistication in all aspects of language use, from vocabulary and syntax to the development and organization of ideas, and they should address increasingly demanding content and sources. Students advancing through the grades are expected to meet each year's grade-specific standards and retain or further develop skills and understandings mastered in the preceding grade.

The problem of the Common Core and the exclusion of imagination-based content in kindergarten writing instruction is relatively simple. Unlike Calkins' writing workshop curriculum, it does not ban imagination-fueled, fantasy, or fiction writing outright. *Significantly, it simply does not list it as standard before third grade.*

Writing standards for all grade levels are divided into three "types and purposes." They are (a) opinion pieces on topics and texts, (b) informative and explanatory texts, and (c) narratives. Expectations of competency increase by grade. Box 8.6 contains narrative standards for K–3.

Because no explanation is provided to justify the exclusion of imaginative writing in the primary grades, we are forced to adopt the language of the Introduction and assign it "non-essential status" in the primary grades.

Box 8.6

- CCSS.ELA-Literacy.W.K.3: Use a combination of drawing, dictating, and writing to narrate a single event or several loosely linked events, tell about the events in the order in which they occurred, and provide a reaction to what happened.
- CCSS.ELA-Literacy.W.1.3: Write narratives in which they recount two or more appropriately sequenced events, include some details regarding what happened, use temporal words to signal event order, and provide some sense of closure.
- CCSS.ELA-Literacy.W.2.3: Write narratives in which they recount a well-elaborated event or short sequence of events, include details to describe actions, thoughts, and feelings, use temporal words to signal event order, and provide a sense of closure.
- CCSS.ELA-Literacy.W.3.3: Write narratives to develop real or imagined experiences or events using effective technique, descriptive details, and clear event sequences.

Discussion

Discussion is guided by the research question: What is the developmental and educational justification for encouraging young children's imagination-based written narratives in early writing instruction? Further, how is it supported or depressed by prevailing curriculum frameworks, standards, and teachers' practices?

Both Calkins' true narrative mandate and the Common Core ELA Standards for kindergarten, as highlighted in this analysis, exemplify exactly what Dewey (1902/1991) warned us against. Each ignores the complex and intellectually active beginning in young children's narrative development in favor of a bare-bones end.

To start, Calkins' true narrative mandate stands on its own to showcase the inappropriate, if not damaging, substitute of ideology for theory. The teacher (Amanda) in the video, for example, not only discards what Harold is "thinking about" (Paley, 1981, p. 66), which is disrespectful enough, but she also ultimately underestimates his capacity as a thinker *and* writer. At the same time, she sets the bar higher than necessary with regard to certain subskills. That is, as we see in the video, Harold's reading of his mostly pictorial story reveals that his encoding skills lag behind his oral storytelling and drawing skills. Yet the research (Clay, 1975; Schickedanz & Collins, 2013) is clear: Harold is not atypical of many 4- to 6-year-olds in this way. This should prompt teachers to make more time in the curriculum for a spectrum of supporting activities, like story dictation; letter formation; encoding of favorite words; phonics, and so on. This is not to say, of course, that children in this age group should not practice independent story writing and drawing, if only to grasp its future potential in their lives (Dewey's "prophetic" possibilities).

Further, Calkins' self-described favorite exemplar should raise several red flags for those not only interested in theory and research-based practice but also fair and meaningful assessment. Calkins offers a simply inexpert opinion of Harold's original story by telling video viewers to note that the story "didn't tell what happened first, next, and last. There really was no story sequence." But the evidence flatly contraindicates her conclusion. Recall the story Harold "read" from his mostly picture-laden book:

> I was eating a hot a dog. Then a burger. Then I ate a cookie. And then I ate sausage. I ate all the food. I love food.

Surely, it is hard to deny Harold's sequencing of events here. Even more troubling is Calkins' failure to give Harold credit for the impressive way in which his story evinces a burgeoning ability to assess the events he wrote about—"I ate all the food"—(Standard W.K.3) *and* a sense of closure—"I love food"—which the standards don't call for until first grade (Standard W.1.3). Further, Calkins' commentary that the stories Harold tells under Amanda's insistence he tell a true story are structurally "better" has no basis in the data either. The original contains the same number of related events as the later two stories, *plus* it contains the aforementioned assessment and closure, which the other two most explicitly do not.

Just as puzzling is Calkins' claim that Harold developed a "felt sense"—by which we assume that she means some sort of internalized understanding—of what storytelling "was like" only *after* Amanda's intervention. Again, this is unsubstantiated by the data. In fact, if we were to permit ourselves conclusions based on Harold's affect, we would see that his initially happy relationship to storytelling plainly surpasses the relationship we see when Amanda moves him on from his food story. In addition, Harold's original story is not only linguistically and narratively more complex than the two Amanda elicits from him, it is, arguably, more interesting from an aesthetic point of view. (It's impossible, of course, to know the source of Harold's food fantasy, but it's hard not to be reminded of Eric Carle's 1969 classic picture book, *The Very Hungry Caterpillar*.)

Digging a little deeper, we also see that Amanda's exaggerated and obviously feigned response to Harold's storytelling throughout obscures two very serious pedagogical breaches that Calkins glosses over. First, not only does Amanda, like Calkins, fail to recognize Harold's narrative accomplishment in his overeating story, she *imposes her diminished assessment of his skills on him*, as shown in his protest that he can't write a story in the way she wants him to write and that he does not know a true story to tell. Second, despite her response to his imagination-based story, Amanda does nothing less than devalue his original story by directing him away from his interest in writing another with the same theme. "It's gotta be a *true* story about Harold." Moreover, in doing so, she very clearly ignores an opportunity to help him practice decontextualized and extended language skills, vocabulary, and the like. Great responses hang in the offing that might have provoked Harold to use his imagination to practice vocabulary and build his decontextualized language. Obvious examples that spring to mind include, "Tell me more about eating so much." Or "I wonder where you found all that food." Or "Did anyone see you gobbling up all that food? What happened then?"

Language theorist and educator James Britton reminds students of writing instruction that "[i]n ordinary favourable [sic] circumstances no one has a greater influence than the teacher in determining what speech is acceptable in his classroom" (1970, p. 134). This is to say that worse than the mistakes of this young teacher and her mentor's faulty interpretation of the role—and potential—of Harold's imagination in learning to write narrative is their complicity, unintentional or not, in the silencing of a small boy's storytelling voice. This is one and the same with silencing the concomitant cognitive, social, and academic benefits that might have accompanied their permission to exercise that voice.

Since no context is provided for any Common Core Standards beyond oblique references to experts and other contributors in the FAQ section, analysis is limited to inference by default. That is, we are forced to conclude that if imaginative writing is an expectation of third graders but *not* of kindergarteners (or first and second graders), the Common Core developers see imaginative narrative only as a subspecialty in writing and not a foundational activity for all writing. This, of course, does not mean that teachers cannot teach imaginative writing if they wish, but given the well-known link between the Common Core, testing, and curriculum development, the reality is that the exclusion of imaginative writing in the K–2 ELA standards means that it will never see the light of day in the curriculum.

Finally, despite the fact that the Introduction to the Common Core ELA Standards specifically calls for children "to show increasing sophistication" in all aspects of language use, we are left to wonder how the absence of, or lack of practice in, imaginative writing before third grade will prepare children to use third-grade-level sophistication in that area when they finally do encounter the expectation.

Implications

As discussed, socioconstructivist theory, as well as research on language development, imaginative play, and writing instruction, allows us to inquire into the educational validity of the practices and recommendations described in the data on Calkins' writing workshop and the Common Core. This analysis suggests that whatever the respective value of Calkins' work or the goals of Common Core in other areas, the exclusion of imagination-based content from narrative writing instruction in the primary grades, particularly in and around the kindergarten year, is contraindicated in theory and practice. Early childhood educators and teacher educators must resist the illogic of standards and practices that neglect what Dewey calls children's "culminating powers and interests" in imagination-based content (1902/1991). We are obligated to view the lost opportunities for stimulating young children's language, academic, and creative achievements as a form of educational malfeasance.

These are strong charges. Yet, as shown, the effects of devaluing young children's imaginative lives are not only theoretical but also extraordinarily real and devastatingly generalizable to the learning potential of tens of thousands of small children across the nation.

References

Applebee, A. (1978). *The child's concept of story*. Chicago, IL: University of Chicago Press.

Berk, L.E., Mann, T.D., & Ogan, A.T. (2006). Make-believe play: Wellspring for the development of self regulation. In D.G. Singer & R.M. Golinkoff (Eds.), *Play = learning: How play motivates and enhances children's cognitive and social-emotional growth* (pp. 124–144). Oxford, UK: Oxford University Press.

Bissex, G. (1980). *Gnys at wrk: A child learns to write*. Cambridge, MA: Harvard University Press.

Bodrova, E., & Leong, D. J. (2006). Developing self-regulation: The Vygotskian view. *Academic Exchange Quarterly, 10*(4), 33–38.

Bodrova, E., & Leong, D.J. (2007). *Tools of the mind: The Vygotskian approach to early childhood education*. Englewood Cliffs, NJ: Prentice Hall.

Bodrova, E., & Leong, D.J. (2008). Developing self-regulation in kindergarten: Can we keep all the crickets in the basket? *Young Children, 63*(2), 56–58.

Bogdan, R., & Biklen, S.K. (2011). *Qualitative research for education: An introduction to theories and methods* (5th ed.). New York, NY: Pearson.

Boscolo, P. (2008). Writing in primary school. In C. Brazerman (Ed.), *Handbook of research on writing: History, society, school, individual, and text* (pp. 293–309). New York, NY: Erlbaum.

Britton, J. (1970). *Language and learning.* London, UK: Lane.

Brown, S., & Vaughn, C. (2009). *Play: How it shapes the brain, opens the imagination, and invigorates the soul.* New York, NY: Penguin.

Bruner, J. (1986). *Actual minds, possible worlds.* Cambridge, MA: Harvard University Press.

Calkins, L.M. (1994). *The art of teaching writing.* Portsmouth, NH: Heinemann.

Calkins, L.M. (2003). *Units of study for primary writing: A yearlong curriculum.* Portsmouth, NH: Heinemann.

Calkins, L.M. (2005). *Big lessons from small writers: Teaching primary writing.* Portsmouth, NH: Heinemann.

Calkins, L.M. (2012). *Pathways to the Common Core: Accelerating achievement.* Portsmouth, NH: Heinemann.

Calkins, L.M. (2013). *Units of study in opinion, information, and narrative writing, Grade K: A Common Core workshop curriculum.* Portsmouth, NH: Heinemann.

Carle, E. (1969). *The very hungry caterpillar.* New York, NY: Penguin Putnam.

Clay, M. (1975). *What did I write?* Portsmouth, NH: Heinemann.

Common Core English Language Arts Standards. (n.d.). Retrieved from http://www.corestandards.org/ELA-Literacy

Common Core State Standards Initiative. (n.d.). Retrieved from http://www.corestandards.org/

Cooper, P. (1993). *When stories come to school: Telling, writing, and performing stories in the early childhood classroom.* New York, NY: Teachers & Writers Collaborative.

Cooper, P.M. (2009). *The classrooms all young children need: Lessons in teaching from Vivian Paley.* Chicago, IL: University of Chicago Press.

Cooper, P.M., Capo, K., Mathes, B., & Grey, L. (2007). One authentic early literacy practice and three standardized tests: Can a storytelling curriculum measure up? *Journal of Early Childhood Teacher Education, 28*(3), 251–275.

Copple, C., & Bredekamp, S.K. (2009). *Developmentally appropriate practice in early childhood programs: Serving children birth through age 8* (3rd ed.). Washington, DC: National Association for the Education of Young Children (NAEYC).

Dewey, J. (1991). *The school and society and the child and the curriculum.* Chicago, IL: University of Chicago Press. (Original work published 1902)

Dickinson, D.K., & Porche, M.V. (2011). Relation between language experiences in preschool classrooms and children's kindergarten and fourth-grade language and reading abilities. *Child Development, 82*(3), 870–886.

Dickinson, D.K., & Sprague, K. (2001). The nature and impact of early childhood environments on the language and early literacy development of children from low income families. In S. Neuman & D.K. Dickinson (Eds.), *Handbook of early literacy* (pp. 263–292). New York, NY: Guilford Press.

Dudley-Marling, C., & Lucas, K. (2009). Pathologizing the language and culture of poor children. *Language Arts, 86*(5), 362–370.

Dyson, A.H. (1997). *Writing superheroes: Contemporary childhood, popular culture, and classroom literacy.* New York, NY: Teachers College Press.

Dyson, A.H. (2003). *The brothers and sisters learn to write: Popular literacies in childhood and school cultures.* New York, NY: Teachers College Press.

Dyson, A.H. (2006). On saying it right (write). *Research in the Teaching of English, 41*(1), 8–39.

Dyson, A.H. (2014). *ReWRITING the basics: Literacy learning in children's cultures.* New York, NY: Teachers College Press.

Dyson, A.H., & Genishi, C. (1993). Visions of children as language users: Language and language education in early childhood. In B. Spodek (Ed.), *Handbook of research in the education of young children* (pp. 122–136). New York, NY: Macmillan.

Dyson, A.H., & Genishi, C. (1994). *The need for story: Cultural diversity in classroom and community.* Urbana, IL: National Council of Teachers of English.

Dyson, A.H., & Genishi, C. (2009). *Children, language, and literacy: Diverse learners in a diverse society.* New York, NY: Teachers College Press.

Engel, S. (1995). *The stories children tell: Making sense of the narratives of childhood.* New York, NY: Freeman.

Erikson, E. (1985). *Childhood and society.* New York, NY: Norton. (Original work published 1950.)

Falk, B. (2012). *Defending childhood: Keeping the promise of early education.* New York, NY: Teachers College Press.

Feinberg, B. (2005). *Welcome to Lizard Motel: Protecting the imaginative lives of children.* New York, NY: Beacon Press.

Freeman, E., & Sanders, T. (1989). Kindergarten children's emerging concepts of writing functions in the community. *Early Child Development & Care, 56,* 81–90.

Geertz, C. (1973). Thick description: Toward an interpretative theory of culture. In C. Geertz (Ed.), *The interpretation of cultures.* New York, NY: Basic Books.

Genishi, C., & Dyson, A.H. (2009). *Children, language, and literacy: Diverse learners in diverse times.* New York, NY: Teachers College Press.

Halliday, J.K. (1975). *Learning to mean.* London, UK: Arnold.

Harwayne, S. (2001). *Writing through childhood: Rethinking process and product.* Portsmouth, NH: Heinemann.

Heath, S.B. (1982). *Ways with words: Language, life and work in communities and classrooms.* Cambridge, MA: Harvard University Press.

Langer, S. (1967–1972). *Mind: An essay on human feeling* (Vols. 1–2). Baltimore, MD: Johns Hopkins University Press.

Lensmire, T. (1994). *When children write: Critical re-visions of the writing workshop.* New York, NY: Teachers College Press.

Lensmire, T. (2000). *Powerful writing, responsible teaching.* New York, NY: Teachers College Press.

Meier, D. (2009). *Here's the story: Using narrative to promote young children's language and literacy learning.* New York, NY: Teachers College Press.

McNamee, G.D. (2015). *The high-performing preschool: Story acting in Head Start classrooms.* Chicago, IL: University of Chicago Press.

Newkirk, T. (2007). Popular culture and writing development. *Language Arts, 84,* 539–548.

Nicolopoulou, A. (1996). Narrative development in social context. In D.I. Slobin, I. Gerhardt, A. Kyratzis, & J. Guo (Eds.), *Social interaction, social context, and language* (pp. 369–390). Hillsdale, NJ: Erlbaum.

Nicolopoulou, A. (2007). The interplay of play and narrative in children's development: Theoretical reflections and concrete examples. In A. Göncü & S. Gaskins (Eds.), *Play and development: Evolutionary, sociocultural, and functional perspectives* (pp. 247–273). Mahwah, NJ: Erlbaum.

Nicolopoulou, A., Cortina, K.S., Ilgaz, H., Cates, C.B., & de Sá, A.B. (2015). Using a narrative and play-based activity to promote low-income preschoolers' oral language, emerging literacy, and social competence. *Early Childhood Research Quarterly, 31*(2), 147–162.

Nicolopoulou, A., McDowell, J., & Brockmeyer, C. (2006). Narrative play and emergent literacy: Storytelling and story-acting meet journal writing. In D.G. Singer, R.M. Golinkoff, & K. Hirsh-Pasek (Eds.), *Play = learning: How play motivates and enhances children's cognitive and social-emotional growth* (pp. 124–144). Oxford, UK: Oxford University Press.

Nicolopoulou, A., & Richner, E.S. (2004). "When your powers combine, I am Captain Planet": The developmental significance of individual- and group-authored stories by preschoolers. *Discourse Studies, 6*, 347–371.

Nicolopoulou, A., Scales, E., & Weintraub, J. (1994). Gender differences and symbolic imagination in the stories of four-year-olds. In A.H. Dyson & C. Genishi (Eds.), *The need for story: Cultural diversity in classroom and community* (pp. 102–123). Urbana, IL: National Council of Teachers of English.

Paley, V.G. (1981). *Wally's stories: Conversations in the kindergarten*. Cambridge, MA: Harvard University Press.

Paley, V.G. (1986). *Mollie is three: Growing up in school*. Chicago, IL: University of Chicago Press.

Paley, V.G. (1988). *Boys and girls: Superheroes in the doll corner*. Chicago, IL: University of Chicago Press.

Paley, V.G. (1990). *The boy who would be a helicopter: The uses of storytelling in the classroom*. Cambridge, MA: Harvard University Press.

Paley, V.G. (1992). *You can't say you can't play*. Cambridge, MA: Harvard University Press.

Paley, V.G. (1997). *The girl with the brown crayon*. Cambridge, MA: Harvard University Press.

Paley, V.G. (2004). *A child's work: The importance of fantasy play*. Chicago, IL: University of Chicago Press.

Pappano, L. (2010). Kids haven't changed; kindergarten has. New data support a return to "balance" in kindergarten. *Harvard Education Letter, 26*(5). Retrieved from http://www.lakesidewaldorfschool.org/pdf/kindergarten_harvard.pdf

Pelligrini, A., & Blatchford, P. (2002). The development and educational significance of recess in schools. *Early Report, 29*(1). Retrieved from: http://www.peacefulplaygrounds.com/pdf/right-to-recess/educational-significance-of-recess.pdf

Piaget, J. (1962). *Play, dreams and imitation in childhood*. New York, NY: Routledge. (Original work published 1945.)

Pritchard, R.J., & Honeycutt, R.L. (2006). The process approach to teaching writing: Examining its effectiveness. In C.A. MacArthur, S. Graham, & J. Fitzgerald (Eds.), *Handbook of research on writing* (pp. 275–290). New York, NY: Guilford Press.

Rogoff, B. (1991). *Apprenticeship in thinking: Cognitive development in social context*. New York, NY: Oxford University Press.

Rosenblatt, L. (2005). *Making meaning with texts: Selected essays*. Portsmouth, NH: Heinemann.

Roskos, K., & Christie, J.F. (2011). The play-literacy nexus and the importance of evidence-based techniques in the classroom. *American Journal of Play, 4*(2), 204–224.

Schickedanz, J., & Collins, M.F. (2013). *So much more than the ABCs: The early phases of reading and writing*. Washington, DC: National Association for the Education of Young Children (NAEYC).

Schwartz, S.L., & Copeland, S.M. (2010). *Connecting emergent curriculum and standards in the early childhood classroom: Strengthening content and teaching practices.* New York, NY: Teachers College Press.

Singer, D.G., Golinkoff, R.M., & Hirsh-Pasek, K. (Eds.). (2006). *Play = learning: How play motivates and enhances children's cognitive and social-emotional growth.* Oxford, UK: Oxford University Press.

Snow, C.E. (1991). The theoretical basis for relationships between language and literacy in development. *Journal of Research in Childhood Education, 6*(1), 5–10.

Snow, C.E., Burns, S.M., & Griffin, P. (Eds.). (1998). *Preventing reading difficulties in young children.* Washington, DC: National Academy Press.

Stake, R.E. (2005). *Multiple case study analysis.* New York, NY: Guilford Press.

Stake, R.E. (2010). *Qualitative research: Studying how things work.* New York, NY: Guilford Press.

Teachers College Reading and Writing Project. (Producer). (2012, December 19). *Providing and then withholding scaffolding to support one [sic] child's understanding of narrative structure.* Retrieved from http://vimeo.com/55954402

Van Allen, R. (1976). *Language experiences in communication.* Boston, MA: Houghton Mifflin.

Vygotsky, L.S. (1978). *Mind in society: The development of higher psychological processes.* Cambridge, MA: Harvard University Press.

Weir, R.H. (1970). *Language in the crib.* The Hague, Netherlands: Mouton. (Original work published 1962.)

Wertsch, J.V. (1991). *Voices of the mind: A sociocultural approach to mediated action.* Cambridge, MA: Harvard University Press.

9

THE DEVELOPMENT OF SUBTEACHER DISCOURSE DURING PRETEND PLAY IN THE WAKE OF READING A STORY

Esther Vardi-Rath, Teresa Lewin, Zehava Cohen, Hadassah Aillenberg, and Tamar Eylon

This chapter focuses on the phenomenon of *subteaching*—i.e., when a pupil positions himself as a teacher and uses discourse strategies similar to those of the teacher. Namely, the child takes on the roles of organizing, explaining, caring, and promoting group processes (Tholander & Aronsson, 2003). This study is a part of a broader study exploring children's discourse during pretend play in the wake of a story (henceforth PPWS) that was conducted at the Kaye Academic College of Education in Beersheba, Israel (Vardi-Rath, Teubal, Aillenberg, & Lewin, 2014). Simply put, PPWS is pretend play where a group of children act out a story they have just heard from a student teacher. The children perform peer discourse without any external adult intervention.

The current study is based on the assumption that pretend play and literacy are interrelated, such that the play can potentially promote academic capabilities in young children (Pellegrini, 2009; Roskos, Christie, Widman, & Holding, 2010). These capabilities are mainly literacy skills such as decontextualized language and high-register language (Blum-Kulka, 2004; Zadunaisky-Ehrlich & Blum-Kulka, 2014).

Throughout the study, we noticed a phenomenon where, during peer discourse, when no adult was present in order to direct and guide the children, some of them stood out and assumed the role of the teacher. Very often, this occurred in situations where the children faced a difficulty, a conflict, or a disagreement during the pretend play and there was a chance of it breaking apart. Thus, the premise is that the primary motivation for talking and functioning as a *subteacher* is to promote the play and prevent its cessation. We argue that this social interaction allows the promotion of oral language, where natural discourse gradually promotes the children's literacy and mediation skills. The activity afforded learning opportunities resulting from incidental learning rather than from systematic instruction and enabled the development and practice of both abilities and knowledge.

The purpose of this chapter is to describe and characterize the discourse of the children acting as subteachers during PPWS. The importance of this phenomenon to child development is threefold: (a) The subteacher discourse indicates that children can sometimes learn from each other, through peer discourse, with no need for adult mediation (Blum-Kulka & Snow, 2004; Kyratzis & Cook-Gumperz, 2008). Thus, the role of the teacher shifts from guiding and teaching to enabling and creating learning opportunities; (b) many characteristics of the subteacher discourse indicate a literate discourse (similar to that of the teacher), which is highly important in nurturing first reading and writing (Blum-Kulka, 2010); and (c) the subteacher phenomenon promotes social skills, such as taking responsibility and initiative and cooperating with and considering others, which are very important to children's future functioning in a democratic society (Pramling-Samuelsson & Kaga, 2008).

Before the presentation and detailed analysis of the activity, we will clarify some concepts in literacy, discursive literacy, pretend play, PPWS, peer discourse, and subteaching.

Theoretical Background

Literacy

The topic of *literacy* has been of concern to psychologists, anthropologists, philosophers, historians, linguists, clinicians, and teachers in recent years. This multidisciplinary approach has led to a reconceptualization of literacy in cognitive, linguistic, social, and cultural terms (Barton, 2007; Olson, 2009; Wagner, Venezky, & Street, 1999). Literacy today has taken on a wide range of meanings and implications, from basic reading and writing skills to the acquisition and manipulation of knowledge via written texts, from metalinguistic analysis of grammatical units to the structure of oral and written texts (Ravid & Tolchinsky, 2002).

Researchers of literacy point out that the notion of literacy includes both the written and the oral modes in a wide range of registers and genres and therefore is suitable for various social functions in several social contexts (Blum-Kulka, 2004, 2010; Olson, 2009; Ravid & Tolchinsky, 2002). They claim that a literate person must understand the sociocultural context of the discourse and adjust himself to it. Therefore, literacy should be studied in a wide variety of contexts rather than merely in the context of deciphering and understanding texts (Snow, Griffin, & Burns, 2006).

Discursive Literacy

Blum-Kulka's (2010) notion of *discursive literacy* includes the use of autonomous, decontextualized language in a variety of oral and written genres as well as the ability to construct textually cohesive and coherent stretches of discourse. She argues that discursively literate texts are typified, in different combinations and to different degrees, by a relatively high level of explicitness, clearly marked textual cohesion and coherence, context sensitivity, lexical preciseness, and syntactic complexity. Discursive literacy is further associated with varying levels of reflexivity—namely, the ability to reflect on and repair language use and to distance the talk from the here and now (Blum-Kulka, 2010).

In recent years, a growing number of studies have shown that an oral literate discourse at a young age may predict children's success in literate discourse missions at an older age (Bergen & Mauer, 2000; Morrow, 1990; Rowe, 1998). Snow (1999), for example, found that children who at the age of 3 participated in conversations transgressing the here and now scored higher on vocabulary and storytelling tests conducted at the age of 5 compared to children who did not participate in such conversations and were immersed in the limited discursive world of the here and now.

In this study, we focused on Blum-Kulka's (2010) notion of discursive literacy and on Ravid and Tolchinsky's (2002) concept of written language as a register as potentially emerging in the oral discourse of children during PPWS.

Pretend Play

Pretend play is the activity by means of which an alternative reality is superimposed on the actual reality in which the players are embedded (Lillard, 2011). When talking about pretend play, we usually refer to free pretend play (Corsaro,1993), when children create an alternative reality through their talk, gestures, prosody, and transformative manipulation of objects (Sawyer, 1997).

Children engage in pretend play in diverse settings that vary in terms of the interaction dimension: *adult–child play*, characteristic of infant–mother play in middle-class Western societies (Lillard, 2011); *single-child play,* making (small) toy figures interact within an individually created imaginary realm (Ilgaz and Aksu-Koç, 2005); and *social pretend play*, involving interaction between peers (Sawyer, 1997), as was the case in our study.

During the play session, the children behave as if they are in an imaginary reality while remaining conscious of their actual surroundings. This enables multiple transitions back and forth from the present reality to the made-up, imaginary world. These multiple transitions are akin to the *literate capacity* referred to by Harris (2000)—i.e., the cognitive processes characteristic of skilled readers as they move back and forth between reality and the world of the text.

We view the degrees of freedom children have to construct and negotiate their own scripts as one of the main characteristics of the pretend play activity. Our assumption is that this affords them an optimal environment for practicing discursive literacy and social skills (Blum-Kulka, 2004; Blum-Kulka & Hamo, 2010; Feigenbaum, 2009; Zadunaisky-Ehrlich & Blum-Kulka, 2014).

Pretend Play in the Wake of Story Reading

Various studies describe children's activity in relation to stories. A number of researchers have studied the impact of storytelling and reading stories on the development of language and comprehension in children aged 3 to 5. These studies show how stories can be used as an effective means to increase early literacy and promote reading comprehension skills (Haven & Ducey, 2007; Morrow, 1990; Phillips, 1999; Rowe, 1998). Cooper (this volume) provides an account of how storytelling and story acting foster children's social competence and their literacy skills. And her findings are reinforced in the study of Nicolopoulou (this volume), who describes how active interplay and cross-fertilization between pretend play and storytelling can significantly promote children's learning and development in a range of domains.

Our study (PPWS) conveys an interaction with a written narrative text read out loud to the children. What differentiates this play around a story from other playing activities is that the children listen to a story and afterward act it out while interacting with their peers, with no adult interference (Vardi-Rath, Teubal, Aillenberg, & Lewin, 2014). The children were totally independent while acting out the story. The degrees of freedom were limited only by the story text, which was a constraining factor. However, the children were free to modify the text as they saw fit. The features characteristic of PPWS involved a number of transitions from the original to the enacted story.

We view the degrees of freedom children have to construct and negotiate their own scripts as one of the main characteristics of the PPWS activity: We assume that this affords a beneficial environment for practicing discursive literacy skills (Blum-Kulka, 2004, 2010; Zadunaisky-Ehrlich & Blum-Kulka, 2010). Our claim is that the task the children take upon themselves (to play the story) is a trigger for cooperation, manifested in a child-to-child interaction that enables them to cope with conflicts, negotiation, creative improvisation, and problem solving while adopting intellectual flexibility (Blum-Kulka, 2005; Blum-Kulka, Huck-Taglicht, & Avni, 2004).

In addition, this task allows the children to develop creativity and imagination and practice social skills such as leadership, sharing, getting along with others, improvising, explaining, listening, and planning (Johnson & Johnson, 1992; Lindsey & Colwell, 2003). Moreover, the task compels them to develop their oral language, as this is their fundamental channel of communication (Blum-Kulka, 2004).

Thus, the activity explored in this study constituted an instance of participation in peer group interaction. In social pretend play, for the play to take place, the group needs share a coconstructed interactional frame: the play frame. This involves negotiation and shifts in definition as the participants interact either by speaking as their play character (*in frame*) or speaking as themselves (*out of frame*). The term *in frame* refers to the imaginary world, while *out of frame* refers to the actual reality context (Sawyer, 1997; Vardi-Rath et al., 2014).

One type of out-of-frame discourse is the *metaplay discourse* (Vardi-Rath et al., 2014). Pellegrini and Galda (1998) have characterized metaplay discourse as involving meta-talk—i.e., talk about linguistic and mental states. They have singled out meta-talk as a crucial aspect of literate language that can predict school-based literacy learning. Metaplay discourse includes children's talk about their play and the stipulation of the imaginary frame (Harris, 2000). During this discourse, the children act out of character as external observers of their pretend play, speaking with their own voices about the characters they play.

Peer Discourse

Peer discourse is defined as a multiparticipant child discourse, egalitarian by nature, based on the common world of children's culture (Blum-Kulka & Hamo, 2010).

Pretend play with peers is the dominant context of language learning from ages 3 to 6 and has a major role in child development (Feigenbaum, 2009; Sawyer, 1997). Observational studies of natural peer discourse among children show that this discourse is a central meaningful arena of sociolinguistic learning and acquiring social and discursive skills (Blum-Kulka & Snow, 2004).

Corsaro (2005) argues that children are active and creative social agents who create their own *peer culture*, thus also affecting adult culture. Corsaro (2000) further emphasizes the fact that during the socialization process, children do not imitate or assimilate adult culture but create an interpretative reproduction of it in an active and creative manner. Thus, ideas taken from the world of adults are attributed new meanings that suit the context within which the children act. In this way, children appropriate this culture, making it their own.

When children enter kindergarten, they begin experiencing speech events with their peers, and an informal peer discourse is developed (Heath, 1983). During these speech events, the children experience the process of producing meaning in a social and cultural context-dependent discourse (Kyratzis & Cook-Gumperz, 2008; Rogoff, 1990; Zadunaisky-Ehrlich, 2011).

Zadunaisky-Ehrlich and Blum-Kulka's study (2014) shows that peer discourse is an optimal arena for nurturing argumentative discourse and, as such, it contributes to the linguistic and literate development of children. This type of discourse is one where participants raise explanations, justifications, and utterances supporting a certain position. It develops in situations of disagreement among the children, or in conflict situations, summoning the examination of differing points of view (Zadunaisky-Ehrlich, 2011).

Subteaching

The phenomenon of subteaching indicates a linguistic conduct that expresses adult pedagogical patterns that children intuitively adopt. As mentioned previously, in subteaching, the child takes on the roles of organizing, explaining, evaluating, and promoting group processes (Tholander & Aronsson, 2003)—i.e., the pupil positions himself as a teacher and uses discourse strategies similar to those of the professional teacher. By appropriating discourses and practices typical of teachers, the subteacher often manages to get his peers to comply with his ideas and methods.

Mehan and Griffin (1980) studied American primary-school children who were participating in a peer-tutoring phase of instructional chains. They show how pupils readily took on the temporarily designated identity of teacher and how they displayed, often in exaggerated ways, the rights and responsibilities of this identity.

As shown in the study of Tholander and Aronsson (2003), this phenomenon regularly appears in pupil small-group work, when pupils position themselves as subteachers and exploit a series of teacher-like strategies. The researchers identified in their study three types of practices, which are, directly or indirectly, linked to informal social control: instruction, evaluation, and disciplinary practices.

One of the instruction practices of the subteacher that Tholander and Aronsson (2003) describe is the *piloting strategy*. They describe it as a teaching strategy whereby the teacher simplifies problems so that pupils are able to solve them by answering a simple chain of questions. This concept can be compared to "scaffolding" (Wood, Bruner, & Ross, 1976). The main difference between the two concepts is that piloting refers specifically to a kind of tutoring that is overdone. Based on their findings, Tholander and Aronsson defined piloting as "a general tendency for detailed and oversimplified guidance on the part of a teacher, instructor, or tutor" (2003, p. 214). Sometimes this leads to types of *teacher talk* that vastly exaggerate the practices of teachers. As the piloting metaphor suggests, the passengers—here, the pupils—become very dependent on the pilot—the subteacher.

This type of subteaching practice is demonstrated in their example of a pupil who pilots her peers as a subteacher by directing the collective writing performed by the group. It is particularly evident where the subteacher willingly provides the pupils with information on what to write while, in turn, the pupils eagerly ask for guidance.

The recent study of Mökkönen (2013) explores the ways in which peers take up a teacher-like discourse to enforce normative uses of language in a classroom. Findings indicate that students draw on subteaching actions to negotiate alignments and sanction others, maintaining social order and constructing situated identities.

Another perspective on teaching in the classroom is the phenomenon of the *teacher as director* (Schonmann, 2006). Schonmann presents a conceptual framework viewing the teaching and learning process as an event that includes elements of drama: text, context, participants, time, and place. The teacher has a wide variety of production and direction options, manifested in two central approaches to theater directing: (a) the improvisation method—the teacher as director realizes

204 Esther Vardi-Rath et al.

the potential of the basic elements at his disposal: text, context, participants, time, and space. The director has no premeditated plan and "gives birth" to the play using what's at hand and (b) the planned and detailed method—the teacher as director prepares a well-defined work plan and tries to match the elements at hand to that plan.

Similarly, Bakhtin (1981, 1986) refers to a phenomenon he calls *voice of authority*, where children reproduce the voices of teachers, friends, and parents that are framed grammatically or prosodically as reported speech or signaled as "imported" in a range of other, more subtle ways.

Asymmetric Social Order in Play Interaction

Children's authority is manifested, among other ways, in studies of social order—namely, of the asymmetric relationships between children. The play arena is one of the contexts in which children negotiate the social order (Goodwin, 1990, 1993). Engagement in play offers a rich set of resources for social organization that can be used by children to establish, reproduce, challenge, and change alignments and hierarchies in their social relations (Kyratzis, 2007).

As in the general play arena, the establishment and use of asymmetrical relationships between players can also be observed in the more specific arena of pretend play. In organizing pretend play, some children may have membership in categories that invoke greater rights than others—such as mother or teacher (Butler, 2008; Kyratzis, 2007). In addition, research has shown how authority and subordination are demonstrated and achieved through the use of linguistic features and speech activities, such as tone and pace of voice, directives, and assessments (Goodwin, 1990; Griswold, 2007; Kyratzis, 2007; Thorell, 1998).

Mediation Among Peers

Children reevaluate and reconstruct their understanding of the world in a social manner through collaboration with their peers. As children assist each other in higher levels of learning, they work in a zone of proximal development (Vygotsky, 1978). When children assist and scaffold each other in working within the zone, they are given an opportunity to perform at levels they cannot achieve on their own. Mediation emphasizes the idea that when children teach each other, they modify a task and offer assistance in completing that task (Tharpe & Gallimore, 1988). Mediation occurs through scaffolding and modeling and is generally prominent between children of different levels of cognitive and/or social understanding, though it may also occur between children of the same competence level.

Several studies have reported that teacher scaffolding increased the amount of literacy activity during play (Morrow & Rand, 1991). Other studies have focused on peer interaction in literacy-enriched play settings (Christie & Stone, 1999;

Neuman & Roskos, 1991). Results indicated that children used a variety of strategies of mediation, such as negotiating and coaching, in order to help each other learn about literacy during play.

In the current study, pupil subteachers are observed using discourse patterns of *teacher talk*. Their choice of words, intonation, behavior, and conduct within and between the various phases of the play allow the observers to infer various behavioral patterns of the subteachers, who endeavor to teach, mediate, explain, support, and solve problems—all this while making sure that the play remains uninterrupted. The purpose of our study is to explore how the phenomenon of subteaching—i.e., how children use the subteacher discourse—is manifested during PPWS.

Methodology

We chose to address the issue of subteaching by means of discourse analysis of young children during PPWS. The methodology is based mostly on the sociolinguistic approach that emphasizes the context of language use in natural situations, without any artificial or laboratory constraints (Schiffrin, 1994; Schiffrin, Tannen, & Hamilton, 2001; van Dijk, 1997).

The premise of this study is that the understanding gained through discourse analysis of children's play in real life will shed light on literate and social processes among children, such as teaching and learning processes, particularly the subteaching phenomenon (Vardi-Rath et al., 2014).

The study is based on ethnographic data gathering—i.e., recording children's discourse during play with no exterior intervention. In the data analysis phase, we chose to integrate qualitative analysis with quantitative descriptions. In other words, we first described the discourse qualitatively and, after finding four styles of subteaching, added a quantitative description that included the frequencies of each style.

Study Design

The study design was as follows: A fairy tale was read by a student teacher to a group of four to five children. The story was read without pauses, enabling the children to get the story as a whole. Immediately after the reading, the student teacher asked the children to go and play the story and supplied neutral artifacts for the children to use at will. The children received no further adult guidance during their play session, which lasted about twenty minutes.

Data Gathering

The PPWS method employed in the study was developed by us in the course of tutoring our student teachers. It was adopted by the educational institutions

206 Esther Vardi-Rath et al.

where the students were training so that the participating children were familiar with it by the time our research began.

During the story playing session, two student teachers (the one who read the story and the other in charge of video recording) sat near the group. The first student teacher wrote down the children's speech and actions, as well as descriptions of play objects and props, while the second made sure that the videotape stand was adequately placed to capture the children as they moved around. After the session, they both produced a transcript combining the information from the written notes and the videotape.

Altogether, 15 transcripts of children's discourse during PPWS were analyzed, both of kindergartners and first graders. Each transcript represents one session of PPWS that took 20 to 30 min. The average scope of each transcript is about 195 speech turns. Altogether, 2,921 speech turns were analyzed, as follows:

Seven groups of children from seven kindergarten classes, aged 4.5 to 6.0 years old
(groups of three to four children)
Eight groups of children from eight first-grade classes, aged 5.5 to 7.0 years old
(groups of three to four children)

All of the kindergarten and first-grade classes are located in Beersheba, a city in the south of Israel. The majority of children come from low-income, working-class families. Pseudonyms are used here for all children.

Creating the Coding Scheme

Processing and analysis were conducted using a coding scheme created especially for this study. The scheme reflects various categories of the subteaching discourse characteristics and is the product of a process completed by a community of learners established in the Teachers' College that includes pedagogical mentors, student teachers, and kindergarten and school teachers.

As mentioned, the coding scheme was created after the qualitative analysis, in which we analyzed the transcripts (along with the student teachers). We wanted to see how the phenomenon of subteaching was manifested. We began by writing down the various characteristics arising from the transcripts and found four types of subteachers, which were at times not easily distinguishable. The transcript analysis was conducted separately (by each of the five researchers), and following this work the individual analyses were compared in order to see whether the process was reliable. When differences arose, we sat together to hone the characteristics of the discourse, especially when there was a need to distinguish between subteachers as social leaders and as directors. Finally, we created quite an accurate list of discourse characteristics, such that there were next to no mistakes in coding. Therefore, the current coding scheme can be replicated.

The types of discourse arising from the analysis are as follows:

1. Subteacher as social leader: The discourse characteristics typical of this type of subteacher were raising play-related suggestions; defining roles; switching roles between participants; making disciplinary comments to children whose behavior interferes with the play ("That's the way it is, the role she gets that's what she has to play"); changing the play development; criticizing play development ("You won't always be what you want to be"); urging other children in order to promote the play; making a large number of speech turns compared to the other children in the group (taking up the stage); and maintaining the rules of the play and the discourse.

2. Subteacher as director: The discourse characteristics typical of this type of subteacher were instructing the children how to perform their roles; giving stage directions promoting the plot ("Now you go there"); explaining the use of props; connecting the play with the story text; giving advice relating to setting; and giving instructions on how the characters should be played and how the story should be timed. Very often the subteacher as director guides the acting child on how and what to say, similar to the role of the prompter ("Come on, say it now").

At certain points, we encountered difficulties in distinguishing between the subteacher as social leader and as director. In such cases, we used one diagnostic question: Was the child acting in order to promote the group play, sensing that otherwise it might stop—that is to say, was the child's perspective rising above the technical details of the play? If so, the child was characterized as a social leader. However, if the child acted in order to improve the performance, he or she was characterized as a director.

3. Subteacher as tutor: The discourse characteristics typical for this type of subteacher were explaining terms and phenomena that are unclear to other children; correcting the children in issues of knowledge of the world ("It's so that children won't open it"); guiding the children about a question that was asked or a problem that was raised; expanding the vocabulary; and guiding the children about the skills required during the play.

4. Subteacher as parent: The discourse characteristics typical to this type of subteacher were helping the children put on their costumes and use props ("Wait honey, I'll fix it for you like a triangle"); expressing love and tenderness toward other children; and demonstrating an ability to attend to other children when in need of help ("I'll help you; it's inside out").

The Children's Language and Translation

The children in this study spoke to one another in Hebrew. The materials were sent to a professional translator who is familiar with the field of play and discourse preschoolers. Note that the transcript materials were submitted to the translator in full in order to provide the context of each segment.

Findings

The transcript analysis showed a high level of use of the subteaching discourse style, with 678 speech turns that make up 23% of all speech turns ($n = 2,921$). This finding indicated that PPWS was a suitable arena for learning processes in which children teach children. This analysis generated four types of subteachers shown in Figure 9.1 (the types) and in Figure 9.2 (a quantitative description of these types).

As shown in Figure 9.2, 45% of all subteacher speech turns were categorized as subteacher as social leader and 42% of these speech turns were categorized as subteacher as director, while subteacher as tutor and as parent comprise only 7% and

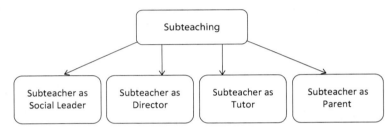

FIGURE 9.1 Coding scheme—subteaching types.

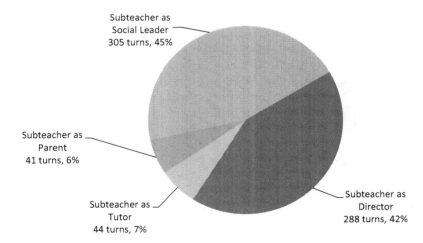

FIGURE 9.2 Distribution of subteacher types ($n = 678$ speech turns).

The Development of Subteacher Discourse **209**

6% of speech turns, respectively. Therefore, the most prominent types of subteaching discourse are the social leader and the director discourses, whereas the tutor and the parent discourses are less frequently seen. Below we will refer to the different types of subteachers and present examples from the children's discourse during PPWS.

Subteacher as Social Leader

This type of subteacher is characteristically an initiator who takes responsibility and leads the play session. He raises suggestions concerning role allocation, initiates steps that promote turning the story into a play, and hastens the rest of the children in order to further the play. In fact, the social leader undertakes responsibility for the whole social happening within the group, even with regard to issues that are not directly related to the play. Oftentimes, the social leader is a dominant type, and this dominance is manifested both in terms of behavior (physical or vocal gestures) and in terms of quantity (amount of speech).

In Example 1, we follow a discourse between children during PPWS following "A Mouse in the House."

Example 1: Subteacher as Social Leader—PPWS Following "A Mouse in the House"

Mirik Snir

Date: March 12, 2003; kindergarten; Beersheba, Israel
Participants: Merav (female, 5.8); Noy (female, 6); Yuval (male, 5.11); Raz (male, 5.6)

1:	**Merav:**	How will we play?
2:	**Merav:**	*[picks up a doll]* **This will be the mouse, it's the smallest.**
3:	**Merav:**	*[picks up a stuffed elephant]* **This is the grandmother.**
...		
8:	**Noy:**	I want to be the mother.
9:	**Merav *[to Noy]:***	**No! You're the sister. And you are the brother** *[to Raz]*.
10:	**Merav:**	**Wait, wait, we will all switch roles,** wait what does the brother do? Oh he doesn't do anything, so pretend you're thinking. *[Raz sits with his finger on his cheek and thinks]*
11:	**Yuval:**	He went to the trap.
12:	**Merav:**	Everyone went to look for a trap. *[Merav and Yuval pick up the book to see what the grandfather said exactly]*
13:	**Yuval:**	*[goes through the pages]* Grandfather sighs.
14:	**Noy:**	*[pointing]* There's the trap, here's a trap in the storeroom.

210 Esther Vardi-Rath et al.

...

18:	**Noy:**	You're the sister! No, you're the grandmother.
19:	**Merav:**	**You won't always be what you what to be.**
20:	**Noy *[to Merav]*:**	And later you will be the father.
21:	**Merav:**	I don't want to.
22:	**Noy:**	**You don't decide here!**
23:	**Yuval:**	I will be the brother.
24:	**Noy:**	You can't, you can't.
25:	**Merav *[to Noy]*:**	**The majority rules.**
26:	**Noy:**	I want to be the sister all the time.
27:	**Merav *[to Noy]*:**	Then you will be the grandmother and the father.
28:	**Noy:**	No!
29:	**Merav:**	No! *[touches Noy]*
30:	**Noy:**	OK, OK, I heard you.
31:	**Merav *[to Yuval]*:**	**He will be a boy, then a girl, and Raz will be a girl, then a boy.**

In this example, we see the children busy with organization, checking out the props, deciding which parts are needed in the play, and who will play whom. When the negotiation begins, Merav takes the role of the social leader and makes resolute decisions:

> "This will be the mouse, it's the smallest" [picks up a doll] (Turn 2)
> "This is the grandmother" [picks up a stuffed elephant] (Turn 3)
> "No! You are the sister [to Noy] and you are the brother [to Raz]" (Turn 9)
> "He will be a boy, then a girl, and Raz will be a girl, then a boy" (Turn 31)

Merav "reads the map" and understands where such decisions might lead, so she stops her decisive demeanor and switches to a different mode of speech: "Wait, wait, we will switch roles, wait what does the brother do? Oh he doesn't do anything, so pretend you're thinking" (Turn 10). Her address, with its proper intonation, draws the attention of her play friends to her. The repetitive use of the word *wait* creates an emphasis that allows her to stop the flow of the conversation in order to focus attention. She suspends the organization of the play to find a smart solution to the question of who shall play which role. Merav acts like a subteacher with a critical perspective on what goes on in the here and now. Then she turns to her playmates in a soothing approach and says: "We will all switch roles" (Turn 10). In other words, on the one hand she makes unilateral decisions (Turns 2, 3, and 9), and on the other hand she uses the word *we* (in the plural), a discourse strategy that emphasizes the inclusiveness of decisions (Turn 10).

Later on, as seen in Turns 18–31, Noy challenges Merav's leadership. She does not silently accept it, and she expresses her objection with resolute statements (Turns 18, 22, and 28). Once differences of opinion are raised, Merav succeeds in

The Development of Subteacher Discourse **211**

interpreting Noy's messages of resistance. In these cases, she is able to establish her leadership by making literal assertions: "You won't always be what you what to be" (Turn 23). Noy identifies Merav's leadership and overtly tries to resist: "You don't decide here!" (Turn 26). Merav, who functions as a subteacher of the social leader type, identifies the potential loss of position and chooses two different strategies: First, she recruits the majority opinion, based on the social–democratic rule "the majority rules" (Turn 31); then, she completely dismisses Noy's opinion and touches her in order to emphasize her point: "No!" (Turn 35). Merav's ability to quickly switch from one strategy to another shows how strongly she controls the situation.

Another aspect that intensifies Merav's social leadership is the number of speech turns she takes during the play. Out of 121 speech turns in this transcript (out of which Example 1 was taken), Merav produced 65 turns. She is very dominant, she has a lot to say, and her presence is extremely prominent in structuring the play. Her role as subteacher is created thanks to her personality and her position as social leader, given to her by the group. The interaction between her and the other children defines her role, without anything being clearly stated. Everyone knows that the social leader Merav is the teacher and that the other members of the group are the pupils.

Another example of a subteacher as social leader can be seen in the following play, where Omer takes on this role:

Example 2: Subteacher as Social Leader—PPWS Following "In a Complicated Street That's Hard to Explain"

Rachel Sarid

Date: April 2, 2003; first grade; Beersheba, Israel
Participants: Odelia (female, 6.11); Omer (male, 6.7); Hanna (female, 6.4); Eden (female, 7)

12:	**Odelia:**	Actually I'm the mother.
13:	**Omer:**	I'm the grandmother. *[the girls laugh at this]*
14:	**Hanna:**	No, I'm the mother. *[she tries to wear a long skirt and Eden helps her]*
15:	**Odelia:**	Hanna, I'm not speaking to you.
16:	**Hanna:**	I'm the mother.
17:	**Omer:**	**Play Evani-Yahu**. *[refers to rock-paper-scissors[1]]*
18:	**Hanna:**	The loser is the mother.
19:	**Omer:**	No, the winner.
20:	**Hanna and Odelia:**	*[play rock-paper-scissors. Hanna wins]*
21:	**Omer:**	She's the mother. *[refers to Hanna]*
22:	**Odelia:**	I want to be the mother!

212 Esther Vardi-Rath et al.

23:	**Omer:**	**That's the way it is, the role she gets that's what she has to play,** I was told to be the father and I agreed.
...		
27:	**Omer:**	Everyone has a role, but we need the boy.
28:	**Hanna:**	I don't want to.
29:	**Omer:**	**So half a turn you go and half a turn she goes.**
30:	**Hanna:**	Just because I have short hair doesn't mean I'm a boy. *[Hanna wears her hair very short]*
31:	**Odelia:**	But Hanna, I gave up for you.
32:	**Hanna:**	No you didn't.
33:	**Odelia:**	Yes I did, yesterday when we played. I always give up for you and you never do.
34:	**Omer:**	**Play Evani-Yahu one more time, and whoever loses—that's that, no acting like a crybaby.**
35:	**Odelia and Hanna:**	*[play rock-paper-scissors. Odelia wins]*
36:	**Hanna:**	Ugh, I'm always the boy.
37:	**Omer:**	**That's the way it is, we said no crybaby.**
38:	**Omer** *[to Eden]:*	Sit down, a cat doesn't stand, doesn't dance Steps.
39:	**Hanna:**	*[takes off the skirt and Odelia wears it]*

After Omer chose himself a role ("I'm the grandmother"), he positions himself in the adult teacher position and uses a directive discourse toward his playmates. He guides the members of his group as to how to properly fill each role in the play. His way of acting indicates his experience and prior knowledge with regard to social skills during a play session. These skills help him when he takes on the role of subteacher in order to determine who will play the mother: "Play Evani-Yahu" (Turn 17). He sets the rules in a decisive and confident tongue: "That's the way it is, the role she gets that's what she has to play" (Turn 23). By doing this, he emphasizes to his friends that they all should act by a certain rule based on social conventions.

In the previous example, Omer is an experienced player who acts according to clear and explicit rules (accepting an external determination such as a game of chance). When a problem arises and one of the group members disagrees with the rules he sets, he once again speaks decisively but also allows some leeway: "Play Evani-Yahu one more time, and whoever loses—that's that, no acting like a crybaby" (Turn 34). When a member of the group insists on her right to speak and emits an "Ugh!" (Hanna, Turn 36), Omer quickly asserts: "That's the way it is, we said no crybaby" (Turn 37). As a subteacher, Omer adopts an "instructional" demeanor by his confident speech, his use of the imperative, and his decisive intonation.

As in the previous example, here, too, Omer uses the plural, or *we* speech, turning the children into partners and seemingly indicating solidarity. However, at the same time, as in the teacher discourse (Vardi-Rath, 2013), this strategy empowers

The Development of Subteacher Discourse **213**

the speaker due to its patronizing tone and emphasizes the speaker's authority in the group.

Another strategy that Omer uses in order to advance the play is offering a compromise. When Hanna refuses to take on the role of the boy, Omer suggests: "So half a turn you go and half a turn she goes" (Turn 29). In the beginning, his offer is rejected because of Hanna's gender considerations ("Just because I have short hair doesn't mean I'm a boy," Turn 30), but later on Omer adopts a different approach and offers the girls an opportunity to re-play the game of chance to decide who will be the boy in the play (Turn 34).

In this case, as in Example 1, the examination of the number of speech turns indicates Omer's dominant position. Approximately a third of the speech turns belong to him (25 out of 69 speech turns). Possibly his being the only boy in a group of girls gives him authority and emphasizes his centrality in the play and the position granted to him thanks to his behavior.

As opposed to the role of subteacher as social leader that is naturally created during the play, there are situations where the children explicitly and willingly empower one of the members of the group. In such cases, one must ask: Is there a correlation between the perceived skills that the children attribute to their peer and his own perceived skills regarding the role he is expected to fulfill? The example below should shed some light on this issue.

Example 3: Subteacher as Social Leader—PPWS Following "Flat to Rent"

Lea Goldberg

Date: November 15, 2004; kindergarten; Beersheba, Israel
Participants: Efrat (female, 5.6); Stav (female, 5.9); Rotem (female, 5.4); Tamar (female, 5.10)

8: **Efrat:** We don't remember, how does it start? *[the story]*
9: **Stav:** **Rotem is the commander, so she will tell us.**
10: **Rotem:** *[picks up the book]*
. . .
20: **Rotem:** **We can't read. How are we supposed to know where to start?**
. . .
39: **Rotem:** *[leafs through the book]* **After the rabbit comes the pig, who wants to be the pig?**
40: **Tamar:** I want to be the pig. I'm the pig and the beetle.
41: **Rotem:** *[leafing through]* **Wait, let me check again.**
42: **Tamar:** *[snorts like a pig; they all laugh]*

In Example 3, we see the issue of maintaining the story sequence with which the children often are faced in PPWS. The children don't remember how "Flat to

Rent" begins, and Stav solves the problem by appointing Rotem as the authority: "Rotem is the commander, so she will tell us" (Turn 9). This natural choice of Rotem might be based on Stav's previous acquaintance of and confidence in her friend's abilities. Rotem accepts the invitation and picks up the book in an act of consent (Turn 10), trying to take on the role. Pretty soon she finds out that playing teacher isn't so simple, and she expresses her lack of confidence: "We can't read. How are we supposed to know where to start?" (Turn 20). However, in the final analysis, the credit Stav gave her proves to be justified, as Rotem quickly recovers and starts to function as she is expected to (Turns 39 and 41). Despite her initial fear due to not knowing how to read, it turns out that the book is her right hand, allowing her to monitor all of the details and lead the play successfully.

Subteacher as Director

Unlike the decisive discourse style typical of the subteacher as social leader, the style of the subteacher as director is more commonly based on advice and guidance given to the children with regard to the play around the narrative text. Sometimes the children understand the PPWS as a theater play in which the plot is presented (Schonmann, 2006). In such cases, the actions of the subteacher are similar to those of a director, instructing the actors how to organize the play, use props, design the set, play the characters, and time the action. It is worth noting that the subteacher as director is not necessarily a leader by nature.

In a PPWS following "Maid Maleen" (Example 4 below), Yuval, one of the participants, acts instructively, characterizing her as a teacher director. Despite Yuval's central position in the play, one can see that her demeanor does not stem from an external supervising position. Her comments are made throughout the play activity such that they do not block the activity but are an integral part of it. She herself plays while instructing, demonstrating, assisting, and mediating, as shown below:

Example 4: Subteacher as Director—PPWS Following "Maid Maleen"

Brothers Grimm

Date: January 14, 2004; kindergarten; Beersheba, Israel
Participants: Yuval (female, 6); Daniela (female, 5.7); Yarden (female, 5.5); Felix (male, 5.10)

22: **Yuval *[to Daniela]*:** First there's . . . Once upon a time there was a king . . . *[takes Daniela's hand]* **You can be the guard for the meantime**.
23: **Daniela:** OK.

The Development of Subteacher Discourse **215**

24: **Yuval** *[to Daniela]*: **Say:** "Marry the king or I'll kill you." **Come on, say it now**.
25: **Yarden:** *[runs after Felix with a cape]*
26: **Felix:** I'm out of the game.
27: **Yuval:** **Come on, say it**. *[runs after Daniela, who moves away]*
28: **Daniela:** What?
29: **Yuval:** **Marry the king or I'll kill you**.
...
61: **Felix** *[to Daniela]*: Now I have to kiss you. *[approaches Daniela to kiss her]*
62: **Yuval:** **No kissing**. *[drags Felix and Daniela and positions them]*
...
65: **Yuval** *[to Felix]*: What do you say, darling? *[whispers to Felix]*
66: **Felix:** What do you say, darling?
67: **Yuval:** **Now you go there**. *[takes Daniela and Felix by the hand]*

Yuval's actions position her as a central axis advancing the play as director, while the screenplay is etched into her mind. She functions as a director who acts according to a predefined plan, as opposed to an improvisation-style director (Schonmann, 1995). She predicts the moves of the play and navigates her friends while strictly maintaining the narrative plot. Like a hardworking ant, she does not rest, reminding her friends what to say and when: "Come on, say it now" (Turn 24). Yuval even functions as a "moral compass" in order to prevent an awkward situation that might sabotage the play: She elegantly bypasses "the kiss obstacle" by saying "no kissing" (Turn 62). Sometimes, in order to be true to the text without sabotaging the continuum, Yuval takes on the role of the prompter (Turn 65). The children accept her instructions without any objection. As the non-official director, she even ensures that every physical or vocal gesture is completed properly where she thinks this is needed for the expressive-emotional aspect of the play.

Subteacher as Tutor

Another style of subteaching is the subteacher as tutor, giving explanations and broadening the knowledge of his pupils. The subject being explained may be related to the play itself (in frame) or to situations of the here and now (out of frame). Within this pattern, children teach their peers, where the knowledgeable child teaches and instructs the others with regard to a certain question or problem, expands their vocabulary, or guides them through actions that are required during the play.

Example 5 shows an orthographic discussion concerning the conventional Hebrew sign for the consonant *j* that has no graphic representation in the standard alphabet.

216 Esther Vardi-Rath et al.

Example 5: Subteacher as Tutor—PPWS Following "Snow White and the Seven Dwarfs"

Adapted by Asi Weinstein

Date: December 25, 2002; first grade; Beersheba, Israel
Participants: Or (male, 6.8); Kobi (male, 6.10)

21: **Or:**   *[finds a note on the floor]* Doesn't it say *jungle?*
22: **Kobi:**   *[looks at Or's note]* Where? There's no *ju*, there's no letter for *ju*. *[in Hebrew]*
23: **Or:**   *G'* is for *ju*.

This example shows Or's literacy mediation. He finds a note on the floor and recognizes the word *jungle*. In reaction, Kobi asks where the letter for *ju* is, because according to his knowledge of the Hebrew alphabet, there is no such letter. From Or's answer, one may infer that he knows such a sign (probably from his own world of knowledge), and as a subteacher he teaches Kobi: "*G'* is for *ju*" (Turn 23), meaning to say: When you see the sign *g'* (he shows it in Hebrew), you should know it sounds like the beginning of the word *jungle*.[2] In fact, they both know the Hebrew orthography, but Or has additional knowledge that allows him to identify words that originate in the other languages.

While playing, children encounter various problems that are not always related to the story they are acting out. Thus, for instance in Example 6, PPWS following "Everyone Is Angry with Me," a discussion develops around one of the props of the play—a bottle of children's antipyretic syrup called Acamoli. As a safety precaution, a complex ability is required to open the bottle in order to prevent children from opening it. As seen in the example, the children compare the syrup (Acamoli) with the same medicine given to adults in the form of pills, Acamol. In this play session, we can identify the style of subteacher as tutor, explaining and guiding his discourse partners with regard to the ability required in the play.

Example 6: Subteacher as Tutor—PPWS Following "Everyone Is Angry with Me"

Nurit Cohen

Date: December 17, 2003; first grade; Beersheba, Israel
Participants: Eden (female, 6.6); Dan (male, 6.8); Amir (male, 6.11)

17: **Eden:**   This won't open. *[tries to open a bottle of Acamoli]*
18: **Dan:**   **It's so that children won't open it.**
19: **Amir:**   *[tries to open the Acamoli safety cap]* How do you open this?

The Development of Subteacher Discourse **217**

20: **Dan:**   You press it down and then open.
21: **Amir:**   **It's Acamoli, not Acamol**.
22: **Eden:**   It's for kids, obviously it's Acamoli.
23: **Dan:**   **Adults have Acamol**, what's the problem?
24: **Amir:**   *[keeps trying to open the bottle]*
25: **Dan:**   **You're still with that Acamoli? Like a little kid trying again
               and again to open**.

The children discuss the design and the function of the medicine bottle while emphasizing the distinction between Acamol for adults and Acamoli for children. In Example 6, we can see two children who function as tutoring subteachers: Dan teaches Eden and Amir that the bottle of Acamoli for children has a special safety cap so that it would be complicated to open ("It's so that children won't open it," Turn 18). In addition, Amir is also a subteacher who functions as a metalinguistic mediator, emphasizing the childish suffix *i* and drawing the children's attention to the different sounds of the words ("It's Acamoli, not Acamol," Turn 21).

In a way, this example can be understood as a constructive learning process, in which the children construct their knowledge based on their experiences. This is quite evident when Amir asks Dan how to open the safety cap (Turn 19) and Dan chooses to guide Amir how to act instead of acting for him ("You press it down and then open," Turn 20).

Subteacher as Parent

Another style of subteaching where the subteacher is granted authority by the children thanks to his behavior and responses is the subteacher as parent. This style is typically characterized by caring behavior manifested in concern, consideration, attention, gentleness, and love (Noddings, 1992). Children of this type oftentimes help other children and are responsive to their needs.

In Example 7, we shall see a subteacher as parent in PPWS following "Little Red Riding Hood."

Example 7: Subteacher as Parent—PPWS Following "Little Red Riding Hood"

Brothers Grimm

Date: May 5, 2005; kindergarten; Beersheba, Israel
Participants: Or (male, 5); Komashi (female, 5.3); Shiri (female, 5.1); Nadav (male, 4.5)

12: **Or:**   Can someone help me close this? *[referring to the
               wolf costume zipper]*

218 Esther Vardi-Rath et al.

13: **Komashi:** **I'll close it, wait it's stuck, here, hold this**.
14: **Or:** Thank you.
15: **Komashi:** What a pretty mother. *[refers to herself]*
16: **Or:** So that my tail won't jump. *[the costume tail]*
17: **Komashi** *[to Shiri]*: **Here I'll put on the scarf for you, like this**, Little Red Riding Hood. *[ties a red cloth around Shiri's waist]*
18: **Shiri:** *[The red scarf falls and she hands it to Komashi]*
19: **Komashi:** This should be on your head, **wait honey, I'll fix it for you like a triangle**. *[the cloth is square]*
20: **Shiri:** Come on, move. *[shoves Nadav, who plays the hunter]*
21: **Nadav:** I'm sick of this old lady.
22: **Komashi:** Who did you say was the wolf?
23: **Or:** Wait I'm fixing the grandmother. *[puts down a doll that represents the grandmother]*
24: **Or** *[to Komashi]*: Dress me.
25: **Nadav:** Here's Little Red Riding Hood's basket. *[a basket of pencils]*
26: **Komashi** *[to Nadav]*: **I'll help you; it's inside out**. *[helps Nadav wear his hunter costume]*
27: **Nadav:** It's not upside down.
28: **Komashi:** **Look! That's how you wear it, give me your hand**.

Komashi's behavior in the play reflects the pattern of a teacher parent who treats the children with motherly care. The way she talks, her tone, and her skillfulness with regard to the complexity of the costumes all give her a special status in the eyes of the children, who naturally turn to her, asking for help. When Or asks, "Can someone help me close this?" (Turn 12), he turns to Komashi, assuming that she would help him, and indeed Komashi's response is motherly and caring. She says, "I'll close it, wait it's stuck, here, hold this" (Turn 13). When there is a problem with Shiri's costume as Little Red Riding Hood, she volunteers to help: "Here I'll put on your scarf, like this, Little Red Riding Hood" (Turn 17). When Shiri's scarf falls, she immediately turns to Komashi (Turn 18), whose response is natural: "This should be on your head, wait honey, I'll fix it for you like a triangle" (Turn 19). Nadav, who feels helpless trying to wear the costume, also receives her dedicated attention: "I'll help you; it's inside out" (Turn 26); "Look! That's how you wear it, give me your hand" (Turn 28).

Komashi's willingness to help and her behavior while helping others (calm, patient, peaceful) naturally grant her the status of the motherly teacher, although this role is not predefined. Her responses produce her status in the play with no premeditation. Her choice of words (e.g., *honey, I'll close it, like this, I'll help you, I'll fix it for you*) clearly indicates that she has appropriated the status of the caring mother that was granted to her by her peers.

Discussion and Conclusion

The present study focused on a special kind of peer interaction: subteaching during pretend play in the wake of a story just having been read to students from a children's storybook (PPWS). In light of the findings, we can say that the subteacher discourse is characterized by a qualitative interaction between peers during which children learn from other children. It is clear that in these peer teaching and learning processes, the children mindfully listen to their peer teachers. It must be noted that the functions of each of the children who acted as subteachers were not predetermined by an exterior authority but rather emerged spontaneously in the social play context. On the one hand, these children established their authority based on their personality and skills, and on the other hand, they were granted authority by the rest of the group as a natural phase of the social interaction, manifested in the group's consent and at times even initiated by the group itself.

In this chapter, we have presented four styles of subteaching: social leader, director, tutor, and parent. Each style is unique. The findings indicate that the two most common types of subteaching during PPWS are the social leader and the director. The prominence of the social leader type is quite understandable. The data analysis shows that very often, the children enter a conflict regarding the play (who shall play whom, who makes decisions about the play, what do you do when the play comes to a stop), and therefore there is a need for a social leader advising the children how to solve the problem and continue the group play.

When the children acted as subteachers as social leaders, they used a wide variety of discourse strategies, such as decisive statements or assertions; soothing language; *we* speech; convincing a majority of group members; resistance, including physical contact; suggesting compromises; and giving a second chance. It is evident that some of these strategies reveal assertiveness borrowed from the world of teaching: decisive assertion, convincing a majority of group members, and resistance. Nevertheless, other strategies infer a softer position and consideration of others: soothing language, *we* speech, suggesting compromises, and giving a second chance.

It could be cautiously claimed that the young leaders used teaching styles that on the one hand indicated assertive and decisive leadership, maybe attesting power and control relations between them and their kindergarten or schoolteachers and on the other hand exhibited care and consideration for others, attesting to the positive, caring, and considerate treatment they received from their teachers (Pianta, 1999).

The subteacher as director style was also quite common among children who functioned as subteachers. This is not surprising, as the nature of the activity was PPWS, such that a large percentage of the children understood the activity as putting on a play in which the plot is presented. This pattern is reminiscent of the teacher as director model and, according to our findings, we may say that the children usually used the improvisation style when directing (Schonmann, 2006). Using their imagination, they invented the props, the time and the place, and

220   Esther Vardi-Rath et al.

often the characters and the text. In doing so, they exhibited intellectual flexibility and improvisation capacities that bring into account the specific context in which the play was held (Sawyer, 2002).

Subteacher Discourse as Literacy Discourse

We wish to argue that the subteacher discourse during PPWS is typically a literacy discourse and as such advances the children toward initial literacy (Blum-Kulka & Snow, 2004). This argument is rooted in a number of findings:

- In the transcripts, we found that in many cases the subteacher was required to understand the level of knowledge and language of his discourse peers, as well as their point of view. The need to adjust oneself to the knowledge level of the discourse peers causes the child to use distanced discourse—i.e., to adapt to the level of explicitness and abstractness of the discourse peers. This ability is pragmatic (Blum-Kulka, 2004) and enables the child to position himself as a teacher and also to receive the compliance and cooperation of the group.
- The better part of the subteacher discourse occurs outside the pretend play frame, meaning that the children refer to the actual reality context, speaking for themselves and not for the fictional character (Sawyer, 1997). This shift is known as the process of mobility between in-frame and out-of-frame interaction: The children suspended their enactment (in-frame interaction) in order to plan, talk about, and explore options and to consider alternatives (out-of-frame interaction) and then return to enacting. These are cognitive processes characteristic of skilled readers as they move back and forth between reality and the world of the text (Harris, 2000). Out-of-frame discourse evolves in a way that can be beneficial to fostering children's discursive literacy and social skills. It includes planning and setting up the pretend play while referring back to the text for role allocation and, above all, making sure that the children's acting ability is good enough for them to enact their roles. One may see this position as an outside observer who is able to watch the play and be critical about it. The ability to exit the imaginary frame and test group processes from the outside on the one hand and on the other hand to enter the imaginary frame and play a role is a critical ability to developing initial literacy skills (Harris, 2000).
- The text is a constraining factor, summoning a decontextualized discourse. The frequency of in-frame/out-of-frame transitions increases when pretend play is based on the enactment of a story text: The text's constraints and distancing factors bring about an increased need for decontextualized discourse. Typically, PPWS offers children multiple degrees of freedom while at the same time demanding that the story text be taken into consideration (Vardi-Rath et al., 2014). The text being read serves as a distancing factor in the children's discourse. It transports the children to a more distant imaginary

world, the text-based play, far from the here and now. This process can be seen as fostering decontextualized discourse, which is essential for children's literacy development (Blum-Kulka & Hamo, 2010; Pellegrini, 2009). As seen in the results analysis, the story text became a backbone for the children's activity, requiring them to play according to its content and structure. This constraint led the children to active collaboration in order to solve problems, thus stimulating their capacity to improvise.

- The subteacher discourse requires an ability to explain, justify, and convince. In particular, the findings analysis shows that conflict between participants might act as a springboard for the development of argumentative skills (Monaco & Pontecorvo, 2014; Zadunaisky-Ehrlich & Blum-Kulka, 2014). Coping with peer conflict without adult interference seems to afford the realization of children's potential to present themselves during negotiations, problem solving, and persuading and supporting their positions with appropriate arguments.

Pretend Play as Promoting Subteacher Discourse

Our findings show that the subteacher discourse was naturally created during peer discourse developing throughout the social play, without any instructions or guidance given by an adult. It is clear that the central motivation to act as a subteacher is promoting the play and preventing its cessation. In addition, we have seen that the subteacher discourse usually appears in situations of conflict, disagreement, or misunderstanding. This also explains why the rest of the group accepts the subteacher's authority, as they share an interest: continuing with the PPWS. The findings also show that, at times, the children appoint the subteacher, specifically when they encounter a deadlock ("Rotem is the commander, so she will tell us"). Therefore, one can say that the phenomenon of subteaching, as it emerges during PPWS, stems naturally from the bottom up and is not imposed on the children externally. This is why the subteaching discourse is relevant to the social world of children (Corsaro, 2000).

Between Two Types of Discourse: Subteacher and Teacher

As expected, many of the subteacher behaviors that we have described previously can be seen among school and kindergarten teachers, including the four subteacher types: social leader, director, tutor, and parent. Children in the education system, particularly preschoolers, are highly affected by the demeanor of their teachers and by their attitude toward the children (Pianta, Hamre, & Stuhlman, 2003). Therefore, we must assume that a child acting as a subteacher reenacts these actions to some extent. If so, we could carefully say that the children may be reflecting their teachers' behaviors in the classroom in a way. And this is why the school or kindergarten teacher discourse is very important, as it affects the way in which the children interact.

The Issue of Hierarchy in Peer Discourse

The scientific literature typically characterizes peer discourse as multiparticipant and egalitarian in nature (Blum-Kulka, 2010). In other words, there is usually no formal differentiation between the children with regard to their authority or hierarchies. In a children's group play, everyone is equal. However, the findings of this study show that despite the natural conditions enabling the development of an egalitarian discourse, the subteacher discourse expressed early signs of authority and hierarchy.

The findings raise questions regarding the issue of authority among preschoolers. This study has demonstrated that although the children are engaged with peer discourse, which is egalitarian and collaborative in nature, there is a naturally occurring hierarchy among the children that is manifested in an asymmetric discourse. This process occurred without the instruction or guidance of the schoolteacher or kindergarten teacher. In light of this finding, it is possible that children need leadership and authority (in the form of a subteacher) in order to promote social processes within the group. We have shown that, in certain situations, even when there is no acting subteacher, the children initiate a "coronation," choosing the most apt leader in their eyes.

In conclusion, the current study reveals the significance of the phenomenon of subteaching occurring during peer discourse, specifically during PPWS. However, above all, it demonstrates the relationship between pretend play and the development of literacy skills among preschoolers. We believe that the curriculum for children at this age should include a lot of play and a lot of peer interaction, both formal and informal. The teacher, of course, has a major role in enabling this interaction and promoting it.

Notes

1 Rock-paper-scissors is a game of chance usually played in order to make decisions and solve conflicts among children.
2 Indeed, the Hebrew alphabet has no unique letter corresponding with the English consonant *j*. However, the Hebrew letter *gimel* with an apostrophe (represented in the example as *g'*) is the conventional way to write that foreign consonant.

References

Bakhtin, M. (1981). *The dialogical imagination.* Austin: University of Texas Press.
Bakhtin, M. (1986). The problem of speech genres (V.W. McGee, Trans.). In C. Emerson & M. Holquist (Eds.), *Speech genres and other late essays* (pp. 60–102). Austin: University of Texas Press.
Barton, D. (2007). *Literacy: An introduction to the ecology of written language* (2nd ed.). Oxford, UK: Blackwell.

Bergen, D., & Mauer, D. (2000). Symbolic play, phonological awareness, and literacy skills at three age levels. In K.A. Roskos & J.F. Christie (Eds.), *Play and literacy in early childhood: Research from multiple perspectives* (pp. 45–62). New York, NY: Erlbaum.

Blum-Kulka, S. (2004). The role of peer interaction in later pragmatic development: The case of speech representation. In R.A. Berman (Ed.), *Language development across childhood and adolescence: Psycholinguistic and crosslinguistic perspectives* (pp. 191–211). Philadelphia, PA: Benjamins.

Blum-Kulka, S. (2005). Modes of meaning-making in children's conversational storytelling. In J. Thornborrow & J. Coats (Eds.), *The sociolinguistics of narrative* (pp. 149–170). Amsterdam, Netherlands: Benjamins.

Blum-Kulka, S. (2010). Introduction: Communicative competence, discursive literacy and peer talk. In S. Blum-Kulka & M. Hamo (Eds.), *Children talk: Communicative patterns in peer talk* (pp. 5–42). Tel Aviv, Israel: The Center for Educational Technology. [in Hebrew]

Blum-Kulka, S., & Hamo, M. (2010). *Child peer talk: Patterns of communication.* Tel Aviv, Israel: The Center for Educational Technology. [in Hebrew]

Blum-Kulka, S., Huck-Taglicht, D., & Avni, H. (2004). The social and discursive spectrum of peer talk. *Discourse Studies, 6*(3), 307–328.

Blum-Kulka, S., & Snow, C. (Eds.). (2004). The contribution of peer talk to pragmatic development. *Special Issue of Discourse Studies, 6*(3), 292–306.

Butler, C.W. (2008). *Talk and social interaction in the playground.* Aldershot, UK: Ashgate.

Christie, J., & Stone, S. (1999). Collaborative literacy activity in print-enriched play centers: Exploring the "zone" in same-age and multi-age groupings. *Journal of Literacy Research, 31*(2), 109–131.

Corsaro, W.A. (1993). Interpretive reproduction in children's role play. *Childhood, 1,* 64–74.

Corsaro, W.A. (2000). Early childhood education, children's peer cultures, and the future of childhood. *European Early Childhood Education Research Journal, 8*(2), 89–102.

Corsaro, W.A. (2005). *The sociology of childhood.* Thousand Oaks, CA: SAGE.

Feigenbaum, P. (2009). Development of communicative competence through private and inner speech. In A. Winsler, C. Fernyhough, & I. Montero (Eds.), *Private speech, executive functioning, and the development of verbal self-regulation* (pp. 105–120). Cambridge, UK: Cambridge University.

Goodwin, M.H. (1990). *He-said-she-said: Talk as social organization among black children.* Bloomington: Indiana University Press.

Goodwin, M.H. (1993). Tactical uses of stories: Participation frameworks within boys' and girls' disputes. In D. Tannen (Eds.), *Gender and conversational interaction* (pp. 165–188). New York, NY: Oxford University Press.

Griswold, O. (2007). Achieving authority: Discursive practices in Russian girls' pretend play. *Research on Language and Social Interaction, 40*(4), 291–319.

Harris, P.L. (2000). *The work of imagination.* Malden, MA: Blackwell.

Haven, K., & Ducey, M. (2007). *Crash course in storytelling.* Westport, CT: Libraries Unlimited.

Heath, S.B. (1983). *Ways with words: Language, life, and work in communities and classrooms.* New York, NY: Cambridge University Press.

Ilgaz, H., & Aksu-Koç, A. (2005). Episodic development in preschool children's play-prompted and direct-elicited narratives. *Cognitive Development, 20,* 526–544.

Johnson, D.W., & Johnson, R.T. (1992). *Advanced cooperative learning.* Edina, MN: Interaction Book.

Kyratzis, A. (2007). Using the social organizational affordances of pretend play in American preschool girls' interactions. *Research on Language and Social Interaction, 40*(4), 321–352.

Kyratzis, A., & Cook-Gumperz, J. (2008). Language socialization and gendered practices in childhood. In P.A. Duff & N. Hornberger (Eds.), *Language socialization: Encyclopedia of language and education* (Vol. 8, pp. 145–157). New York, NY: Springer.

Lillard, A. (2011). Mother–child fantasy play. In A.D. Pellegrini (Ed.), *The Oxford handbook of play* (pp. 284–295). New York, NY: Oxford University Press.

Lindsey, E.W., & Colwell, M.J. (2003). Preschoolers' emotional competence: Links to pretend and physical play. *Child Study Journal, 33*(1), 39–52.

Mehan, H., & Griffin, P. (1980) Socialization: The view from classroom interactions. *Sociological Inquiry, 50*(3–4), 357–392.

Mökkönen, A.C. (2013). An ethnographic study of language socialization and choice in a first and second grade English medium classroom in Finland. *Journal of Immersion and Content-Based Language Education, 1*(2), 279–295.

Monaco, C., & Pontecorvo, C. (2014). Explanatory discourse and historical reasoning in children's talk. In A. Cekaite, S. Blum-Kulka, V. Grover, & E. Teubal (Eds.), *Children's peer talk: Learning from each other* (pp. 87–106). Cambridge, UK: Cambridge University Press.

Morrow, L., & Rand, M. (1991). Preparing the classroom environment to promote literacy during play. In J. Christie (Ed.), *Play and early literacy development* (pp. 141–165). Albany: State University of New York Press.

Morrow, L.M. (1990). Small group story readings: The effects on children's comprehension and responses to literature. *Reading Research and Instruction, 29*(4), 1–17.

Neuman, S., & Roskos, K. (1991). Peers as literacy informants: A description of young children's literacy conversations in play. *Early Childhood Research Quarterly, 6*(2), 233–248.

Noddings, N. (1992). *The challenge to care in schools: An alternative approach to education.* New York, NY: Teachers College Press.

Olson, D.R. (2009). Language, literacy and mind: The literacy hypothesis. *Psykhe, 18*(1), 3–9.

Pellegrini, A.D. (2009). *The role of play in human development.* New York, NY: Oxford University Press.

Pellegrini, A.D., & Galda, L. (1998). *The development of school-based literacy: A social ecological perspective.* London, UK: Taylor & Francis.

Pianta, R.C. (1999). *Enhancing relationships between children and teachers.* Washington, DC: American Psychological Association.

Pianta, R.C., Hamre, B., & Stuhlman, M. (2003). Relationships between teachers and children. In W. Reynolds & G. Miller (Eds.), *Comprehensive handbook of psychology: Educational psychology* (Vol. 7, pp. 199–234). New York, NY: Wiley.

Phillips, L. (1999). *The role of storytelling in early literacy development* (ERIC Document Reproduction Service No. ED444147). Retrieved from http://files.eric.ed.gov/fulltext/ED444147.pdf

Pramling-Samuelsson, I., & Kaga, Y. (Eds.). (2008). *The contribution of early childhood education to a sustainable society.* Paris, France: United Nations Educational, Scientific, and Cultural Organization (UNESCO). Retrieved from http://www.oei.es/decada/unesco_infancia.pdf

Ravid, D., & Tolchinsky, L. (2002). Developing linguistic literacy: A comprehensive model. *Journal of Child Language, 2*, 419–448.

Rogoff, B. (1990). *Apprenticeship in thinking: Cognitive development in social context.* New York, NY: Oxford University Press.

Roskos, K.A., Christie, J.F., Widman, S., & Holding, A. (2010). Three decades in: Priming for meta-analysis in play-literacy research. *Journal of Early Childhood Literacy, 10*(1), 55–96.

Rowe, D.W. (1998). The literate potentials of book-related dramatic play. *Reading Research Quarterly, 33*(1), 10–35.

Sawyer, R.K. (1997). *Pretend play as improvisation: Conversation in the preschool classroom.* Mahwah, NJ: Erlbaum.

Sawyer, R.K. (2002). Improvisation and narrative. *Narrative Inquiry, 12*(2), 321–351.

Schiffrin, D. (1994). *Approaches to discourse.* Oxford, UK: Blackwell.

Schiffrin, D., Tannen, D., & Hamilton, H.E. (Eds.). (2001). *The handbook of discourse analysis.* Oxford, UK: Blackwell.

Schonmann, S. (1995). *Theatre of the classroom.* Tel Aviv, Israel: Cherikover. [in Hebrew]

Schonmann, S. (2006). *Theatre as a medium for children and young people.* Dordrecht, Netherlands: Springer.

Snow, C.E. (1999). Facilitating language development promotes literacy learning. In L. Eldering & P. Leseman (Eds.), *Early education and culture* (pp. 141–162). New York, NY: Falmer Press.

Snow, C.E., Griffin, P., & Burns, M.S. (2006). *Knowledge to support the teaching of reading: Preparing teachers for a changing world.* Washington, DC: National Academy Press.

Tharpe, R.G., & Gallimore, R. (1988). *Rousing minds to life: Teaching, learning, and schooling in a social context.* New York, NY: Cambridge University Press.

Tholander, M., & Aronsson, K. (2003). Doing subteaching in school work: Positioning, resistance and participation frameworks. *Language and Education, 17,* 208–234.

Thorell, M. (1998). *Politics and alignments in children's play dialogue: Play arenas and participation.* Linköping, Sweden: Linköpings Universitet.

van Dijk, T.A. (1997). The study of discourse. In T.A. van Dijk (Ed.), *Discourse as structure and process* (pp. 1–34). London, UK: SAGE.

Vardi-Rath, E. (2013). Multifaceted solidarity—Teacher discourse analysis from the perspective of politeness styles. In B. Alpert & S. Shlasky (Eds.), *A close look at the school and the classroom: Ethnographic studies in education* (pp. 439–474). Tel Aviv, Israel: The MOFET Institute. [in Hebrew]

Vardi-Rath, E., Teubal, E., Aillenberg, H., & Lewin, T. (2014). "Let's pretend you're the wolf!": The literate character of pretend-play discourse in the wake of a story. In A. Cekaite, S. Blum-Kulka, V. Grover, & E. Teubal (Eds.), *Children's peer talk: Learning from each other* (pp. 63–87). Cambridge, UK: Cambridge University Press.

Vygotsky, L.S. (1978). *Mind in society: The development of higher psychological processes.* Cambridge, MA: Harvard University Press.

Wagner, D.A., Venezky, R.L., & Street, B.V. (Eds.). (1999). *Literacy: An international handbook.* Boulder, CO: Westview Press.

Wood, D., Bruner, J.S., & Ross, G. (1976). The role of tutoring in problem solving. *Journal of Child Psychology and Psychiatry and Allied Disciplines, 17,* 89–100.

Zadunaisky-Ehrlich, S. (2011). Argumentative discourse of kindergarten children: Features of peer talk and children-teacher talk. *Journal of Research in Childhood Education, 25*(3), 248–267.

Zadunaisky-Ehrlich, S., & Blum-Kulka, S. (2010). Peer talk as a "double opportunity space": The case of argumentative discourse. *Discourse & Society, 21,* 211–233.

Zadunaisky-Ehrlich, S., & Blum-Kulka, S. (2014). "Now I said that Danny becomes Danny again"—A multifaceted view of kindergarten children's peer argumentative discourse, language play, peer group improvisation, and L2 learning. In A. Cekaite, S. Blum-Kulka, V. Grover, & E. Teubal (Eds.), *Children's peer talk: Learning from each other* (pp. 23–41). Cambridge, UK: Cambridge University Press.

10

THE NATURAL WORLD AS CONTENT FOR INTERCONNECTION AND DIVERGENCE OF PRETENSE AND STORYTELLING IN CHILDREN'S PLAY

Kumara Ward

Introduction

Play-based curriculum approaches are widely recognized by researchers and educators in the early childhood sector as fundamental to children's learning and to children being active participants in the learning process (Australian Curriculum Asssment and Reporting Authority [ACARA], 2010; Arthur, Beecher, Death, Dockett, & Farmer, 2014; Dockett & Fleer, 1999; Fleer et al., 2006; Hamilton & McFarlane, 2005; Hedges, 2000; Isenberg & Jalongo, 1993). Accordingly, they are implemented in various forms throughout childcare settings in Australia. Play-based approaches are also embedded in the Early Years Learning Framework (EYLF; Department of Education, Employment and Workplace Relations [DEEWR], 2009), which guides practice in all settings across the country. That they are included in this national framework document underscores the recognition of the role of play in children's learning, identity, and development. While play is recognized as something that all children do, the type of play and its content vary depending on physical context, social grouping, sociocultural backgrounds of the children and their development, interests, and funds of knowledge (Arthur et al., 2014; Fleer et al., 2006; Göncü, 1993; Little, 2010; Riojas-Cortez, 2001; Rogers & Evans, 2006).

The play that this chapter explores is the self-selected play of four groups of children in preschools in Sydney, Australia, who were participating in my doctoral research study for the academic year of 2009 (Ward, 2011).[1] This research asked the following question (subsequently unpacked into subquestions): In what ways can educator-generated creative arts experiences, using content from the natural world, assist children in learning about the natural world? The aim of the research was primarily to investigate education for sustainability (EfS) in the early childhood curriculum and the use of educator-generated, arts-based pedagogies, not specifically to analyze children's play. However, the answers to the questions the research asked were particularly evident in the children's play, which reflected their understandings of the natural world and their attitudes toward it. In addition, and as a result of the increased curriculum content about the natural world, the social dynamics evident in the children's play reflected those that existed in the local natural world (Ward, 2011).

The content about the natural world was introduced into the classroom through storytelling and other arts-based pedagogies. The research design specifically included data collection based on observations of the children's play, built on the premise that elements of the additional curriculum content would be evident in their play. These data revealed specific new and ongoing play content focused on the natural world that included knowledge of new subject matter; relationships and negotiations between species and objects; role-plays of animal, insect, or elemental characters; and rules of the play that echoed the dynamics of the subject in the natural world. This occurred early in the period of the research and raises some interesting questions about triggers for children's play and the way in which children embrace new influences, situations, and content. It also invites further discussion about storytelling as early childhood pedagogy.

The ways in which the content about the natural world in the children's curriculum interconnected with their daily lives in their preschool setting and the ways in which this content triggered a divergence of subject matter and complexity in their play will form the overall structure of this discussion. Engaging with the arts-based pedagogies (Brinkman, 2010; Edwards, 2010; Eisner, 2002; McArdle, 2012; Russell-Bowie, 2009; Wright, 2012) that underpinned the storytelling and the programmed creative arts experiences used in this research will assist in understanding the play and pretense (Dockett & Fleer, 1999; Göncü, 1989, 1993; Hedges, 2000; Lillard, 2001; Riojas-Cortez, 2001; Rogers & Evans, 2006) that the children engaged in. Theories of identity, place, and belonging (Orr, 2005; Somerville, 2012; Tooth & Renshaw, 2009) and posthumanist theories of common worlds and relational materialism (Haraway, 1994; Hultman & Lenz Taguchi, 2010; Taylor, 2011) will also be used to highlight the impact of environment and context in play. Given that play occurs in context and in a physical environment, discussion about the value of increased content about the natural world as an intrinsic element of children's physical environment and identity will also be included. Theories related to biophilia (Wilson, 1984) and ecopsychology (Roszak, Gomes, & Kanner, 1995) will provide the lenses for this discussion.

Method

There were four preschools and eight educators engaged in this research. Two educators from each preschool—one bachelor qualified (10 years of experience or more) and one vocational education and training (VET) support educator (also 10 years of experience or more)—agreed to research and engage in creatively rendering information about their local natural environments and to include this in their daily programs with the children. They did so over an 11-month period in 2009 (see Ward, 2011). This process was scaffolded through a teacher educator, participatory action research process (Ponte, Ax, Beijaard, & Wubbels, 2004), where I, as teacher educator, modeled example processes for the participating educators for developing self-generated stories and creative arts experiences based on factual research about the local natural environment. The first step modeled in this process was story creation and storytelling.

The preschool educators collaborated with me in the story development process initially by contributing information about the children's interests in the animals or insects in the natural world, what flora and fauna was in focus in the locality, and the story content that interested them. I then added this information to my own research of the local natural environment and created a story for each setting and for each visit. The characters and settings of each story subsequently became the subject matter for experiences in other arts modes such as drama, dance, music, and visual arts. After three to four research visits, the educators took over the process of researching their local environments and, as per the process articulated previously, first expressed their detailed environmental knowledge by creatively rendering it into self-generated stories and, from there, into experiences in other arts media. For example, one educator started her storytelling journey by creating and telling stories about the common wombat. She began by researching the wombat habitat, life cycle, and behaviour in her local area and creatively weaving this information into a story. After an alliterative naming of her main character, Wilma Wombat, she wove an adventure story that included other characters and elements of the lives led by wombats and the challenges they faced in finding food, overcoming obstacles, eating poisonous weeds, and avoiding cars (Wilma lived in the nearby Royal National Park, where there were picnic sites and cars). Wilma and her friends were drawn, painted, acted, sculpted, and played (see Figures 10.1 and 10.2).

The process exemplified previously includes factual research of subject matter and habitat and creative rendering of this material into stories and, from there, into other arts experiences and was repeated in all of the preschools. Subsequently, the children self-selected these characters and story elements and expressed them in their play.

There was a wide range of data collected by both the educators and myself. Data collected by the educators included reflective journal entries, photographs and written observations of the children's responses and interactions during stories, creative experiences and at play, their own planning materials, creative artifacts and props, feedback from families, and artifacts created with the children. The data I collected included video footage of the sessions with the children (presented by me or the educators), notes of phone calls with educators to plan the

FIGURE 10.1 Children's sculptures of wombats in the Royal National Park, headfirst in burrows.

FIGURE 10.2 Four-year-old girl playing at camping in the Royal National Park, holding Pinky Pad Possum, who lived in the tree near Wilma Wombat.

sessions, e-mail records of contact with the educators, journal notes created after each session, and photographs of the artifacts created by the educators and the children that reflected the stories and their characters. These included sculptures, drawings, paintings, or new songs based on the session content. A questionnaire was also conducted with the educators at the beginning of the visits (February) and at the end of the visits (December), capturing variances in responses and representing a rich source of data (Goodwin & Goodwin, 1996). Categories of data across all data types emerged and were gradually adjusted and finally confirmed in consultation with the participants (Creswell, 2002).

Restoring the Voice of Nature Through Arts-Based Pedagogies

Nature, as an interactive meaning-making entity, is silent. The extent to which we as a species privilege language and texts with meaning making and as a vehicle for enacting consciousness and intersubjectivity means that the natural world, with no voice or text, remains outside of our conscious interactions and is largely unheeded (Elliott & Davis, 2009). However, understanding nature as *place* (Somerville, 2012) was inherent in this research project, and the educators and children gave their place a voice through investigation, storytelling, and creative arts experiences. As in posthumanist theories (Dolphijn & van der Tuin, 2012; Haraway, 1994) that attribute agency to nonhuman objects, this process provided a platform for revoicing nature by experiencing it through creative, physical, affective, and cognitive processes and encounters. The educators and the children in this project investigated other ways of knowing nature and pathways toward connection or **eco**nnection through arts-based pedagogies that encouraged the participants to imagine, embody, render into story, mold, shape, and enact elements of their natural world and to reinterpret their understanding of it through these processes.

The arts foster creativity and innovation, engage and promote problem solving, transfer and adapt knowledge and skill, and are fundamental in early childhood (Edwards, 2010; Isenberg & Jalongo, 2009; Russell-Bowie, 2009; Wright, 2012). Early childhood educators support children to see themselves as inherently creative, as agents who can do, make, and create art (Isenberg & Jalongo, 2009; Wright, 2012). The arts are applicable to all areas of sensory experience (Department of Education and Training of New South Wales, 2010; Russell-Bowie, 2009) and, as such, are inherently playful. When a child pretends to be a monster, they will walk with arms wide and take big, loud steps. When a child pretends to be a mother duck, they are engaged in role-play and pretense and in embodying and empathizing with an element of the natural world. The act of embodiment is an example of connecting with a situated being in place (Somerville, 2012)—in this case, the mother duck. The content of the role-play and the earnestness with which the child becomes the mother duck reflects knowledge and empathy and builds on the child's ecopsychological identity (Roszak, 1998).

Similarly, a drawing can contain many symbolic elements and be underpinned by a narrative representing a pretend scenario (Wright, 2010). The arts can also be seen as an additional way of knowing, thinking, and innovating that encompasses affective realms of being (Wilson, 2010; Wright, 2012). Eisner (2002) reminds us of the capacity afforded by the arts to reengage with and stabilize memories of lived experiences and to communicate them through the arts. This reengaging with subject matter to explore, investigate, or make sense of is a recognized feature of play (Dockett & Fleer, 1999). In this instance, the arts were used as a vehicle to introduce content about the natural world into the program. This, in turn, engendered play that reflected the children's connection with and learning about the natural world. The connection to and embodiment of the natural world exhibited in the children's play is consistent with Somerville's (2012) concept of *postmodern emergence*, where place is understood through a variety of creative modes that, combined, generate a deep knowing and belonging to place.

What Does the Natural World Have to Do With Play?

The natural environment is an overlooked influence in a child's life (Louv, 2006; White & Stoecklin, 2008). Edward O. Wilson (1984) claims that we have a biophilic connection with the natural world that is manifest through unconscious recognition of our shared biology and an inner sense of connection to and identification with the natural world. Primary experience is the most direct means of experiencing the natural world and, as fundamentally biological beings, we yearn for these biophilic experiences (Wilson, 1984). The groundswell of voices that champion the right for children to be able to play outdoors and in unstructured environments (Ballantyne & Packer, 2009; Gill, 2004, 2005a, 2005b, 2006, 2007a, 2007b, 2007c; Louv, 2006; Phenice & Griffore, 2003; Pyle, 2002; Roszak, 2001; Tooth & Renshaw, 2009; Warden, 2005) further highlights the importance of these experiences. The natural world is also a primary and multifaceted play context (Malone, 2004), but the absence of content or opportunity in many early childhood programs for connecting children with their local natural environments (Elliott & Davis, 2009) perpetuates the ongoing disconnect between human beings and place (Orr, 2005; Sobel, 2005) and affects children physically, affectively, and cognitively. What has been clearly demonstrated by studies conducted by many of these advocates is that children are stronger, fitter, happier, more cognitively dexterous, and more capable of environmental stewardship when they can and do spend time outdoors. They also show that children, through this kind of activity and play, become effective risk assessors in their own right (Gill, 2007b; Warden, 2012).

There are a number of psychologically oriented paradigms that advocate spending time in nature. They include deep ecology (Naess, 1989; Seed, Macy, Fleming, & Naess, 1988), ecofeminism (Gaard, 1993; Gomes & Kanner, 1995; Shiva, 2005), theories of place and belonging (Somerville, 2012; Tooth & Renshaw, 2009; Wattchow & Brown, 2011), and a key theory embraced by this research project: ecopsychology (Roszak, 1998). Ecopsychology (Roszak, 2001; Roszak et al., 1995) emerged as a new branch of psychology, yet it goes much further than conventional psychology in that it attributes an ecological unconscious to humankind. This is an inner knowing that we are part of the planet, the solar system, and the universe. It involves an understanding that we all share in the life of our planet, its history, its composition, and its place in the cosmos. This awareness is current when we are born but, for most of us, it becomes clouded by what

The Natural World as Content **233**

could be called *urban alienation*. This condition is one that causes us to lose our sense of environmental reciprocity, which is, of course, impossible to have if we do not recognize the extent to which we are dependent on, or part of, the natural environment (Roszak, 1998). The aim of ecopsychology is to "heal the more fundamental alienation between the recently created urban psyche and the age-old natural environment" (Roszak, 1998, p. 4). Children, according to Roszak, have an innate sense of wonder for the natural world that can be nurtured through direct experiences in the natural world and through the arts. This assists in developing the "ecological ego" (Roszak, 1998, p. 4) that matures as the child grows with a sense of environmental ethics and aesthetic appreciation that encompasses social and political dimensions.

Fritjof Capra (1999) connects the development of aesthetic appreciation to nature and highlights this capacity as one of the key filters through which we mediate experiences of the world in general. Our interactions with the natural world stimulate this aesthetic appreciation and this in turn supports our ability to recognize the characteristics of pattern, form, colour, sound, and movement (p. 5). He claims that the study of patterns, particularly as they relate to living systems or the environment, is central to understanding ecology and should be a key factor in education for all children. This is a key element of what Capra (1999) calls *ecoliteracy*.

All children's lived experiences include elements of the natural world to some degree. This includes elements of the natural world in or adjacent to urban settings such as parks and beaches and rural, agricultural, and wild settings. However, when early childhood educators talk about reflecting children's lives, it is often through poststructural theories or sociocultural or ecological approaches (Bronfenbrenner, 1994; Fleer et al., 2006) that include the key elements and influences of family and culture, extended family, early childhood or school settings, churches, community services, the state, and the broader cultural values within which these elements exist. What this ever-increasing pattern of influence omits is the natural world on which all these institutions and groupings stand. Many children have limited primary experiences in the natural world. However, the flexibility, multiple media options, and evocative representations of nature that are possible within the arts make the arts a powerful means of investigating, exploring, interpreting, and connecting with the natural world and experiencing its form, colour, variety, wisdom, and wonder (Somerville, 2012; Wilson, 2010). The local natural environment is a fundamental contextual feature of children's lives and, as this research shows, becomes a key feature in their awareness and play when creatively incorporated into the curriculum. Playing out stories and content about the natural world then becomes an effective means of reinforcing children's eco-psychological (Roszak, 2001) and biophilic (Wilson, 1984) connections and of experiencing the full ecological settings and context of their lives.

Context of the Play

Children play and learn in cultural, social, environmental, and political contexts (Arthur et al., 2014; Berk & Winsler, 1995; Bronfenbrenner, 1979; Fleer et al., 2006; Rogoff, 1990). The environments, interactions, and play affordances children encounter in early childhood settings, where they may spend up to 5 days per week, render them as significant reference points and places of *being* to which children's view of the world is firmly rooted. Throughout this research, the place context was enhanced as the children were told, and shared in creating, unique stories that were set in the natural environment local to them and populated by locally occurring flora and fauna.

After the story and programmed creative arts experiences, the children were able to engage freely with boxes of natural materials (incorporated as part of the research), which consisted of bark, stones, driftwood, pinecones, feathers, other seed pods, and large pieces of plain and patterned cloth to use as backdrops. These materials were left at the preschools, and the educators also gathered additional natural materials for the children to play with.

The first time these materials were available, the children were so intense in their exploration of them that the bark was shredded, the dried leaves were crushed, and the driftwood was in pieces (see Figure 10.3). This deconstruction of the materials occurred simply through the children feeling, exploring, and testing the qualities of the materials—stroking, pulling, tearing, and snapping as if exploring their own inherent biophilic connection to them. Having done so, the children quickly settled into self-initiated play with these materials and began to tell each other elements of the story or stories they had heard earlier—complete with the verbal intonations (i.e., vocalisms) and body language cues that characterize pretense (Göncü, 1989). Having thoroughly examined the natural materials, the children then arranged them into story scenes to support the play (see Figure 10.4). The multimodal exploration or postmodern emergence (Somerville, 2012) that the children engaged in during this play was generated through the content of the story, the targeted arts experience that explored the story content, and inanimate objects. This is consistent with posthumanist paradigms (Haraway, 1991; Hultman & Lenz Taguchi, 2010; Panelli, 2010), which describe the relationship between human and nonhuman actors (in this case, inanimate objects), each with distinctive characteristics and their own unique agency, which is performed within their interactions. That is to say, the child in *nature play* is not the only actor or agent—the nonhuman actors or objects with which they engage can have causal qualities and influence. The child's ability to respond to the nonhuman actors or agents within the story or play context is also, according to Egan (1997), a natural feature of their predisposition toward creative language, metaphor, and imagination. That these experiences and materials had agency in prompting the children to behave in particular ways is indisputable. What is most interesting is

The Natural World as Content 235

FIGURE 10.3 The natural materials in the aftermath of discovery and exploration.

FIGURE 10.4 A deliberate child-initiated play scene using existing and additional natural resources.

that the materials were used in a variety of ways and attributed with many qualities, rendering them ideal for pretense scenarios.

The children were behaving as if they were in the story, creating the story and pretending to be the story characters, and in doing so reflecting behavioural (Lillard, 2001) and metarepresentational (Friedman & Leslie, 2007; Friedman, Neary, Burnstien, & Leslie, 2010) theories of play behaviour and pretense.

Initially, the children's play closely reflected the storylines as told by the educators, where a child would narrate parts of the story and the others would act it out. However, after a period of 3 months, they began to create their own stories using familiar characters and engage in negotiated role-play. This is consistent with developing complexity in children's social play that includes intersubjectivity or negotiated narrative forms, roles, and rules (Göncü, 1993;Vygotsky, 1978). The main difference here was that the subject matter and acts of the play did not rely solely on the children's individual funds of knowledge but encompassed their shared experiences of the story and the creative arts experience that followed it. For example: The preschool child who listened to their educator's story about the cockatoos and heard about the challenges these birds had in finding a nest, who then drew a picture of the cockatoo's new home in the tree trunk, or who sculpted the newly laid eggs in clay, could be said to have experienced the content cognitively, affectively, and kinaesthetically (McArdle, 2012; Russell-Bowie, 2009; Wright, 2012). Having such a multilayered experience allowed for proficient manipulation of the details of the story and seemed to generate unlimited possibilities for embellishment or extension of the characters and settings. Within the first 3 months of the research, the children were taking the characters and the settings and creating play stories with each other that represented the behaviour the animal or insect might exhibit and the natural habitats they were situated in. The children were also anthropomorphizing the affective states of the characters in the play scenarios, and this appeared to provide additional scope for understanding the play character's motivations and social interactions (Littledyke, 2008; White & Stoecklin, 2008).

Nature Play

Play has been theorized and categorized in many ways over the last century, and my main purpose here is to highlight the social and environmental context of the children's play and the funds of knowledge they brought to it. While the intention here is to avoid subscribing to developmental sequences in play, the following paragraphs discuss some of the social iterations of the play that occurred following nature story episodes in the preschools. In the reflection on solitary play, it is implicit that this type of play can occur at any age and that we can learn much about the child's metacognitive and affective processes through their pretense. The negotiation implicit in group play is discussed in the context of the nature stories, and the rules related to role-play are also a focus. The addition of the stories as a trigger for the play adds a dimension, as the context for the role-play, whether solitary or in a group, is directly related to the stories without being constrained by them. The content about nature is a feature of the children's self-selected play topics—albeit strongly influenced by the classroom experiences that focus on the natural world.

Solitary Play

Initially, the children's play reflected the stories that the researcher or the educators told. In Preschool 1, the educators had created a play scene depicting Deepwater

FIGURE 10.5 David resting in the river play scene with a comfort toy.

Creek. This comprised a long piece of blue cloth for the river, with patterned green cloth for the grassy riverbank and many real seed pods, rocks, bark, and shells. One child decided that he would take a soft toy koala into the river and lie down (see Figure 10.5). He rocked back and forth for a few minutes and then got up and went to play with the other children. This solitary play followed a story about a Saint Andrew's Cross spider that was immature and not very practiced at building webs—therefore being uncomfortable and hungry for much of the time. The spider, after choosing many unsuitable places to attempt web building, gradually learned that it needed to get older so that it could weave the characteristic white cross in the center of the web to hold it together, and then its web-building exploits would be more successful. What motivated the child to take the soft toy and lie down in the creek and rock is unclear, but he had never demonstrated behaviour like this before in the preschool. Whether it was a biophilic association with comfort, perhaps a sense of belonging in place, or the story contained a metaphor or an analogy related to other aspects of his life is hard to say. It does seem to be an ecopsychological identification or empathy with the story content. It is worth noting that this behaviour was observed on three separate occasions in three different preschools, each time after a story that contained underpinning messages about physical comfort and having one's needs met for shelter, nesting, or, in the case of the spider, creating a web for catching life-sustaining food.

Another example of solitary pretend play was that of Luke (see Figure 10.6) in Preschool 2 kneeling in a play scene created by the children using the large pieces of material and the natural resources provided. Luke had just heard a story about Croaka Loka, the green tree frog and a number of other animals that lived in or around the pond in which he lived. Luke went to the toy box and found a plastic

FIGURE 10.6 Luke vocalizes the talk of the echidna.

echidna and brought it back to the play scene. He then went and drew an echidna, cut it out, and placed it in the play scene so the first one could have a friend with which to play. During this process, Luke became the voice of the echidnas and introduced them to the other animals in the pond, where they (collectively voiced by him as well) proceeded with a story narrative of his making. This is an example of individual role-play with a narrative and an example of the child following his own play agenda (Rogers & Evans, 2006) but within the context of the play scene triggered by the story and the materials. Clearly, content, context, opportunity, and materials were all enabling aspects of this play scenario. The reflection of biophilic, ecopsychological, and relational materialist or posthumanist theories are also lenses through which this play episode (and many others throughout the research) could be interpreted.

Group Play

In Preschool 4, the educator told a story of Dibble Duck, Dabble Duck, and Paddle Quack—three young ducks with downy backs (yes, this became the lead line in the song). This was a serialized story and was being told well into the academic year at the time when the educators were developing complex, often ongoing story narratives. The story had finished and the children had free time to go and play. They took off to another part of the room but first had to negotiate who was going to be the mother duck and lead the others. In the absence of agreement for one mother duck, there were now three, and they marched off with those that were baby ducks trailing behind them (see Figure 10.7). The story that followed in their play used the same characters as those in the story the educator had developed, but they had different adventures when redeveloped for their play, demonstrating the children's choices of subject matter (they chose to use the established characters) and storyline—an important element of role-play according to the children in Rogers and Evans' (2006) study. The intricate machinations of the role assignment were reenacted daily, as the children replayed similar scenarios daily for a number of weeks. Such variations are also consistent with the importance of choice in good role-play (Rogers & Evans, 2006). This engagement of a number of players with a group-devised narrative demonstrated complex learning and negotiation with numerous references to the material "learned" through the stories. So even though the children were playing with and adding to the curriculum content that was offered to them through the stories, they were demonstrating detailed knowledge of their local environment, the species with whom the ducks interacted, and the ducks' habitats and social dynamics.

FIGURE 10.7 Three mother ducks leading the ducklings.

Social Dynamics and Rules

The children's use of the story characters reflected the characteristics and behaviours of the animal, insect, or phenomenon in question. They also reflected the rules and power relationships that exist in the natural world. After a story and drama and movement session in Preschool 4 about cicadas and the way in which they fly in the sunlight once their wings have dried, four boys decided that they would continue playing. While two of the children started out curled up on the floor with "wet wings," they told the other two that they had to be the sun. This meant that the other two boys had to dart around being sunrays to dry the wings of the emerging cicadas—in other words, the requirements of the biology of the cicada characters dictated the roles of the other players. When one of the cicadas told a sun dancer he could be a cicada, too, he replied—"No, I am the sun, I have to fly around and dry your wings" (Ward, 2011). This postmodern, performative (Barad, 2003) exploration of the natural world reflects multifaceted connections to biophilic understandings, ecopsychological behaviour, natural phenomena situated in place (Somerville, 2012), and metacreative learning of the subject matter—in this case, through drama, dance, and story.

Another play episode in Preschool 1 saw a group of girls playing a family of kookaburras, which had an affective emphasis. The baby kookaburras were soon to fledge, and they were worried that they would not know how to fly. The mother and father kookaburras reassured them that they would be fine, that they would teach them what they needed to do, and that there would be opportunities for short flights for practice. This was a storyline taken from the educator's story. Again, later in the research process, the children played the storyline over and over. It is hard to say whether this repeated play was to consolidate the content of the story or if it touched an archetypal nerve about insecurity and learning new things. As the story was replayed and embellished over a number of weeks, it expanded to include a number of kookaburra families. This involved a great deal of negotiation about who would be the parents, what aspects of life the parents had to teach the baby kookaburras, the extent to which the babies could or should ask for help, and the things they should know already (see Figure 10.8). This is a good example of the children anthropomorphizing the animals in question and attributing to them human-like emotions in response to the challenges they faced. This emotional understanding of their play subjects was still integrated with the real-life challenges a kookaburra might face and was an example of what the kookaburras might say if they could speak and we could hear them. As Littledyke (2008), in discussing environmental education, says, anthropomorphizing is constructive if it assists the children in understanding the animals in question.

The educators also reported changes in the groupings of children, saying that the normal affinity or gender groupings were not so obvious. Instead, the children were just as likely to be grouped by their interest in the play or creative arts

FIGURE 10.8 Two girls play kookaburra families teaching the young to fly.

exploration they were engaged in. Some of these friendships were temporary. For example, when the children in Preschool 1 created beeswax butterflies after a story where a monarch butterfly was the main character, they put their butterflies onto a display area and engaged them as players by giving them voices and using them like puppets. Other groups became more established, engaging in repeat episodes of play on a shared topic of interest, and intersubjectivity became the glue for the groups, resulting in shared sustained thinking (Siraj-Blatchford, Taggart, Sylva, Sammons, & Melhuish, 2008) and complex learning.

These examples show that the children were indeed playing the curriculum content and, in turn, learning much about the natural world. The modeled behaviour and focus on stories told by the educators became the everyday stuff of the children's engagement in play, whether it was pretend play using props and role-play or play with creative materials for art exploration and meaning making. Preschool 4 tracked the children's self-initiated drawings over a 3-day period and found that 17 of 27 drawings were of plants, animals, and insects that were interacting in an intentional narrative on the page. That is, the children had engaged in play in their drawings where the narrative was in visual form and the drawn elements on the pages created the stories. These drawn relationships were based on the children's new knowledge of the natural world and the real interactions that occur within it. When considering the now-outmoded dichotomous view of children's play and work, particularly when it comes to classroom pedagogy (Lim,

2010), it is clear that these activities are both play and content learning and are drawn directly from the children's lived experience.

Findings

Two themes that emerge from this chapter are the importance of place with the natural world as context and the embodiment of place, nature, culture, and knowledge as content for play. Place became a key factor when the children began to refer to the stories and their characters as "our stories." The key point at which this happened was when the educators began to tell the stories instead of me telling them—3 to 4 months into the research. While the children attended to my stories (they were situated in their local area and reflected local flora and fauna and their own interests), the stories the educators developed and told had much greater impact. This is a significant indication of the importance of the relationships between the educators and the children and the extent to which they shared the place, space, and daily content of their lives. The attachment inherent in these relationships (Robinson, 2008) was further emphasized by the attachment and sense of belonging to place (Morgan, 1987; Orr, 2005; Prohansky & Fabian, 1987; Pyle, 2002; Somerville, Dundas, Mead, Oliver, & Sulter, 1994; Tooth, 2006; Vaske & Kobrin, 2001). The story threads representing the natural world (Tooth, 2006) wove their way into the children's perceptions of where they lived and who they were in the place. The incidents of play expressing story content increased dramatically. The attachment to the story characters and the empathy the children had for them was heightened, and the demand for repeated or serialized episodes of the stories was articulated daily. The children took the stories home; their parents began asking questions about the content and subsequently began taking their children to see the story characters in their local neighbourhood on weekends. This included visits to the Royal National Park, where wallabies and wombats were seen, and the beach, where seagulls, dolphins, and turtles were in focus. This content filtered into family lives in other ways as well. The educator in Preschool 4 recorded the following anecdote:

> Fiona's mum (name withheld) said her (Fiona's) dad was watching a fishing show on the weekend. When they caught the Leatherjacket Fiona said, 'I hope that's not Lester'!
>
> *(Ward, 2011, p. 121)*

These occurrences indicate that there is scope for community storymaking about place, generated by the preschool as a hub of place awareness, and are consistent with the studies of rendering place as a community activity conducted by Somerville et al. (1994). The children were clearly engaged with the natural world surrounding them as they played, enacted, and became the various objects and life forms within it.

Being in the natural world and having primary experience of natural phenomena have been part of early childhood education philosophy since its inception. This experience, combined with an adventurous spirit, was seen to build character and confer useful knowledge about life. This was evident in Owen's infant schools and Frobel's kindergartens and later in the educational writings of Dewey (Elliott & Davis, 2009; Spodek & Saracho, 1996). The historical notion of nature being good for children and, in addition, of children having a "pure nature" is also exemplified in the writings of Rousseau (1762). It's ironic that, collectively, these ideas have positioned nature as separate. They have created a nature–culture divide, where children are seen as inherently pure and natural but without access to or understanding of nature and yet in need of it (Taylor, 2011). This is still the basis of much of the advocacy to promote children's rights to connect with and spend time in nature and the outdoors.

While the notion that nature is good for children is supported by this research, the contemporary lenses of relational materialism (Hultman & Lenz Taguchi, 2010) and posthumanist paradigms (Panelli, 2010; Taylor, 2011) provide new ways for understanding and valuing children's play in or about nature. Through their play, the children were engaged in nonhuman encounters (Panelli, 2010; Taylor, 2011). The children were playing with natural materials, fluttering in excitement when pretending to be silk moths, moving like an eel, or pretending to swim in the sea while a playmate narrated the play (see Figures 10.9 and 10.10). The children were incorporating experiences of moving, singing, drawing, or sculpting their play subjects in relation to their previous experiences in the natural world.

The materials and concepts with which the children worked and played had particular qualities that exposed and elucidated the subjects in the imagined playscape. Concepts such as the "sundancers" for sunrays or "rush roar" to characterize the wind (see Figure 10.11) were readily incorporated into the children's play

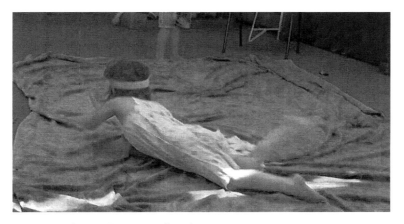

FIGURE 10.9 Catherine "swimming" in the ocean.

FIGURE 10.10 Two boys swimming like eels.

FIGURE 10.11 Alex is the wind!

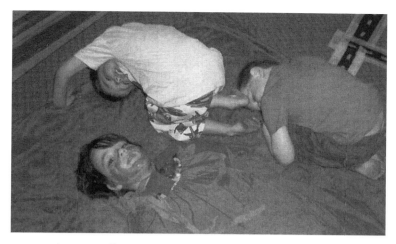

FIGURE 10.12 A group of boys investigate what it is like to be green in a green world.

with full roles and responsibilities. One group of children went so far as to play at camouflage. They had observed camouflage in nature and then played at being green insects, such as crickets and grasshoppers (see Figure 10.12). This process engaged the children in sinking into and feeling what it was like to be immersed in the green foliage that filled their play conception of nature. What conceptions or deep-seated knowing that we are part of nature does this engender? The words of Barad in an interview with Dolphijn and van der Tuin (2012) resonate here: "Matter feels, converses, suffers, desires, yearns and remembers" (p. 59). Whether the subject of the play was animal, insect, or element, it had agency. It became part of the interwoven life of the children's experience of the natural world as the children embodied it with all their senses and with their metarepresentations of pretense (Friedman et al., 2010), creating nature–culture play (Haraway, 1991; Taylor, 2011).

Conclusion

This chapter has described the development of new and significant play by preschool children who were engaged in a curriculum that featured the natural world and whose educators implemented this content using arts-based pedagogies. The close relationship between the arts and children's play has been established by examining the various ways in which play can be identified in arts experiences and the manner in which the arts themselves can be playful. The ubiquitous nature of play—as something children do—has been reiterated as a contextual and sociocultural enactment, and further contextual significance has been attributed to the natural world. The relevance of knowing and experiencing the natural world and the contribution this makes toward children's health, well-being, and sense of identity has been argued, as has the importance of place and identity in developing a sense of belonging.

The many examples of children's play highlight the extent to which the children readily incorporated their new experiences of the natural world, initially reflecting the storylines proffered by the educators and then embellishing and recreating their own stories using familiar settings and characters. The children demonstrated detailed learning of their local natural environments and played the characters in these environments physically, affectively, and cognitively through their interactions and through their use of the arts. The metarepresentations in their pretense incorporated social rules and dynamics from the natural world. Children used these in their play and as models of behaviour in other interactions.

The children's immersion in play with nonhuman elements of the natural world significantly erased the boundaries inherent in the nature–culture divide. The arts-based experiences of the nonhuman agents provided the children with deep insight into these actors. The children reflected these with a sensitivity and commitment that is consistent with intense enactment through pretense and play. The knowing and knowledge that resulted from this intense playing of their place and its elements led to a deep sense of belonging and connection with their preschool setting and its situatedness in their local natural world. This demonstrates a synergy of work and play and highlights the value of meaningful content and play coming together as significant elements of the children's lived experience.

Finally, this chapter demonstrates the power of story and place. For these children, the stories became the content that they lived, through the arts experiences and through their play. The children's use of story followed as a natural extension in their play, and they populated their negotiated and pretend worlds with nature and cultures that were alive with possibilities.

Note

1   Pseudonyms are used for the children where names are mentioned.

References

Arthur, L., Beecher, B., Death, E., Dockett, S., & Farmer, S. (2014). *Programming and planning in early childhood settings* (6th ed.). South Melbourne, VIC, Australia: Cengage Learning Australia.

Australian Curriculum Assssment and Reporting Authority (ACARA). (2010). Draft of K-12 Australian Curriculum in English, History, Mathematics and Science. Retrived from http://www.australiancurriculum.edu.au/home

Ballantyne, R., & Packer, J. (2009). Introducing a fifth pedagogy: Experience-based strategies for facilitating learning in natural environments. *Environmental Education Research, 15*(2), 243–262.

Barad, K. (2003). Posthumanist performativity: Toward an understanding of how matter comes to matter. *Signs: Journal of Women and Culture in Society, 28*(3), 801–831.

Berk, L., & Winsler, A. (1995). Scaffolding children's learning: Vygotsky and early childhood education. Washington, DC: National Association for the Education of Young Children (NAEYC).

Brinkman, D.J. (2010). Teaching creatively and teaching for creativity. *Arts Education Policy Review, 111*(2), 48–50. http://dx.doi.org/10.1080/10632910903455785

Bronfenbrenner, U. (1979). *The ecology of human development: Experiments by nature and design.* Cambridge, MA: Harvard University Press.

Bronfenbrenner, U. (1994). Ecological models of human development. In T. Husén & N. Postlethwaite (Eds.), *International encyclopedia of education* (2nd ed., Vol. 2, pp. 37–43). Oxford, UK: Elsevier.

Capra, F. (1999, March). *Ecoliteracy: The challenge for education in the next century.* Paper presented at Liverpool Schumacher Lectures, Liverpool, England. Retrieved from http://ccccnsw.org.au/rattlerresources/ecoliteracy.pdf

Creswell, J. (2002). *Research design: Qualitative, quantitative, and mixed method approaches.* London, UK: SAGE.

Department of Education, Employment and Workplace Relations (DEEWR). (2009). The Early Years Learning Framework: Belonging, being & becoming. Canberra, ACT, Australia: Council of Australian Governments.

Department of Education and Training of New South Wales. (2010). Curriculum key learning areas K-6: Learning and teaching. Retrieved from http://www.schools.nsw.edu.au/learning/k_6/index.php

Dockett, S., & Fleer, M. (1999). *Play and pedagogy in early childhood: Bending the rules.* London, UK: Harcourt.

Dolphijn, R., & van der Tuin, I. (2012). *New materialism: Interviews and cartographies.* Ann Arbor, MI: Open Humanities Press.

Edwards, L. (2010). *The creative arts: A process approach for teachers and children* (5th ed.). Upper Saddle River, NJ: Merrill.

Egan, K. (1997). The arts as the basics of education. *Childhood Education, 73*(6), 341–345. http://dx.doi.org/10.1080/00094056.1997.10521136

Eisner, E.W. (2002). *The arts and the creation of mind.* New Haven, CT: Yale University Press.

Elliott, S., & Davis, J. (2009). Exploring the resistance: An Australian perspective on educating for sustainability in early childhood. *International Journal of Early Childhood, 41*(2), 65–77.

Fleer, M., Edwards, S., Hammer, M., Kennedy, A., Ridgway, A., Robbins, J., & Surman, L. (2006). *Early childhood learning communities: Sociocultural research in practice.* Frenchs Forest, NSW, Australia: Pearson Education.

Friedman, O., & Leslie, A.M. (2007). The conceptual underpinnings of pretense: Pretending is not "behaving-as-if." *Cognition, 105,* 103–124.

Friedman, O., Neary, K.R., Burnstien, C.L., & Leslie, A.M. (2010). Is young children's recognition of pretense metarepresentational or merely behavioural? Evidence from 2- and 3-year-olds' understanding of pretend sounds and speech. *Cognition, 115,* 314–319.

Gaard, G. (Ed.). (1993). *Ecofeminism: Women, animals, nature.* Philadelphia, PA: Temple University Press.

Gill, T. (2004, September 23). Bred in captivity. *The Guardian.* Retrieved from http://www.theguardian.com/society/2004/sep/20/childprotection

Gill, T. (2005a, August 3). In need of an unlevel playing field [Comment]. *The Guardian.* Retrieved from http://www.theguardian.com/comment/story/0,3604,1541383,00.html

Gill, T. (2005b, September 23). Let our children roam free. *Ecologist Online*. Retrieved from http://www.paee.net/pdfs/Tim%20Gill%20-%20Let%20Our%20Children%20Roam%20Free.pdf

Gill, T. (2006). *Growing adventure: Final report to the Forestry Commission*. Bristol, UK: Forestry Commission England.

Gill, T. (2007a). Can I play out . . . ? Lessons from London Play's Home Zones Project, London, UK: London Play.

Gill, T. (2007b, September). *Growing up in a risk averse society*. Paper presented at the Come and Play Outside Symposium, University of Western Australia, Perth, WA, Australia.

Gill, T. (2007c). Playing it too safe. *RSA Journal: The Journal of the Royal Society for the Encouragement of Arts, Manufactures & Commerce, 154*, 46–51.

Gomes, M.E., & Kanner, A.D. (1995). The rape of the well maidens. In T. Roszak, M.E. Gomes, & A.D. Kanner (Eds.), *Ecopsychology: Restoring the mind, healing the earth* (pp. 111–115). San Francisco, CA: Sierra Club.

Göncü, A. (1989). Models and features of pretense. *Developmental Review, 9*, 341–344.

Göncü, A. (1993). Development of intersubjectivity in the dyadic play of preschoolers. *Early Childhood Research Quarterly, 8*, 99–116.

Goodwin, W.L., & Goodwin, L.D. (1996). *Understanding quantitative and qualitative research in early childhood education*. New York, NY: Teachers College Press.

Hamilton, N., & McFarlane, J. (2005). Children learn through play. *Putting Children First, 14*, 8–10.

Haraway, D. (1991). Situated knowledges: The science question in feminism and the privilege of partial perspective. In D. Haraway (Ed.), *Simians, cyborgs, and women: The reinvention of nature* (pp. 183–201). New York, NY: Routledge. Retrived from http://muse.jhu.edu/journals/configurations/v002/182.181haraway.html

Haraway, D. (1994). A game of cat's cradle: Science studies, feminist theory, cultural studies. *Configurations, 2*, 59–71.

Hedges, H. (2000). Teaching in early childhood: Time to merge constructivist views so learning through play equals teaching through play. *Australian Journal of Early Childhood, 24*(4), 16–21.

Hultman, K., & Lenz Taguchi, H. (2010). Challenging anthropocentric analysis of visual data: A relational materialist methodological approach to educational research. *International Journal of Qualitative Studies in Education, 23*(5), 525–542. http://dx.doi.org/10.1080/09518398.2010.500628

Isenberg, J., & Jalongo, M. (1993). *Creative play and expression in the early childhood curriculum*. New York, NY: Macmillan.

Isenberg, J., & Jalongo, M. (2009). *Creative thinking and arts-based learning: Preschool through age four* (5th ed.). Upper Saddle River, NJ: Pearson.

Lillard, A.S. (2001). Pretend play as twin earth: A social-cognitive analysis. *Developmental Review, 21*, 495–531.

Lim, M.-Y.S. (2010). Reconsidering the play-work dichotomy in pedagogy. In M. Ebbeck & M. Waniganayake (Eds.), *Play in early childhood education: Learning in diverse contexts* (pp. 141–156). Sydney, NSW, Australia: Oxford University Press.

Little, H. (2010, November–December). *Finding the balance: Early childhood practitioners' views on risk, challenge and safety in outdoor play settings*. Paper presented at the Australian Association for Research in Education Conference, Melbourne, VIC, Australia. Retrieved from http://hdl.handle.net/1959.14/153913

Littledyke, M. (2008). Science education for environmental awareness: Approaches to integrating cognitive and affective domains. *Environmental Education Research, 14,* 1–17.

Louv, R. (2006). *Last child in the woods: Saving our children from nature deficit disorder.* Chapel Hill, NC: Algonquin Books of Chapel Hill.

Malone, K. (2004). "Holding environments": Creating spaces to support children's environmental leanring in the 21st century. *Australian Journal of Environmental Education, 20*(2), 53–66.

McArdle, F. (2012). The visual arts: Ways of seeing. In S. Wright (Ed.), *Children, meaning-making and the arts* (2nd ed., pp. 30–56). Frenchs Forest, NSW, Australia: Pearson.

Morgan, S. (1987). *My place.* Fremantle, WA: Fremantle Arts Centre Press.

Naess, A. (1989). *Ecology, community and lifestyle: An outline of ecosophy.* Cambridge, UK: Cambridge University Press.

Orr, D.W. (2005). Place and pedagogy. In M. Stone & Z. Barlow (Eds.), *Ecological literacy: Educating our children for a sustainable world* (pp. 85–95). San Francisco, CA: Sierra Club Books.

Panelli, R. (2010). More-than-human social geographies: Posthuman and other possibilities. *Progress in Human Geography, 34*(1), 79–87.

Phenice, L.A., & Griffore, R.J. (2003). Young children and the natural world. *Contemporary Issues in Early Childhood, 4*(2), 167–171.

Ponte, P., Ax, J., Beijaard, D., & Wubbels, T. (2004). Teachers' development of professional knowledge through action research and the facilitation of this by teacher educators. *Teaching and Teacher Education, 20*(6), 571–588.

Prohansky, H.M., & Fabian, A.K. (1987). The development of place identity in the child. In C.S. Weinstein & T.G. David (Eds.), *Spaces for children: The built environment and child development* (pp. 21–40). New York, NY: Plenum Press.

Pyle, R. (2002). Eden in the vacant lot: Special places, species and kids in the neighbourhood of life. In P. Kahn, Jr. & S. Kellert (Eds.), *Children and nature: Psychological, sociocultural, and evolutionary investigations.* Cambridge, MA: MIT Press.

Riojas-Cortez, M. (2001). Preschoolers' funds of knowledge displayed through sociodramatic play episodes in a bilingual classroom. *Early Childhood Education Journal, 29*(1), 35–40.

Robinson, M. (2008). *Child development and behaviour from birth to eight: A journey through the early years.* Berkshire, UK: Open University Press.

Rogers, S., & Evans, J. (2006). Playing the game? Exploring role play from children's perspectives. *European Early Childhood Education Research Journal, 14*(1), 43–55.

Rogoff, B. (1990). *Apprenticeship in thinking: Cognitive development in social context.* New York, NY: Oxford University Press.

Roszak, T. (1998). Ecopsychology: Eight principles. Retrieved from https://soulcraftwisdom.wordpress.com/2012/04/29/ecopsychology-eight-principles/

Roszak, T. (2001). *The voice of the Earth: An exploration of ecopyschology* (2nd ed.). Grand Rapids, MI: Phanes Press.

Roszak, T., Gomes, M.E., & Kanner, A.D. (Eds.). (1995). *Ecopsychology: Restoring the mind, healing the mind.* San Francisco, CA: Sierra Club Books.

Rousseau, J. (1762). *Emile.* Paris, France: La Haye, J. Néaulme.

Russell-Bowie, D. (2009). *MMADD about the arts: An introduction to creative arts education* (2nd ed.). Sydney, NSW, Australia: Pearson Prentice Hall.

Seed, J., Macy, J., Fleming, P., & Naess, A. (1988). *Thinking like a mountain: Towards a council of all beings.* Philadelphia, PA: New Society.

Shiva, V. (2005, November). Two myths that keep the world poor. *Ode Magazine,* 1–3.

Siraj-Blatchford, I., Taggart, B., Sylva, K., Sammons, P., & Melhuish, E. (2008). Towards the transformation of practice in early childhood education: The Effective Provision of Pre-School Education (EPPE) project. *Cambridge Journal of Education, 38*(1), 23–36.

Sobel, D. (2005). *Place-based education: Connecting classrooms and communities.* Great Barrington, MA: The Orion Society.

Somerville, M. (2012). The critical power of place. In G.S. Cannella & S. Steinberg (Eds.), *Critical qualitative research reader* (pp. 67–81). New York, NY: Lang.

Somerville, M., Dundas, M., Mead, M., Oliver, J., & Sulter, M. (1994). *The sun dancin': People and place in Coonabarabran.* Canberra, ACT, Australia: Aboriginal Studies Press.

Spodek, B., & Saracho, O.N. (1996). Culture and the early childhood curriculum. *Early Child Development and Care, 123*(1), 1–13.

Taylor, A. (2011). Reconceptualizing the "nature" of childhood. *Childhood, 18*(4), 420–433. http://dx.doi.org/10.1177/0907568211404951

Tooth, R. (2006). *Growing a sense of place: Storythread and the transformation of a school* (Unpublished doctoral dissertation). University of Queensland, Brisbane, QLD, Australia.

Tooth, R., & Renshaw, P. (2009). Reflections on pedagogy and place: A journey into learning for sustainability through environmental narrative and deep attentive reflection. *Australian Journal of Environmental Education, 25,* 95–104.

Vaske, J., & Kobrin, K.C. (2001). Place attachment and environmentally responsible behaviour. *Journal of Environmental Education, 32*(4), 16–21.

Vygotsky, L.S. (1978). *Mind in society: The development of higher psychological processes.* M. Cole, V. John-Steiner, S. Scribner, & E. Souberman (Eds.), Cambridge, MA: Harvard University Press.

Ward, K. (2011). *The living curriculum: A natural wonder: Enhancing the ways in which early childhood educators scaffold young children's learning about the environment by using self-generated creative arts experiences as a core component of the early childhood program* (Unpublished doctoral dissertation). University of Western Sydney, Sydney, NSW, Australia.

Warden, C. (2005). *The potential of a puddle.* Auchterarder, Perthshire, Scotland: Mindstretchers.

Warden, C. (2012). *Nurture through nature: Working with children under 3 in outdoor environments* (2nd ed.). Auchterarder, Perthshire, Scotland: Mindstretchers.

Wattchow, B., & Brown, M. (2011). *A pedagogy of place: Outdoor education for a changing world.* Clayton, VIC, Australia: Monash University Publishing.

White, R., & Stoecklin, V.L. (2008). Nurturing children's biophilia: Developmentally appropriate environmental education for young children. Retrieved from http://www.whitehutchinson.com/children/articles/nurturing.shtml

Wilson, E.O. (1984). *Biophilia.* Cambridge, MA: Harvard University Press.

Wilson, R. (2010, May–June). Aesthetics and a sense of wonder. *Child Care Exchange,* 24–26.

Wright, S. (2010). *Understanding creativity in early childhood.* London, UK: SAGE.

Wright, S. (2012). *Children, meaning-making and the arts.* Frenchs Forest, NSW, Australia: Pearson.

PART III

Pretense and Storytelling in Cross-Cultural Development

11

USING NARRATIVES AND DRAWINGS TO ASSESS CREATIVITY IN PRESCHOOL-AGE CHILDREN

Candice M. Mottweiler

Understanding the emerging creativity of young children and how it relates to various aspects of development and personality are topics of interest for parents, educators, and researchers (see Jalongo & Hirsh, 2012; Korn-Bursztyn, 2012). But while the creative potential of young children might appear obvious from their colorful drawings, original stories, and elaborate games of pretense, there are significant challenges to conducting empirical research in this area. The goals of this chapter are to consider various definitions of creativity and how they apply to young children and to report the results of a study that was guided by this analysis. For the study, two new measures of creativity were designed to avoid some of the issues that have been problematic in past research assessing the creativity of preschool-age children.

Defining Creativity

The most widely accepted definition of *creativity* among psychologists involves the creation of products that are both *novel* and *appropriate* (Sawyer, 2012). On this view, to be judged as creative, a product must be novel (i.e., original, unique, or unexpected in some way), but novelty alone is not sufficient because it does not control for odd or bizarre ideas that have no value. Therefore, appropriateness is also required—to be judged as creative, a product must be a successful solution for a given problem and be valued for its usefulness or effectiveness.

The definition of creativity as the intersection of novelty and appropriateness has been applied to products along a wide continuum, from the masterpieces of art and science to clever solutions for everyday problems. However, there is debate over how broad or narrow the definition should be. For example, Csikszentmihalyi's (1996) description of creativity requires the product to be new and valuable to *the world*. This *Big C* creativity is typically limited to individuals who have become experts from years of experience and are capable of generating products that revolutionize their fields. While preparation and learning in a domain might be crucial for finding the unique and creative directions that underlie important creative achievements, a significant limitation of this model is that it excludes the experiences of most people. In particular, children—who lack expertise and are unlikely to know which things are novel to the world, let alone be able to create something that is novel to the world—are not considered capable of creativity.

While the world may not benefit from a preschooler's masterpiece, it is problematic to assume that preschoolers are incapable of creative thought. Young children frequently create products that are new and interesting to *them* personally and that are useful in the entertainment they provide to the children as well as others in their lives. This fits with an everyday, or *little c*, model of creativity that focuses on innovation in generating solutions for everyday problems and the formation of ideas that have not been considered previously by *the self* (rather than by society at large; Kaufman & Beghetto, 2009; Runco, 1996). Even very young children are capable of this type of creativity, and therefore this is the most appropriate level for creativity research with children.

Measuring Creativity

It is readily apparent when watching children that creative endeavors provide them with joy and entertainment (Russ, 2014), but is there value in children's creativity beyond the positive affect produced by this experience? For example, do early creative behaviors lead to creativity later in life? Research with adults in which they are asked to report on their childhood activities provides some evidence for this possibility (Goldstein & Winner, 2009; Hill & Clark, 1998; Hoff, 2005; Kidd, Rogers, & Rogers, 2010; Schaefer, 1969). For example, Root-Bernstein and Root-Bernstein (2006) interviewed adults recognized for their creativity (i.e., recipients of MacArthur Fellowships) and found that they were more likely than undergraduate students to recall engaging in the creative activity of generating elaborated imaginary worlds when they were children. Similarly, Taylor, Hodges, and Kohányi (2003) found that a high percentage of adult fiction writers recalled having created an imaginary companion as children.

These results suggest that early creative activities and behaviors might have meaningful consequences later in life and highlight the importance of understanding the developmental progression of creativity in childhood. However, to understand early creativity, it is crucial to conduct research with children themselves rather than relying on retrospective reports from adults who are often biased and/or incomplete in their recall of childhood activities. For example, many adults have forgotten their imaginary companions or report a biased selection of details about their past activities that they have heard from family stories. Retrospective reports cannot be considered reliable accounts of what children actually do. Thus, the study reported here was conducted with the children themselves rather than with adults recalling their childhoods.

Examining creativity in young children and determining its correlates in childhood is a necessary step for the larger goal of investigating the development of creativity across time. However, there are special challenges for the direct assessment of creativity in children. In order to better understand the origins of creativity, it is necessary to identify effective and appropriate tools for use with young populations. In what follows, the strengths and weaknesses of various approaches for assessing children's creativity are discussed. For the study reported here, this analysis guided the decisions (a) to use laboratory tasks rather than to interview teachers or the children themselves about their engagement in creative pursuits and (b) to evaluate products children created during the laboratory session using the consensual assessment technique (Amabile, 1982) instead of the more common strategy of assessing the uniqueness and fluidity of children's performance on divergent thinking tasks.

Adult and Self-Reports

Some measures ask teachers or other adults to rate children on creativity or other characteristics believed to be associated with creativity. For example, teachers are sometimes asked to rate the frequency of individual students' overall creative behaviors (Li, Poon, Tong, & Lau, 2013). Other measures, such as Barnett's (1990) Children's Playfulness Scale, ask teachers to rate students on characteristics considered important for creativity, such as physical spontaneity, social spontaneity, cognitive spontaneity, sense of humor, and manifest joy.

One of the benefits of this approach is that teachers have experience with many different children, giving them a basis for judging children's varying abilities and limitations. However, some research suggests that teachers' ratings are influenced by the halo effect, in which some children are seen as better in all domains, causing variables such as children's likeability or intelligence to affect the teachers' ratings of student creativity (see Karwowski, Gralewski, Lebuda, & Wiśniewska, 2007). While teacher reports of creativity shed light on how children's creativity is perceived by adults, given the inherent biases in this type of data, there are problems in using this approach to assess children's creative ability or potential.

In some studies, the children themselves have been asked to report on their creative activities. For example, the Creative Activities Checklist (Runco, 1987) is a self-report measure that asks children to indicate how often they participate in various creative activities, including literature, music, drama, arts, crafts, and science. However, a major limitation with self-report measures is that they rely on the insight of the individual to recognize and accurately report on his or her own behaviors. Young children are often poor informants of their skills and the frequencies of their various activities. The issue of accuracy, in addition to children's limited creative accomplishments, is likely a reason why this method is rarely implemented with young children and was not considered for the present study.

256 Candice M. Mottweiler

Observations of Creativity

Observing children's actual behavior helps overcome some of the aforementioned limitations. Several qualitative studies have closely observed the creative behaviors of children in naturalistic settings, such as preschools (Holmes & Geiger, 2002; Robson & Rowe, 2012; Trawick-Smith, Russell, & Swaminathan, 2011). For example, Cremin, Chappell, and Craft (2013) examined the stories spontaneously generated by preschool children and identified inclusions of fantastical or "what if" content within their narratives. One of the general findings of this methodology is that even very young children demonstrate behaviors indicative of creative thought, such as telling stories that are created completely by the children, with made-up characters, unique settings, and novel plot twists. While these studies provide rich descriptions of individual children's creativity, it is difficult to employ quantitative methods or analyses with products that are so diverse. In order to complement the findings of qualitative research, it is important to employ creativity measures that are standardized and thus allow comparison of responses across children.

Divergent Thinking Tasks

By far the most commonly used measures for assessing creativity across age groups are divergent thinking tasks, which are intended to capture participants' mental flexibility to generate numerous possibilities (Runco, Dow, & Smith, 2006; Torrance, 2000). This ability is deemed particularly important for creativity and is therefore routinely used as a measure of creative ability or potential (see Silvia et al., 2008; Torrance, 1974). In divergent thinking tasks, participants are asked to generate as many solutions as possible for a given problem. For example, in the Alternative Uses Task, individuals are asked to generate as many uses as possible for an everyday object, such as a brick or a newspaper.

Participants' responses are then scored for the number of solutions generated (fluency) as well as how many of those solutions are not mentioned by other participants in the study (uniqueness; Wallach & Kogan, 1965). The interpretation of these scores is straightforward: The greater the fluency and the greater number of unique ideas generated, the more creative the individual is assumed to be. The ease of scoring and its relative objectivity might account in part for the heavy usage of these types of tasks. Another benefit of these measures is that they assess everyday creativity and thus do not require special skills or expertise, making it possible to assess and compare a larger range of individuals instead of focusing only on experts in a given field.

However, divergent thinking tasks have been criticized in recent years on several counts. These tasks often fail to predict real-world creativity, both concurrently as well as across time (see Sawyer, 2012); divergent thinking task performance appears to be easily manipulated and influenced (Dziedziewicz,

Olędzka, & Karwowski, 2013; Sawyers, Moran, Fu, & Milgram, 1983); and these measures focus on the novelty of ideas, while the appropriateness of ideas is generally neglected, despite appropriateness being a fundamental criterion of creativity (Zeng, Proctor, & Salvendy, 2011).

These limitations warrant caution in using and interpreting these measures. Nonetheless, they are used extensively and likely have some utility in research with adults and older children. However, when divergent thinking tasks are used with young children, additional issues emerge, and it is questionable whether these types of tasks are appropriate (Ward, 1968). Some evidence suggests that young children are unable to relate to these types of tasks and have great difficulty in generating meaningful responses (Busse, Blum, & Gutride, 1972). Although there have been attempts to make tasks easier by including more visual stimuli and decreasing the need for verbal responses (Tegano, Moran, & Godwin, 1986; Torrance, 1981), these adaptations do not address some core concerns. For instance, Smogorzewska (2012) argues that young children generally do not understand the purpose of divergent thinking tasks, which likely leads to a lack of interest or motivation to engage in the task. This is problematic, as the importance of making creativity measures for children fun, inherently interesting, easy to understand, and easy to complete has been heavily emphasized (Amabile, 1996; Starkweather, 1964; Wallach & Kogan, 1965). As Starkweather (1971) stated, "The goal [in designing creativity measures] was always the development of a game which the child would want to play" (p. 246).

In addition, Torrance (2000) argues that creativity measures should be natural to the experiences of young children. This is problematic for divergent thinking tasks—identifying *all* the ways something can be used, perceived, or acted on does *not* reflect the natural experiences of young children. The unfamiliarity of this kind of request might make the task seem strange, regardless of the stimuli used. Also, research on children's counterfactual reasoning (which involves considering various alternatives to reality) suggests that generating alternatives is cognitively challenging for young children and might be too difficult for many to execute effectively (Beck, Robinson, Carroll, & Apperly, 2006; Guajardo & Turley-Ames, 2004). If participants have difficulty grasping the basic demands of a task, it should be considered inappropriate. It is essential that precautions be taken when determining assessments for children by taking into account skills and experiences that likely vary as a function of age and developmental level.

In summary, despite the frequent use of divergent thinking tasks when studying young children's creativity, they are likely inappropriate for this age group. These are likely strange and unfamiliar tasks for young children that do not match their naturalistic experiences, which might limit their understanding of the task demands as well as their enjoyment of the task. Divergent thinking scores are associated with age and are likely reflective of developing cognitive abilities, such as executive functioning, counterfactual reasoning, and verbal ability, rather than creative potential. In fact, divergent thinking scores are often not correlated with pretend play, an activity that is theoretically linked to creativity, as it requires children to transform reality in ways that are often novel and entertaining (Fein, 1987; Gelman & Gottfried, 2006; Runco & Pina, 2013; Russ, 2014). Lillard et al. (2013) conclude that there is not convincing support for the claim that pretend play facilitates creativity in preschool children. However, given that most of the studies used divergent thinking tasks, it is possible that poor measurement led to the null results.

This suggests that in order to understand preschool-age children's creativity, it is important to identify and develop alternative methods for assessing creativity in this age group.

Consensual Assessment Technique

Amabile's (1982) consensual assessment technique overcomes many of the aforementioned problems with divergent thinking tasks. In this approach, participants are asked to complete a product that generally does not require specialized skills (e.g., create a collage, tell a story). The completed products are then assessed for creativity by appropriate judges who provide subjective ratings of creativity on a Likert scale. These ratings are based on their own intuitions and ideas about creativity. The only instructions given to judges are to use the full rating scale and to focus on comparing the creativity of available responses within the study (as opposed to using some external standard of creativity). Amabile argues that measuring creativity in this way is valid because the method is similar to how creativity is assessed in the real world.

The consensual assessment technique avoids potentially incomplete definitions of creativity or an overemphasis on specific components by not defining creativity per se. Arguably, a subjective rating of creativity takes into account all the aspects of creativity that are meaningful for a judge. This approach would be problematic if everyone had different perspectives or definitions of creativity, but the consensual assessment technique tends to produce highly reliable scores across judges, suggesting that judges tend to agree about what is creative (Amabile, 1996). Another benefit is that this method does not suffer from some of the problems of scoring fluency (e.g., potential confounds with verbal ability) and uniqueness (e.g., including bizarre or ordinary ideas as unique). Instead of generating multiple responses, the participant decides on an approach to the problem and then develops a single solution that can then be judged for creativity.

The consensual assessment technique is ideal for developing creativity measures for young children because it flexibly allows for a large range of tasks, such as age-appropriate activities that are familiar to children and can be easily adapted. For example, drawing, storytelling, and building with blocks are activities that are familiar, fun, and interesting for most young children. These activities are also readily understandable for children, as they have likely encountered these activities numerous times before. In addition, given that these activities are part of the natural experiences of early childhood, it is unlikely that they require cognitive skills that are beyond the average preschooler's abilities.

The Development of Two Measures of Preschool-Age Children's Creativity

Considering these various issues and concerns helped to inspire and shape new age-appropriate tasks for preschool-age children that would hopefully be effective in capturing creativity and that could be used to investigate the role of creativity in children's lives and how it develops over time. Both tasks were included in a study with seventy-five 4- and 5-year-old children (38 boys, 37 girls). The children were all native English speakers with no known developmental disorders, primarily from European American, middle-income families, reflective of the local demographics where the study was conducted. Children were asked to create both stories and drawings—two different types of products that involve familiar activities for preschool children and that could be judged for creativity using Amabile's (1982) consensual assessment technique.

Narrative Creativity Task

The narrative task was adapted from the MacArthur Story Stem Battery (Emde, Wolf, & Oppenheim, 2003), which is used for assessing family relations and emotional difficulties in young children. In this task, an experimenter tells the beginning of a story with the use of dolls (that match the child's gender) and props and then asks children to finish the story. This task provided some structure while allowing for a wide range of responses. In the present study, a story stem about two dolls finding a magical key was designed to elicit a range of narratives that could be assessed for creativity. The experimenter "walked" two small dolls along a felt path on the table while narrating, "Susan and Jane are going for a walk outside when they see a key. Susan says, 'What's this on the ground?' Jane says, 'It's a key. I wonder if it's magic.'" Then the experimenter asked the child, "Can you show me and tell me what happens now?"

Almost all of the children were able to complete the task and had no difficulty with its demands. The children also appeared to enjoy the activity. Even children whose responses were coded as less creative often seemed interested in and entertained by the dolls. Note that this task did not involve generating alternatives—children provided a single completion for a story stem that was then transcribed and coded following Amabile's (1982) consensual assessment technique. Three judges rated the subjective creativity of each narrative on a scale from 1 to 5. The judges were instructed to use the full range of the rating scale and compare the narratives to those of other children within the study (as opposed to using some external standard). In addition, it was suggested that the ratings of creativity should not be based solely on verbal ability or talkativeness. Other than these considerations, judges were instructed to use their own ideas and intuitions about creativity (as opposed to having a definition of creativity provided). Children provided a wide range of completions for this task. Examples of story completions that were rated as highly creative included:

Five-year-old boy: Okay. And his brother picks up the key, shoves it in his hand and they were going to have a tug-of-war. And whoever got the key from tug-of-war, got to be magically pulled onto the key and go to Disneyland when they are just little. So, they decided to play tug-of-war. Oh! But the boy lost it. And the key was on the ground and it flew away. The key dropped on a cold place by here, right here. It was right here until it decided to go back to its family, so it flew back and went under the road. And then, his brother spotted something. "What is that lump on the road?" And then he opened it up. "Ahh! Another key brother! We are just finding keys today. We both get to go to Disneyland. Come on, let's go." And they magically flew quicker to Disneyland . . . *[child acts out narrative with dolls and props throughout]*

Five-year-old boy: The key . . . opens up their body and takes their hearts out and then locks them up. *[child demonstrates the key opening the hearts on the dolls]* . . . And then the key goes back on the ground. It falls.

Four-year-old girl: And then the key flies and then hides in carpet and Susan, she don't know. And Susan says, "Where is the key now? Oh, I think something is under the rug. Huh . . . ? Oh, there you *[key]* are. We're gonna use you and then . . . But where do you go? Do you go to a door? I don't think he wants a door" . . . *[child hums for a minute, then makes a fist with her hand and places it on the table]* "Here is a rock! Does it have a ### in it? Except it is glowing." *[child acts out dolls touching the "rock"]* "Hey! There is the key!" *[child places key on doll's head]* "There! It's flying! It's flying! It's in your hair somewhere. Where is that key now? Where where? . . . ##### key gone. Huh? Oooooh, oh there you are, key! Key is right here . . . Oh! I am trying to get you, key! Key! Come back here!" *[child acts out dolls chasing the key]* "Key! Come back here! Now, key, never go away." *[child acts out the doll "catching" the key and then using it to open a door]* Chik chik. "Oh! It's a door to her home! I am going outside." "Me too!"

In contrast, examples of story completions that were rated as less creative included:

Four-year-old boy: They pick it up and see if it's magic, but it's not. They said, "What? It can't do magic?!?" . . . And they say, "Oh, I'm going home." And then he picks it up and hided it. "Look what I brought home—the key." And then he doesn't want to show it to his mom. So they keep it behind their back. They take the sidewalk and they put in a new sidewalk. *[child acts out narrative with dolls and props throughout]*

Five-year-old girl: They can both hold on to it like that and hold on to it. They can. I don't know if they can do that *[child tries to make both dolls hold onto key]* #### not. Then they can do that. Oh! . . . Well, I don't know, they can just hold on to it and say something and that will do it. Maybe they can stand on the path. . . . It's hard. *[child struggles to make dolls stand on path with key]*

Five-year-old girl: She picks up the key and umm . . . Oh, then she has to go with the key . . . that was magic . . . back. . . . Then they came back and the key was gone. *[child walks dolls back and forth down the length of the path]*

Drawing Creativity Task

The children also completed a drawing task that was included in the study in order to have a measure of creativity that was less verbally demanding than the storytelling task. This task was based on Karmiloff-Smith's (1990) procedure for assessing children's drawing development, in which children are asked to draw real and pretend versions of the same object (e.g., a real person and a pretend person). In the present study, children were asked to draw a real person and a "pretend person, a person that couldn't exist, a person that is made up." After the children completed the drawings, they were asked to describe what they had drawn. Similar to the narrative task, three judges reviewed children's solutions to this task, including both drawings and the children's verbal descriptions of their drawings, and rated them for subjective creativity for each child's overall approach to this task on a scale from 1 to 5. In addition, judges were recommended to not make creativity ratings based solely on drawing ability, but were otherwise instructed to use their own definitions of creativity. Children provided a range of solutions for this task that could be judged for creativity. For example, several children drew a pretend person that deviated a great deal from their real person drawing, such as a simple stick figure for the real person and an "egg" character for the pretend person, while other children generated two virtually identical drawings. See Figures 11.1a–11.1d for examples of the children's drawings.

FIGURE 11.1A Real person.

FIGURE 11.1B Pretend person.

FIGURE 11.1C Real person.

FIGURE 11.1D Pretend person.

264 Candice M. Mottweiler

Pretend Play and Narrative Structure Tasks

Another goal of this study was to investigate how creativity scores derived from the narrative and drawing tasks might be related to other childhood activities. In particular, this study focused on children's elaborated role-play (i.e., pretending in which children imagine and act out the part of another individual on a regular basis in the form of imaginary companions or pretend identities taken on by children). The children and parents were interviewed about the children's role-play activities following the procedure developed by Taylor, Carlson, Maring, Gerow, and Charley (2004), in which children were asked if they had a "pretend friend" as well as if they pretended to be "another person or an animal." When children replied in the affirmative, they were asked a series of questions regarding the details of the character. Parents were additionally interviewed to clarify whether children might be confused and also provide additional details about the characters created by their children. All of these interviews were then later coded for whether children had imaginary companions (i.e., invisible friends or personified objects) and/ or pretend identities. In addition, the raters coded the creativity of each character following the consensual assessment technique on a scale from 1 to 5.

Finally, given that this study examines children's narratives for creativity, it is important to also identify and control for the effects of children's ability to structure and organize narratives. In other words, is the creativity of a narrative distinct from how well it is organized? In order to answer this question, a previously developed measure of children's ability to structure narratives was used (Reilly, Bates, & Marchman, 1998). This task involves Mayer's (1969) *Frog, Where Are You?*, a picture book that follows an easily identifiable plot about a boy who loses his pet frog and the series of events following in search of the frog. In this task, children looked at the pages in the book and were asked to describe what was happening on each page. Children's responses were later transcribed and coded for whether they included beginning, middle, and ending elements of the plot (for a total possible score of 0 to 6; Reilly et al., 1998).

Results

The results of this study showed (as in past research with the consensual assessment technique) narrative creativity and drawing creativity to both produce high levels of agreement across the three judges. In addition, narrative creativity and drawing creativity were correlated, suggesting that while they are very different tasks, both appear to have tapped a similar core ability believed to be reflective of creativity. Scores for both measures of creativity were also higher for children who described engaging in elaborated forms of role-play (e.g., having an imaginary companion) and were both further related to how creative the role-play characters were judged to be. This provides some validity for these measures, as creating an imaginary companion is often thought to be a highly creative activity.

While the ability to form well-structured stories during this task was associated with age and other developmental abilities, it was not related to either measure of creativity. This suggests that the creativity measures are not simply a function of children's ability to tell well-structured stories but are instead reflective of a distinct ability.

These results suggest that the narrative task and drawing task were generally accessible to the children, enjoyable, and successfully elicited a range of responses that were reliably coded for creativity. In addition, creativity scores on these tasks corresponded with reports of engaging in creative behaviors outside the laboratory (i.e., engaging in elaborated role-play), providing some validation for these measures.

While these new measures show promise, they are not without limitations. In this study, drawing creativity was correlated with age, while narrative creativity was correlated with verbal ability, suggesting that some developmental skills (e.g., drawing ability, verbal ability) likely influenced judges' creativity ratings. However, when age and verbal ability were statistically controlled, the creativity measures continued to be related to each other and children's elaborated role-play, suggesting that while developmental abilities are likely involved, they are not driving the results. Overall, these and similar measures hold promise for future research examining children's creativity.

Future Directions and Conclusion

Future research will benefit from exploring and expanding on narrative and drawing measures of creativity as well as surveying other activities familiar to young children that could be assessed for creativity, such as building with blocks (Holmes & Geiger, 2002), making collages (Amabile & Gitomer, 1984), and gross motor activities (Torrance, 2000). In addition, it would be beneficial to systematically examine children's perceptions of creativity tasks: Are the creativity tasks seen by children as fun and enjoyable? Do children describe the tasks as easy to understand and complete or as challenging and difficult? The answers to these questions are important for determining whether measures should continue to be used in future research. The present study aimed to address the apparent weaknesses of divergent thinking tasks and appeared to have been successful in its approach; however, systematic evaluations of children's experiences of a range of creativity measures (including the narrative and drawing tasks used in the present study as well as those used in divergent thinking tasks) would prove insightful in this regard.

In addition, longitudinal research is necessary to identify the potential trajectories of early creative behaviors and how they might lead to adult creativity. To begin addressing this issue, a follow-up assessment of preschool children (who participated in the study described previously) several years later when the children are approximately twelve years of age will be conducted. The goal of this follow-up is to examine how early creative behavior might predict later creative behavior and activities. In particular, it will investigate how creativity at Time 1 is related to a larger battery of creativity tasks when the children are older at Time 2. The follow-up battery will include tasks similar to the narrative task and drawing task described here. In addition, it will include divergent thinking tasks to explore differential patterns for divergent thinking in comparison to tasks that employ the consensual assessment technique. For example, the children will be asked to list all of the uses that they can think of for a brick. Additionally, as in Time 1, at Time 2 the study will explore how creativity in laboratory tasks corresponds with real-world creative activities, including imaginary companions and the generation of elaborate imaginary worlds. This study will hopefully shed light on how creativity develops across time in childhood.

Another area that deserves attention is the role of social content in creativity measures. Most divergent thinking tasks include content focused on objects or abstract concepts. For example, listing uses for a brick (a common divergent thinking task) does not typically bring ideas about the social world into mind. This contrasts with the creativity tasks included in the present study: Telling a story about two characters and drawing people both involve content about the social world. It is possible that the social content included in these tasks could have made them more accessible for the children and might have led to a specific pattern of results that might not replicate if the study included creativity tasks that focused on objects. Exploring these possibilities in future studies in which children complete batteries of creativity measures that vary in the amount of social content included would provide clarity on this issue. For example, a possible creativity task that might be effective in assessing nonsocial aspects of creativity could involve asking young children to create interesting structures with blocks. This differentiation will be looked at in the longitudinal follow-up of this study; the battery of creativity tasks is designed to vary in this regard to examine potential differentiation. For example, children will be asked to complete the drawing task as described previously (with social content). In addition, the children will complete a collage task in which they will be provided with colorful shapes and asked to make an "interesting, silly design" (with no cues that indicate social content).

While the ability to identify early creativity is a positive goal, it is essential to remain cautious of how the information is interpreted and utilized, particularly in educational settings. While it is important to identify gifted children and provide them with the resources and opportunities to enhance their skills, it is equally important to not leave children behind as "ungifted" (Runco, 2003). Creativity likely develops at different rates and becomes apparent within different domains. Assessing children's individual creative strengths and at different points in their development will likely help in this regard. In addition, while creativity is a useful attribute to engender, it is not the only valuable trait that leads to later success (Ward, 1974). It is necessary to research and foster creativity in concert with other skills and behaviors, such as perseverance, executive functioning, and social skills.

In conclusion, creativity is a complex construct that creates challenges when defining and measuring it, with additional challenges arising when young children are involved. This has led to the conclusion that the most common measures of creativity (i.e., divergent thinking tasks) are inappropriate for young children. Some of the issues of past measures have been addressed in the new creativity tasks developed in a recent study (Mottweiler & Taylor, 2014). However, questions remain about the most effective ways to measure creativity, and these should be explored in future research. In order to move forward with this work, it is important to develop and use measures of creativity that make sense to the children being asked to use them, not just the researchers who study creativity. Investing effort in understanding young children's creativity is valuable in that it will help with developing strategies to enhance children's creativity, which will likely prove invaluable as they prepare for adulthood in a rapidly changing world.

Author Note

This research was supported by a National Science Foundation Graduate Research Fellowship awarded to Candice M. Mottweiler.

References

Amabile, T.M. (1982). Social psychology of creativity: A consensual assessment technique. *Journal of Personality and Social Psychology, 43,* 997–1013.

Amabile, T.M. (1996). *Creativity in context: Update to The Social Psychology of Creativity.* Boulder, CO: Westview Press.

Amabile, T.M., & Gitomer, J. (1984). Children's artistic creativity: Effects of choice in task materials. *Personality and Social Psychology Bulletin, 10,* 209–215. http://dx.doi.org/10.1177/0146167284102006

Barnett, L.A. (1990). Playfulness: Definition, design, and measurement. *Play & Culture, 3,* 319–336.

Beck, S.R., Robinson, E.J., Carroll, D.J., & Apperly, I.A. (2006). Children's thinking about counterfactuals and future hypotheticals as possibilities. *Child Development, 77,* 413–426.

Busse, T.V., Blum, P., & Gutride, M. (1972). Testing conditions and the measurement of creative abilities in lower-class preschool children. *Multivariate Behavioral Research, 7,* 287–298.

Cremin, T., Chappell, K., & Craft, A. (2013). Reciprocity between narrative, questioning and imagination in the early and primary years: Examining the role of narrative in possibility thinking. *Thinking Skills and Creativity, 9,* 135–151. http://dx.doi.org/10.1016/j.tsc.2012.11.003

Csikszentmihalyi, M. (1996). *Creativity: Flow and the psychology of discovery and invention.* New York, NY: HarperCollins.

Dziedziewicz, D., Oledzka, D., & Karwowski, M. (2013). Developing 4- to 6-year-old children's figural creativity using a doodle-book program. *Thinking Skills and Creativity, 9,* 85–95. http://dx.doi.org/10.1016/j.tsc.2012.09.004

Emde, R.N., Wolf, D., & Oppenheim, D. (2003). *Revealing the inner worlds of young children: The MacArthur Story Stem Battery and parent-child narratives.* New York, NY: Oxford University Press.

Fein, G.G. (1987). Pretend play: Creativity and consciousness. In D. Görlitz & J.F. Wohlwill (Eds.), *Curiosity, imagination, and play: On the development of spontaneous cognitive motivational processes* (pp. 281–304). Hillsdale, NJ: Erlbaum.

Gelman, S.A., & Gottfried, G.M. (2006). Creativity in young children's thought. In J.C. Kaufman & J. Baer (Eds.), *Creativity and reason in cognitive development* (pp. 221–243). New York, NY: Cambridge University Press.

Goldstein, T.R., & Winner, E. (2009). Living in alternative and inner worlds: Early signs of acting talent. *Creativity Research Journal, 21,* 117–124. http://dx.doi.org/10.1080/10400410802633749

Guajardo, N.R., & Turley-Ames, K.J. (2004). Preschoolers' generation of different types of counterfactual statements and theory of mind understanding. *Cognitive Development, 19,* 53–80.

Hill, O.W., & Clark, J.L. (1998). Childhood fantasy, creativity, and an internal epistemic style. *Journal of Social Behavior & Personality, 13,* 177–183.

Hoff, E. (2005). Imaginary companions, creativity, and self-image in middle childhood. *Creativity Research Journal, 17,* 167–180. http://dx.doi.org/10.1080/10400419.2005.9651477

Holmes, R.M., & Geiger, C.J. (2002). The relationship between creativity and cognitive abilities in preschoolers. In J.L. Roopnarine (Ed.), *Conceptual, social-cognitive, and contextual issues in the fields of play: Play & culture studies* (Vol. 4, pp. 127–148). Westport, CT: Ablex.

Jalongo, M.R., & Hirsh, R.A. (2012). Reconceptualizing creative thought processes in young children: An integrative review of the research. In O.N. Saracho (Ed.), *Contemporary perspectives on research in creativity in early childhood education* (pp. 89–108). Charlotte, NC: Information Age.

Karmiloff-Smith, A. (1990). Constraints on representational change: Evidence from children's drawing. *Cognition, 34,* 57–83. http://dx.doi.org/10.1016/0010-0277(90)90031-E

Karwowski, M., Gralewski, J., Lebuda, I., & Wiśniewska, E. (2007). Creative teaching of creativity teachers: Polish perspective. *Thinking Skills and Creativity, 2,* 57–61. http://dx.doi.org/10.1016/j.tsc.2006.10.004

Kaufman, J.C., & Beghetto, R.A. (2009). Beyond big and little: The Four C model of creativity. *Review of General Psychology, 13,* 1–12. http://dx.doi.org/10.1037/a0013688

Kidd, E., Rogers, P., & Rogers, C. (2010). The personality correlates of adults who had imaginary companions in childhood. *Psychological Reports, 107,* 163–172. http://dx.doi.org/10.2466/02.04.10.PR0.107.4.163-172

Korn-Bursztyn, C. (2012). *Young children and the arts: Nurturing imagination and creativity.* Charlotte, NC: Information Age.

Li, W.L., Poon, J.C.Y., Tong, T.M.Y., & Lau, S. (2013). Psychological adjustment of creative children: Perspectives from self, peer and teacher. *Educational Psychology, 33,* 616–627. http://dx.doi.org/10.1080/01443410.2013.824069

Lillard, A.S., Lerner, M.D., Hopkins, E.J., Dore, R.A., Smith, E.D., & Palmquist, C.M. (2013). The impact of pretend play on children's development: A review of the evidence. *Psychological Bulletin, 139,* 1–34. http://dx.doi.org/10.1037/a0029321

Mayer, M. (1969). *Frog, where are you?* New York, NY: Dial Books for Young Readers.

Mottweiler, C.M., & Taylor, M. (2014). Elaborated role play and creativity in preschool age children. *Psychology of Aesthetics, Creativity, and the Arts, 8,* 277–286.

Reilly, J.S., Bates, E.A., & Marchman, V.A. (1998). Narrative discourse in children with early focal brain injury. *Brain and Language, 61,* 335–375. http://dx.doi.org/10.1006/brln.1997.1882

Robson, S., & Rowe, V. (2012). Observing young children's creative thinking: Engagement, involvement, and persistence. *International Journal of Early Years Education, 20,* 349–364. http://dx.doi.org/10.1080/09669760.2012.743098

Root-Bernstein, M., & Root-Bernstein, R. (2006). Imaginary worldplay in childhood and maturity and its impact on adult creativity. *Creativity Research Journal, 18,* 405–425. http://dx.doi.org/10.1207/s15326934crj1804_1

Runco, M.A. (1987). Interrater agreement on a socially valid measure of students' creativity. *Psychological Reports, 61,* 1009–1010. http://dx.doi.org/10.2466/pr0.1987.61.3.1009

Runco, M.A. (1996). Personal creativity: Definition and developmental issues. In M.A. Runco (Ed.), *Creativity from childhood through adulthood: The developmental issues: New directions for child development* (pp. 3–30). San Francisco, CA: Jossey-Bass.

Runco, M.A. (2003). Education for creative potential. *Scandinavian Journal of Educational Research, 47,* 318–324.

Runco, M.A., Dow, G., & Smith, W.R. (2006). Information, experience, and divergent thinking: An empirical test. *Creativity Research Journal, 18,* 269–277. http://dx.doi. org/10.1207/s15326934crj1803_4

Runco, M.A., & Pina, J. (2013). Imagination and personal creativity. In M.Taylor (Ed.), *The Oxford handbook of the development of imagination* (pp. 379–386). New York, NY: Oxford University Press.

Russ, S.W. (2014). *Pretend play in childhood: Foundation of adult creativity.* Washington, DC: American Psychological Association.

Sawyer, R.K. (2012). *Explaining creativity: The science of human innovation* (2nd ed.). New York, NY: Oxford University Press.

Sawyers, J.K., Moran, J.D., Fu, V.R., & Milgram, R.M. (1983). Familiar versus unfamiliar stimulus items in measurement of original thinking in young children. *Perceptual and Motor Skills, 57,* 51–55. http://dx.doi.org/10.2466/pms.1983.57.1.51

Schaefer, C.E. (1969). Imaginary companions and creative adolescents. *Developmental Psychology, 1,* 747–749. http://dx.doi.org/10.1037/h0028270

Silvia, P.J., Winterstein, B.P., Willse, J.T., Barona, C.M., Cram, J.T., Hess, K.I., . . . Richard, C.A. (2008). Assessing creativity with divergent thinking tasks: Exploring the reliability and validity of new subjective scoring methods. *Psychology of Aesthetics, Creativity, and the Arts, 2,* 68–85. http://dx.doi.org/10.1037/1931-3896.2.2.68

Smogorzewska, J. (2012). Storyline and Associations Pyramid as methods of creativity enhancement: Comparison of effectiveness in 5-year-old children. *Thinking Skills and Creativity, 7,* 28–37. http://dx.doi.org/10.1016/j.tsc.2011.12.003

Starkweather, E.K. (1964). Problems in the measurement of creativity in preschool children. *Journal of Educational Measurement, 1,* 109–114.

Starkweather, E.K. (1971). Creativity research instruments designed for use with preschool children. *The Journal of Creative Behavior, 5,* 245–255.

Taylor, M., Carlson, S.M., Maring, B.L., Gerow, L., & Charley, C.M. (2004). The characteristics and correlates of fantasy in school-age children: Imaginary companions, impersonation, and social understanding. *Developmental Psychology, 40,* 1173–1187.

Taylor, M., Hodges, S.D., & Kohányi, A. (2003). The illusion of independent agency: Do adult fiction writers experience their characters as having minds of their own? *Imagination, Cognition and Personality, 22,* 361–380. http://dx.doi.org/10.2190/FTG3-Q9T0-7U26-5Q5X

Tegano, D.W., Moran, J.D., & Godwin, L.J. (1986). Cross-validation of two creativity tests designed for preschool children. *Early Childhood Research Quarterly, 1,* 387–396. http:// dx.doi.org/10.1016/0885-2006(86)90015-3

Torrance, E.P. (1974). *Torrance Tests of Creative Thinking: Norms—technical manual*. Bensenville, IL: Scholastic Testing Services.

Torrance, E.P. (1981). *Thinking creatively in action and movement*. Bensenville, IL: Scholastic Testing Service.

Torrance, E.P. (2000). Preschool creativity. In B.A. Bracken (Ed.), *The Psychoeducational Assessment of Preschool Children* (pp. 349–363). Boston, MA: Allyn & Bacon.

Trawick-Smith, J., Russell, H., & Swaminathan, S. (2011). Measuring the effects of toys on the problem-solving, creative and social behaviours of preschool children. *Early Child Development and Care, 181,* 909–927. http://dx.doi.org/10.1080/03004430.2010.503892

Wallach, M.A., & Kogan, N. (1965). *Modes of thinking in young children*. New York, NY: Holt, Rinehart & Winston.

Ward, W.C. (1968). Creativity in young children. *Child Development, 39,* 737–754.

Ward, W.C. (1974). Creativity (?) in young children. *The Journal of Creative Behavior, 8,* 101–106.

Zeng, L., Proctor, R.W., & Salvendy, G. (2011). Can traditional divergent thinking tests be trusted in measuring and predicting real-world creativity? *Creativity Research Journal, 23,* 24–37. http://dx.doi.org/10.1080/10400419.2011.545713

12

A CULTURAL–HISTORICAL READING OF IMAGINATION AND CREATIVITY IN YOUNG CHILDREN'S SHARED NARRATIVE CREATIONS ACROSS CULTURAL CONTEXTS

Sue March, Liang Li, and Gloria Quiñones

> The development of a creative individual, one who strives for the future, is enabled by creative imagination embodied in the present.
>
> *(Vygotsky, 2004, p. 88)*

Imagination and creativity are seen as central to play, pretense, and story, but the full significance of children's narratives is lost when we view them as "just stories." Pretense and storytelling are intricately linked with the specific cultural contexts in which young children live and develop. Children from completely different cultural backgrounds create shared narratives together with other children and adults in their daily lives. In this chapter, we examine the process of generation of children's shared narratives through collective imagination with others. We explore this in the context of a conversation in a Mexican community, the shared narration of a child's drawing in a Chinese family, and a shared imaginary situation in a play event in an Australian family. We are interested in the role of imagination in the process of creating those shared narratives across cultural contexts.

According to Kangas, Kultima, and Ruokamo (2011), narratives can be represented as drawings, descriptions, and discussions about the environment of children's dreams and connected everyday activities (p. 71). In contrast to the intentional nature of storytelling, narratives in the lives of very young children tend to be embedded in conversations (Bredikyte, 2011). Cultural–historical researchers have considered how communication, or the use of language, depends on our imagination (Connery, John-Steiner, & Marjanovic-Shane, 2010). The importance of imagination and creativity is foregrounded in these studies. For example, Connery et al. (2010) explain how, by collaborating creatively and in a community of players, we are able to understand different life situations. Lobman (2010) encourages educators to see pedagogy as a creative and imaginative activity where students and teachers work together. She explains how we need to "create moments of ordinary creativity even under constraining conditions" (p. 205). Mottweiler (this volume) shows that it is important for researchers to carefully consider the abilities and everyday social experiences of young children when processing creativity measures. Siraj-Blatchford and Siraj-Blatchford (2011) also note that the role of creativity and imagination is increasingly seen as important in education and concur with the need for more focus on everyday creativity, or creativity "with a little c" (p. xxii). All these researchers agree that imagination and creativity are a collective initiative.

The relation between dialogue and narrative has also been foregrounded in the literature. Kellogg (2014), for example, sees narrative and dialogue as both linked and separate aspects of storytelling. Examining the narrative structure in the sociodramatic play of 5-year-old children in United Kingdom preschool environments, Sawyer (2011) analysed the connections between improvisational dialogue and narrative structure, arguing that the narratives that emerged from these forms of collaborative improvisation were "collective social products" (p. 29). They were not reducible to the sum of the individual contributions of the participating children but rather emerged in the turn-by-turn dialogue of a collaborative social process. Truman (2011) also found that group interaction and collaboration assisted the creative process in relation to music lessons, and she examines the generative aspect of creativity. In Finland, Bredikyte (2011) draws our attention to the role of dialogue and narrative in relation to young children's collective play and artistic pursuits. The literature suggests that the relation between dialogue and narrative can be understood through a cultural–historical reading of imagination development.

Our theoretical orientation leads us to investigate how young children's shared narratives are generated in three different cultural contexts using Vygotsky's concept of combinatorial creativity (2004). Here, we define narrative as the aspect of storytelling that is embedded in everyday shared conversations, or dialogues, with others. Siraj-Blatchford and Siraj-Blatchford (2011) highlight the need to elaborate the relation between the theoretical concepts of creativity, narrative, and collaboration (Kangas et al., 2011; Sawyer, 2011) in light of Vygotsky's (2004) seminal work, and they emphasise the combinatorial nature of imagination in this conception. We focus on what we believe to be the essence of this process: the relation between imagination and narrative. In each case study, we will see that imagination is the key to narrative, transforming the children's experiences and impressions from their rich cultural contexts and embedded imaginary situations to create ever more abstract and generalised narratives.

Elsewhere in the literature, imagination and play are linked to children's everyday environments. Gaskins (2014) notes that some children grow up in adult-centric and others in child-centric everyday environments; some children participate in formal learning; and, for others, learning takes place in informal settings. She

A Cultural–Historical Reading **273**

contrasts the experience of children who do not have the opportunity to participate in the work of their parents with those who are part of the adult-centric world around them and questions the impact that growing up in such different settings has on the nature of children's play. El'konin (2005) explored this in relation to the historical development of role-play, noting the relation between play and imagination. We question what impact these different cultural orientations might have on children's imagination and shared narrative creation.

In each case study, we see a very different role of the parents. In each case study, we see a different strategy from the researcher. But in each case study, the role of the researcher in unfolding the narrative can be understood through a cultural–historical reading of children's imagination development. Each researcher is attuned to the cultural values and conditions created for their focus child's development. Seeing the future possibility in the present moment, they work within the values and expectations of their respective cultural communities to progress the children's shared narratives, carefully adopting an appropriate communication style. It is this reciprocal relation between the researcher and the child, within their broader culture, that extends the narrative beyond the dialogue.

Our studies are also concerned with the collective, shared nature of children's narrative creation (the process of creating a narrative). Our focus is on how shared narratives are generated in the very different cultural contexts of the everyday lives

FIGURE 12.1A Mayra in her rural Mexican community.

FIGURE 12.1B Yi and her mother in Yi's study room in their Chinese home.

FIGURE 12.1C Oliver and Nessie in their Australian playroom.

of our focus children and with the role of the adults in this process, including the role of the researcher. In her rural Mexican village, 5-year-old Mayra[1] is allowed to roam the streets, chatting with the researcher, Gloria, with no family present. This contrasts sharply with the more controlled and directed style of 4-year-old Yi's mother in her Chinese community in Australia. These two cases enable us to see more clearly the embedded cultural values and practices in 4-year-old Oliver's Western play situation. This familiar Australian play situation in turn enables us to see the role of imagination in narrative creation and allows us to consider the role of imagination in the Mexican and Chinese heritage situations. We consider the importance of children's shared narratives in the process of their development as members of society (see Faulkner & Coates, 2011) in these different cultural contexts.

A Cultural–Historical View on Imagination, Creativity, and Shared Narratives

We foreground the role of imagination and creativity in children's narratives as they develop in relation to the social and material conditions of their everyday lives in different cultural communities (Vygotsky, 1994). Vygotsky (2004) referred to the concept of imagination and creativity as a *dialectical relation*, in which each can only be thought of in relation to the other and such that each gives meaning to the other. Vygotsky (1987) saw imagination, like thinking, as a complex psychological system, "based on the unification of several functions in unique relationships" (p. 348). He asserts the place of imagination as central to children's meaning making and creativity and as being oriented to the future.

Children make meaning of social relations and interpret everyday experience through imagination. In our case studies, we examine the complex system of imagination and narrative creation in the meaning making and creative storytelling of children in their everyday lives in three different cultural settings. According to Vygotsky (2004), imagination, or fantasy (in the psychological sense), forms the "basis of all creative activity" (p. 9). In fact, he saw it as "an important component of absolutely all aspects of cultural life, enabling artistic, scientific, and technical creation alike" (p. 9). Vygotsky (2004) used another term for creative activity, calling it *combinatorial* (p. 9), noting that children do not simply reproduce their experiences from everyday life but that they creatively rework impressions they have acquired through their experience, combine them, and use them to construct a new reality based on the child's own sense of the situation. As observed by van Oers (2013) in a preschool class, under the teacher's support, "a boy first built houses and then spurted the fire engine from the other side of the room to the burning house to extinguish the fire and rescue the people" (p. 245). This boy did not simply copy what he had experienced. He did not just push a toy fire engine around the classroom; he created a new reality by imagining himself as a firefighter using tools to rescue people. As van Oers (2013) argued, a narrative has emerged here. This boy had his own sense and awareness of the situation in which a firefighter rescues people from a burning house. He used tools such as a toy fire engine and combined what he had experienced to creatively reconstruct this situation, forming a narrative of the imagined situation. This process can be conceptualised as *combinatorial creativity*, which is important to children's narrative creations.

As a child's imagination develops and they gain more experience in the world and creatively combine this experience with the objects and ideas around them, plots start to develop and play assumes a narrative character, as in van Oers' (2013) example of the firefighter narrative. Rather than disappearing, each form of play is incorporated into the next level, a further combination of lived experience, which continues Vygotsky's full circle of creativity. Rich experiences support the child in transforming *director play* (pretending a block is a fire truck) into *image play* (pretending to be the firefighter) into *plot role-play* (pretending the house is on fire, putting out the fire, and rescuing the people; Fleer, 2013; Kravtsova, 2010; Vygotsky, 1966). We see here that imagination and pretense are at the heart of play. In these narrative-rich role-play scenarios, children "flicker" (El'koninova, 2002) between play (being the firefighter) and metaplay (planning what is going to happen next). Play and the visual arts are interconnected forms of early childhood creativity.

Children's cultural experiences shape their imagination and creativity. In drawing, children rebuild and reconstruct the meaning of their experience to show a new reality through narrative. Ahn and Filipenko (2007) have investigated how young children's narratives reflect the way they construct meaning about their lived experiences. They have argued that "narrative is a portrait drawn by children interweaving many functions and attitudes and incorporating a number of voices" (p. 287). Children's narratives present not only what children have seen or heard but also how they feel and how they make sense of their lived experience (Owoki & Goodman, 2002; Robbins, 2007). In play and storytelling, children are able to describe the characters and the relations in the world through their creativity in visual arts (Ahn & Filipenko, 2007).

Other forms of narrative development include the practice of walking around. Christensen (2003) found that through walking around, children would develop an "emplaced" narrative knowledge of their local area. For example, children would rehearse routes when put into bed at night and through regularly walking to school, they imagined games that involved not stepping on certain cracks in paving stones. All these researchers acknowledge the importance of the adult's shared awareness of narrative development in children. Play, drawing, and walking as cultural practices support children in developing their narratives and help us as educators and researchers to understand children's worlds.

Combinatorial Creativity Across Cultural Contexts in a Cultural–Historical Research Approach

In examining the case studies in this chapter, we centre our investigation on the role of combinatorial creativity and imagination in children's narrative creation as we seek to uncover the conditions that families and communities create to support the development of imagination and narratives in children's daily lives. The three case studies (Yin, 2003) have been selected from our PhD studies in different cultural communities (Li, 2012; March, 2016; Quiñones, 2013). Our PhD research has focused on understanding children's perspectives and understanding their everyday lives (see Hedegaard, Aronsson, Hojholt, & Ulvik, 2012). We use case studies of children's life experiences, as it is important for us as cultural–historical researchers to understand children's life conditions.

The following three case examples are analysed using a cultural–historical approach. First, we introduce the life conditions, cultural values, and communication styles of each cultural community. We then explain the role of imagination and the role of the adult or researcher in entering into the child's narratives through imagining. We do not aim to generalise each cultural community but rather offer the reader different cultural scenarios on how children, with the support of the adult or researcher, generate and extend their narratives and imagining together. Research shows that the role of the researcher has not been theorised (Fleer, 2014b; Quiñones, 2014), and we believe that there is scope to further theorise the researcher's role in relation to children's development of imagination.

Acknowledging the role of the researcher is the first of three key principles of cultural–historical research. In this chapter, we examine the importance of the researcher in imagining *with* the child to generate and develop a shared narrative. All three studies were conducted using a cultural–historical visual video methodology (Hedegaard & Fleer, 2008; Li, 2014), and the data discussed in this chapter were generated using video observations. Use of video observation techniques is the second key principle in this approach, which allows the researcher to retrace and recreate the path of development of a given process observed in the data (in these cases, the process of narrative creation). The third key principle is rigorous data analysis through three iterative stages, from initial interpretation, through applying the theoretical concepts in a situated practice analysis, to thematic interpretation (see Fleer, 2014a) to generate a systematic and synthetic analysis of each case individually and the three cases together. The essential first step in this process was the careful selection of one segment of data that represents an episode of narrative creation on the part of the children in relation to their social and material environment (Vygotsky, 1994). Using the three iterative stages, we analysed the three case studies together in relation to the dialectical concept of imagination and creativity.

In the first case study, oral storytelling is explored as the third author, Gloria, accompanies a 5-year-old Mexican girl, Mayra, on a walk through her neighbourhood. In the second, a 4-year-old Chinese girl living in Australia, Yi, is narrating a story based on a picture she has painted, supported by her mother and prompted by the second author, Liang. In the third case study, two Australian children, Oliver and Nessie, aged 4 and 5 years, are playing with Lego (colourful plastic building blocks) and striving to create a narrative role-play together, observed by the first author, Sue, who collaborates with Oliver who, in turn, understands his role as showing Sue "how he plays Lego." We examine the family values and practices that contribute to the different conditions for developing imagination and creating narratives in each case. Together, these case studies show that children's narratives are both collectively imagined and culturally constructed.

Analysis of Case Examples

Case Example 1: Mayra's Narrative

Mexican Cultural Values and Communication Styles

In order to understand children's perspectives, we need to consider that "children's perspectives may also involve an exploration and analysis of children's life conditions, and children's social participation under different social conditions" (Hedegaard et al., 2012, p. ix; Göncü & Vadeboncoeur, this volume). In the following case example, we show how Mayra has different life conditions that allow her to have good geographical knowledge of her community (see Figure 12.1a) and to engage in narrative, as this is an everyday practice her mother and uncle engage in. Mayra uses verbal and nonverbal language such as pointing to express herself in the process of shared narrative creation. She poetically uses words to rhyme, almost like singing, which is also another important cultural value in her family, as she explains that her uncle sings every day and that everyone, including the researcher, has heard him.

Mayra lives in a village in the north of Mexico. The village has 20 houses, a park, an unfinished church, and two small stores. She is 5 years old and lives with her brother, mother, and stepfather in a small room next to a house. Mayra enjoys walking in the community, and this is the only mode of transportation in the community. She has two uncles; one is visually impaired, and the other works in the fields. Her mother and her uncle with visual impairment spend a considerable amount of time together talking about people in the community and about news heard on the television or radio. The family values cooking for themselves rather than asking for food from others. In this community, a common practice is to ask for support from others; however, being self-sufficient and being able to cook for oneself without asking others for food is important and shows pride in being able to provide food for one's family without the help of others. The value of being self-sufficient is important in this family. These values are expressed in Mayra's narratives with the researcher. We will see that parental values have been shaped through participation in this adult-centric, informal-learning-oriented social condition (Gaskins, 2014).

A Shared Narrative Generated Through the Imagination of Community Life

The following narrative shows how the researcher and child shared a narrative around the community. The previous day, the researcher had promised to visit Mayra the following day. But Mayra had walked from her house to the researcher's home to come and see her first. The conversation starts while walking back to Mayra's home.

R: I heard someone sang . . . was it your uncle?

M: Mmhh *[affirming]*

R: He likes to sing?

M: Yes . . . *[my uncle]* he sometimes sing, when it's at night he likes to sing . . . yes . . . *[my uncle]* he sometimes sing, when it's at night he likes to sing . . .

R: Yes.

M: Later today he is going to sing, I don't know why *[pause]* look here! There is a small path that goes until there *[points out]* . . .

R: This way is easier?

M: Yes *[shows]* the little road comes that way to my godmother's house *[points]* and there is my house . . .

R: Ah that's another way that takes you to your house . . .

M: And I come and buy Coca-Colas here and I go this other way . . .

R: And who is there? *[as they come closer to her house]*

M: My uncle is with my mum talking, sometimes he comes here and talks to my mum and she gives him food to eat . . .

In this dialogue, it can be seen how the researcher is able to progress Mayra's narrative creation as she recounts her knowledge about the community, her everyday world. Mayra creates a story about where places are located. We have discussed how creating a story is a combinatorial or creative act. Mayra poetically shares her knowledge with the researcher through this narrative creation. The adult, in this case the researcher, is interested in her and sensitive and responsive towards Mayra. Mayra is able to imagine and communicate to the researcher the paths she takes to different places in the community. In this combinatorial act, Vygotsky (2004) explains how individuals do more than reproduce impressions of what was experienced; individuals have their own idea, images, and picture of what it looks like. Mayra, through the process of narrative creation, shares

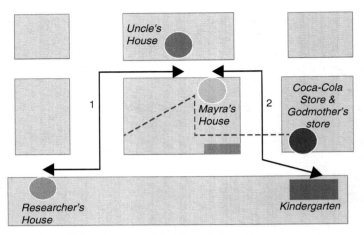

FIGURE 12.2 Map of Mayra's geographical knowledge of her community.

enthusiastically all the paths and surprises of making one's way around the community. In turn, the researcher has to imagine the different places in the community, and the researcher is able to create new images, which Vygotsky (2004) explains is a second type of combinatorial act. After this conversation took place, the researcher made an image of her interpretation of the path that Mayra had imagined (see Figure 12.2). Vygotsky (1987), drawing on the observation of Russian poet A.S. Pushkin, notes that "imagination is as necessary in geometry as it is in poetry" (p. 153).

In this case study, we see that, through shared narrative creation, the researcher is able to draw on Mayra's imagination and emplaced knowledge of her neighbourhood (Christensen, 2003) to help develop Mayra's imagination and construct a spatial (abstract geographical) representation of Mayra's daily life in her community. Through the narrative, we can see Mayra's ability to imagine through her storytelling. The researcher has an everyday understanding and has learned about Mayra's everyday world though listening to her narrative. When analysing the dialogue, she is able to be more aware of Mayra's imagination in the process of explaining detailed geographical accounts but also to imagine the ways and routes that are important when living in this rural community.

Role of the Researcher in Progressing the Shared Narrative

Through her cultural upbringing in Mexican communities, the researcher is able to "tune in" to Mayra's stories and help her develop her imagination and storytelling through narrative creation. The role of the adult, such as the researcher, is important in showing genuine interest in the narratives created by children. Narratives emerge in everyday conversations. This is a value shared in this Mexican

FIGURE 12.3 Yi's drawing.

community, where everyday conversations created by the participants are transformed into narratives. Mayra's narrative is a creative act based on elements of her everyday cultural world, such as living in a small rural community. In Mayra's narratives, she relates aspects of her life such as the people who are important to her. Therefore, her everyday experiences allow Mayra to imagine through the process of sharing this narrative with the researcher beyond a dialogue.

Case Example 2: A Shared Narrative Generated in the Activity of "Draw and Tell a Story"

In this case example, we see how 4-year-old Yi's narrative takes the form of a story, as she is narrating the drawing she has made, retelling the story based on the known plot of a Chinese idiom[2] (traditional Chinese short story with a simple moral). The conversation that follows shows Yi's imagination in her drawing, her narrative creation through retelling the story, and how cultural values impact daily communication styles. When the researcher, Liang, arrived at Yi's family house for an interview, Yi's mother invited her to go to Yi's study room (Figure 12.1b), where Yi's drawing was on the desk (Figure 12.3). Yi's mother told the researcher that Yi attends drawing classes. Then, Yi's mother explained to the researcher that Yi had completed her drawing and had told her first story. Her mother wanted Yi to retell the story to the researcher. The dialogue between Yi and her mother was transcribed and translated from Chinese into English and is explained in the following section.

M: When she started to draw, she only drew a sky, a worm, and a chicken on the paper. She did not draw others. Then, I said that your drawing is quite boring. Then she asked what it is "boring", I told her that it means not many things on the picture. Then she said that the chicken is eating the worm.

282 Sue March, Liang Li, and Gloria Quiñones

Y: I first drew the sun, rainbow, then chicken and worm.
M: Yes, you continued drawing a sky and grass on the floor.
Y: Then, I also drew a girl.
M: Yes. I told you it is too boring. So you continued drawing a cloud and a bird. Then, she drew a tree and a nest. Then I asked her to tell a story.

In this dialogue, Yi's mother explains the drawing process and how she encouraged her to finish the drawing with a meaningful context. Meanwhile, Yi's mother started to open the dialogue in order to stimulate Yi to tell her own story and how she finished the drawing. With her mother's support, Yi started to talk and tried to correct her mother. As her mother mentioned, Yi enjoys correcting others. A narrative has been generated through their dialogue and the explanation of Yi's drawing. Noting the literature, Mackenzie and Veresov (2013) point out that "talk and drawing often overlap as *mutually transformative processes* [emphasis added]" (p. 22).

Yi began to narrate her drawing and explain what was happening in the drawing, developing her narrative thinking. An imaginary situation had also been created in her drawing. In the following dialogue between Yi and the researcher, Liang indicates Yi's narrative creation.

R: You drew a daytime. Who is the girl?
Y: It is me.
R: Is the chicken eating the worm or catching the worm?
Y: Yes. The bird as well.
R: What is the bird doing?
Y: The bird mother is also catching the worm. They are fighting to catch the worm.
R: Then, what are you doing?
Y: I was looking at them at the beginning, then I saw some thing on the tree, eggs, the bird eggs. *[she points to the nest on the tree]* some thing I want to take them home.
R: Oh, you want to take them home.
Y: Yes. Then I can boil and eat them.
R: You want to eat them!
Y: some thing, the bird mother came back and found his babies are gone.
R: Oh. The bird mother found her eggs are gone, she must be very upset.
Y: Yes. I gave the eggs to Mum and Dad to eat.
R: Did you name this drawing?
Y: I forgot to name it.
R: Oh. It is OK. You see that bird mother must be very upset, she must look for her babies.
Y: Yes. She came to our house and found the eggs in the house.
R: Oh. She flyed to the house.

Y: Yeah. She saw the three eggs. She thought it is bird's . . .

R: Yes. These are her babies. Did you return the eggs to the bird?

Y: No. They were boiled . . .

It can be seen that drawing supported Yi's imagination and narrative creation. Through Liang's questions, Yi was able to engage in a further conversation and tell the story of the drawing that included a beginning, a development, and a conclusion. This episode raises questions about how she can retell the story using her drawing and leads us to think about the cultural values and living conditions Yi has been experiencing in her everyday life.

Chinese Cultural Values and Communication Style

The Chinese context and bedtime story routine provide a literacy environment for Yi to develop her own story through imagination. Yi's family values storytelling in developing Yi's language and literacy. And this, in turn, becomes a generative opportunity for developing Yi's narrative thinking. Yi's social environment and lived experience have dramatically influenced her abstract narrative creation.

Using Drawing to Imagine Family Life to Create a Shared Narrative

Vygotsky (1987) notes that creative activity "is accessible to the child at a young age. If we consider the products of this creativity in drawing or story telling, it quickly becomes apparent that this imagination has a directed nature" (p. 346). We note that the story Yi created includes characters, movement, affective dimensions and emotions, and background. Imagination supported her to tell the story and improve her narrative creation. It is of particular importance to our consideration of imagination in a psychological sense that Yi imagined herself as assuming the role of herself in the story, along with her other family members. As Vygotsky (1998) argued, Yi's drawing by combining separate objects in a creative way allowed Yi to "crystalise" a new reality, which in turn helped her create a narrative as a further combinatorial act. For instance, her mother had previously mentioned that Yi has an allergy to eggs. In her imaginary situation, Yi boiled the eggs for her parents rather than for herself. This further confirms that the creation of the drawing comes from reality, from children's everyday life.

Yi is the narrator for her own drawing and imagination. As argued by Kangas et al. (2011): "Through narratives, children structured and organized their experience and the products of their imaginations into entities through which their created environments acquired meaning" (p. 73). Through the narrative, Yi has restructured her own everyday experience and her products of imagination; i.e., drawing. This is consistent with Mottweiler's (this volume) arguments on the need to consider the abilities and everyday social experiences of young children when

284 Sue March, Liang Li, and Gloria Quiñones

processing creativity measures. Children's everyday life determines the transformation process from reality to creativity.

Role of Adults in Progressing Shared Narratives

Rogoff (2003) notes that Chinese parenting includes caring, devotion, and support, as well as strict discipline and control. Her mother's communication style shows that she instructed Yi on her drawing and narrative thinking. The tone she used was like a teacher talking to a child, similar to "teacher-pupil talk" (Burns & Radford, 2008, p. 196). In actuality, Yi's mother had been a primary schoolteacher for 11 years, which may have influenced her communication style at home.

Compared to her mother, the communication style between Liang and Yi shows evidence of collaboration in coconstructing a narrative. Liang used the question-led talking style to encourage Yi's narrative creation in telling the story. Here, Liang has shared imaginative thinking with Yi, which enabled her to ask particular questions. It has been argued by Kangas et al. (2011) that the role of the researcher is important in "creating appropriate conditions for children's collaborative creativity by being encouraging, inventive, and creative" (p. 71). Liang used questions and discussions to actively respond to and extend Yi's imagination and enhance her narrative thinking.

Case Example 3: A Shared Narrative Generated Through Play With Lego

Anglo-Australian Cultural Values and Communication Styles

In this case study, we see that cousins Oliver (4 years old) and Nessie (5 years old) draw on objects and roles from their surrounding cultural environment in creating their narratives. Oliver's playroom contains an array of toys, including artefacts depicting both real-life and transmedia fictional elements, such as Lego and other construction blocks; police vehicles; boats; child-sized furniture replicating that in a typical house from their community, such as a couch and a school desk; various dolls and soft toys reflecting their culture; a small mat on which they sit to play; and a box of dress-ups. These are typical in Western communities where the parents' work (in this case, that of a designer) is far removed from the everyday skills that children can participate in directly, and children learn their culture through imaginative play with toys.

Parental values are shaped through participation in child-centric, formal-learning-oriented social conditions (Gaskins, 2014). The parents' values are reflected in their provision of a dedicated play space for the children, in setting up play partners, and in his mother's habit of placing objects around the house to "trigger" Oliver's imagination. The family has just moved into a quiet street in a small seaside town,

A Cultural–Historical Reading **285**

and Oliver is allowed to ride his bike outside on the dirt road, where his mother can see him while she is gardening. In contrast to Mayra, he is not allowed to go beyond his mother's line of sight. His cousin Nessie lives nearby. There is another child of Oliver's age living in the same street, and the families are getting to know each other. Thus, childhood is valued in this community and is important to the organisation of family life.

Imagination and Shared Narrative Creation in Play

Much of Oliver and Nessie's 40-minute play episode takes the form of a nonverbal narrative, which Bredikyte (2011) considers an important, but underrecognized, form of narrative. The children unhurriedly construct Lego vehicles and props and gradually negotiate a shared (spoken) narrative about police officers and the consequences of bad behaviour. The following dialogue takes place near the beginning of the play episode (see Figure 12.1c) in the children's playroom.

N: Could you help me, Oliver? *[sifts through the pieces of Lego in the box]* Actually, could I build something? *[picks up a road works sign and looks at Oliver]* Shall I build the road? Where's going to be the road? *[pointing]* Over there?

O: *[looks in direction Nessie is pointing]* Um . . . yes.

N: *[placing the piece]* So, there's roadworks in the road.

O: *[holding up the black Lego construction]* And this is the roadwork car? Here?

N: *[picking up a larger toy truck]* And maybe you could truck, maybe you could truck . . . maybe the trucks could help, yeh?

O: *[looking between Nessie's larger truck and his beginning Lego construction]* Um, I only need Lego ones.

N: Do you have any. . . *[picking up a toy (non-Lego) car]* . . . and there's a car. A car to help them. *[picks up another non-Lego car]*

O: *[looks and considers, but shakes his head]* Mmm, not a car. Not a car.

N: OK. *[puts them down]*

O: Um, ah. You just build it first then I work out what to, to put on it? OK?

N: Yes. *[sits down beside Oliver and starts building]* Um, could those go on the road?

O: Um, no, no, no. 'Cos that's too little. I don't need little things.

In this dialogue, we can see how the children's interactions support their joint striving to create a narrative together—a collectively imagined recombining of their shared and individual impressions from their daily life and culture. Nessie makes suggestions—"So there's roadworks in the road"—in a singsongy voice, indicating pretense (Lillard, 2007) and prompts the story plot forwards, while Oliver uses his experience of building Lego models with his father to make the props to support the narrative. Importantly, long sections of the narrative take place without speaking, and we can only wonder what the children are thinking as they select the "right" pieces and put together newly imagined Lego models.

Peer relations throughout the play episode reveal the complexity of the children's imitation of roles from their family and community as well as the broader societal roles that children draw on from their surrounding cultural environment in creating their narratives. Oliver combines many positions simultaneously, both imaginary and real world. The children seem to "flicker" (El'koninova, 2002) effortlessly between play and metaplay, between dialogue, as they try out storylines, and more abstract narratives as they plan and build the props for the play, sometimes seeming to occupy both positions at once. Oliver, simultaneously imitating the role of his father from their joint experience of constructing Lego kits together and complying with his assigned position of "He's in charge. . . . He's the captain" evaluates the size and fit of the pieces: "Um, no, no, no. 'Cos that's too little. I don't need little things." These examples illustrate Vygotsky's (1987) point that children's realistic and imaginative thinking processes "develop as a unity" in early childhood (p. 348).

Tacit Role of Researcher in Progressing Shared Narrative

The role of the researcher is acknowledged as, on this second visit to the family home, Oliver is keen to "show Sue how we play Lego." On the previous visit, he and his mother had shown the researcher the dedicated playroom, and Oliver's mother had described how she values the children's imagination. Sue had explained the purpose of her research, in language Oliver could understand, as "wanting to learn about how he and other children play."

As the children played on the mezzanine-level playroom on this visit, Sue was sensitive to the fact that Oliver's mother was downstairs listening and that she valued the children being encouraged to play together. Sue's role was instrumental in generating the joint narrative play between the two children, as she looked for opportunities to encourage the two children to play together rather than alongside each other. Her orientation alerted her to the possibility of an imaginative role-play developing, and when Oliver asked Sue to help him find some pieces, she suggested that Nessie help him instead. A different kind of narrative or play episode might have ensued had Sue collaborated directly with Oliver rather than encouraging Nessie's involvement. In this way, Sue creatively incorporated the values of Oliver's family into the play situation.

We have seen through the three case studies that dialogues are an important element in knowing about children's everyday worlds. They allow narrative development, and children are able to create and imagine as they interact with other children and adults. The next section discusses important dimensions to be considered in the combinatorial creativity in children's narratives.

Discussion

Children's Shared Narratives Are Culturally Constructed

We ask in relation to these examples: How can we read culture in narratives? We discuss how children's narratives are culturally constructed. We see that Mayra's narrative shows her affective relation to everyday life in her community through her imagination. Yi, in her drawing, also narrated a story arising from her culture and her affective relation to her shared reading time with her mother. The combinatorial creation in her drawing supported her to develop this narrative, which includes a bird, a worm, her parents, and herself as characters together with a plot based on a Chinese idiom. Combinatorial creativity is also noted in the way the Lego kits and minifigures embody the multimedia narratives that derive from a complex web of commercial interests and have been interpreted by the manufacturers for children. These narratives are taken up by the children and creatively reworked into Oliver and Nessie's narrative. Thus, imagination in the form of combinatorial creativity is essential to understanding each case.

In addition, the children bring their own characteristics and skills developed through their participation in their cultural community to generate their narratives. Mayra has developed spatial awareness of her neighbourhood and a chatty, lyrical ease in conversing with the researcher through the cultural practice of walking and talking. In her creative drawing, Yi combines what she experiences in her cultural life and uses the skills acquired in her participation in community drawing classes to show her own awareness of everyday life and to construct a new story. Oliver brings his skill with Lego, developed through his family practice of building Lego kits with his father, in which they have developed their own shared language ("one-ies," "two-ies," etc., denoting the size of each block). These skills and orientations are incorporated into the narratives of the children and combined with the other objective and subjective elements of their stories.

Therefore, children's everyday cultural life has oriented their combinatorial creativity and has driven their narrative generation. Our analysis of three different cultural cases has shown that children's rich cultural experiences help them develop a more complex combinatorial creativity and construct intricate and complicated narratives.

The Combinatorial Creativity of Lived Experience in Children's Shared Narratives

As we have discussed, children's combinatorial creativity (Vygotsky 2004) means that in terms of what they have experienced, children combine objects, memories, and impressions to make new meaning for themselves and to develop a new reality for themselves and others. We have seen how, in Mayra's case, she experiences and then imagines important places in her community and her affection for the adults in her life as she shares this with the researcher. Yi creates a new reality in her drawing, which includes birds, a worm, eggs, her parents, and herself. The new reality that is crystalised in her drawing and further reworked in her story about the drawing not only demonstrates the emotional bonds in her everyday life but also incorporates her impressions from this experience. Similarly, Oliver and Nessie, in their shared Lego play, collectively imagine, negotiate, and create a new story around police officers, using toys to represent community roles that they cannot experience directly, as outlined in El'konin's (2005) theory of role-play. They use their imagination to change the meaning of the objects, and this mutually transformative process helps develop their imagination. As Vygotsky (2004) outlined, a child's play is not simply an echo of what he or she has experienced but is also a creative reworking of what he or she has seen and heard in reality.

Although Mayra's narrative is not a story by Engel's (1995/1999) definition of being communicated intentionally (rather, it is embedded in the conversation), it has required an imaginative act to combine the various impressions and elements from her social and material reality and create a narrative of her life in her community. This creative act would not be evident in a laboratory study with narrow parameters of what constitutes children's imagination but is revealed through these qualitative studies in naturalistic settings. In a complex sentence produced by Oliver in the full transcript of his play, "Let's go, matey, 'coz I've finished," he combined different kinds of thinking, flickering between dialogue as he assumed the role and his impression of the voice of a police officer, formed from his surroundings, and abstract thinking in planning and constructing Lego models. He and Nessie also further reworked the narrative device of the road trip into an imagined journey of police officers with their prisoners (Figure 12.4).

Collective imagination (see Fleer, 2010, 2013) is an important aspect of the development of these children's narratives. In Yi's narrative, themes are not necessarily incorporated literally but are creatively reworked: Yi understood that she has an allergy to eggs in reality, so she boiled the eggs for her parents in the imaginary situation that she created. In Mayra's narrative, only those elements of her neighbourhood that come into view or are important to her narrative account of her daily life are mentioned. When Oliver picks up a red parrot figure from the floor, even though it is an element from his local environment that the two children had seen that morning, the potential story element is not taken up by his play partner, Nessie, whereas the idea of "My car's on fire," which is generated when he picks up a similar object representing a flame, is more congruent with the shared imaginary situation that the two children are creating together and is incorporated into the narrative. Thus, the logic of the narrative also dictates the elements to be recombined into the shared narrative. We have seen that, in the three cases, children's shared narratives have been developed through their collective imagining with others. Children's cultural lived experience has been clearly embedded through their combinatorial creativity into their narrative constructions.

FIGURE 12.4 Oliver and Nessie create a shared narrative together.

The Role of Family and Adults in Children's Combinatorial Creativity and Narrative Development

We ask what conditions are created by the families and communities to support the development of combinatorial creativity and narrative creation. We have seen that, in the case of Mayra's family and community, they value oral storytelling outside the home as part of their everyday life and entertainment, and the value of being self-sufficient is expressed through the narratives. These are all influential in Mayra's narrative accounts of her life in the community. The case of Yi's narrative shows that her family values storytelling in children's development and narrative creation. One of the important routines in Yi's family is that of the bedtime story. Yi's mother expressly chooses Chinese idiomatic stories for shared reading, and this genre was reflected in her creative drawing and story. Also, Yi attends weekend drawing classes. Her development of drawing skills provides Yi with the possibility to express her rich narrative in her drawing. Oliver's family values children's imaginative play and creates the conditions for this to "emerge" by providing the space, time, materials, and social environment (e.g., peer play partners) to foster this. However, the adults do not participate directly in the children's imaginative play in this example. The dedicated play space, coupled with the provision of Lego and other toys, supports the children's development of creativity. The opportunities for one-on-one and small-group play with his sister and cousin ensure a gentle, noncompetitive environment to nurture Oliver's imagination. Therefore, like Yi's family, Oliver's family values have influenced his opportunities for narrative creation and creative thinking.

We can see the importance of providing children with rich cultural experiences, as this affords rich accounts in their narratives. These narrative accounts and combinatorial creativity can be seen through play, drawing, and walking, which are everyday practices that children engage in with peers and adults. Everyday practices were also important in helping the researchers to make sense of the children's worlds.

In each case, the researcher's cultural attunement is significant. As Mayra's poetical lyricism unfolds on the walk around her neighbourhood, Gloria's supportive "uh, huh" or "hmm, I see" is enough to encourage Mayra's storytelling, whereas in Yi's case, a more direct question—"Is it a bird?"—is required to draw out Yi's imagination. Sue's communication with Oliver is tacit and nonverbal. Oliver looks to Sue as he joins two Lego pieces together in an unspoken "Look, this is how we make a story out of Lego," and Sue reciprocates with her facial expression and by focusing the video camera on the piece he is showing her. Liang and Gloria both demonstrate the creativity of the researcher who shares in the imaginary situation with the children, seeing the future possibility in the present moment. They creatively combine elements from each child's real and imagined worlds to help generate and support the narrative creation. Oliver and Nessie are conscious of Sue's position as a researcher and that they are being observed by video. The position the children adopt in relation to the researcher is one of demonstrating how they play with Lego as participants in a study. The researcher's orientation alerts her to the possibility of an imaginative narrative role-play developing, which she facilitates in response to opportunities provided by the children and the developing storyline. The adults, through their questioning and positioning, assist in eliciting narratives and encouraging the children to include new dimensions of imaginative thinking. The children's narrative creation has been valued by the adults in their lives.

The central role of imagination and the dialectical relation between the children's activities and their imagination development has been elucidated in each context. Together, these case studies have shown that children's narratives are both collectively imagined and culturally constructed, that the role of combinatorial creativity is central to narrative creation, and that children's narratives relate to their everyday life. The main point of analysing these three case studies together in relation to the dialectical concept of imagination and creativity has been to show that different cultural contexts have necessitated different culturally attuned strategies on the part of the adults in order to support children's development of imagination and shared narratives. We believe that this is a fruitful area for further research.

Acknowledgements

We would like to gratefully acknowledge the valued supervision of Professor Marilyn Fleer in each of our PhD studies and thank her for feedback on early drafts of this chapter. We would like to thank the editors and reviewers of this volume for their valuable feedback and support and thank the children and families who participated in our studies. Thanks also to Professor Pia Christensen for her advice and feedback on early versions. We also acknowledge the support of scholarships from the Australian Postgraduate Award (APA) and the Monash Graduate Research Scholarship (MGRS).

Notes

1 Pseudonyms are used throughout.
2 "When the snipe and the clam grapple, the fisherman profits" is a Chinese idiom: It's a fine day. The sun is shining brightly. A clam is sleeping on the bank of a small river. A bird sees the clam, and she gives it a good peck. The bird tries to take out her beak, but the clam doesn't open his shell. They fight for a long time. The bird still can't take out her beak. They're both tired. A young man is coming their way. The bird tries to fly away, but she can't fly with the heavy clam. Finally, the man gets both of them and carries them home for dinner.

References

Ahn, J., & Filipenko, M. (2007). Narrative, imaginary play, art, and self: Intersecting worlds. *Early Childhood Education Journal, 34*(4), 278–289.

Bredikyte, M. (2011). *The zones of proximal development in children's play* (Unpublished doctoral dissertation). University of Oulu, Kajaani, Finland.

Burns, A., & Radford, J. (2008). Parent–child interaction in Nigerian families: Conversation analysis, context and culture. *Child Language Teaching and Therapy, 24*(2), 193–209.

Christensen, P. (2003). Place, space and knowledge: Children in the village and the city. In P. Christensen & M. O'Brien (Eds.), *Children in the city: Home, neighbourhood and community* (pp. 69–84). London, UK: Routledge Falmer.

Connery, M.C., John-Steiner, V.P., & Marjanovic-Shane, A. (Eds.). (2010). *Vygotsky and creativity: A cultural-historical approach to play, meaning making, and the arts*. New York, NY: Lang.

El'konin, D.B. (2005). On the historical origin of role play. *Journal of Russian and East European Psychology, 43*(1), 49–89.

El'koninova, L.I. (2002). The object orientation of children's play in the context of understanding imaginary space-time in play and in stories. *Journal of Russian and East European Psychology, 39*(2), 30–51.

Engel, S. (1999). *The stories children tell: Making sense of the narratives of childhood*. New York, NY: W.H. Freeman. (Original work published 1995)

Faulkner, D., & Coates, E. (2011). *Exploring children's creative narratives*. London, UK: Routledge.

Fleer, M. (2010). *Early learning and development: Cultural-historical concepts in play*. Melbourne, VIC, Australia: Cambridge University Press.

Fleer, M. (2013). *Theorising play in the early years.* Port Melbourne, VIC, Australia: Cambridge University Press.

Fleer, M. (2014a). Beyond developmental geology: A cultural-historical theorization of digital visual technologies for studying young children's development. In M. Fleer & A. Ridgway (Eds.), *Visual methodologies and digital tools for researching with young children: Transforming visuality: International perspectives on early childhood education and development* (Vol. 10, pp. 15–34). Dordrecht, Netherlands: Springer.

Fleer, M. (2014b). A digital turn: Post-developmental methodologies for researching with young children. In M. Fleer & A. Ridgway (Eds.), *Visual methodologies and digital tools for researching with young children: Transforming visuality: International perspectives on early childhood education and development* (Vol. 10, pp. 3–14). Dordrecht, Netherlands: Springer.

Gaskins, S. (2014). Children's play as cultural activity. In L. Brooker, M. Blaise, & S. Edwards (Eds.), *SAGE handbook of play and learning in early childhood* (pp. 31–42). Los Angeles, CA: SAGE.

Hedegaard, M., Aronsson, K., Hojholt, C., & Ulvik, O.S. (2012). Introduction. In M. Hedegaard, K. Aronsson, C. Hojholt, and O.S. Ulvik (Eds.), *Children, childhood, and everyday life: Children's perspectives* (pp. vii–xii). Charlotte, NC: Information Age.

Hedegaard, M., & Fleer, M. (2008). *Studying children: A cultural–historical approach.* New York, NY: Open University Press.

Kangas, M., Kultima, A., & Ruokamo, H. (2011). Children's creative collaboration: A view of narrativity. In D. Faulkner & E. Coates (Eds.), *Exploring children's creative narratives* (pp. 63–85). London, UK: Routledge.

Kellogg, D. (2014). *The great globe and all who it inherit: Narrative and dialogue in story-telling with Halliday, Vygotsky and Shakespeare.* Rotterdam, Netherlands: Sense.

Kravtsova, E.E. (2010, July). *Play in non-classical psychology of L. S. Vygotsky.* Paper presented at the 3rd International Vygotsky Summer School, Lesnaya Pol'ya, Moscow Region, Russia.

Li, L. (2012). *Family involvement in preschoolers' bilingual heritage language development: A cultural-historical study of Chinese-Australian families' everyday practices* (Unpublished doctoral dissertation). Monash University, Melbourne, VIC, Australia.

Li, L. (2014) A visual dialectical methodology: Using a cultural-historical analysis to unearth the family strategies in children's bilingual heritage language development. In M. Fleer & A. Ridgway (Eds.), *Transforming visuality: Researching childhood* (pp. 35–53). Dordrecht, Netherlands: Springer.

Lillard, A. (2007). Guided participation: How mothers structure and children understand pretend play. In A. Göncü & S. Gaskins (Eds.), *Play and development: Evolutionary, sociocultural, and functional perspectives* (pp. 131–153). Mahwah, NJ: Erlbaum.

Lobman, C. (2010). Creating developmental moments. In M.C. Connery, V.P. John-Steiner, & A. Marjanovic-Shane (Eds.), *Vygotsky and creativity: A cultural-historical approach to play, meaning making, and the arts* (pp. 199–214). New York, NY: Lang.

Mackenzie, N., & Veresov, N. (2013). How drawing can support writing acquisition: Text construction in early writing from a Vygotskian perspective. *Australasian Journal of Early Childhood, 38*(4), 22–29.

March, S. (2016). *A study of fairy tales as a source of child development in early childhood education* (Unpublished doctoral dissertation). Monash University, Melbourne, VIC, Australia. Manuscript in preparation.

Owoki, G., & Goodman, Y.M. (2002). *Kidwatching: Documenting children's literacy development.* Portsmouth, NH: Heinemann.

Quiñones, G. (2013). *Vivencia perezhivanie in the everyday life of children* (Unpublished doctoral dissertation). Monash University, Melbourne, VIC, Australia.

Quiñones, G. (2014). A visual and tactile path: Affective positioning of researcher using a cultural-historical visual methodology. In M. Fleer & A. Ridgway (Eds.), *Visual methodologies and digital tools for researching with young children: Transforming visuality* (pp. 111–128). Dordrecht, Netherlands: Springer.

Robbins, J. (2007, February). *Young children thinking and talking: Using sociocultural theory for multi-layered analysis*. Paper presented at the Learning and Socio-Cultural Theory: Exploring Modern Vygotskian Perspectives International Workshop, University of Wollongong, Wollongong, NSW, Australia.

Rogoff, B. (2003). *The cultural nature of human development*. Oxford, UK: Oxford University Press.

Sawyer, R.K. (2011). Improvisation and narrative. In D. Faulkner & E. Coates (Eds.), *Exploring children's creative narratives* (pp. 11–38). London, UK: Routledge.

Siraj-Blatchford, I., & Siraj-Blatchford, J. (2011). Creativity, communication, collaboration and curriculum: A Vygotskian perspective. In D. Faulkner & E. Coates (Eds.), *Exploring children's creative narratives* (pp. xxi–xxv). London, UK: Routledge.

Truman, S.M. (2011). A generative framework for creativity: Encouraging creative collaboration in children's music composition. In D. Faulkner & E. Coates (Ed.), *Exploring children's creative narratives* (pp. 200–224). London, UK: Routledge.

van Oers, B. (2013). An activity theory view on the development of playing. In I. Schousboe & D. Winther-Lindqvist (Eds.), *Children's play and development: Cultural-historical perspectives* (pp. 231–250). Dordrecht, Netherlands: Springer.

Vygotsky, L.S. (1966). Play and its role in the mental development of the child. *Voprosy Psikhologii, 12*(6), 62–76.

Vygotsky, L.S. (1987). Thinking and speech (N. Minick, Trans.). In R.W. Rieber & A.S. Carton (Eds.), *The collected works of L.S. Vygotsky: Problems with general psychology* (Vol. 1, pp. v–285). New York, NY: Plenum Press.

Vygotsky, L.S. (1994). The problem of the environment. In R. van der Veer & J. Valsiner, (Eds.), *The Vygotsky reader* (pp. 338–354). Cambridge, MA: Blackwell.

Vygotsky, L.S. (1998). *Child psychology* (R.W. Rieber, Trans., Vol. 5). New York, NY: Kluwer Academic and Plenum.

Vygotsky, L.S. (2004). Imagination and creativity in childhood. *Journal of Russian and East European Psychology, 42*(1), 7–97.

Yin, R.K. (2003). *Case study research: Design and methods* (3rd ed., Vol. 5). London, UK: SAGE.

13

RETURNING TO PLAY

The Critical Location of Play in Children's Sociocultural Lives

Artin Göncü and Jennifer A. Vadeboncoeur

Introduction

After a period of inactivity, interest in play is on the rise again. Thirty years after the publication of the first review paper on play in 1983 in the *Handbook of Child Psychology*, the same source is now publishing the second review paper after having disregarded play for three decades (i.e., Lillard, 2015). Currently, a proliferation of associations and journals organize scholarly communities that address play— including the International Play Association, the National Institute for Play, *The International Journal of Play*, and *The American Journal of Play*—and play has increasingly become a worthwhile topic for scholars from across disciplines (e.g., Brown, 1998; Corsaro, 2011; Goldman, 1998; Sutton-Smith, 1979). There is a growing emphasis on the importance of understanding play in the toy industry, as evidenced in publications such as those of the Lego Foundation (cf. Gauntlett & Thomsen, 2013). Also, increasing access to technology and video gaming has created an awareness of the diversity of play environments for both child and adult users (e.g., Barab, Gresalfi, & Ingram-Goble, 2010; Gee, 2007). Further, and with significant relevance to the focus of this book, there are scholars in developmental psychology and early childhood education addressing the developmental course of this activity and its place at home, in the classroom, and across contexts (e.g., Brooker, Blaise, & Edwards, 2014; Clark, 2003; other chapters in this volume). A subset of these scholars are advancing research that locates play in the social and cultural contexts of children's lives (e.g., Fleer, 2013; Göncü, 1999; Haight & Miller, 1993).

The return to play, however compelling from the perspectives of both research and practice, has been focused mostly on the possible contributions of play to human development and on instituting play as an educational and developmental tool, rather than on the examination of play itself. A quick look at the recent play literature provides support for this observation. For example, some play scholars have argued that play equals learning (cf. Singer, Golinkoff, & Hirsh-Pasek, 2006), and others have stated that play is necessary for healthy and happy living (cf. Brown, 1998). Consistent with these efforts and in support of them, international organizations such as the United Nations Children's Fund (UNICEF) and the International Play Association have aimed to ensure that all children have access to play opportunities in order to benefit from it universally. The current excitement around play thus appears to relate to its instrumental use—for example, to use play for learning, for healthy living, or for the development of creativity. Our sense is that there is still much more to learn and understand about play before it can be assumed, in the language of some, to cause or produce a particular range of beneficial outcomes for all children.

As scholars who have devoted their careers to the study of play and child development, and as those who have witnessed the contributions of play to children's development in different personal and professional contexts (cf. Göncü, 2013; Vadeboncoeur, in press), we certainly support these efforts. However, we also feel that the intense focus on the benefits of play at the expense of a more thorough examination of play itself merely maintains an incomplete portrayal of this enigmatic activity. In addition, we recognize that much of the work on the contributions of play to learning and development, however insightful and convincing, is based on both anecdotal evidence (e.g., Brown, 1998) and systematic research. While insights from personal experience often motivate research, it is crucial for any field to establish itself on a foundation of systematic inquiry. Unfortunately, even some of the work that populates our journals includes conceptual confusion, differing theoretical interpretations, and minimal methodological clarity (Lillard et al., 2013). These issues place the arguments on the importance of play as well as the benefits of play in a vulnerable position.

In our view, the research on play has reached a point in its own development to warrant closer and more critical study. Although research examining universal, developmental, and variable aspects of children's pretend play exists (e.g., Haight, Wang, Fung, Williams, & Mintz, 1999), to date, with notable exceptions (e.g., Gaskins, 1999; Lancy, 2008), much of the research on play tends to assume it to be an unconstrained and universal activity that exists outside of cultural understandings and contextual limitations on children and childhood. This often results in the advancement of overgeneralized claims about how play contributes to children's learning and development. Basically, without knowing whether or how children from different cultures and communities participate in this activity, scholars are at risk of finding in their research only what they recognize as play. Historically, this has contributed to identifying children from low-income and non-Western communities as deficient in comparison with their middle-income and Western peers and articulating recommendations for incorporating play as an intervention to address what children and/or their material conditions lack. In doing so, researchers have frequently discounted local considerations about play and child-hood that were not available to them and, as a result, potentially misrecognized different manifestations of play in unique sociocultural milieus. Current research on childhood extends the effort to take these concerns seriously (e.g., Corsaro, 2011; Wells, 2009); however, much of the literature still assumes that play is a universal activity of individual children that occurs as separate from and/or is uninfluenced by their sociocultural lives (e.g., Lillard et al., 2013).

This chapter builds on previous calls for culturally contextualizing research on play so that a comprehensive understanding of this activity becomes possible, thus enabling more informed judgments about its role in education, development, and everyday life. The chapter locates play as an economically structured, contextually driven, and culturally value-laden activity. As such, the affordances for play and its manifestations present cultural variations. In the following paragraphs, drawing from Göncü's conceptualization of play as a cultural activity (e.g., Göncü, Jain, & Tuermer, 2007; Göncü, Tuermer, Jain, & Johnson, 1999), we argue that children's competing activities of work, chores, and schooling must be considered in under-standing the degree to which and the forms through which children in different communities engage in play. Then, we describe pretend play as a culturally expres-sive activity, arguing that how play manifests itself varies as a function of cultural traditions and roles specific for children in relation to adults. Finally, in the last section, we offer a research and policy agenda that attends to the role of narrative in pretend play and the significance of sustained engagement in research on play. This provides an initial framework for future work on pretend play, its correlates, and its benefits.

Situating Children's Play in Their Lives: The Economic and Value Context of Play

Our interest in describing children's activities that compete with their play derives from descriptions of children in what some scholars call the majority world (e.g., Kağitçibaşi, 1996). Caregivers, psychologists, and educators of the Western world (e.g., North America, Europe, and Australia) generally focus on children's school-ing, their play, and their performance on experimental tasks as indices of their learning and development. Notwithstanding the conflicts about the relative con-tributions of these activities to children's learning and development, this focus is not seen as inappropriate since activities that define childhood, at least in the early and elementary school years, are limited to those that promote children's learn-ing. Now, we aim to illustrate that in contrast to the Western communities, in the majority world (i.e., the low-income, non-Western communities) what is deemed appropriate for children's learning and participation is highly varied and often regulated by cultural norms and expectations that differ. In our view, an under-standing of the variations of activities that are available for children in different communities is necessary because they may have relevance to the availability of play and manifestations of play. Moreover, an appreciation of the variation in definitions of children and childhood throughout the world may enable us to see and understand aspects of children and childhood in our own communities that we may otherwise overlook. In what follows, we attend to children in the majority world first and then take a closer look at children in North America.

One type of activity that has a significant bearing on the degree to which play is available to children involves actual income-producing activity both by children and their caregivers. Problematic in and of itself and little understood as it may be, children's labor exists in many different parts of the world. The Western world has been informed of children's labor either in the context of abuses in sweatshops through international organizations, such as UNICEF, or as part of work that highlights the contributions of labor activities to children's cognitive development (for a review, see Rogoff, 2003). However, there is less research on what work means in given contexts; how it is understood by children, caregivers, and employers; what type of work is deemed acceptable for children of different ages, if any; and how work competes with children's other activities, such as play and schooling (as an exception, see Larson & Verma, 1999).

In the research that is available to date, children participate in the workforce in many different parts of the world, and their economic contributions may take many different forms. Some examples involve engagement in trade as vendors. For example, scholars reported that children of early and elementary school age sell candy and woven goods in Brazil (e.g., Nunes, 1992; Saxe, 1988) and a range of goods in India (Sitabkhan, 2008) and Indonesia (Dewayani, 2013) with the purpose of making an economic contribution to the well-being of their families. Other examples involve the employment of children as novices under the tutelage of experts with the purpose of developing skills to be put into use to provide income. For example, Göncü, Ozer, and Ahioglu (2009) described how young children, boys and girls alike, work alongside experts both to acquire skills needed in small businesses, such as tailoring clothes and cutting hair, and to learn the ethical practices needed for a respectable and successful business. Further, the third kind of economic activity in which children participate relates to their work with their families. Usually, this takes place in communities with a subsistence economy, and children work either in agriculture or animal husbandry or at home (Gaskins, 1999; Göncü et al., 2007; Rogoff, 2003).

Although an indirect economic contribution, a second major category of work in which children participate is household chores. Evidence exists that children both in the majority and the Western world have responsibilities regarding taking care of household chores. For example, children in low-income European American, African American, and Turkish peasant communities participate in household chores doing a variety of tasks, such as doing the dishes and cleaning up after themselves (Göncü et al., 2007). Others in different communities in Central

America participate in cooking, making tortillas, and taking care of their younger siblings, among other things (Gaskins, 1999; Rogoff, 2003). Household chores are required of children by parents across income levels, although what differs, perhaps, is the extent to which specific chores are a necessity for the functioning of the family. For example, if a child attends to cooking, cleaning, and child minding, these activities allow parents to focus their energies on other spheres of work that may directly receive a wage. Given the important contribution that children make through their household work as well as the extent to which this shapes their other daily activities, this topic deserves more study (see Goodnow, 1988; Shweder et al., 2006).

Just as children's direct and indirect economic activities may relate to their involvement in play, caregivers' work also relates to the kinds of provisions that adults make for their children's play. There is now a fairly substantive body of evidence showing that a consideration of adults' work reveals significant knowledge that explains variations in children's engagement in play. For example, unlike some Western caregivers who make provisions for play by creating places in homes and purchasing toys for their children to play with, many non-Western caregivers may not be able to make provisions for children's play to the same extent given affordability and availability of space in the home and toys for purchase. Some low-income families do not have the income to buy toys, as was visibly evident in a low-income community in Turkey (Göncü et al., 2007). In addition, research conducted in many communities, such as those in Mexico (Gaskins, 1999), Guatemala, and India (Rogoff, Mistry, Göncü, & Mosier, 1993) reported that in communities that rely on a subsistence economy, adult workloads are heavy and therefore, do not always have the time or energy to play with children after long stretches of work. Also, it is not unreasonable to assume that some parents may see their role differently—for example, primarily in terms of their responsibilities for providing for their family—and may see the child's peers and/or extended family members as primary playmates (for a discussion of cultural variation in parental roles, see Shweder et al., 2006). In different cultural contexts, along with making note of differences from Western perspectives on objects, spaces, and joint play activities with parents, research also needs to be conducted into the extent to which play simply looks different—for example, play with repurposed items like boxes and natural items like sticks—how play moves across differing contexts, and how interactions between adults and children are playful, as when grandparents tell stories.

Research on children and families in other cultures is particularly informative in relation to social practices closer to home. Researchers have long noted the ways in which Western children face cultural expectations regarding their accomplishments that may have little to do with child development knowledge per se and/or provide little room for individual variations in development (cf. Elkind, 1981). In the United States, 30 years of standards-based reforms have narrowed what education and learning are taken to mean, as well as "what counts" as time well spent in schools with at least two results. First, children have less access to learning through play activities and simulations in K–12 schooling, including the reduction or removal of recess completely (Pellegrini, 2005, 2009), and play-based early childhood programs are consistently under threat from the pressure to begin direct instruction in literacy and numeracy earlier (Cooper, this volume; Jeynes, 2006; Russell, 2011). Second, some parents have begun to overschedule their children, especially children from middle-income and affluent families for whom the additional cost of enrichment activities is, perhaps, less of a burden (Rosenfeld & Wise, 2000). These children are engaged in additional educational tasks and private lessons of all sorts, in part because parents are eager to provide learning opportunities and also in part because of concerns over unstructured time (see, for discussion, Ginsburg, The Committee on Communications, & The Committee in Psychosocial Aspects of Child and Family Health, 2007). School-like activities are even beginning to populate after-school programs in an effort to equip children to succeed in the kinds of tasks privileged in school settings (Nocon & Cole, 2006). In some families, this may occur given a need of working parents for childcare to support their paid work commitments. In some middle-income and more affluent families, while children do not contribute to their families through work and parents may have fewer paid work commitments, their time may be so highly structured with after-school and enrichment activities that some children experience stress and pressure that is exacerbated by their isolation from parents and reduced time for play with siblings and peers (Lareau, 2011; Luthar & Becker, 2002). The intensification of learning as academic learning reflects a cultural paradox and ambivalence in the United States: Play is both romanticized as free time, and yet time for unstructured play is reduced in favor of additional academic lessons.

While some children are burdened by the overscheduling of enrichment activities to the point that it is experienced as if it were work, other children from low-income families and families who contribute economically through family-owned farming and ranching businesses are actually working (Fan, Huston, & Pena, 2014). In such cases, even in North America, the opportunities for pretend play as defined in Western scholarship may be limited. Historically, given claims that children contribute centrally in family businesses like farms and ranches, school programming dovetails with seasonal harvests. In some areas of the United States, the school attendance of children from family farms is waived in order to enable them to work for their families. Since 1938, federal labor laws in the United States have excluded child farmworkers from labor protections that are routinely provided to children in other industries—for example, children as young as 12 years old can work legally with a parent's permission and/or alongside a parent (Fair Labor Standards Act). Some children have responsibilities in lifestyles that are more similar to than different from their low-income and family farming counterparts in other cultures. As a result, many children across the globe, and not just outside of North America, as well as across social classes find their time limited by their commitments to family livelihoods and may therefore have less time for play. In these cases, it seems likely that pretend play is intertwined with everyday life wherever it occurs in the world; how these responsibilities and contexts shape play deserves more study.

In order for us to understand how pretend play occurs and what forms it takes, we need to conduct research across these varied cultures and contexts to learn from cultural groups and better understand the role of culture in shaping play and affordances for play. As noted by Rogoff, Morelli, and Chavajay (2010), developmental research has primarily involved children from European American and middle-class backgrounds, thus resulting in a biased perspective on what is considered the norm for children's lives. Importantly, as much as it may not occur to us, in some cultures and communities, children's play may be embedded in their work and/or household activities. In addition, children's play may more often than not include heterogeneous agemates and/or may be integrated into other community activities, rather than, as in the United States, with children more frequently segregated into homogeneous age groups (Rogoff et al., 2010). Sometimes, unable to see beyond our Western values that seem to identify play and work as distinct and dichotomous categories of activities—with play as some-thing that children do and work as something that adults do—we do not recog-nize their potential overlapping and/or continuous manner. It is not unreasonable to find that children create a world of play while they work or that what begins as play can become experienced as work.

The purpose of these descriptions is to bring to the attention of the scholarly community that children are busy people and are busier in some cultures and communities than others. Children differ in the ways they contribute to family life, the kinds of responsibilities they have, and the extent to which the family and/or community relies on the contributions of children. Along with culture, research on play needs to take into account economic structure and the responsi-bilities that children have in relation to adults that bear directly and/or indirectly on the livelihoods of families. Children's economic responsibilities are ineluctably linked with the extent to which they have time to engage in play and educational activities. Economic structures intersect with culture and matter in ways that are often overlooked in research. Indeed, play is not the "free" activity—in the sense of individual and autonomous—that it is sometimes romanticized to be. As we gain cultural understandings of children's lives, idealized notions of childhood as a time of free play need to be questioned on several grounds, along with nar-row and idealized notions of play as an expression of freedom and individual self-fulfillment. Children's opportunities to engage in pretend play are constrained by what is expected of them by their cultural communities and their families. Fur-thermore, as we discuss in the next section, even the desire to engage in play and the expression of specific play themes are constrained by children's experiences.

Play as a Culturally Expressive Activity

To achieve an understanding of children's play that does not separate children from the cultures and communities in which they grow requires consideration of the ways in which play finds its forms of expression across different cultural contexts. The Western scholarship on play has privileged pretend play as an activity with benefits for children's learning and development. This is evident across the literature. For example, in her review of play for the *Handbook*, Lillard (2015) recognized different play kinds but focused on pretend play following the scholarly emphasis placed on pretend play. In addition, a glance at research on play's developmental and educational correlates as well as research on play intervention indicates that the research focus has been almost always on pretend play. Finally, in applied settings such as preschool classrooms and play therapy rooms, adults' focus is often constrained to activities that take place on the exploration–pretend play continuum.

There are many reasons for this. For one, the play theories that have dominated scholarship on this activity in the Western world privileged pretend play as an activity with significance for survival. Psychologists like Vygotsky (1967), and Piaget (1945), as well as psychiatrists (e.g., Freud, 1961; Winnicott, 1971) and anthropologists (e.g., Bateson, 1955), considered pretend play to be an activity that is necessary for children's optimal development. The majority of these theorists saw pretend play as an activity necessary for affective and cognitive mastery over experience and encouraged its examination. For another, the world of educational practice privileged pretend play because of its symbolic nature and its assumed relevance to the development of academic skills that require functioning with decontextualized symbols, such as math and literacy. A wide variety of early childhood curricula ranging from the Vygotskian school (e.g., Bodrova & Leong, 1998; Göncü, Main, & Abel, 2009) to Piagetian constructivists (e.g., DeVries & Zan, 2012) gave priority to pretend play as an educational tool and as preparation for school environments.

In addition to privileging pretend play, the Western scholarship privileged a specific definition of pretend play. The commonly accepted definition of pretend play relied on the separation of the meaning of an object or action from the object or action itself. When children can separate meaning from object or action, they can impose a new meaning, and this developing ability has been valued specifically in relation to the ways in which it prepares children to participate in other representational activities. Pretend play often covered the activity of repurposing an object or an action—for example, using a banana as a phone—or performing a role representative of a specific cultural role—for example, playing "Mommy" or "Daddy" and pretending to feed a doll as if it were a living infant. These examples show the child separating himself or herself from the concrete context and performing with objects, actions, and roles in ways other than those dictated by the context. From a Vygotskian perspective (1967), an imaginary situation enables the child to link roles with rules that provide a context for activity, such as eating at a restaurant or performing the role of a doctor and giving a stuffed animal a shot. Frequently, objects are repurposed in ways that reflect the lived experiences of children, and the roles enacted by children reflect the roles that others have played in their lives. In this way, much of the literature emphasizes pretend play as an activity of sense making that is ineluctably linked with the sense making of a particular culture and with attention to the cognitive and affective work of children as they reenact previous experiences in an effort to prepare themselves for new ones (Göncü, Abel, & Boshans, 2010).

Examining play from this limited angle with a focus on pretend play has led to narrow definitions of this rich activity that have produced misunderstandings of other cultures as well as communities within Western culture. In early research from the 1970s, when the Western definition and descriptions of pretend play were not found in other communities, these communities and children were perceived as deficient and subjected to play interventions (McLoyd, 1982). Interestingly, when the intervention studies revealed results in the expected directions, they were interpreted as justification for their institution to help the children who needed to be taught directly how to play. The possibility that this intervention research may only have been teaching children a specific kind of pretend play and therefore a way of playing that is simply different from their own kind of play was not considered. In other words, we don't know to this day if the intervention research taught children to play in "a middle-class way" as opposed to helping them develop competence in culturally relevant skills to represent their realities in a symbolic and playful way.

To their credit, Sutton-Smith and Brice-Heath (1981) offered a conceptualization of pretend play as a cultural activity. Their goal was to counter the ethnocentric bias in the scholarship at the time, including the privileging of certain kinds of pretend play. They stated that pretend play emerges as an extension of broader cultural traditions, and in making this point they contrasted oral and literate traditions. For these authors, in communities where oral traditions dominate, life is narrated in terms of spoken words, and children's representations are primarily confined to daily experiences and the social roles embedded in them. In contrast, however, in communities where the literate traditions are dominant, children are exposed to symbols that are represented mostly in texts and therefore are often different from daily experiences. When children are exposed to print, their play becomes filled with characters that may be mythical in origin or not confined solely to quotidian experiences. The work of Sutton-Smith and Brice-Heath played a pioneering role in bringing the significance of culture to our attention in appreciating different manifestations of play. However, it, too, offered a limited view on how culture may influence pretend play because of its consideration of pretend play from a Western perspective and conceptualization of cultural influences only in terms of two broad categories.

There is now evidence that communities with dominant oral traditions are not limited to representations of daily experiences in their pretend play. Work in anthropology provides rich evidence that cultures with oral traditions rely on many different kinds of mythical meanings in celebrations involving symbolic representations. For example, Goldman (1998) illustrated that, in relation to children from communities in the Southern Highlands Province of Papua New Guinea, representations of mythical characters, such as ogres and tricksters, in Huli myths do enable children to go beyond daily experiences to learn from the imagined experiences of others.

Also, it is important to note that the play of children in the middle-class Western world is not necessarily only populated by magical and mythical characters. Quite contrary to this claim, there is ample evidence that children's pretend representations are filled with examples from their concrete daily experiences. Perhaps more than a difference between the medium of oral traditions and/or literacy, at issue here is a societal difference between nonindustrialized cultures, where formal schooling may be less likely to be an available and expected activity for children, and industrialized cultures, where schooling and schooling activities tend to dictate what counts as appropriate ways for children to spend their time. The extent to which formal schooling is an expected and valued feature of children's lives may shape the opportunities for and the expression of representational activities, including those that are highlighted in pretend play.

If we understand pretend play as a representational activity, it becomes reasonable to argue that representations can take place in many different ways and through different mediums, including, for example, the real and imagined stories shared through oral traditions and folktales as well as those written in fairy tales and texts. Following this line of reasoning, the first author examined how cultural traditions influence children's pretend play representations. In one example, Göncü et al. (2007) expanded the distinction offered by Sutton-Smith and Brice-Heath (1981) to illustrate how features of oral traditions make their way into children's pretend play. Research with low-income African American, European American, and Turkish peasant children from this perspective revealed forms of pretend play that were not previously identified in the Western literature. For example, the authors argued that teasing—often avoided as a form of insult in middle-class communities and discouraged as a form of acceptable activity—can be a play form when it is fun filled (see also Miller, 1986, for a discussion of teasing as a form of play). As such, teasing is a highly sophisticated form of representational pretend play in which the signifier and the signified occur in an overlapping manner. When a child calls his friend a *bald-headed roach* with a smile on his face, he does so with the belief that his friend will see the humor in his utterance and will respond in kind. This is, in fact, what happened in the research: Two 4-year-old children used words to communicate nonliteral meanings in constructing a playworld for themselves. A second example involved playing with music and rhythm, a play form—called *sound and rhythm play*—in which children used a sound or a tune and then made variations of it (Göncü et al., 2007). Analogous to jazz music in its form, this kind of play also involves representation in that every improvisation of the original tune is an attempt to represent it in the same manner; the child represents the role adopted for play as in being a doctor. For example, one of the children began his play by singing the logo of a radio station *WGCI, dot i* . . . and then made variations of it by singing it at various pitches and through improvisations.

Notwithstanding the ongoing discussions about what constitutes symbolic representation, we are arguing that there are different ways of representing our realities in play and that the manner of representation as well as what is represented in play is influenced by the player's cultural experiences and traditions. As such, when the focus is pretend play, we need to take into account not only our own definition of what pretend play is but also how pretend play may be understood and enacted by those whom we study. In addition, we may want to shift our focus to include other representational activities like improvisation and the use of metaphor to examine the ways in which pretense is embedded in multiple activities that may not look at all like play. Improvisation has been taken up across contexts and the life span for a number of different purposes: from representational play with children (e.g., Sawyer, 1997), to pedagogy with children between the ages of 11 and 16 described as having Asperger's syndrome (Murray, 2011), to a form of social therapy with children and youth (LaCerva & Helm, 2011), as well as a method of reducing test anxiety (Lobman, 2013). Pretense in language play can also take the form of teasing, sarcasm, and other kinds of humor that enable both identity and boundary making (Günthner, 2011; Lee, 2000).

In our effort to illustrate the cultural bias involved in the conceptualization of play with emphasis on the idealization of pretend play, we make the following additional points. First, it is important to recognize that the use of pretense is not only limited to play and, indeed, occurs throughout life in a range of different types of contexts (Haight et al., 1999; Roopnarine & Davidson, 2015). For example, Göncü and Jain (1999) found that middle-class Turkish mothers in the city of Ankara used pretense both in play and also as a means of control in their interactions with their 12- to 24-month-olds. The data were collected when the mothers and their children explored novel objects provided by the researchers, engaged in unstructured play, and during the feeding and dressing of children. The analyses revealed that while mothers and toddlers pretended together in play initiated by either party, the mothers also created pretend situations in order to accomplish their chores. For example, one mother pretended that a spoon full with food was a plane landing from the sky onto the ground that "happened to be" the child's mouth. When the child looked amused at the "plane," it landed in the child's mouth, facilitating the mother's work of feeding the child. Though the authors initially considered the use of pretense-as-control in this manner as potentially specific only to this middle-class Turkish community, informal inquiry in Chicago with middle-class U.S. mothers identified it as a common practice in Chicago as well. As another example, a colleague shared the following story about a friend who had brought his 3-year-old son for a brief visit (L. Stirling, personal communication, September 2014). The son was getting bored and kept asking if they could leave. The child said, "When are we leeeeaving. I want to go home." The father held out his bare wrist and, pretending, said, "Look, see that watch?" The child replied without hesitation, "Yes." The father continued, gesturing on his bare arm, "We'll leave when this hand gets around to here." The intentional use of pretense by adults to enable goal-directed actions with children is a generative area of study.

In addition, sometimes children incorporate themes in pretend play that potentially shun or bully playmates, and there may be cultural differences in both the themes themselves and the way themes shape action. This is important because, along with other romanticized notions of play as free from constraint and autonomous, the Western cultural perspective on pretend play assumes that play is always innocent, linking a child's innocence with the innocence of play. However, there is some evidence that this is not always the case. In work aiming to describe preschoolers' classroom activities (cf. Göncü & Weber, 2000), the first author witnessed an incident where the teacher intervened in children's pretend play in which one of the children was about to become the house pet. Upon inquiring of the teacher, the researchers learned two things. First, that sometimes withdrawn or rejected children were assigned the role of the house pet and that this did not help them to feel more integrated in the play group. Second, in her experience, even for a member of the peer group, being assigned the role of the house pet often became a mechanism for rejection. Given this experience, the teacher stepped in to redirect this particular group of children if and when they began to assign the role of house pet to other children in pretend play. Berk, Mann, and Ogan (2006) have noted the importance of monitoring pretend play and not assuming that everything that is created by children is innocent. This perspective makes sense, in particular, when situating children's lives in worlds created by adults and leads to the recognition that, just as play is not the free and unfettered activity we have sometimes taken it to be, children must have guidance with some play themes, particularly potentially harmful or violent ones.

To sum up, our existing notions of play are highly biased, with pretend play privileged as the dominant form of play. This privileging may result from the relationship between pretend play and symbolic representation that is valued as preparation for formal schooling in Western cultures. In addition, the tendency is to assume that play is a free, autonomous, and innocent activity that exists outside of children's relations with adults and responsibilities within different activities. We often do not reflect upon the various cultural manifestations and expressions of pretense in and across a range of activities as opportunities that are equal in value, but different in kind, to Western notions of pretend play. This bias reflects itself both in research on cultural differences between Western and non-Western cultures and in the examination of pretense and play across cultures. We feel that consideration of various uses of pretense will provide a more comprehensive and fair understanding of this activity as well as its place in child development, learning, and education.

Research and Policy Agenda on Play, Correlates, and Benefits

Returning to play means not just attending to play again, but also inquiring into our definitions of pretend and representation in an attempt to recognize them in potentially new and culturally responsive ways. We have located play as an economically structured, contextually driven, and culturally value-laden activity and argued that play is a culturally expressed activity. From this perspective, then, rather than narrowing scholarship to a single, universal, Western cultural view of pretend play and designing ever more narrow laboratory experiments to better understand the developmental consequences of play, our position is that we need to learn how children situated in different economic and cultural communities engage in play and the qualities of play that are taken as significant, including pretense, the imposition of meaning onto objects, actions, and roles, and attend to the ways in which representation is supported through different kinds of play and other activities. To date, play has been assumed to look one way. In contrast, we are advocating for research that asks instead how opportunities to play surface in different cultures, what is considered play and what it looks like, to what extent engaging in any form of play enables learning and development that is culturally valued, and to what extent engaging in play challenges cultural norms and expectations.

Here, we advance an approach to moving the research and policy agenda forward with four overlapping points. First, it is important to recognize that children are not "free" or autonomous; for that matter, neither are adults. Together, children and adults participate in activities that contribute to the maintenance of families, communities, and cultures. Social activities—like working, household chores, school, and play—take on value differently in relation to economic conditions, and this may or may not be proportionate to the way children actually spend their time. For example, it is possible that a child could live in a culture that values play but may not be able to engage in specific forms of play given the economic conditions of her family and/or community. As a result, we are suggesting that future research focus on children's play not as an activity owned by individual children but rather as a social activity of children that is expressed in a web of relationships involving the social, cultural, and economic structure of their communities. More specifically, even if we choose to focus on play as a psychological mechanism through which we aim to understand the development of individual children, as in play therapy, we cannot ignore the sociocultural context that influences both the opportunities for and the expressive forms through which play takes place. In research practice, our approach requires consideration of children's family and community expectations; opportunities and requirements for learning, school, and labor; understanding and openness to diverse expressions of gender; and the contexts of meaning and material conditions that shape children's lives.

Second, and related to the first, a more comprehensive understanding of children's play as a sociocultural activity requires that we analyze play more generally—thus, not simply pretend play—in relation to cultural forms of language, like scripts and narratives, that provide enabling conditions for early childhood learning and development. Positioning play as a social narrative constructed in dialogue, rather than analyzing it in terms of isolated and/or decontextualized variables, enables us to attend to and document the various ways in which play is situated to further describe the web of relationships that support it in differing communities and cultures and to examine closely the relationship between play and narrative development. Consideration of play as narrative reveals several important features of this activity that have not yet been understood. One feature that has been addressed in a limited number of theoretical works, and even fewer research studies, is that children's play narratives can be likened to a story with a plot. Drawing upon this line of work in play (e.g., Bruner, 1986; Nicolopoulou, this volume; Paley, 1990), as well as those on play as script (e.g., Bretherton, 1984; Göncü, 1993; Nelson, 2007) and play as improvisation (e.g., Sawyer, 1997), children practice the taking on of roles and ways of performing culturally valued actions through play. Over time, their competence grows and they come to see themselves and be seen by others as competent participants in families and communities. A thread that binds these sorts of activities together is composed of narrative and, more specifically, the plot summary of culturally significant stories.

Third, to this we propose, further, that we expand notions of narrative to include variations in narrative genre that reflect cultural variations and values, as well as inquire more deeply into the ways discourse weaves together pretense with everyday practices (e.g., Goldman, 1998; Göncü, 1993). Children's play is inclusive of a number of culturally situated narrative genres through which children address sociocultural experiences and concerns, as well as personal ones, with the purpose of working toward and developing shared meanings. A close look at children's play reveals that children construct narratives in a wide range of activities that vary from what we call *rough and tumble* to *imaginative* play and that these narratives may be mapped to familial and cultural preferences for fables; folktales or tall tales; and/or myths that emerge in storytelling, reading, and ritual. So far, we have undertheorized the different ways in which narrative genres may be used in different forms of play and everyday practices that include pretense and representation, and this may, in part, be one way to gain a sense of cultural variation.

Granted, we know that pretend play involves a language expressing transformations of objects, actions, and roles. We know that rough and tumble play involves manipulation of action and physical contact with the purpose of communicating its playfulness rather than serious intent and ongoing verbal and physical language to ensure that the play partner is having fun and is not hurt, which would call off the activity. Finally, we know that language play involves manipulation of features of language from syntax to pragmatics, as well as the incorporation of metaphor and particular intonation and emphases. However, and across each of these forms of play, we do not know how verbal and physical communication is woven together through discourse to construct a narrative and/or how children's discourse and actions may be shaped by the variety of cultural narratives that they have heard and/or read. In future work, considering play as reflecting a variety of narrative genres, we need to focus on how children construct stories in their play, what kind of stories children construct, the significance and meaning of these stories for children, and the potentially heterogeneous cultural sources that are woven into play. And this research on play as a representational activity must be expanded to include forms of play beyond pretend play, such as physical and language play. This may enable us to better understand how children represent and interpret their concerns and experiences in their playworlds, as well as how they communicate with one another when doing so, by drawing upon and recounting cultural narratives. With an interdisciplinary stance, we may even be able to construct bridges between how children represent their worlds in play and the means of representation in their worlds shared with adults.

Fourth, our belief is that an examination of children's play narratives in relation to social and cultural contexts will reveal significant insights about how play can be used as an educational, a therapeutic, and even an artistic device. Once we have a better sense of localized understandings, for example, of which and how narratives are drawn upon to guide play, it may be easier to make recommendations to parents and preschool teachers about how they can enter and exit play scenarios with an eye toward maximizing the benefits of allowing children the broadest range of directorial decision making while minimizing the potential for harm. Moreover, an understanding of elements of play narratives and genres may enable us to construct informed hypotheses about the correlates and consequences of play. For example, when teasing is considered a play form, it might be possible to find relations between it and other uses of language. Basically, what we are suggesting here is that if we focus on the substance of play (e.g., metaphoric use of language) rather than its general form (e.g., pretend), we may be able to understand better both what children do when they play and how such activity is related to other areas of their development.

In conclusion, while we appreciate the position of the United Nations, along with pediatricians who advocate for the necessity of play in every child's life, we are concerned that this approach may not reflect a cultural understanding of children's lives or the ways in which play may look in different cultures and may also be used in potentially harmful ways—for example, dictating play therapy to intervene in play in ways to ensure that children's play fits one specific cultural model. Universalized approaches to anything, not just play, are easy to challenge because they do not reflect differences in living conditions, cultural values, and children's contributions to their families and communities. Rather than mandating a Western notion of play, a different approach may be to address three related goals:

- Working to understand children's lives better through sustained engagement and ethnographic research. The places least likely to meet acultural, ahistorical, and universal perspectives on play are most likely to be places where children work to support their families and communities both inside and outside the majority world. Learning about their lives will require careful and culturally responsive research that inquires into the way pretense and representation emerge in everyday activity.
- Working to reduce inequity and poverty and increase access to basic human rights, such as access to clean water, safety, and housing. Academics and activists alike have noted that extreme poverty is the world's worst human rights crisis (Khan, 2009), a crisis that interferes with the attainment of living conditions that afford possibilities for all human rights to be met—among them, access to play.
- Working to understand how children's life conditions are expressed in their narratives, and the relation between these narratives and culturally privileged narrative genres, may help us reduce our Western ethnocentrism and enable us to describe more fairly the activities of children from the majority world.

This understanding, we hope, will also guide us to construct sensitive local theories about children's play and the relationships between forms of play and learning and development, schooling and work, and family and community participation, rather than passing judgment on children and cultural groups who do not engage in play the way "we do."

References

Barab, S.A., Gresalfi, M., & Ingram-Goble, A. (2010). Transformational play: Using games to position person, content, and context. *Educational Researcher, 39*(7), 525–536.

Bateson, G.A. (1955). A theory of play and fantasy. *Psychiatric Research Reports, 2,* 39–51.

Berk, L.E., Mann, T.D., & Ogan, A.T. (2006). Make-believe play: Wellspring for development of self-regulation. In D.G. Singer, R.M. Golinkoff, & K. Hirsh-Pasek (Eds.), *Play = learning: How play motivates and enhances children's cognitive and social-emotional growth* (pp. 74–100). Oxford, UK: Oxford University Press.

Bodrova, E., & Leong, D.J. (1998). Development of dramatic play in young children and its effects on self-regulation: The Vygotskian approach. *Journal of Early Childhood Teacher Education, 19*(2), 115–124.

Bretherton, I. (1984). *Symbolic play: The development of social understanding*. New York, NY: Academic Press.

Brooker, L., Blaise, M., & Edwards, S. (2014). *SAGE handbook of play and learning in early childhood*. Thousand Oaks, CA: SAGE.

Brown, S. (1998). Play as an organizing principle: Clinical evidence and personal observations. In M. Bekoff & J.A. Byers (Eds.), *Animal play: Evolutionary, comparative, and ecological perspectives* (pp. 243–260). Cambridge, UK: Cambridge University Press.

Bruner, J. (1986). *Actual minds, possible worlds*. Cambridge, MA: Harvard University Press.

Clark, C.D. (2003). *In sickness and in play: Children coping with chronic illness*. New Brunswick, NJ: Rutgers University Press.

Corsaro, W.A. (2011). *The sociology of childhood* (3rd ed.). Thousand Oaks, CA: SAGE.

DeVries, R., & Zan, B. (2012). *Moral classrooms, moral children: Creating a constructivist atmosphere in early education*. New York, NY: Teachers College Press.

Dewayani, S. (2013). What do you want to be when you grow up? Self-construction in Indonesian street children's writing. *Research in the Teaching of English, 47*(4), 365–390.

Elkind, D. (1981). *The hurried child: Growing up too fast too soon*. Reading, MA: Addison-Wesley.

Fan, M., Huston, M., & Pena, A.A. (2014). Determinants of child labor in the modern United States: Evidence from agricultural workers and their children and concerns for ongoing public policy. *Economics Bulletin, 36*(1), 125–145.

Fleer, M. (2013). *Play in the early years*. New York, NY: Cambridge University Press.

Freud, S. (1961). *Beyond the pleasure principle*. New York, NY: Norton.

Gaskins, S. (1999). Children's daily lives in a Mayan village: A case study of culturally constructed roles and activities. In A. Göncü (Ed.), *Children's engagement in the world: Sociocultural perspectives* (pp. 25–60). New York, NY: Cambridge University Press.

Gauntlett, D., & Thomsen, B.S. (2013). *Cultures of creativity: Nurturing creative mindsets across cultures*. Billund, Denmark: The Lego Foundation.

Gee, J.P. (2007). *What video games have to teach us about learning and literacy*. New York, NY: Palgrave Macmillan.

Ginsburg, K.R., The Committee on Communications, & The Committee in Psychosocial Aspects of Child and Family Health. (2007). The importance of play in promoting healthy child development and maintaining strong parent-child bonds. *Pediatrics, 119*(1), 182–191.

Goldman, L. (1998). *Child's play: Myth, mimesis, and make-believe*. New York, NY: Berg.

Göncü, A. (1993). Development of intersubjectivity in social pretend play. *Human Development, 36,* 185–198.

Göncü, A. (1999). Children's and researchers' engagement in the world. In A. Göncü (Ed.), *Children's engagement in the world: Sociocultural perspectives* (pp. 3–24). Cambridge, UK: Cambridge University Press.

Göncü, A. (2013). Discovering self in play. In R. Lake & C. Connery (Eds.), *Constructing a community of thought: Letters on the scholarship, teaching and mentoring of Vera John-Steiner* (pp. 50–54). New York, NY: Lang.

Göncü, A., Abel, B., & Boshans, M. (2010). The role of attachment and play in young children's learning and development. In K. Littleton, C. Wood, & J. Small Staarman (Eds.), *International handbook of psychology in education* (pp. 35–72). London, UK: Emerald Group.

Göncü, A., & Jain, J. (1999, April). *The construction and meaning of pretense in mother-child interaction*. Paper presented at the meeting of Society for Research in Child Development, Albuquerque, NM.

Göncü, A., Jain, J., & Tuermer, U. (2007). Children's play as cultural interpretation. In A. Göncü & S. Gaskins (Eds.), *Play and development: Evolutionary, sociocultural, and functional perspectives* (pp. 155–178). Mahwah, NJ: Erlbaum.

Göncü, A., Main, C., & Abel, B. (2009). Fairness in participation in preschool. In D. Berthelsen, J. Brownlee, & E. Johansson (Eds.), *Participatory learning in the early years* (pp. 185–202). New York, NY: Routledge.

Göncü, A., Ozer, S., & Ahioglu, N. (2009). Childhoods in Turkey: Social class and gender differences in schooling, labor, and play. In M. Fleer, M. Hedegaard, & J. Tudge (Eds.), *The world yearbook of education 2009: Childhood studies and the impact of globalization: Policies and practices at global and local levels* (pp. 68–85). New York, NY: Routledge.

Göncü, A., Tuermer, U., Jain, J., & Johnson, D. (1999). Children's play as cultural activity. In A. Göncü (Ed.), *Children's engagement in the world: Sociocultural perspectives* (pp. 148–170). New York, NY: Cambridge University Press.

Göncü, A., & Weber, E. (2000). Preschoolers' classroom activities and interactions with peers and teachers. *Early Education and Development, 11,* 93–107.

Goodnow, J.J. (1988). Children's household work: Its nature and functions. *Psychological Bulletin, 103,* 5–26.

Günthner, S. (2011). The dynamics of communicative practices in transmigrational contexts: "Insulting remarks" and "stylized category animations" in everyday interactions among male youth in Germany. *Text and Talk, 31*(4), 447–473.

Haight, W.L., & Miller, P.J. (1993). *Pretending at home: Early development in a sociocultural context.* Albany: State University of New York Press.

Haight, W.L., Wang, X., Fung, H.H., Williams, K., & Mintz, J. (1999). Universal, developmental, and variable aspects of young children's play: A cross-cultural comparison of pretending at home. *Child Development, 70*(6), 1477–1488.

Jeynes, W. (2006). Standardized tests and Froebel's original kindergarten model. *Teachers College Record, 108*(10), 1937–1959.

Kağitçibaşi, C. (1996). *Family and human development across cultures: A view from the other side.* Mahwah, NJ: Erlbaum.

Khan, I. (2009). *The unheard truth: Poverty and human rights.* New York, NY: Norton.

LaCerva, C., & Helm, C. (2011). Social therapy with children with special needs and their families. In C. Lobman & B.E. O'Neill (Eds.), *Play and performance: Play and culture studies* (Vol. 11, pp. 180–197). Lanham, MD: University Press of America.

Lancy, D. (2008). *The anthropology of childhood: Cherubs, chattel, changelings.* Cambridge, UK: Cambridge University Press.

Lareau, A. (2011). *Unequal childhoods: Class, race, and family life* (2nd ed.). Berkeley: University of California Press.

Larson, R.W., & Verma, S. (1999). How children and adolescents spend time across the world: Work, play, and developmental opportunities. *Psychological Bulletin, 125*(6), 701–736.

Lee, C.D. (2000). Signifying in the zone of proximal development. In C.D. Lee & P. Smagorinsky (Eds.), *Vygotskian perspectives on literacy research: Constructing meaning through collaborative inquiry* (pp. 191–225). Cambridge, UK: Cambridge University Press.

Lillard, A.S. (2015). The development of play. In R. Lerner (Ed.), *Handbook of child psychology and developmental science,* Vol. 2 (pp. 1–44). New York, NY: John Wiley and Sons.

Lillard, A.S., Lerner, M.D., Hopkins, E.J., Dore, R.A., Smith, E.D., & Palmquist, C.M. (2013). The impact of pretend play on children's development: A review of the evidence. *Psychological Bulletin, 139*(1), 1–34. http://dx.doi.org/10.1037/a0029321

312 Artin Göncü and Jennifer A. Vadeboncoeur

Lobman, C. (2013). "I feel nervous . . . very nervous": Addressing test anxiety in inner city schools through play and performance. *Urban Education, 49,* 329–359.

Luthar, S.S., & Becker, B.E. (2002). Privileged but pressured? A study of affluent youth. *Child Development, 73,* 1593–1610.

McLoyd, V. (1982). Social class differences in sociodramatic play: A critical review. *Developmental Review, 2,* 1–30.

Miller, P. (1986). Teasing as language socialization and verbal play in a white working-class community. In B. Schieffelin & E. Ochs (Eds.), *Language socialization across cultures* (pp. 199–212). Cambridge, UK: Cambridge University Press.

Murray, P. (2011). Playing with Asperger's syndrome: "We're not supposed to be able to do this, are we?" In C. Lobman & B.E. O'Neill (Eds.), *Play and performance: Play and culture studies* (Vol. 11, pp. 155–179). Lanham, MD: University Press of America.

Nelson, K. (2007). *Young minds in social worlds: Experience, meaning, and memory.* Cambridge, MA: Harvard University Press.

Nocon, H., & Cole, M. (2006). School's invasion of "after-school": Colonization, rationalization, or expansion of access? In Z. Bekerman, N.C. Burbules, & D. Silberman-Keller (Eds.), *Learning in places: The informal education reader* (pp. 99–121). New York, NY: Lang.

Nunes, T. (1992). Ethnomathematics and everyday cognition. In D.A. Grouws (Ed.), *Handbook of research on mathematics teaching and learning* (pp. 557–573). New York, NY: Macmillan.

Paley, V.G. (1990). *The boy who would be a helicopter: The uses of storytelling in the classroom.* Cambridge, MA: Harvard University Press.

Pellegrini, A.D. (2005). *Recess: Its role in education and development.* Mahwah, NJ: Erlbaum.

Pellegrini, A.D. (2009). *The role of play in human development.* New York, NY: Oxford University Press.

Piaget, J. (1945). *Play, dreams and imitation in childhood.* New York, NY: Norton.

Rogoff, B. (2003). *The cultural nature of human development.* New York, NY: Oxford University Press.

Rogoff, B., Mistry, J., Göncü, A., & Mosier, C. (1993). Guided participation in cultural activity by toddlers and caregivers. *Monographs of the Society for Research in Child Development, 58,* 1–179.

Rogoff, B., Morelli, G.A., & Chavajay, P. (2010). Children's integration in communities and segregation from people of differing ages. *Perspectives on Psychological Science, 5*(4), 431–440.

Roopnarine, J.L., & Davidson, K.L. (2015). Parent-child play across cultures: Advancing play research. *American Journal of Play, 7*(2), 228–252.

Rosenfeld, A.A., & Wise, N. (2000). *The over-scheduled child: Avoiding the hyper-parenting trap.* New York, NY: St. Martin's Press.

Russell, J.L. (2011). From child's garden to academic press: The role of shifting institutional logics in redefining kindergarten education. *American Educational Research Journal, 48*(2), 236–267.

Sawyer, R.K. (1997). *Pretend play as improvisation: Conversation in the preschool classroom.* Mahwah, NJ: Erlbaum.

Saxe, G.B. (1988). The mathematics of child street vendors. *Child Development, 59,* 1415–1425.

Shweder, R.A., Goodnow, J., Hatano, G., Levine, R., Markus, H., & Miller, P. (2006). The cultural psychology of development: One mind, many mentalities. In W. Damon (Ed.), *Handbook of child psychology* (6th ed., pp. 865–938). Hoboken, NJ: Wiley.

Singer, D.G., Golinkoff, R.M., & Hirsh-Pasek, K. (Eds.). (2006). *Play = learning: How play motivates and enhances children's cognitive and social-emotional growth*. New York, NY: Oxford University Press.

Sitabkhan, Y. (2008, April). *Child vendors on the trains in Mumbai, India: A comparative case study*. Poster session presented at the 2008 Research Pre-Session of the National Council of Teachers of Mathematics (NCTM), Salt Lake City, UT.

Sutton-Smith, B. (1979). *Play and learning*. New York, NY: Garden Press.

Sutton-Smith, B., & Brice-Heath, S. (1981). Paradigms of pretense. *Quarterly Newsletter of the Laboratory of Comparative Human Cognition, 3*(3), 41–45.

Vadeboncoeur, J.A. (in press). *Vygotsky for educators: Unifying theory and practice*. New York, NY: Lang.

Vygotsky, L.S. (1967). Play and its role in the mental development of the child. *Soviet Psychology, 5*(3), 6–18.

Wells, K. (2009). *Childhood in global perspective*. Malden, MA: Polity Press.

Winnicott, D.W. (1971). *Playing and reality*. New York, NY: Basic Books.

CONTRIBUTORS

Hadassah Aillenberg, PhD, is engaged in musical education in the Early Childhood Program in the Kaye Academic College of Education, Beer-Sheva, Israel, and is a former head of the Music Department. She is a member of the teaching staff at the Integration Institute, Bar-Ilan University, Israel. She researches children's discourse analysis.

Justine Cassell, PhD, is associate vice-provost of technology strategy and impact at Carnegie Mellon University and director-emerita of the Human Computer Interaction Institute. Cassell's current research examines how the sociocultural underpinnings of learning can improve technology-enhanced learning tools.

Mahwish Chaudry holds a master's in clinical psychology from La Trobe University. She works as a psychologist in a school assisting children diagnosed with intellectual disabilities as well as in private practice.

Zehava Cohen, MA, is a lecturer and pedagogical mentor in the Kaye Academic College of Education, Beer-Sheva, Israel. She is a former head of the Early Childhood Department in the college, and her main research interests are sociodramatic play in early childhood and peer discourse analysis in children.

Patsy (Patricia M.) Cooper, PhD, is an associate professor of early childhood education at Queens College at the City University of New York. She is the author of *The Classrooms All Young Children Need: Lessons in Teaching from Vivian Paley*, as well as articles and chapters related to the fair and meaningful teaching of young children.

316   Contributors

Cristina Costescu, PhD, is a research assistant in the Department of Clinical Psychology and Psychotherapy at Babeş-Bolyai University. Her major interest is in designing and testing the effectiveness of different types of interventions based on technology for children with autism spectrum disorder (ASD).

Daniel David, PhD, is a university professor of psychology at Babeş-Bolyai University; director of the International Institute of Advanced Studies in Psychotherapy and Applied Mental Health; research director of the Albert Ellis Institute, New York; and associate professor at Mount Sinai School of Medicine, New York.

Cheryl Dissanayake, PhD, is the founding director of the Olga Tennison Autism Research Centre—Australia's first research center dedicated to ASDs established in 2008. She has been an autism researcher since 1984 and has established and led an active research program since joining the School of Psychological Science at La Trobe University in 1996.

Susan Douglas, PhD, is a research associate at the University of Melbourne. She is a developmental linguist with a particular interest in the language acquisition of children with ASD. Her research is focused on syntactic and semantic acquisition, narrative development, and the discourse of pretend play.

Tamar Eylon, MA, is a lecturer and pedagogical mentor in the Early Childhood Program at the Kaye Academic College of Education, Beer-Sheva, Israel. She is a former coordinator of a program fostering linguistic and mathematic literacy for deprived children and currently researches the discourse analysis of young children within pretend play.

Artin Göncü, PhD, is professor emeritus in the College of Education at the University of Illinois. He is a developmental psychologist and early childhood educator whose current research projects examine the role of community and school influences on children's play, teacher education and professional development, and pretend play in mother–child interaction.

Teresa Lewin, PhD, is head of the training program in the Kaye Academic College of Education, Beer-Sheva, Israel. She is a pedagogical counselor and lecturer who teaches developmental literacy. Her research areas are language and pedagogical innovation.

Liang Li, PhD, is a lecturer in the Faculty of Education at Monash University, Australia. Her research interests focus on play and pedagogy, child development, and visual methodology.

Contributors **317**

Neil Maclean, PhD, is an anthropologist at the University of Sydney. His recent work addresses the relationship between intimacy and ethnographic method and the implication of disability and personhood. He is currently working on life histories of adults in Asperger support groups.

Sue March is a research assistant and PhD candidate in the Faculty of Education at Monash University. Her research interests include fairy tales, multiage groups, child development, and early childhood science and technology using cultural–historical theory.

Candice M. Mottweiler is a doctoral student in the psychology department at the University of Oregon. Her research is focused on the development of imagination and creativity.

Ageliki Nicolopoulou, PhD, is professor of psychology at Lehigh University, Bethlehem, PA. She is a sociocultural developmental psychologist whose research interests include the role of play and narrative in children's development, socialization, and education.

Gloria Quiñones, PhD, is a lecturer in the Faculty of Education at Monash University, Australia. Her research interests focus on infants and toddlers, play, pedagogy, emotions, and visual methodologies. Gloria is the co-author of the book *Early Childhood Pedagogical Play: A Cultural–Historical Interpretation Using Visual Methodology*.

Ramona Simut is a PhD candidate in the Clinical and Life Span Psychology Department of Vrije Universiteit Brussel. Her research is focused on the impact of a social robot on a social story intervention for children with ASDs.

Karen Stagnitti, PhD, is professor in the School of Health and Social Development at Deakin University. She has worked with families with children with autism for over 30 years. In the last 20 years, she has developed a play intervention for children.

Lesley Stirling, PhD, is associate professor of linguistics and applied linguistics at the University of Melbourne. Drawing on a background in cognitive science, she has been researching communication in autism for more than a decade, focusing on the discourse analysis of children's stories and play interactions.

Andrea Tartaro, PhD, is an assistant professor of computer science at Furman University in Greenville, SC. Her research focuses on how interactive technology can support social interaction and positive behavior change.

318 Contributors

Jennifer A. Vadeboncoeur, PhD, is associate professor of human development, learning, and culture at the University of British Columbia. Her research explores learning and development in student–teacher and child–parent relationships from a Vygotskian perspective.

Bram Vanderborght, PhD, is professor at the Robotics Research Group at Vrije Universiteit Brussel, working on human–robot interaction. He is principal investigator of the Development of Robot-Enhanced Therapy for Children with Autism Spectrum Disorders (DREAM) project and has a European Research Council (ERC) grant. He is a member of the Young Academy.

Johan Vanderfaeillie, PhD, is associate professor at Vrije Universiteit Brussel in the Faculty of Psychology and Educational Sciences in the Department of Clinical and Lifespan Psychology. He is promoter of the Centre of Youth Care Research of Vrije Universiteit Brussel. The research of this center focuses on the assessment process, care processes, and outcomes of (Flemish) special youth care.

Esther Vardi-Rath, PhD, is a senior lecturer at the Kaye Academic College of Education, Beer-Sheva, Israel, and a former head of the Early Childhood Department in the college. She currently coordinates the teaching and instruction program at the MOFET Institute, and her research investigates classroom discourse and discourse analysis during peer interaction.

Kumara Ward, PhD, lectures in curriculum and pedagogy in the School of Education at the University of Western Sydney. Her research interests include nature education and its role in identity; well-being and sustainability; place-based education; and development of the naturalist intelligence, metacognition, and art-based pedagogies.

INDEX

Please note that page numbers in bold indicate defined terms.

academic development 177
acting 17, 53, 120, 140, 201, 207, 212, 216, 217; *see also* story-acting practice
acting ability 220
action characters 155
action-event frame item **128**, 148
actions item **128**, 135, 141, 147
ADOS *see* Autism Diagnostic Observation Schedule (ADOS)
adult-child play **200**
adult culture 202
adult reports of child creativity 255
adults: children drawn to singsong speech of 52; in children's combinatorial creativity and narrative development 289–90; creativity and 254, 255; engaged in pretend play 56; narrative activity (pretend play and storytelling as modes of) and 4, 8, 9, 17, 19; as play partners 45; in progressing shared narratives 284; returning to play and 296, 298, 300, 301, 305, 306, 308; scaffolding learning from 178
affect attribution item **128**, 138, 147
affective capacities 150
Ahioglu, N. 297
Ahn, J. 276
Aillenberg, H. 198, 315
Aksu-Koç, A. 8

Altemeier, W. A. 34
Alternative Uses Task **256**
Amabile, T. M. 258, 259
amanuensis 155, 164–6
ambiguity of truths 53
American Journal of Play, The 294
American Psychiatric Association (APA) 31, 72, 73, 96, 101, 117, 124
Anglo-Australian example 284–6, 287, 288, 289–90
animacy **32**, **125**
Applebee, A. 126, 130, 132, 134, 138, 141, 180
Applied Behavior Analysis (ABA) 97
appropriateness **253**
Aronsson, K. 203, 277
Art of Teaching Writing, The 185, 186
arts-based pedagogies 228, 231–2, 245
ASD *see* autism spectrum disorder (ASD)
ASD symptomatology 44
as if quality **32**
Asperger, H. 167
Asperger's disorder 31, 37
Astell, A. 56
Astington, J. W. 40
asymmetric social order in play interaction 204
Atlas, J. A. 33
attachment figure 52
attentional control 42

320 Index

attribution of absent or false properties **32**, 36
attribution of animacy **32**, **125**
attribution of imaginary properties **125**
attribution of mental processes at the imaginal level **138**
attribution of psychological states **133**
augmented reality 74; *see also* virtual and augmented reality
Australia study: conclusion to 245–6; context of the play in 234–6; findings from 242–5; group play in 238–9; method for 228–30; self-selected play of four groups of children in preschools in 227–8; social dynamics and rules in 240–2; solitary play in 236–8
authorable virtual peer (AVP) 72, 83, 84, 91; *see also* virtual peer for children with ASD
authoring interface 88–9
authoring the virtual peer **73**, 80, 88–9, 90, 92
Autism Diagnostic Observation Schedule (ADOS) **85**, 86, 92, 101
autism parenting 154
autism spectrum disorder (ASD): defined **31**, **117**; family, narrative, and *see* family (ASD, narrative, and); features of 73; intersection of pretense and storytelling in children with *see* pretense and storytelling intersection in children with ASD; intervention approaches for 74–6; Learn to Play program and 57–60; narrative, family, and *see* family (ASD, narrative, and); as neurological impairment 153; play, narrative, and children with *see* play, narrative, and children with ASD; pretend play in children with *see* pretend play in children with ASD; pretense and storytelling in *see* pretense and storytelling in ASD; social robots and *see* social robots; technologies for 74–6; virtual peer for children with *see* virtual peer for children with ASD
autistic mannerisms 83
Avatar 160, 163

Bakhtin, M. 204
Baldwin, J. M. 149
Bamburg, M. 64
Barab, S. 77

Barad, K. 245
Barnett, L. A. 255
Baron-Cohen, S. 35, 37, 44, 57
Barrington, G. 123
Barry, L. M. 107
Barry, T. D. 74
Bates, E. A. 264
Beghetto, R. A. 254
beliefs: beliefs about 53; influence of bias on 53; narrative and 54; role-play dimension of pretend play and 140; theory of mind and 51, 53
belonging 228, 232, 237, 242, 246
Benson, M. S. 8, 15
Berk, L. E. 179, 305
Bers, M. U. 77
bias 254, 255, 300, 302, 304, 305, 306
Big C creativity **254**
biolooping **153**, 154
blocks 179, 258, 265, 266, 278, 284
bluffing 53
Blum-Kulka, S. 199, 200, 202
Bodrova, E. 179
Boscolo, P. 184
Boucher, J. 36, 38, 46, 56
Bovee, J. 149
Boyd, B. 8
Brady, N. C. 44
brain 56, 66, 69
Bredikyte, M. 272, 285
Brice-Heath, S. 302, 303
Brierly, L. M. 33
Britton, J. 192
Brooks, R. 53
Bruner, E. 121
Bruner, J. 13, 126, 127
bullying 305
Burlew, S. B. 107

CA *see* chronological age (CA)
Calkins, L. 176, 177, 185, 186, 187, 190, 191, 192, 193
Capps, L. 119
Capra, F. 233
Carey, L. 54
Carlson, S. M. 40, 264
Carruthers, P. 46
CARS *see* Childhood Autism Rating Scale (CARS)
cartoons 63, 86, 153, 155, 158, 162, 163
cartoon task **86**
Casey, S. 59

Cassell, J. 72, 77, 315
change: ASD and 97, 108
Chappell, K. 255
character accent 164
character figurines 8
character representation 13–14, 15, 16
characters: action 155; creativity and 256, 261, 264, 266, 276, 283, 287, 302, 303; family (ASD, narrative, and) and 152, 153, 155–9, 162, 163; in fully developed narrative 13; imagination and 276; in inter- and intrapersonal relations category 128, 135; narrative activity and 9, 13, 22; natural world and 228, 229, 230, 235, 236, 239–43, 246; play, narrative, and children with ASD and 54, 56, 58, 61, 63–6, 68–9; pretense and storytelling intersection in children with ASD and 119, 121, 125–36, 138–42; subteacher discourse during PPWS and 201–2, 207, 214, 220
Charley, C. M. 264
Charman, T. 35, 37, 57
Chaudry, M. 31, 57, 315
Chavajay, P. 300
Childhood Autism Rating Scale (CARS) 124
Child-Initiated Pretend Play Assessment 60
Child Language Data Exchange System (CHILDES) 125
Children's labor 297–300
Children's Playfulness Scale **255**
Chinese example 281–4, 287, 288, 289–90
choice time 17
Christensen, P. 276
Christie, J. F. 181
chronological age (CA) **33**
classificatory looping **153**, 154
coaching 205
Codes for the Human Analysis of Transcripts (CHAT) 125
coding scheme 40, 122, 206–7, 208
cognition: Leo study and 167; narrative activity and 7, 23; nonverbal 44–5; social 83; theory of 178; verbal 42–4
cognitive attribution item **128**, 147
cognitive capacities 150
cognitive development 52
cognitive flexibility 39
cognitive functioning 96
cognitive functioning item **128**, 129, 148
cognitive model 51

cognitive skills 32, 51, 258
Cohen, Z. 198, 315
collaboration 204, 221, 272, 284
collaboration in pretend play narratives 139–40
collaborative creativity 284
collaborative improvisation 272
collaborative narratives 76
collaborative pretense with peers 46
collaborative production of the plot 117
collaborative social pretend play 45, 122
collaborative social process 272
collaborative storytelling 3
collages 265, 266
Collins, A. 79
Coltman, P. 56
combinatorial creativity: across cultural contexts in cultural-historical research approach 277–8; in Chinese example 283; defined **275–6**, **287**; of lived experience in children's shared narratives 286, 287–8; in Mexican example 279, 280; narrative development and 289–90; role of family and adults in 289–90; Vygotsky and 272
comic strip conversations 74
Common Core State Standards in English Language Arts 177, 189–90, 191, 193
Common Core State Standards Initiative 176, 177, 185, 192
communication: imagination and 271; interpersonal 96; metaplay 14; nonverbal 53–4, 102, 290; oral language and 201; physical 308; social 31, 72, 73, 74, 83, 117, 142; social attention and 38; social behavior and 99; social-cognitive item and 138; social interaction and 97; verbal 53–4, 102, 308
communication style 273, 277, 278–9, 281, 283, 284–5
complementarity 7, 10–11, 24
complication 119, **155**, 157, 158, 159–60, 161, 164
comprehension questions 105, 106, 107, 115
comprehension skills 8, 180, 201
computer game designers 163
computer games 76
computers: personal 74
computer technology 98
Connery, M. C. 271
Connolly, J. A. 32

322 Index

consensual assessment technique 255, **258**, 259, 264, 266
constructionism **72–3**, 76–7
constructionist theory 72, 73, 76, 78, 90
content: in imaginative storytelling 181–4
convergence 10–11, 16–19, 24
conversational exchanges 53
conversational narrative **54**, 119, 120, 121, 126, 141
conversational skills 74
conversations: narratives embedded in 271
Cooper, P. 175, 201, 315
Corsaro, W. A. 202
Costall, A. 150
Costescu, C. 316
Craft, A. 255
Craik, D. 56
Creative Activities Checklist **255**
creative thinking 290
creative writing 76
creativity: ASD and 40, 85, 86, 92, 122; Big C **254**; as central to play 271; collaborative 284; combinatorial *see* combinatorial creativity; cultural-historical reading of *see* cultural-historical reading in children's shared narratives; defined **253–4**, **258**, **259**; drawings to assess *see* creativity in preschool-age children (narratives and drawings to assess); everyday model of **254**; little c model of **254**; narratives to assess *see* creativity in preschool-age children (narratives and drawings to assess); natural world and 231; observations of 256; subteacher discourse during PPWS and 201; in typical development 32
creativity in preschool-age children (narratives and drawings to assess): conclusion to 265–7; defined **253–4**; development of two measures of 259–65; future directions of 265–7; measuring 254–8
creativity scores 264, 265
creativity task: drawing 261–3, 264, 265, 266; examining children's perceptions of 265; narrative 259–61, 264, 265, 266
Cremin, T. 256
Cross, B. 163, 164
cross-cultural development *see* pretense and storytelling in cross-cultural development

cross-fertilization 7, 10–11, 13, 16–19, 21–4, 201
crossover **155**
Csikszentmihalyi, M. 253
cultural-historical reading in children's shared narratives: adults in children's combinatorial creativity and narrative development in 289–90; combinatorial creativity in *see* combinatorial creativity; discussion in 287–8; examples in 278–86; family in children's combinatorial creativity and narrative development in 289–90; introduction to 271–5
cultural-historical research approach, combinatorial creativity across 277–8
cultural-historical view on imagination, creativity, and shared narratives 275–6
culturally expressive activity: play as 301–6
cultural norms item **128**, 135, 147
cultural relations 129
culture: adult 202; Applebee and 180; ASD and 32, 51, 52, 162, 163; Dyson and 187; narrative activity and 9, 18, 19; in narratives 287; natural world and 233; Paley and 184; peer 202; play in different 306

Damrad-Frye, R. 64
David, D. 96, 316
Davidson, K. L. 304
DBR *see* design-based research (DBR)
decentering **77**
decentration **32**
decontextualisation **32**
decouple **40**
deep ecology 232
Delves, K. 123
descriptions 271
design-based research (DBR) 77, 78, 79, 85, 90, 92
design conjecture 78
design goals 79–80
design sessions 79
design study for virtual peer for children with ASD: design conjecture in 78; design goals for 79–80; method for 78–9; participants for 80–3; research phases for *see* Research phases for design study for children with ASD; setting for 80
developmental psychology 4, 294

Dewey, J. 176, 183, 184, 193, 243
Dewey's theory of motivation in
learning 176
Diagnostic and Statistical Manual of Mental Disorders (DSM-5) 31, 45, 117
Diagnostic and Statistical Manual of Mental Disorders (DSM-IV-TR) 101, 122, 124
dialectical relation 275, 290
dialogue 128, 154, 155, 272, 273, 279–82, 285–6, 288, 307
Dickinson, D. K. 180
director play **276**
discourse strategies 198, 203, 210, 219
discursive literacy **199–200**, 201, 220
discursive narrative 8, 16, 19, 119, 120, 123, 130, 131–2, **140**
Dissanayake, C. 52, 57, 125, 316
divergent thinking scores 257
divergent thinking tasks **256–8**, 265, 266, 267
dolls 61, 85, 128, 179, 259, 284
Dolphijn, R. 245
Donnelly, J. 149
Douglas, S. 8, 45, 54, 117, 122, 123, 168, 316
Down syndrome 36, 39
Doyle, A. B. 32
dramatic play 9, 175, **176**; *see also* pretend play
draw and tell a story activity 281–4
drawing: to assess creativity in preschool-age children *see* creativity in preschool-age children (narratives and drawings to assess); containing symbolic elements 231; in different cultures 281–4, 287–8, 289–90; from Göncü's conceptualization of play as a cultural activity 296; to imagine family life to create a shared narrative 283–4; independent writing and 175, 182; meaning of experiences through 276; narratives represented as 271; natural world and 230, 231, 241; showing emotion 67
drawing creativity task 261–3, 264, 265, 266
Dudley-Marling, C. 180
Dunn, J. 149, 151
Dunn, L. M. 43
Dyson, A. H. 180, 187

Early Years Learning Framework (EYLF) 227
ecofeminism 232
ecoliteracy **233**
ecological ego **233**
ecology 232, 233
econnection 231
economic and value context of play 296–300
ecopsychology 228, **232–3**
education for sustainability (EfS) 227
effectiveness: creativity and 253; defined **97**; of social robots 98; of Social Stories 74, 98, 109, 110
efficacy **97**, 98; defined **97**; cf social robots 98; of social skills groups 74; of Social Stories 110
Egan, K. 234
Eisner, E. W. 231
El'konin, D. B. 273, 288
El'konin's theory of role-play **288**
emotional cues 52, 54
emotions: ASD and 52–3, 79, 102, 105, 106, 128, 138; drawings showing 59, 64–7, 283; narrative activity and 14; natural world and 240; by robot 116
empathizing–systemizing theory **97**, 98
enacted narrative 119, 120, 130, 131–2, **140**
enacting 63, 120, 220
encoding 119, 128, 181–4, 191
Engel, S. 8, 14, 288
English Language Arts 189–90
entertainment 254, 289
Erikson, E. 178, 179
Erikson's psychosocial theory of human development **179**
Ethnography of Autism Project 151
Evans, J. 239
events item **128**, 135, 141, 147
event structure item **128**, 148
everyday model of creativity **254**
executive functioning 32
executive functioning hypothesis 32, 40, 41–2, 46, 257, 266
executive function position **52**
experimental theater 18
experimentation 9, 178, 180, 183
experts 192, 254, 256, 297
exploration-pretend play continuum 301
expressive language 36, 43. 79, 81, 82, 83, 89, 124

324 Index

Expressive Vocabulary Test (EVT-2) **82**
Eyal, G. 167
Eylon, T. 198, 316

face-to-face storytelling 84
family: in combinatorial creativity
  and narrative development 289–90;
  culture and 271, 275, 278–9, 283–7,
  289–90; difficulty or instability in 21;
  disorganization and instability in 18;
  Henry case study and 62; natural world
  and 233, 240, 242; returning to play and
  298–300, 306, 307, 309
family (ASD, narrative, and): ASD children
  respond more positively with 151;
  introduction to 149–50; Leo study and
  see Leo study
family relationships 15, 259
family stories 254
family structure 52
fantasy **275**; *see also* imagination
fantasy-inspired thoughts **175–6**
fantasy play 9, **55**; *see also* pretend play
Fein, G. 118, 126, 127, 147
Fernandez, M. C. 34
Fewell Play Scale 39
figurines 8, 11, 14, 20, 21, 75, 85, 119
Filipenko, M. 276
films 63, 153, 163
Fishel, P. T. 34
Fleer, M. 276, 291
Fleming, K. K. 44
flexibility: ASD and 39, 40, 41, 122;
  cognitive 39; intellectual 201, 220;
  mental 256
focused chains **126–7**
Freeman, S. 122
free play task **85**
Friedman, O. 245
Frith, C. D. 56
Frog, Where Are You? 264

Galda, L. 202
games 63, 74, 76, 77, 80, 96, 153, 155, 162,
  163, 276
Gaskins, S. 272
gaze following 53
general cognitive development
  hypothesis 42
generativity 41, 42
genetics 52
Genishi, C. 180

Gerow, I. 264
gestures 57, 75, 86, 89, 153, 188, 200, 209
Giffin, H. 120, 129
Glaubman, R. 118, 126, 147
goal-directed behaviour 42
Goffman, E. 151
Goldman, L. 303
Goldman, S. 54, 64
Göncü, A. 142, 294, 296, 297, 303,
  304, 316
Goodman, Y. M. 276
Gould, J. 33
Graves, D. 185
Gray, C. 154
Griffin, P. 203
gross motor activities 265
group play 142, 207, 219, 222, 236,
  238–9, 290
group programs **74**, 85, 92

Haag, G. 161
habituation with the robot 105
Hacking, I. 153, 154, 167
halo effect **255**
Handbook of Child Psychology 294, 301
Harel, I. 90
Harris, P. L. 8, 200
Hart, B. 164
Head Start classrooms 11, 18, 19, 21–3
heaps **126–7**
Henry case study 60–8
Hepburn, S. 39
hierarchy in peer discourse 222
high-functioning autism (HFA) 54
Hobson, J. A. 39, 40, 96, 122
Hobson, R. P. 39, 40, 122
Hodges, S. D. 254
Honeycutt, R. L. 185, 186
*How Do I Ask Questions When I Play With
  Others?* 116
Hughes, A. 43
Hughes, C. 52
human peers 72, 76
humor 255, 303, 304

Ilgaz, H. 8
imaginary **128**
imaginary companion 254, 264, 266
imaginary friends 40, 55
imaginary object present **32**
imaginary situation 178, 271, 272, 282,
  283, 288, 290, 301

imaginary world 200, 202, 254, 266, 286
imagination; *see also* fantasy: as central
to play 271; communication and
271; cultural-historical reading of *see*
cultural-historical reading in children's
shared narratives; deficits in 31; defined
275; Leo study and 161, 167; narrative
activity and 7, 9, 10, 22, 23; subteacher
discourse during PPWS and 201, 219;
theory of mind scores and 40
imagination-based episode 179
imaginative play; *see also* pretend play:
defined 45, **55**, **125**; imaginative writing
and 180; involving absent objects or
imaginary characters **125**; psychosocial
development and 179; rough and
tumble to 307; socioconstructivist
learning and 178
imaginative storytelling from kindergarten
writing instruction: Common Core
in 176, 177, 185, 189–93; content
in 181–4; discussion about 190–3;
encoding in 181–4; findings in 185–6;
implications regarding 193; introduction
to 175–7; language development in
180–1; method for 177–8; motivation
to learn in 181–4; psychosocial
development 178–9; socioconstructivist
learning in 178; symbolic thought in
179–80; writing workshop curriculum
in 185–9
imaginative thinking 178, 179, 181, 284,
286, 290
imaginative writing 176, 177, 180, 185,
186, 190, 192–3
imagined world 9, 129, 290
independent writing 175, 182, 183
Index of Productive Syntax (IPSyn) **124**
individualistic ideology 187
individual-level analysis 108
infant-mother play **200**
in frame **201**, 215, 220
inhibition 41, 42
initiative *versus* guilt stage 179
integration **32**
intellectual disabilities 33, 35, 37, 43
intellectual flexibility 201, 220
intentionality 53
intentions: role-play dimension of pretend
play and 140
inter- and intrapersonal relations category
128, 135, 147

International Journal of Play, The 294
International Play Association 294, 295
Internet 74
interpersonal communication 96
intervention 57, 58, 69, 73, 192, 198, 205,
295, 301, 302
intervention approaches 74–6
intervention sessions 105
iterative sessions 79, 92

Jain, J. 304
Jameso, H. 56
Jarrold, C. 34–6, 46, 150
Jefferson System transcription
conventions 155
Jenkins, J. M. 40
Johnsen, K. 92
Johnsen, M. 92
joint pretence 53
joy 254, 255
Jurassic Park 163

Kangas, M. 271, 283, 284
Kaplan, N. 77
Karmiloff-Smith, A. 261
Kasari, C. 122
Kashi, G. 118
Kaufman, J. C. 254
Kavanaugh, R. D. 8, 14
Kellogg, D. 272
Kelly, R. 38, 41
Kidd, E. 55
Kientz, J. A. 74
kindergarten writing instruction:
imaginative storytelling from *see*
imaginative storytelling from
kindergarten writing instruction
Kohányi, A. 254
Konstantareas, M. M. 42, 43, 44, 45
Koresh, R. 118
Kravtsova, E. E. 276
Kultima, A. 271

labor: children's 297–300
Labov, W. 119, 155
Lander, R. 56
landscape of action 13
landscape of consciousness 13, 16
language; *see also* literacy: communication
and 271; expressive 36, 43, 79, 81, 82,
83, 89, 124; narrative activity and 7, 23;
nonverbal 278; oral 16, 18, 198, 201;

326 Index

participant **180**; receptive 43, 44, 79, 81, 82, 83, 89; spectator **180**; subteaching and 207–8; theory of 178; verbal 278; written 200
language ability 73, 80, 82, 83, 90, 124
language ability scale 82
language development: imaginative storytelling and 177, 178, 180–1, 193; play enhances 96; pretend play for children with ASD and 32, 43
language disorder 34, 54
language item **128**, 147
language skills 18, 21, 43, 180, 192
leadership 201, 210–11, 219, 222
learning process 97, 106, 203, 205, 208, 217, 219, 227
learn/learning: as academic learning 299; Dewey's theory of motivation in 176; motivation to 176, 181–4; play equals 295, 296, 299, 307; socioconstructivist 178
Learn to Play program 57–60, 68, 69
Lee, A. 39, 122
Leekam, S. 52, 54
Lego Foundation 294
Legos 278, 284–6, 287, 288, 289–90
Leiter International Performance Scale—Arthur Adaptation 44
Lemanek, K. L. 34
Leong, D. J. 179
Leo study: amanuensis in 155, 164–6; background for 149; case history in 152–4; complication in 155, 159–60; conclusion of 167–8; how is Leo's Pretend different in 162–4; intentionality in 152; looping in 166–7, 167; narrative devices employed in 150; orientation in 155–9; Pretend in 150, 151, 152, 154–5, 156, 165, 166, 167; prosthetic environment and 150; resolution in 155, 159, 160–1
Leslie, A.M. 32, 51, 52
Lewin, Teresa 198, 316
Lewis, V. 36, 38, 42, 56
Li, L. 278, 281–4, 290, 316
Libby, S. 36
Likert scale 258
Lillard, A. S. 257, 301
Lilley, R. 168
linguistic development 52
literacy; *see also* language: defined **199**; discursive **199–200**, 201, 220; mediation

and 204–5; narrative activity and 16; pretend play and 198; returning to play and 299, 301, 303; socioconstructivist learning and 178; subteaching during PPWS and 198, 199–200
literacy development 181, 221
literacy discourse: subteacher discourse as 220–1
literacy skills 180, 183, 198, 201, 220, 222
literate capacity **200**
little c model of creativity **254**
Littledyke, M. 240
Lobman, C. 271
locale-spatial item **128**, 147
looping **153**, 154, 166–7, 167
low-income preschools 19, 21–3
Lucas, K. 180

MA *see* mental age (MA)
MacArthur Story Stem Battery 259
Mackenzie, N. 282
Maclean, M. 159
Maclean, N. 57, 63, 149, 317
majority world 296, 297, 309
make a story task **85**
make-believe play **55**, **176**; *see also* pretend play
managing play 14
Mann, T. D. 179, 305
March, S. 271, 286, 290, 317
Marchant, J. L. 56
Marchman, V. A. 264
Maring, B. L. 264
Marvel Character Guide 155, 156
math 76, 301
Mayer, M. 264
McCune, L. 42
McNamee, G. D. 180
mean length of utterance (MLU) **124**
media 56, 119–20, 152, 155, 187
mediation: adult 199; among peers 204–5
mediation skills 198
Mehan, H. 203
Meltzoff, A. 53
memory 33, 42
mental age (MA) **33**
mental flexibility 256
mental states 14, 15, 51–4, 55, 62, 68, 128, 202
mental state terms **51**
mental state verbs **52**
metacognitive skills 72, 73, 76, 77

metacommunication 120, 122, 129, 135, 136, 142
metalinguistic reflection 76–7
metalinguistic skills **77**; *see also* metacognitive skills
metaplay communication and interaction 14
metaplay discourse **202, 276**
metarepresent **40**
metarepresentation **51**, 52, 55, 56
metarepresentational hypothesis 40–1
metatalk **202**
Mexican example 278–81, 287, 288, 289–90
middle-class preschools 18, 19–21
Mifsud, J. 38, 43
Miller, P. J. 303
miniculture 17
MLU *see* mean length of utterance (MLU)
mobile devices 74
modeling 204
Mökkönen, A. C. 203
moral dilemmas 53
Morelli, G. A. 300
motivation: Dewey's theory of 176; to learn 176, 181–4; of Leo 164; to pretend or imagine in play 178; of subteacher 198, 221; theory of mind and 51
motivation and engagement 97, 157
Mottweiler, C. M. 253, 267, 272, 283, 317
Moulthrop, S. 77
MSEL *see* Mullen Scales of Early Learning (MSEL)
Mullen Scales of Early Learning (MSEL) 44
multimedia 74
Mundy, P. 35
Murray, D. 185
music 304
mutually transformative process 282

narrative activity (pretend play and storytelling as mode of): from complementarity to convergence in 10–11; complementary narrative emphases in 14–15; conclusion to 23–4; introduction to 7; low-income preschools in 21–3; making sense of this pattern in 13; middle-class preschools in 19–21; narrative in play and story in 7–10; *Promoting Convergence, Cross-Fertilization, and Development:*

Reports from a Preschool Storytelling and Story-Acting Practice in 16–19; as separate from storytelling 11–12
narrative coherence 130, 141
narrative creation **273**, 275, 277, 279, 280, 283, 289
narrative creativity task 259–61, 264, 265, 266
narrative descriptions 79
narrative development 181, 191, 276, 286, 289–90, 307
narrative enactment 16
narrative-rich role-play 276
narratives: ASD, play, and *see* play, narrative, and children with ASD; to assess creativity in preschool-age children *see* creativity in preschool-age children (narratives and drawings to assess); collaborative 76; conversational **54**, 119, 120, 121, 126, 141; cultural-historical reading of imagination and creativity in children's shared *see* cultural-historical reading in children's shared narratives; defined **54–5**, **119**, **186**, **271**, **272**, **276**; dialogue and 272; discursive 8, 16, 19, 119, 120, 123, 130, 131–2, **140**; enacted 119, 120, 130, 131–2, **140**; episodes of 126; of Henry case study 64–8; to illustrate social situations and responses 74; as narrative type 126–7; oral 117, 123; personal **54**; play, children with ASD, and *see* play, narrative, and children with ASD; play, culture, and 307, 308; in play and story 7–10; pretend play *see* pretend play narrative; primitive **126–7**; requirements for 13; shared *see* shared narratives; storytelling *vs.* 271
narrative scenario 8, 13, 16, 19, 20, 21, 23, 118, 119
narrative sequences 155
narrative sophistication 132–7, 141
narrative structures 8, 55, 123, 132, 161, 187, 272
narrative structure tasks 264
narrative thinking 282, 283, 284
National Institute for Play 294
nativistic position **52**
natural inputs 74
natural world: assisting children in learning 227–8, 229; as content for interconnection and divergence of pretense and storytelling in children's

328 Index

play *see* pretense and storytelling in children's play (natural world and); play and 232–3; through arts-based pedagogies 231–2
nature 231–2, 233, 243, 245
nature play 234, 236–42
negotiated pretense 122
negotiating 205
negotiating play 14
neuroscience 69
Newkirk, T. 187
New Social Story Book: Illustrated Edition, The 103
Nickelodeon 155
Nicktoons 155, 157
Nicolopoulou, A. 7, 56, 118, 120, 140, 179, 201, 316
Nielsen, M. 125
nonhuman encounters 243
nonverbal cognition 44–5
nonverbal communication 53–4, 102, 290
nonverbal language 278
Norrick, N. 121
novelty **253**

Object Permanence test 44
objects item **128**, 135, 141, 147
object substitution **32**, **37**, 38, 51, 60, **125**
observations: of creativity 255–6
Ochs, E. 119
Ogan, A. T. 179, 305
oral language 16, 18, 198, 201
oral narrative 117, 123
oral traditions 303
orientation 119, 121, 126, 138, **155**, 155–9
out of frame **201**, 215, 220
overlap and interchange: thematic disjunction *vs.* 11–12
Owoki, G. 276
Ozer, S. 297
Ozonoff, S. 41

paintings 230
Paley, V. G. 9, 16, 19, 118, 175, 176, 181, 182
Papert, S. 90
parenting 154, 284
participant language **180**
participant observation **151**
participants: for social robots 101; for virtual peer for children with ASD 80–3
participatory design (PD) 78

Pathways to the Common Core: Accelerating Achievement 185
Peabody Picture Vocabulary Test—Revised (PPVT–R) 43, 80, 81
peer conflict 221
peer culture 202
peer discourse 198–9, **202**, 221, 222
peer group interaction 201
peer interaction 72, 73, 74, 142, 204, 219, 222
peer-mediated training 97
peer relations 286
peers: collaborative pretense with 46; human 72, 76; mediation among 204–5; pretend play and 200; virtual *see* virtual peer for children with ASD
Pellegrini, A. D. 202
personal computers 74
personal narratives **54**
Peter, M. 57, 69
physical communication 308
physical world category **128**, 135, 147
Piaget, J. 118, 178, 180, 301
pictures 64, 68, 74, 101
piloting strategy **203**; *see also* scaffolding
place: context of play and 234; importance of 242; nature as 231, 232; theory of 232
planning: virtual peer for children with ASD and 78
play: adult-child **200**; in children's sociocultural lives *see* returning to play; as culturally expressive activity 296, 301–6; defined **9**, **306**; developmental processes and 150; director **276**; dramatic 9, 175, **176** *see also* pretend play; economic and value context of 296–300; equals learning 295; goals in understanding 309; group 142, 207, 219, 222, 236, 238–9, 290; imaginative *see* imaginative play; infant-mother **200**; interest on rise regarding 294 *see also* returning to play; location of *see* returning to play; make-believe **55**, **176** *see also* pretend play; natural world and 232–3; nature 234, 236–42; policy agenda on 306–9; pretend *see* pretend play; representational **55**, 304 *see also* pretend play; research and policy agenda on 295–6, 306–9; research limited on ASD and storytelling and 150; returning to *see* returning to play; rhythm **304**; rough and tumble 307,

308; self-selected 227; single-child **200**; situating children's 296–300; as social narrative constructed in dialogue 307; sociodramatic 118, 272; solitary 236–8; sound and rhythm **304**; story based **176** *see also* pretend play; symbolic **32** *see also* pretend play; symbols in 51 *see also* object substitution; in toy industry 294; value context of 296–300; visual arts and 276

play, narrative, and children with ASD: conclusion to 68–9; Henry case study of 60–8; introduction to 51–4; pretend play and 55–60

play actions 55–63, 68

play as improvisation 307

play as script 307

play-based curriculum approaches 227

playfulness 39–40, 122, 255, 308

playful pretense 40, 122

play idea 55

play intervention 69, 301, 302

play-literacy nexus 181

play/story communicate item **128**, 148

play scenarios 8, 14, 15, 19, 21, 55, 56, 68, 139, 236, 238, 276, 308

play scenes 51, 57, 59–64, **60**, 235–8

play scripts 56, 58, **60**, 61, 140

play sequences 60, 63, 68, 125, 126

play theories 301

play therapy 301, 307, 309

playworld 9, 303, 308

plot: in fully developed narrative 13; in Leo study 153, 158, 159, 162, 163, 164; storytelling and 117, 120, 126; subteacher discourse during PPWS and 207, 214, 215, 219

plot construction 13–14, 15, 16

plot development 140, 141, 159, 164

plot twists 158, 256

policy agenda on play 306–9

Pop, C. A. 101

postmodern emergence **232**, 234

PPVT-R *see* Peabody Picture Vocabulary Test—Revised (PPVT–R)

"Prehistory of Written Language" (1978) 184

Pre-school age children: narratives and drawings to assess creativity in *see* creativity in preschool-age children (narratives and drawings to assess)

preschools: low-income 19, 21–3; middle-class 18, 19–21; observations in 10, 11, 18; upper-middle-class 19

Prescott, S. J. 37, 38

pretend person 261, 262, 263

pretend play: ASD and 55–60; in children with ASD *see* pretend play in children with ASD; collaborative social 45, 122; as cultural activity 302; defined **10**, **32**, **33**, **55**, **125**, **176**, **178**, **200**, **301–2**; differences between storytelling and 10, 15; with figurines 14; integrating elements of narrative scenario in 16; intersubjectivity in 14; involves language expressing transformations 308; language and 42–4; literacy and 198; as mode of narrative activity *see* narrative activity (pretend play and storytelling as mode of); narrating 117; pretense and 150; reciprocity and 72; as representational activity 303; similarities between storytelling and 9, 13, 15; social 5, 8, 45, 46, 53, 122, 127, 133, **200**, 201; social development and 44; social robots and 96; subteaching during *see* subteacher discourse during PPWS; in typical development 32–3

pretend play and narrative structure tasks 264

pretend play deficits 33–44

pretend play in children with ASD: discussion regarding 45–6; introduction to 31; nonverbal cognition and 44–5; pretend play deficits in 33–44; pretend play in typical development for 32–3; studies supporting intact pretend play in 36–40

pretend play in the wake of story (PPWS): defined **198**, **201–2**; subteacher discourse during *see* subteacher discourse during PPWS

pretend play narrative 15, 20, 23; Bruner and 121; collaboration in 139–40; conversational narratives and 119, 121; defined **118**; developmental stage and sophistication of 126; drama and 121; forming discussions and conclusions about 140–1; identified for analysis on basis of criteria of 125; identifying and analyzing results of 129–40; production of 126; verb acquisition and 123

Index

pretense and storytelling across cultural contexts 271

pretense and storytelling in ASD: family in *see* family (ASD, narrative, and); intersection of *see* pretense and storytelling intersection in children with ASD; play, narrative, and children with ASD in *see* play, narrative, and children with ASD; pretend play in children with ASD in *see* pretend play in children with ASD; social robots as storytellers in *see* social robots; virtual peer for children with ASD in *see* virtual peer for children with ASD

pretense and storytelling in children's play (natural world and): conclusion for 245–6; context of the play in 234–6; findings in 242–5; in four groups of children in preschools in Sydney, Australia *see* Australia study; introduction to 227–8; method for 228–30; natural world and 232–3; nature play in 236–42; restoring voice of nature through acts-based pedagogies in 231–2

pretense and storytelling in cross-cultural development: cultural-historical reading in children's shared narratives in *see* cultural-historical reading in children's shared narratives; location of play in children's sociocultural lives in *see* returning to play; returning to play in *see* returning to play; using narratives and drawings to assess creativity in preschool-age children *see* creativity in preschool-age children (narratives and drawings to assess)

pretense and storytelling intersection in children with ASD: conclusion for 140–2; defined **118–23**; discussion of 140–2; introduction to 117–18; method for 123–9; results in 129–40

pretense and storytelling in the classroom: imaginative storytelling from kindergarten writing instruction in *see* imaginative storytelling from kindergarten writing instruction; pretense and storytelling in children's play *see* pretense and storytelling in children's play (natural world and); subteacher discourse during PPWS *see* subteacher discourse during PPWS

primary representation 40, 51

primitive narratives **126–7**

Pritchard, R. J. 185, 186

Probo (robot) 100, 102–3, 106

Promoting Convergence, Cross-Fertilization, and Development: Reports from a Preschool Storytelling and Story-Acting Practice 16–19

props 206, 207, 210, 214, 259

prosthetic environment **150**

protodeclarative pointing 60

Providing and Then Withholding Scaffolding to Support One [sic] Child's Understanding of Narrative Structure 187

psychology 232, 294

psychosis 34

psychosocial development 177, 178–9, 180

Pushkin, A. S. 280

quasifamily relationships 15

Quiñones, G. 317

Quirmbach, L. M.

Rakoczy, H. 53

RATs *see* robot-assisted therapies (RATs)

Ravid, D. 200

RCC *see* robot control center (RCC)

RDLS *see* Reynell Developmental Language Scale (RDLS)

realistic **128**

realistic-imaginal scale (RIS) 132–7, 147–8

realistic-imaginative continuum **129**

reality: pretend play and 200; virtual and augmented 74, 76, 98

real person 262, 263

receptive language 43, 44, 79, 81, 82, 83, 89

reciprocity: defined **72**; environmental 233; social-emotional 141

reciprocity with technology and storytelling: virtual peer for children with ASD as *see* virtual peer for children with ASD

Reddy, V. 150

reenacting 63

Reese, E. 10

reflection: virtual peer and 78

reflexivity **200**

Reichow, B. 97

Reilly, J. S. 264

Renfrew Action Picture Test 36

representational activity, play as 303–4, 308

representational play **55**, 304; *see also* pretend play

research and policy agenda on play 295–6, 306–9

researcher: importance of 277; in progressing shared narrative 280–1, 286; role of 277

research phases for design study for children with ASD: development of authoring interface as 88–9; generalizing with children of varying abilities as 89–92; task development as 84–8

resolution 54, 63, 64, 67, 68, 119, 121, **155**, 159, 160–1

response measurement 106–7

returning to play: defined **306**; economic and value context of play in 296–300; introduction to 294–6; play as culturally expressive activity in 296, 301–6; research and policy agenda on play, correlates, and benefits in 295–6, 306–9; situating children's play in their lives in 296–300

Reynell Developmental Language Scale (RDLS) 43

rhyme 278

rhythm 304

rhythm play *see* sound and rhythm play

Richner, E. S. 179

RIS *see* realistic-imaginal scale

Robbins, J. 276

robot-assisted therapies (RATs) 98–101

robot control center (RCC) 102

robotics 74

robotic systems 98

robots: social *see* social robots

Roby, A. 55

Rogers, S. 239

Rogers, S. J. 39, 41, 44

Rogoff, B. 284, 300

role-play **32**, **125**, 236, 239, **264**, 273, 276, 288

role-play exercises **74**

roles item **128**, 147

role taking 32

Root-Bernstein, M. 254

Root-Bernstein, R. 254

Rosenblatt, L. 181

Roskos, K. 181

Roszak, T. 233

rough and tumble play 307, 308

Rousseau, J. 243

Runco, M. A. 254

Ruokamo, H. 271

Ruskin, E. 43

Rutherford, M. 39, 41, 44

SACS *see* Social Attention and Communication Study (SACS)

SAGE 77

Sandoval, W. A. 90

sarcasm 304

Sawyer, R. K. 14, 272

scaffolding 163–4, 178, 181, 203, 204

Scales, E. 179

scenarios 152, 153

Schonmann, S. 203

Schuler, A. 122

Schutz, A. 152

Schweder, R. A. 298

scoring fluency 258

sculptures 230

self-reports 255

self-selected play 227

sense of belonging 237, 242, 246

sensors 74

sequences **126–7**

set, design the 214

set shifting 42

setting: creativity and 256; growing up in different 273; natural world and 229, 236, 246; for social robots 101; for virtual peer for children with ASD 80

setting up play 14

shared active surfaces 74

shared narratives: cultural-historical reading of imagination and creativity in children's *see* cultural-historical reading in children's shared narratives; cultural-historical view on 275–6; as culturally constructed 287–8; examples of 278–86

shared pretense 45,122

Sherman, T. 35

Sherratt, D. 57, 59, 69

shunning 305

Sigman, M. 34, 35, 43

Silverman, C. 151

simulation theory **52**

Simut, R. 96, 317

single-child play **200**

Siraj-Blatchford, I. 272

Siraj-Blatchford, J. 272

332 Index

Sixth Sense program 154
Smith, P. 36, 46
Smogorzewska, J. 257
Snow, C. E. 200
social activities 306
Social Attention and Communication Study (SACS) 38
social awareness 53, 83
social capacities 150
social cognition 83
social-cognitive item **128**, 138, 147
social communication 31, 72, 73, 74, 83, 117, 142
social communication skills 74
social-cultural content category **128**, 135, 147
social development 44
social dynamics and rules 240–2
social-emotional development 181
social impairments 78, 79, 80, 81, 83, 99
social information 97
social interaction: play, narrative, and children with ASD 52, 56, 57, 58, 61, 63; social robots for children with ASD 96, 97, 98, 99, 102, 109; subteacher discourse during PPWS 198, 219; virtual peer for children with ASD 72–8, 80, 83, 90
social interaction skills 74, 75, 76, 77
sociality 167
social motivation 83
social pretend play 5, 8, 45, 46, 53, 122, 127, 133, **200**, 201
social relations 10, 17, 128, 134, 135, 147, 150, 183, 204, 275
social relations item **128**, 135, 147
Social Responsiveness Scale (SRS) **83**
social robots: conclusions regarding 108–10; future directions of 108–10; introduction to 96–101; method for 101–7; results regarding 107–8; social story with the emotions by 116; as storytelling agent 98; treatment integrity with 115
social skills 32, 58, 74, 76, 96, 100, 199–201, 212, 220, 266
social skills groups **74**, 79, 85
social skills picture stories 74
social skills program 80, 92
social skills treatments 97, 98, 110
Social Stories 74, **97**, 103, 106

Social Story intervention 97–8, 101, 108–10
socioconstructivist learning 178
socioconstructivist theory **178**, 181, 193
sociocultural lives (location of play in children's) *see* returning to play
sociodramatic play 118, 272
socioemotional skills 7
solitary play 236–8
Solomon, O. 151, 162, 163
Somerville, M. 232, 242
songs 230
sound and rhythm play **304**
spectator language **180**
speech item **128**, 147
Spillane, A. 97
spontaneity 63, 68, 255
Sprague, K. 180
Squire, K. 77
SRS *see* Social Responsiveness Scale (SRS)
Stagnitti, K. 51, 53, 56, 59, 158, 317
Stake, R. E. 177
Stanley, G. C. 42, 43, 44, 45
Starkweather, E. K. 257
Star Wars 163
Steiner, B. 77
Stirling, L. 8, 45, 54, 117, 122, 123, 168, 317
Stone, W. L. 34
story-acting practice 11, 12, 16–19, 21, 22, 201
story based play **176**; *see also* pretend play
storyboarding **138**
story listening 106
story/storytelling: across cultural contexts 271; basic structures of children's 126–7; collaborative 3; defined **9, 10**; dialogue and narrative 272; differences between pretend play and 10, 15; face-to-face 84; fantasy play and 9; imaginative *see* imaginative storytelling from kindergarten writing instruction; integrating elements of narrative scenario in 16; as mode of narrative activity *see* narrative activity (pretend play and storytelling as mode of); within pretend play 117; pretense and *see entries beginning* pretense and storytelling; Probo for 100, 102–3; reciprocity with technology and *see* virtual peer for children with ASD; research limited on ASD and interactive play and 150; role

in general development and academic achievement 181; similarities between pretend play and 9, 13, 15; social robots as *see* social robots; story-acting practice and 11, 12, 16–19, 21, 22, 201; technology and *see* technology; thematic disjunction *vs.* overlap and interchange in 11–12; as type of narrative form 127; virtual peer for children with ASD and *see* virtual peer for children with ASD

story task **86**

storytelling agent 98

storyworld 9

structural features of play or stories category **128**, 148

structure tasks: narrative 264; pretend play 264

studies of effectiveness **97**, 98

studies of efficacy **97**, 98

subject-plot role-play 276

subteacher: as director 207, 208, 214–15, 219; as parent 207, 208, 217–18, 219; as social leader 109, 207, 208, 209–14, 219; as tutor 207, 208, 215–17, 219

subteacher discourse during PPWS: coding scheme for 206–7, 208; conclusion of 219–22; data gathering for 205–6; discussion regarding 219–22; examples of 209–18; findings regarding 208–9; introduction to 198–9; as literacy discourse 220–1; mediation among peers in 204–5; methodology of 205–8; pretend play as promoting 221; purpose of chapter regarding 199; study design for 205; styles of 205, 208–19; teacher discourse and 221; theoretical background of 199–204

subteaching **198, 202–4**

superpowers 152

Sutton-Smith, B. 302, 303

symbolic capacities 150

symbolic play **32**; *see also* pretend play

symbolic representation 305

symbolic thought 179–80

symbols in play 51; *see also* object substitution

Tartaro, A. 72, 317

task development 84–8

Taylor, M. 40, 254, 264

teacher as director **203**

teacher discourse 221

Teachers College Reading and Writing Workshop Project (TCRWP) 176, 177, 185, 186, 187, 206

teacher talk **203, 205**

teasing 304

technology: for ASD 74–6; computer 98; design of virtual peer for children with ASD as *see* virtual peer for children with ASD; play and 294

television (TV) 18, 56, 57, 67, 68

Teubal, E. 198

theater: experimental 18

thematic disjunction *vs.* overlap and interchange 11–12

themes: in middle-class preschools 19; in pretend play 305

themes item **128**, 135, 147

theory: of belonging 228, 232; of child development 278; of cognition 178; empathizing-systemizing **97**, 98; of human development **179**; of identity 228; of language 178; of mind 32, **40**, **51**, 52, 53, 54, 55, 69; of motivation in learning (Dewey's) 176; of place 228, 232; of place and belonging 232; play 301; related to ecopsychology 232; of role-play **288**; simulation **52**; regarding social pretend play and storytelling 127; socioconstructivist **178**, 181, 193

theory theory position **52**

Thiemann-Bourque, K. S. 44

thinking: creative 290; groups and 241; higher level 59; imagination and 275; imaginative 178, 179, 181, 284, 286, 290; narrative 282, 283, 284; through visual and verbal descriptions of ideas 78

thinking tasks, divergent **256–8**, 265, 266, 267

Tholander, M. 203

time reference item **128**, 148

Torrance, E. P. 257

toy industry 294

toys 39, 42, 57, 60–1, 75–6, 101, 125, 128

transcripts 206

translation 207–8

Trawick-Smith, J. 120

treatment integrity 107, 115

Truman, S. M. 272

T scores 83

unfocused chains **126–7**

Ungerer, J. A. 34, 35, 43

334 Index

uniqueness 258
United Nations Children's Fund
  (UNICEF) 295, 297, 308
*Units of Study for Primary Writing: A Yearlong
  Curriculum* 185
*Units of Study in Opinion, Information, and
  Narrative Writing, Grade K: A Common
  Core Workshop Curriculum* 185
unstructured activities **74**
upper-middle-class preschoolers 19
urban alienation **233**

Vadeboncoeur, J. A. 294, 318
Vanderborght, B. 96, 101, 318
Vanderfaeillie, J. 96
van der Tuin, I. 245
van Oers, B. 276
Vardi-Rath, E. 198, 318
verb acquisition 123
verbal cognition 42–4
verbal communication 53–4, 102, 308
verbal language 278
verbal mental age (VMA) 35
Veresov, N. 282
video 74, 153, 155, 177, 187, 191
video game/gaming 18, 155, 160, 294
video modeling 97
virtual and augmented reality 74,
  76, 98
virtual peer for children with ASD:
  authorable 84, 91; authoring the **73**,
  80, 88–9, 90, 92; background regarding
  73; constructionism and 72–3, 76–7;
  defined **72**; design research and 77;
  design study for *see* design study for
  virtual peer for children with ASD;
  human peers and 76; implementation in
  88; introduction to 72–3; metalinguistic
  reflection and 76–7; picture of 75;
  reciprocity and 72; technology
  and 74–6
virtual reality environments 98
visual arts 276
voice of authority **204**

Volkmar, F. R. 97
Vygotsky, L. S. 10, 118, 126, 178, 179, 180,
  184, 272, 275, 276, 279, 280, 283, 287,
  288, 301

Waletzky, J. 155
walking around 276
Wang, P. 97
Ward, K. 227, 318
wearables 74
Wechsler Preschool and Primary
  Scale of Intelligence (WPPSI–R or
  WPPSI–III) 124
we-intentionality 53, 54
Weintraub, J. 179
Wells, G. 9
Westby, C. 51
what if content 256
Whitebread, D. 56, 59
Whitehead, C. 56
Wilson, E. O. 232
Wing, L. 33, 34
Wisconsin Card Sorting Test 42
Wizard of Oz (WoZ) setting **102**
Wolf, D. P. 14
Wolfberg, P. 122
working memory 42
WoZ setting *see* Wizard of Oz (WoZ)
  setting
writing: creative 76; imaginative 176, 177,
  180, 185, 186, 190, 192–3; independent
  175, 182, 183
writing instruction: kindergarten
  see imaginative storytelling from
  kindergarten writing instruction
writing workshop **185**, 193
writing workshop curriculum 185–9
written language 200
Wu, M. 78

Yeates, S. R. 33
Young, G. S. 39

Zadunaisky-Ehrlich, S. 202